Latin American Writers

THIRTY STORIES

Latin American Writers

THIRTY STORIES

Edited by
Gabriella Ibieta

Drexel University

ST. MARTIN'S PRESS   NEW YORK

Senior editor: Catherine Pusateri
Development editor: Edward Mitchell-Hutchinson
Managing editor: Patricia Mansfield-Phelan
Project editor: Erica Appel
Production supervisor: Katherine Battiste
Text design: Barbara Balch
Cover design: Jeanette Jacobs
Cover art: Tarsila do Amaral, Lagoa Santa, 1925. Julio Bogoricin Imoveis. São
  Paulo. Photograph: Sotheby's.

For information, write:
St. Martin's Press, Inc.
175 Fifth Avenue
New York, NY 10010

ISBN: 0-312-07524-3

Acknowledgments

"The Wilderness" from *The Exiles and Other Stories* by Horacio Quiroga,
translated by David Danielson with the assistance of Elsa K. Gambarirri.
Copyright © 1987. By permission of the University of Texas Press.
  "The Circular Ruins," "Death and the Compass," and "Emma Zunz" from
Jorge Luis Borges: *Labyrinths.* Copyright © 1962, 1964 by New Directions
Publishing Corporation.
  "The Hill Called Mambiala" by Lydia Cabrera. From *Contemporary
Women Authors of Latin America: New Translations,* ed. by Doris Meyer and
Margarite Fernandez Olmos. Copyright © 1983 by Brooklyn College Press.
Reprinted with permission of the editors.

*Acknowledgments and copyrights are continued at the back of the book on pages 355–356,
which constitute an extension of the copyright page.*

For Ariana

Preface

SINCE THE PURPOSE of this anthology is to introduce students and general readers to the contemporary Latin American short story, I have included texts that represent the more established canon within the literature as well as less familiar works that are nonetheless culturally significant. The stories have been arranged chronologically by author's date of birth and are preceded by biographical notes. A general introduction offers an overview of the major literary currents and themes within the Latin American short story as represented in this collection.

I have selected texts generally defined as short stories or short fiction. For this reason, I have not included excerpts from novels by such major writers as Miguel Angel Asturias, Guillermo Cabrera Infante, and Mario Vargas Llosa, to mention only a few. Twenty-two authors have been selected: twelve men and ten women. This represents an effort to correct the mistaken assumption that the large majority of Latin American writers are male and to recognize the significant contributions of Latin American women writers.

When more than one text by an author has been chosen, the criteria have been as follows: In the case of well-known writers with a long history of major publications (Borges, Cortázar, García Márquez), I have chosen two or three texts that represent significant themes and obsessions; in the case of less well-known but nonetheless major writers (Lispector, Piñera), I have chosen two texts that represent different aspects of their work; in the case of Rey Rosa, a young and innovative writer, I felt that two texts would not only enrich readers' appreciation of his themes and techniques but would also help to provide a general idea of very current trends in the Latin American short story.

The major geographical regions within Latin America have been represented by eleven countries: South America (Argentina, Brazil, Chile, Colombia, Ecuador, Paraguay, Uruguay); Central America (Guatemala); North America (Mexico); the Caribbean (Cuba, Puerto Rico). Although not all the countries of Latin America have been included, the selection covers a wide spectrum that exemplifies national and regional differences.

As is inevitably the case with a work of this nature, there are regrettable omissions. I would like to note, however, that for some authors (Alejo Carpentier and Armonía Somers, for example), difficulties with permissions could not be overcome.

Working on this anthology has given me the welcome opportunity to select and compile texts that I have taught and loved. I would like to thank those who have helped me in its production: my friend and former department head at Drexel University, Burton Porter, for his savvy suggestions and encouragement, and for much-needed released time; my research assistant at Drexel, Carol Kaapu, for her diligence and accuracy; my editors at St. Martin's Press, Mark Gallaher, Cathy Pusateri, Edward Mitchell-Hutchinson, and Erica Appel for their advice, kind patience, and good humor; and my husband, best friend, and most astringent critic, Miles Orvell, for his intellectual acumen, moral support, and gourmet meals. Finally, special thanks to my three-year-old daughter, Ariana, who makes me laugh and reminds me of the relationship between literature and life with her most constant demand: "Read me a book."

Gabriella Ibieta

Contents

Introduction

GIVEN THE VARIETY of Latin America's national and regional characteristics, it is a difficult though not impossible task to present a coherent vision of its contribution to world literature within the genre of the contemporary short story. The texts selected for this anthology are representative of the major themes and styles developed in Latin America during the twentieth century.

In the nineteenth century, the Latin American short story exhibited characteristics of both Romanticism and Realism, often at the same time. Although the genre was not clearly defined, such writers as Esteban Echevarría, Tomás Carrasquilla, and Manuel Gutiérrez Nájera, among others, produced excellent short narratives that reflected national and regional interests as well as aesthetic currents.

With Horacio Quiroga's collection, *Jungle Tales* (1918), the Latin American short story made a quantum leap. His psychological acumen and penchant for the grotesque, combined with his realistic settings in the South American jungle (as in "The Wilderness," included in this anthology), give him a unique place as an important precursor to the concept of modernity within the genre.

We can distinguish four main currents within the modern Latin American short story, each represented in this collection: the fantastic, social realism, magical realism, and female discourse. The fantastic concerns itself with the exploration of unreal or uncanny settings and characters, often with the purpose of creating an alternate meaning for everyday reality. Social realism may be defined as a preoccupation with issues of social injustice and a depiction of Latin America's economic and political problems. Works typical of social realism in Latin America have usually offered unfavorable portrayals of militaristic and repressive regimes, or have offered fictional accounts of political insurgence. Magical realism is a term that has posed innumerable problems to scholars and critics; for our purposes, I would suggest a somewhat simplified and general definition of magical realism as the tendency to introduce unexpected and often supernatural elements in a work that is otherwise realistic in its depiction of the natural world and its elements. (The early novels of Cuban writer Alejo Carpentier are considered classic examples of magical realism.) A fourth, more recent, modality in the development of the genre has been

1

introduced by women writers predominantly concerned with the problems of a female discourse.

A leading figure in the development of fantastic literature, Jorge Luis Borges is represented here by "The Circular Ruins," "Death and the Compass," and "Emma Zunz." His short fiction from the 1930s and 1940s revolutionized the genre in ways that are still discernible today in the work of younger writers. His explorations in the realm of the fantastic, through highly original settings and characters, express a metaphysical dimension through a limpid, cerebral style that is concerned primarily with the creation of particular codes of meaning.

Borges's innovations within fantastic literature were further developed by such writers as Julio Cortázar and Virgilio Piñera. Cortázar's stories add a new element: the juxtaposition of the unreal with everyday situations ("Secret Weapons") or the exaggeration of reality to present an absurd vision of the world ("The Southern Thruway"). In a somewhat different vein, Virgilio Piñera also uses elements of the fantastic in his work, particularly the theme of the double ("The One Who Came to Save Me") to express an uncanny vision of reality.

The prevailing influence of Borges on the Latin American short story is also present in the work of Rodrigo Rey Rosa ("The Truth" and "Xquic"). The youngest writer represented in this anthology, Rey Rosa uses irony in his manipulation of the seemingly fantastic to make strong political statements, adding a new twist to this particular mode of writing.

A major exponent of social realism in the short story is Lino Novás Calvo ("The Dark Night of Ramón Yendía"), whose depictions of persecuted, marginalized characters have been highly praised. Juan Rulfo's "Tell Them Not to Kill Me" and Augusto Roa Bastos's "The Prisoner" express a similar preoccupation with political repression and social injustice, although it should be added that both authors are also well-known for their experimentation with less conventional narrative forms.

The third current within modern Latin American literature, magical realism, overlaps the fantastic in some respects. A distinct characteristic of magical realism, however, is its close preoccupation with the Latin American experience. "Monologue of Isabel Watching It Rain in Macondo" by Gabriel García Márquez captures the oppressive and incessant presence of Colombia's tropical climate through the main character's "magical" thinking. Two other stories associated with magical realism and included here are "The Day We Were Dogs" by Elena Garro and "In a Flemish Garden" by Carlos Fuentes.

Many of the stories already mentioned have a prominent place within the period in Latin American literature known as the "Boom." Although this term resists definition and has been the object of both praise and derision by literary critics, one cannot escape it. The literature of the Boom reflects an intense period of experimentation by Latin American writers during the 1960s, mostly in the novel but also in the short story. The term also alludes to the rapid internationalization of Latin American literature during this period, when a series of major works by Latin Americans were published one after the other to critical acclaim and were quickly translated into foreign languages. Authors associated with the Boom and represented in this anthology are Julio Cortázar, José Donoso ("The Walk"), Carlos Fuentes, and Gabriel García Márquez. Precursors to the Boom are Juan Rulfo and Juan Carlos Onetti; the latter's preoccupation with obsession and psychological anguish is represented here by "The Image of Misfortune."

While the work of Latin American women writers has been largely neglected, especially during the flourishing period of the Boom, their contributions have been significant and constitute a fourth category. Included in this anthology are two important figures from the earlier part of the century, Lydia Cabrera ("The Hill Called Mambiala") and María Luisa Bombal ("New Islands"). Cabrera's work on and with Afro-Cuban folklore defies classification and remains unique within the genre, while Bombal has been claimed by younger women writers as instrumental in the development of a female discourse within Latin American literature.

Writers like Clarice Lispector ("The Imitation of the Rose" and "The Departure of the Train"), and Rosario Castellanos ("Cooking Lesson") have explored the particular experience of Latin American women through works that challenge preconceived, stereotyped images of women. Alicia Yáñez Cossío has dealt with the theme of motherhood and the genre of science fiction, although the selection included here, "Sabotage," is a political satire.

Among the younger generation of Latin American women writers, Nélida Piñón ("Adamastor") occupies a special place for her lyrical, often hermetic explorations of language, especially as reflected in her novels. Highly experimental in nature, the works of Luisa Valenzuela ("Strange Things Happen Here") and Cristina Peri Rossi ("The Influence of Edgar Allan Poe on the Poetry of Raimundo Arias") combine an interest in

Latin American politics with a particularly female discourse. Rosario Ferré's "Sleeping Beauty" inscribes the childhood story in a humorous critique of Latin American middle-class values, in which the protagonist challenges the traditional female roles assigned by her social class.

The stories collected in this volume present an encompassing, coherent vision of the contemporary Latin American short story, and it is my hope that they will inspire the reader to explore further this rich realm.

ARGENTINA: Jorge Luis Borges, Julio Cortázar, Luisa Valenzuela

BRAZIL: Clarice Lispector, Nélida Piñón

CHILE: María Luisa Bombal, Jose Donoso

COLOMBIA: Gabriel García Márquez

CUBA: Lydia Cabrera, Lino Novás Calvo, Virgilio Piñera

ECUADOR: Alicia Yáñez Cossío

GUATEMALA: Rodrigo Rey Rosa

MEXICO: Juan Rulfo, Elena Garro, Rosario Castellanos, Carlos Fuentes

PARAGUAY: Augusto Roa Bastos

PUERTO RICO: Rosario Ferré

URUGUAY: Horacio Quiroga, Juan Carlos Onetti, Cristina Peri Rossi

Horacio Quiroga

1878–1937

HORACIO QUIROGA, LATIN America's master of the modern short story, was born in Salto, Uruguay, on December 31, 1878. His life was punctuated by violence and tragedy, including his father's death in a hunting accident and the suicides of his stepfather and his first wife. During his youth, Quiroga attended the University of Montevideo, founded a literary magazine, traveled to Paris, and started a long career as a writer. In 1906, he settled in the tropical jungle region of Misiones in northern Argentina, which would become the source and setting for most of his work. For the next thirty years, Quiroga would divide his time between Misiones and Buenos Aires. His short-story collection *Cuentos de amor, de locura y de muerte* (1917; Tales of love, madness, and death), influenced by Guy de Maupassant and Edgar Allan Poe, marked the beginning of his literary fame. In his stories, Quiroga combined careful descriptions of the Misiones jungle with a bizarre and tragic sense of life, all told in a sparse and controlled narrative style. Among his best known collections are: *Cuentos de la selva* (1918; *South American Jungle Tales,* 1922); *La gallina degollada y otros cuentos* (1925; *The Decapitated Chicken and Other Stories,* 1976); and *Los desterrados* (1926; *The Exiles and Other Stories,* 1987). Afflicted by cancer, Quiroga committed suicide in 1937.

The Wilderness

Translated by J. David Danielson

THE CANOE GLIDED along the edge of the woods, or what might seem to be woods in all that darkness. More by instinct than from any clue, Suber-

7

casaux felt its nearness, for the gloom was a single impervious block, starting at the rower's hands and extending up to the zenith. The man knew his river well enough so as to not be unaware of where he was, but on such a night, and under threat of rain, landing his craft in the midst of piercing *tacuara* canes and patches of rotten reeds was very different from going ashore in his own little port. And Subercasaux was not alone in his canoe.

The atmosphere was sultry to the point of asphyxiation. In no direction his face might turn could he find a little air to breathe. And at that moment, clearly and distinctly, some raindrops pattered in the canoe.

Subercasaux raised his eyes, looking vainly into the sky for a tremor of brightness or the fissure of a lightning bolt. All afternoon, and now as well, one could not hear a single thunderclap.

"Rain for the whole night," he thought. And turning to his companions, who kept silent at the stern:

"Put on your rain-capes," he said briefly. "And hold on tight."

In fact, the canoe was now bending branches as it moved along, and two or three times the portside oar had skidded on a submerged limb. But even at the price of breaking an oar, Subercasaux stayed in contact with the foliage, since if he got five meters offshore he could go back and forth all night in front of his port, without managing to see it.

Skimming the water at the very edge of the woods, the rower advanced a while longer. The drops were falling more densely now, but also at greater intervals. They would cease abruptly, as if they had fallen from who-knows-where, and then begin again, large, warm, and separate, only to break off once more in the same darkness and the same atmospheric depression.

"Hold on tight," repeated Subercasaux to his two companions. "We've made it home."

For he had just caught a glimpse of the mouth of his port. With two vigorous strokes of the oars he propelled the canoe onto the clay bank, and as he fastened the craft to its post his two silent companions jumped to the ground, which in spite of the darkness was easy to see, since it was covered with myriads of shiny little worms that made its surface undulate with their red and green fires.

As far as the top of the bluff—which the three travelers climbed in the rain, at last compact and uniform—the soaking clay shone phosphorescently. But then they were shut in again by the darkness, and in its midst had to search for the sulky they'd left resting on its shafts.

The saying "You can't even see your hands in front of your eyes" is made to order. And on such nights the momentary flash of a match is of no use but to deepen the dizzying darkness right afterward, to the point of making you lose your balance.

They found the sulky, nevertheless, but not the horse. And leaving his two companions on guard next to one of the wheels—where they stood motionless under their drooping capes, noisily spattered by rain—Subercasaux went off among the painful thorns to the end of the trail, where he found his horse, tangled up in its reins, of course.

He hadn't taken more than twenty minutes to look for the animal and bring it in, but when he sought his bearings in the vicinity of the sulky—saying: "Are you there, kids?" and hearing: "Yes, daddy"—Subercasaux became fully aware, for the first time that night, that the two companions he had abandoned to the night and the rain were his two children, aged five and six, who didn't stand as high as the hub of the sulky wheel, and who were huddled together, dripping water from their rain-capes, and calmly waiting for their father to return.

Finally they were on their way home, chattering and happy. When moments of worry or danger had passed, Subercasaux's voice was very different from the one he used to speak to his youngsters when he had to address them as grown-ups. Now it had lowered by two tones, and no one there would have thought, upon hearing the tenderness of their voices, that the man then laughing with the children was none other than the one with the curt and harsh accent of a half an hour before. And now the real talkers were Subercasaux and his daughter, since the little boy—the baby of the family—had fallen asleep on his father's knees.

II

Subercasaux usually got up at daybreak; and though he did it noiselessly, he was well aware that in the next room his boy, as much of an early riser as he was, had been lying with his eyes open for quite a while, waiting to hear his father before he got out of bed. And then the unchanging ritual of morning greetings would begin, passing from one bedroom to the other:

"Good morning, daddy!"

"Good morning, my dear little boy!"

"Good morning, darling little daddy!"

"Good morning, spotless little lamb!"

"Good morning, little mouse with no tail!"

"My little raccoon!"

"Little daddy armadillo!"

"Little cat-face!"

"Little snake-tail!"

And in this colorful style it would go on for a good while longer—till, once they were dressed, they would go have coffee under the palms, while the little lady kept on sleeping like a stone, till the sun in her face awakened her.

With his two young children—in their temper and training handiwork of his own—Subercasaux considered himself the happiest father on earth. But this he had achieved at the cost of greater grief than usually experienced by married men.

Abruptly, as things happen that are inconceivable for their appalling unfairness, Subercasaux had lost his wife. He was suddenly left alone, with two little children who hardly knew him, and in the same house, built by him and fixed up by her, where every nail and every brushmark on the wall was a sharp reminder of shared happiness.

The next day he found out, when he chanced to open the wardrobe, what it is to all of a sudden see your already buried wife's underthings; and on a hanger, the dress that she never had time to try out.

He went through the urgent and fateful need, if you want to go on living, to destroy every last trace of the past, when with his eyes set and dry he burned the letters he had written to his wife, and she had saved since their courtship with more devotion than her big-city clothes. And that same afternoon he found out, at last, what it's like to be finally worn out from sobbing, and hold back in your arms a young child who's struggling to get loose so he can go play with the cook's little boy.

Hard, that was terribly hard . . . But now he was laughing with his two kids, who along with him formed a single person, given the uncommon way in which Subercasaux brought up his children.

The youngsters, for example, had no fear of the dark, nor of being alone, nor of anything that contributes to the terror of babies raised at their mother's skirts. More than once night descended when Subercasaux still wasn't back from the river, and the children lit the wind-lantern to wait for him, unworrying. Or they would wake up alone in the middle of a furious storm that kept them blinded behind the windowpanes, only to go back to sleep again at once, secure and confident of their daddy's return.

They feared nothing, except what their father warned them they should fear; and at the top of the list, naturally, were snakes. Free as they were, exuding health and stopping to look at everything with eyes as big as those of happy puppies, they wouldn't have known what to do for a moment without their father's company. But if, when he left, he let them know he was going to be gone for such and such a time, the kids were content to stay and play together. Similarly, if on their long joint trips through the woods or on the river Subercasaux had to go off for some minutes or hours, they would quickly improvise a game, and wait for him unfailingly in the same place, in this way repaying, with blind and cheerful obedience, the confidence their father placed in them.

They went horseback-riding on their own, and this from the time the boy was four years old. Like all free creatures, they were perfectly aware of their limits, and never went beyond them. Sometimes, alone, they would get as far as the Yabebirí, to the pink sandstone cliff above the river.

"Make sure of the terrain and sit down afterward," their father had told them.

The cliff rises straight up to a height of twenty meters from deep and shaded waters which cool the crevices at its base. There on top, tiny as they were, Subercasaux's youngsters would approach the edge, testing the stones with their feet; and, once secure, sit down and let their sandals frolic over the abyss.

Naturally, Subercasaux had achieved all this in successive stages, each one of them charged with its own anxieties.

"Some day a kid'll get killed on me," he said to himself. "And for the rest of my days I'll be asking myself if I was right to bring them up this way."

Yes, he was right. And among the few consolations of a father left alone with motherless children, the greatest is being able to raise them in accordance with a single course of conduct.

Subercasaux was therefore happy, and the children felt warmly bound to that big man who would play with them for hours on end, teach them to read on the floor with large heavy letters made of red lead, and sew up the rips in their pants with his huge toughened hands.

From sewing gunnysacks in the Chaco, when he was a cotton planter there, Subercasaux had retained both the custom of sewing and his pleasure in it. He sewed his own clothes, those of his children, the holsters for his revolver, and the sails of his canoe—all with cobbler's thread, and knotting every stitch. So it was that his shirts could tear at any point except where he had tied his waxen thread.

When it came to games, the children both recognized their father as a master, especially in his way of running on all fours—so outlandish that it made them shout with laughter right away.

Since in addition to his regular activities Subercasaux was a restless experimenter, whose interests took a new tack every three months, his children, constantly at his side, were acquainted with a lot of things not usually known to children of that age. They had seen—and sometimes helped in—the dissection of animals, the making of *creolina,* the extraction of latex from trees to seal their raincoats; they had seen their father's shirts dyed all sorts of colors, the construction of eight-ton outworks for the study of cements, the making of superphosphates, orange wine, *yerba* dryers of the Mayfarth type, and the suspension of a car-cable from the woods to the bungalow, hung at ten meters above the ground, along which the youngsters would then go flying down to the house in little cable-cars.

Around that time Subercasaux had been attracted to a vein or deposit of white clay left exposed by the last great retreat of the Yabebiri. From the study of this clay he had gone on to the others of the region, which he fired in his pottery-ovens—constructed, of course, by him. And if he had to get data on cooking, vitrification, and the like, using specimens of no particular form, he preferred to experiment with pots, masks, and imaginary animals, in all of which his children helped him with great success.

At night, and on stormy afternoons when it was really dark, the factory moved into high gear. Subercasaux would light the oven early, and the experimenters, shrunk by the cold and rubbing their hands, would sit down in its warmth to model clay.

But the smaller of his ovens easily generated 1,000°C in two hours, and at this point, every time they opened the door to feed it, a veritable bolt of fire that burned their lashes came out of the white-glowing hearth. So the ceramics-makers would retreat to a far end of the workshop, till the icy wind that came whistling in between the shafts of *tacuara* in the walls would drive them back, workbench and all, to get cooked with their backs to the oven.

Except for the youngsters' naked legs, which now took the blasts of heat, everything went along well. Subercasaux had a weakness for prehistoric pots; the little girl preferred to model fancy hats; and the boy, without fail, made snakes.

Sometimes, however, the monotonous snore of the oven didn't cheer them up enough, and then they turned to the gramophone, and the same old records in use since Subercasaux's marriage, which the kids had abused with all sorts of needles, nails, thorns, and bits of *tacuara* that they themselves would sharpen. By turns, each of them would take charge of attending the machine, which amounted to automatically changing records without even lifting their eyes from the clay, and resuming their work right away. When all the records had been played, it was another's turn to repeat exactly the same operation. They didn't even listen to the music anymore, since they knew it perfectly by heart; but the noise entertained them.

At ten o'clock the ceramics-makers considered their task concluded, and rose to proceed for the first time to the critical inspection of their works of art, since till all of them had finished not the slightest commentary was allowed. And then it was quite a sight to see the jubilation over the ornamental fantasies of the little lady, and the enthusiasm aroused by the boy's relentless collection of snakes. After which Subercasaux would put out the fire in the oven, and all holding hands they would run through the icy night to their house.

III

Three days after the nocturnal canoe-trip we've told about, Subercasaux was left without a servant girl; and this incident, trifling and inconsequential anywhere else, altered the life of the three exiles in the extreme.

In the first moments of his bereavement Subercasaux had been able to count on the help of a fine woman to raise his children, the same cook who wept and found the house too lonely at the death of her mistress.

The next month she left, and Subercasaux went through all sorts of grief to replace her with three or four sullen girls pulled out of the back country, and who'd only stay a few days, because they found their boss's character too harsh.

Subercasaux, as a matter of fact, was partly guilty, and he admitted it. He spoke with the girls just barely enough to make himself understood, and what he said had an excessively masculine logic and precision. When they swept the dining room, for example, he cautioned them to also sweep around every leg of the table. And this, expressed so sparingly, exasperated and fatigued the girls.

For the space of three months he couldn't even get a girl to wash the dishes for him. And in those three months Subercasaux learned a bit more than how to bathe his children.

He learned, not how to cook, because he already knew that, but how to scour pots and pans with the very sand of his patio, squatting in the icy wind, which made his hands turn blue. He learned to interrupt his work again and again to run and take the milk off the fire or open the smoking oven; and he also learned to bring in three buckets of water (not a one less) from the well at night, to wash his kitchenware.

This problem of the three inescapable buckets was the substance of one of his nightmares, and it took him a month to realize that he couldn't do without them. In the first days he had naturally put off cleaning pots and dishes, which he piled up side by side on the floor, so as to wash them all at once. But after wasting a whole morning on his haunches scraping burned cooking vessels (they all got burned), he opted for cook-eat-and-scrub, a three-step process the delights of which aren't known to husbands either.

He really had no time left for anything, especially during the short days of winter. Subercasaux had entrusted the children with keeping the two bedrooms in order, a job they did passably well. But he himself didn't feel he had spirit enough to sweep the patio: a scientific, radial, circular, and exclusively feminine task, which—though he knew it was basic to well-being in huts in the wilderness—transcended his patience.

In that loose, undisturbed sand, turned into a plant-laboratory by the climate of alternating rains and burning sun, the sand-fleas spread so much that you could see them crawling over the shoeless feet of the children. Subercasaux, though he always wore *stromboots,* paid a heavy tribute to the fleas. Almost always lame, he would have to spend a whole hour after the midday meal with his boy's feet in his hands, blinded by sun in the patio or on the veranda and splattered by rain. When he finished with the youngster it was his own turn; and when he stood up at last, with bended back, the boy would call him again because three new fleas had bored deep into the skin of his feet.

Luckily, the girl seemed to be immune; there was no way her little toenails could tempt the fleas, seven out of ten of which fell by right to the boy and only three to his father. But those three were too many for a man whose feet were the key to the rustic life he led.

Sand-fleas, in general, are more harmless than snakes, botflies, and even the little *barigüis.* They walk high on their legs across the skin, and all of a sudden pierce it swiftly, going down to the raw flesh, where they make a little pouch that they fill with eggs. Neither the extraction of the flea nor of its nest is usually troublesome, nor do its bites go bad more than might be expected. But for every hundred clean fleas there's one that carries an infection, and with that you have to be careful.

Subercasaux had such an infection in one of his toes—the insignificant little toe of his right foot—and couldn't manage to subdue it. From a little pink hole it had grown to a swollen and terribly painful split along the edge of his toenail. Iodine, bichloride, hydrogen peroxide, formalde-hyde—there was nothing he had failed to try. He wore his shoes, however, but didn't leave the house; and his endless labors in the woods were now reduced, on rainy afternoons, to slow and silent walks around the patio, when as the sun went down the sky would clear, and the woods, outlined against the light like a shadow pantomime, would come nearer and nearer in the superbly pure air till it touched your very eyes.

Subercasaux realized that in other living conditions he could have conquered the infection, which only called for a little rest. The afflicted man slept badly, shaken by chills and sharp pains late at night. At daybreak he would finally fall into a very heavy sleep, and at that moment would have given anything to stay in bed till even as late as eight o'clock. But the little boy was as much of an early bird in winter as in summer, and Subercasaux would get up shaking with fever to light the Primus stove and prepare the coffee. Then there was the midday meal, and the scrubbing of pots. And for diversion, at noon, the endless saga of his youngster's fleas.

"Things can't go on this way," Subercasaux finally said to himself. "At all costs I have to get a maid."

But how? During his married years this terrible concern with servant girls had been one of his regular anxieties. The girls would come and go, as we've said, without saying why, and this when there was a lady of the house. Subercasaux would abandon all his tasks and stay on his horse for three days, galloping along the trails from Apariciocué to San Ignacio, after any useless girl who might want to wash the diapers. At last, some day at noon, he would emerge from the woods with a halo of horseflies around his head, and his horse's neck ragged and bloody—but triumphant. The girl would arrive the next day, astraddle behind her father, with a bundle; and exactly a month later would leave with the same bundle, on foot. And Subercasaux would again put aside his hoe or machete to go get his horse, already waiting and sweating motionless in the sun.

Those were bad experiences, that had left him with a bitter taste, and now had to start up again. But which way would he go?

During his nights of sleeplessness Subercasaux had already heard the distant rumbling of the woods, battered by rain. Spring is usually dry in Misiones, and winter very rainy. But when the pattern is reversed—something always to be expected of the climate in Misiones—the clouds disgorge a meter of rain in three months, of the meter and a half supposed to fall in all the year.

They were already almost hemmed in. The Horqueta, which cuts across the road to the shore of the Paraná, had no bridges at all at that time and was passable only at the wagon ford, where the water fell in foamy rapids over round and shifting stones, trod by horses quaking with fear. And this under normal conditions; for when the stream had to take on the rain of a seven-day storm, the ford was submerged under two fathoms of racing water, strung out in deep bands which suddenly broke up and coiled into whirlpools. And the settlers from the Yabebirí, detained on their horses before the flooded grassland, watched dead deer go by, revolving as they floated on. It was like this for ten or fifteen days.

The Horqueta could still be crossed when Subercasaux decided to go out; but in his state he didn't dare cover such a distance on horseback. And after all, what was he likely to find in the direction of Cazador Creek?

Then he remembered a young fellow he'd employed at one time, bright and hard-working as few are, who had told him laughing—the very day he arrived, as he scrubbed a frying pan in the dirt—that he'd stay for a month, because his boss needed him, but not one day more, because that was no work for a man. The fellow lived at the mouth of the Yabebirí, across from Toro Island, and that meant a strenuous trip; for if the Yabebirí plays its game of dropping and rising up again, the eight-hour stretch of rowing will crush the fingers of anyone who's not already used to it.

Subercasaux made his decision, however. And despite the threatening weather went down to the river with his children, with the cheerful air of one who finally sees the open sky. The youngsters repeatedly kissed their father's hand, as they usually did when they were full of joy. Despite his feet and all the rest, Subercasaux kept up all his courage for his children— but for them it was something very different to take a hike with their daddy through the woods aswarm with surprises, and then run barefoot along the shore, over the warm and springy mud of the Yabebirí.

There what they expected awaited them: the canoe full of water, which had to be bailed out with the usual scoop and the gourds for keeping bugs that the children always slung over their shoulders when they went into the woods.

Subercasaux was so hopeful that he wasn't disturbed enough by the dubious look of the muddied waters—of a river where you can usually see the bottom as far as two meters down.

"The rains," he thought, "still aren't coming down hard with the southeaster . . . It'll be a day or two before it rises."

They kept on working. Standing in the water on both sides of the canoe, they bailed away as best they could. Subercasaux, at the start, hadn't dared to take off his boots, which kept sticking in the deep mud, so badly that it caused him great pains to pull out his foot. Finally he took them off, and with his feet free and sunk like wedges in the stinking mud, he finished bailing out the canoe, turned it over, and cleaned off the bottom, all in two hours of feverish activity.

Ready at last, they left. For an hour the canoe glided along more rapidly than the rower would have liked. He was rowing badly, braced by a single foot, his naked heel scarred by the edge of the supportbeam. And even so he was moving fast, because the Yabebirí was racing now. Finally, the sticks swollen with bubbles starting to fringe the backwaters, and the moustache of straw caught up against a big root, led Subercasaux to realize what was going to happen if he waited another second to veer the prow toward his port.

Servant girl, young man . . ., a rest at last! . . ., and more hopes gone. So he rowed without losing a stroke. The four hours he spent, tortured by worry and fatigue, going back up a river he'd gone down in an hour, in air so rarefied that his lungs gasped in vain—only he could thoroughly appreciate. When he got to his port the warm and frothy water had already risen two meters above the beach. And down the channel came dead branches, half submerged, their tips bobbing up and sinking in the sway.

The travelers reached the bungalow when it was already close to dark, though barely four o'clock, and just as the sky, with a single flash from its zenith to the river, at last disgorged its huge supply of water. They had supper at once and went to bed exhausted, under the clamor on the metal roof, which was hammered all night by the deluge with unrelenting violence.

IV

At daybreak, a chill to the bone awoke the master of the house. Till then he had slept like a block of lead. Contrary to what was usual since he'd had the infected toe, his foot hardly hurt at all, despite the exertions of the day before. He took the raincoat tossed on the bedstead and pulled it on top of him, and tried to go back to sleep.

Impossible. The cold went straight through him. The frost inside spread outward to all his pores, now turned into needles of bristling ice, a sensation he got from the slightest rub against his clothes. Curled up in a ball, assailed all up and down his spinal cord by intense and rhythmic waves of cold, the ailing man watched the hours go by with no success at getting warm. Luckily, the children were still asleep.

"In the state I'm in you don't do dumb things like yesterday's," he kept telling himself. "These are the consequences . . ."

As a distant dream, a pricelessly rare bliss he once possessed, he fancied he could spend all day in bed, warm and rested at last, while at the table he heard the noise of the cups of *café con leche* that the servant—that first great servant woman—was setting before the children . . .

Stay in bed till ten, at least! . . . In four hours the fever would pass, and even his lower back wouldn't hurt so much . . . What did he need, after all, to get well? A little rest, nothing more. He'd said that himself ten times . . .

The day was moving on, and the sick man thought he heard the happy noise of the cups, amid the heavy throbbing of his leaden temples. What a delight to hear that noise! . . . He would rest a little, finally . . .

"Daddy!"

"My dear boy . . ."

"Good morning, sweet little daddy! You're not up yet? It's late, daddy."

"Yes, my love, I was just getting up . . ."

And Subercasaux got dressed in a hurry, reproaching himself for his laziness, which had made him forget his children's coffee.

The rain had finally stopped, but without the slightest breath of wind being left to sweep away the prevailing humidity. And at noon it started again—a warm, tranquil, monotonous rain, which dissolved the valley of the Horqueta, the sown fields and the grasslands, in a misty and extremely dreary film of water.

After lunch the kids entertained themselves by renewing their stock of paper boats, which they had used up the afternoon before. They made hundreds of them, fitting them inside each other like ice-cream cones, ready to be tossed into the wake of the canoe, when they went out on the river again. Subercasaux took advantage of the chance to go to bed for a while, where he at once resumed his curled-up posture, lying motionless with his knees against his chest.

Again, on his temple, he could feel the enormous weight that held it to the pillow, so firmly that the pillow seemed to form an integral part of his head. How good he felt that way! Oh, to stay one, ten, a hundred days without moving! The monotonous drumming of the water on the metal roof lulled him toward sleep, and in its murmur he could hear distinctly, so well as to extract a smile, the tinkling of the cutlery being handled swiftly by the servant in the kitchen. What a servant he had! . . . And he heard the noise of the dishes, dozens of plates, cups, and pots that the servants—there were ten of them now!—scraped and scrubbed with dizzying speed. What a joy to be nice and warm at last, in bed, without a single, not a single worry! . . . When, at what previous time had he dreamed of being sick, with an awful problem? . . . How foolish he'd been! . . . And how nice it is like this, listening to the noise of hundreds of spotless cups . . .

"Daddy!"

"Darling girl . . ."

"I'm getting hungry, daddy!"

"Yes, sweetheart, right away . . ."

And the sick man went out in the rain to fix coffee for his children.

Without being quite sure what he had done that afternoon, Subercasaux watched the night come on with intense delight. He did remember that the delivery-boy hadn't brought milk that afternoon, and that he'd looked at his wound a long while, without noting anything special about it.

He fell into bed without even undressing, and in no time the fever laid him low again. The boy that hadn't come with the milk . . . Crazy! . . . Now he was fine, perfectly fine, resting.

With only a few days more of rest, even a few hours more, he'd get well. Right! Right! . . . There's justice in spite of everything . . . And also a little compensation . . . for someone who'd loved his children as he had . . . But he'd get up healthy. A man can get sick sometimes . . . and need to rest a little. And what a rest he was having now, to the lull of the rain on the metal roof! . . . But hadn't a month gone by already? . . . He ought to get up.

The sick man opened his eyes. He saw nothing but darkness, pierced by flashing specks that shrank and expanded by turns, approaching his eyes moving swiftly to and fro.

"I must have a very high fever," said the sick man to himself.

And he lit the wind-lantern on the night-table. The humid wick sputtered on for some time while Subercasaux kept his eyes on the roof. From far away, very far away, came the memory of a night like this when he was very, very sick . . . How silly can you get? . . . He was healthy, because when a man who's only tired is lucky enough to hear from his bed the furious clinking of the kitchen service, it's because the mother is watching over her children . . .

He woke up again. From the corner of his eye he saw the lighted lantern, and after a hard effort to focus his attention, recovered his self-awareness.

In his right arm, from his elbow to the tips of his fingers, he now felt intense pain. He tried to bring up his arm but couldn't do it. He pushed away the raincoat, and saw his livid hand, traced in streaks of violet; frozen, dead. Without closing his eyes, he thought a while about what that meant, along with his chills and having rubbed the open vessels of his wound against the foul mud of the Yabebirí, and then he came to the clear, absolute and conclusive understanding that his whole being was dying too, that he was passing into death.

A great silence fell within him, as if the rain, the noise, and the very rhythm of things had abruptly fallen back toward the infinite. And as though he were already detached from himself, he saw far off in a landscape a bungalow totally cut off from all human aid, where two small children, with no milk and all alone, were left abandoned by God and men, in a most iniquitous and dreadful state of helplessness.

His little children . . .

With a supreme effort he sought to wrest himself out of that torment which made him grapple, hour after hour and day after day, with the fate of his beloved children. In vain he would think: Life has higher forces that escape us . . . God provides . . .

"But they won't have anything to eat!" his heart would cry out tumultuously. And he would be dead, lying right where he was and witnessing that unprecedented horror . . .

But, in spite of the livid daylight reflected from the wall, darkness began to engulf him again, with its dizzying white dots, which receded and came back again to pulsate in his very eyes . . . Yes! Of course! He'd had a dream! It shouldn't be allowed to dream such things . . . Now he was going to get up, rested.

"Daddy! . . . Daddy . . . My dear little daddy! . . ."

"My son . . ."

"Aren't you going to get up today, daddy? It's very late. We're really hungry, daddy!"

"My little boy . . . I'm not going to get up just yet . . . You kids get up and eat some crackers . . . There's still two left in the can . . . And come back afterward."

"Can we come in now, daddy?"

"No sweetheart . . . Later I'll make the coffee . . . I'll be calling you."

He still got to hear the laughing and chatter of his children as they got up, and then a *crescendo* reverberation, a dizzy jingling that radiated from the core of his brain and went on to throb in rhythmic waves against his dreadfully aching skull. And that was all he heard.

He opened his eyes again, and as he did so felt his head falling toward the left, so freely that it surprised him. He no longer felt any reverberation at all. Only a growing but painless trouble with judging the distance of objects . . . And his mouth held wide-open to breathe.

"Kids . . . Come here right away . . ."

In no time the children appeared at the half-opened door, but viewing the lighted lantern and their father's countenance, came forward silently with their eyes opened wide.

The ailing man was still brave enough to smile, and as he made that awful face the children opened their eyes still wider.

"Kids," said Subercasaux when he had them at his side. "Pay attention, sweethearts, because you're big now and can understand everything . . . I'm going to die, kids . . . But don't be distressed . . . Soon you'll be grown-ups, and you'll be good and honest . . . And then you'll remember your daddy . . . Be sure you understand, my dear children . . . In a while I'll die, and you won't have a father anymore . . . You'll be alone in the house . . . But don't be alarmed or afraid . . . And now good-bye, my children . . . You're going to give me a kiss now . . . One kiss each . . . But quickly, kids . . . A kiss . . . for your daddy . . ."

The children left without touching the half-opened door, and went to linger in their room, looking out on the drizzle in the patio. They didn't stir from there. The girl alone, glimpsing the import of what had just come to pass, would pout from time to time with her arm at her face, while the boy distractedly scratched the window frame, uncomprehending.

Neither one nor the other dared to make any noise.

But at the same time there wasn't the slightest noise from the next room, where for three hours their father, with his shoes and clothes on under his raincoat, had been lying dead in the light of the lantern.

1923

Jorge Luis Borges

1899–1986

ONE OF THE most distinguished and innovative of contemporary writers, Jorge Luis Borges was born in Buenos Aires on August 24, 1899, into a wealthy family. An English grandmother instilled in him a love for English language and literature. He was educated in Switzerland, attended Cambridge University in England, and lived briefly in Spain before returning to Buenos Aires in 1921. During the next fifteen years, Borges would become a well-known poet, founder of three literary magazines, and an active member of the Argentine cultural avant-garde. In the late 1930s, he started writing the sort of text that would make him famous: short prose pieces, which he called *ficciones* (fictions), metaphysical explorations into the fantastic and into the nature of reality. Borges is also well known for his essays, later poetry, and Spanish translations of such authors as Faulkner, Gide, and Kafka. During the 1940s, he opposed Nazism in pro-German Argentina, as well as the government of Juan Perón, suffering persecution and an official lack of recognition for his work. After Perón's fall, Borges became director of the National Library of Argentina and Professor of English and North American Literature at the University of Buenos Aires. Borges suffered from a hereditary disease, which left him almost totally blind toward the latter part of his life. Having achieved an international reputation as a major writer, Borges lectured widely all over the world until his death in 1986. Although he wrote many texts that deal particularly with Argentine history and culture, Borges is best known as the author of cerebral, precisely constructed fictions that transcend national boundaries. One of his major themes is his conception of the universe as a labyrinth within which human beings construct their own personal labyrinths or destinies. Another important obsession for Borges is the image of the eternal recurrence, or the circular conception of historical time. Selected texts from the collections *Ficciones* (1944; Fictions); *El aleph* (1949; The aleph); and *Otras inquisiciones* (1960; Other inquisitions) appear in English translation in the volume *Labyrinths. Selected Stories and Other Writings* (1964). A more recent anthology is *Borges: A Reader* (1981).

The Circular Ruins

Translated by James E. Irby

And if he left off dreaming about you . . .

Through the Looking Glass, VI

No ONE SAW him disembark in the unanimous night, no one saw the bamboo canoe sinking into the sacred mud, but within a few days no one was unaware that the silent man came from the South and that his home was one of the infinite villages upstream, on the violent mountainside, where the Zend tongue is not contaminated with Greek and where leprosy is infrequent. The truth is that the obscure man kissed the mud, came up the bank without pushing aside (probably without feeling) the brambles which dilacerated his flesh, and dragged himself, nauseous and blood-stained, to the circular enclosure crowned by a stone tiger or horse, which once was the color of fire and now was that of ashes. This circle was a temple, long ago devoured by fire, which the malarial jungle had profaned and whose god no longer received the homage of men. The stranger stretched out beneath the pedestal. He was awakened by the sun high above. He evidenced without astonishment that his wounds had closed; he shut his pale eyes and slept, not out of bodily weakness but out of determination of will. He knew that this temple was the place required by his invincible purpose; he knew that, downstream, the incessant trees had not managed to choke the ruins of another propitious temple, whose gods were also burned and dead; he knew that his immediate obligation was to sleep. Towards midnight he was awakened by the disconsolate cry of a bird. Prints of bare feet, some figs and a jug told him that men of the region had respectfully spied upon his sleep and were solicitous of his favor or feared his magic. He felt the chill of fear and sought out a burial niche in the dilapidated wall and covered himself with some unknown leaves.

The purpose which guided him was not impossible, though it was supernatural. He wanted to dream a man: he wanted to dream him with minute integrity and insert him into reality. This magical project had exhausted the entire content of his soul; if someone had asked him his own name or any trait of his previous life, he would not have been able to answer. The uninhabited and broken temple suited him, for it was a minimum of visible world; the nearness of the peasants also suited him, for they would see that his frugal necessities were supplied. The rice and fruit of their tribute were sufficient sustenance for his body, consecrated to the sole task of sleeping and dreaming.

At first, his dreams were chaotic; somewhat later, they were of a dialectical nature. The stranger dreamt that he was in the center of a circular amphitheater which in some way was the burned temple: clouds of silent students filled the gradins; the faces of the last ones hung many centuries away and at a cosmic height, but were entirely clear and precise. The man was lecturing to them on anatomy, cosmography, magic; the countenances listened with eagerness and strove to respond with understanding, as if they divined the importance of the examination which would redeem one of them from his state of vain appearance and interpolate him into the world of reality. The man, both in dreams and awake, considered his phantoms' replies, was not deceived by impostors, divined a growing intelligence in certain perplexities. He sought a soul which would merit participation in the universe.

After nine or ten nights, he comprehended with some bitterness that he could expect nothing of those students who passively accepted his doctrines, but that he could of those who, at times, would venture a reasonable contradiction. The former, though worthy of love and affection, could not rise to the state of individuals; the latter pre-existed somewhat more. One afternoon (now his afternoons too were tributaries of sleep, now he remained awake only for a couple of hours at dawn) he dismissed the vast illusory college forever and kept one single student. He was a silent boy, sallow, sometimes obstinate, with sharp features which reproduced those of the dreamer. He was not long disconcerted by his companions' sudden elimination; his progress, after a few special lessons, astounded his teacher. Nevertheless, catastrophe ensued. The man emerged from sleep one day as if from a viscous desert, looked at the vain light of afternoon, which at first he confused with that of dawn, and understood that he had not really dreamt. All that night and all day, the intolerable lucidity of insomnia weighed upon him. He tried to explore the jungle, to exhaust himself; amidst the hemlocks, he was scarcely able to manage a few snatches of feeble sleep, fleetingly mottled with some rudimentary visions which were useless. He tried to convoke the college and had scarcely uttered a few brief words of exhortation, when it became deformed and was extinguished. In his almost perpetual sleeplessness, his old eyes burned with tears of anger.

He comprehended that the effort to mold the incoherent and vertiginous matter dreams are made of was the most arduous task a man could undertake, though he might penetrate all the enigmas of the upper and lower orders: much more arduous than weaving a rope of sand or coining the faceless wind. He comprehended that an initial failure was inevitable. He swore he would forget the enormous hallucination which had misled him at first, and he sought another method. Before putting it into effect, he dedicated a month to replenishing the powers his delirium had wasted. He abandoned any premeditation of dreaming and, almost at once, was able to sleep for a considerable part of the day. The few times he dreamt during this period, he did not take notice of the dreams. To take up his task again, he waited until the moon's disk was perfect. Then, in the afternoon, he purified himself in the waters of the river, worshiped the planetary gods, uttered the lawful syllables of a powerful name and slept. Almost immediately, he dreamt of a beating heart.

He dreamt it as active, warm, secret, the size of a closed fist, of garnet color in the penumbra of a human body as yet without face or sex; with minute love he dreamt it, for fourteen lucid nights. Each night he perceived it with greater clarity. He did not touch it, but limited himself to witnessing it, observing it, perhaps correcting it with his eyes. He perceived it, lived it, from many distances and many angles. On the fourteenth night he touched the pulmonary artery with his finger, and then the whole heart, inside and out. The examination satisfied him. Deliberately, he did not dream for a night; then he took the heart again, invoked the name of a planet and set about to envision another of the principal organs. Within a year he reached the skeleton, the eyelids. The innumerable hair was perhaps the most difficult task. He dreamt a complete man, a youth, but this youth could not rise nor did he speak nor could he open his eyes. Night after night, the man dreamt him as asleep.

In the Gnostic cosmogonies, the demiurgi knead and mold a red Adam who cannot stand alone; as unskillful and crude and elementary as this Adam of dust was the Adam of dreams fabricated by the magician's nights of effort. One afternoon, the man almost destroyed his work, but then repented. (It would have been better for him had he destroyed it.) Once he had completed his supplications to the numina of the earth and the river, he threw himself down at the feet of the effigy which was perhaps a tiger and perhaps a horse, and implored its unknown succor. That twilight, he dreamt of the statue. He dreamt of it as a living, tremulous thing: it was not an atrocious mongrel of tiger and horse, but both these vehement creatures at once and also a bull, a rose, a tempest. This multiple god revealed to him that its earthly name was Fire, that in the circular temple (and in others of its kind) people had rendered it sacrifices and cult and that it would magically give life to the sleeping phantom, in such a way that all creatures except Fire itself and the dreamer would believe him to be a man of flesh and blood. The man was ordered by the divinity to instruct his creature in its rites, and send him to the other broken temple whose pyramids survived downstream, so that in this deserted edifice a voice might give glory to the god. In the dreamer's dream, the dreamed one awoke.

The magician carried out these orders. He devoted a period of time (which finally comprised two years) to revealing the arcana of the universe and of the fire cult to his dream child. Inwardly, it pained him to be separated from the boy. Under the pretext of pedagogical necessity, each day he prolonged the hours he dedicated to his dreams. He also redid the right shoulder, which was perhaps deficient. At times, he was troubled by the impression that all this had happened before . . . In general, his days were happy; when he closed his eyes, he would think: *Now I shall be with my son.* Or, less often: *The child I have engendered awaits me and will not exist if I do not go to him.*

Gradually, he accustomed the boy to reality. Once he ordered him to place a banner on a distant peak. The following day, the banner flickered from the mountain top. He tried other analogous experiments, each more daring than the last. He understood with certain bitterness that his son was ready—and perhaps impatient—to be born. That night he kissed him for the first time and sent him to the other temple whose debris showed white downstream, through many leagues of inextricable jungle and swamp. But first (so that he would never know he was a phantom, so that he would be thought a man like others) he instilled into him a complete oblivion of his years of apprenticeship.

The man's victory and peace were dimmed by weariness. At dawn and at twilight, he would prostrate himself before the stone figure, imagining perhaps that his unreal child was practicing the same rites, in other circular ruins, downstream; at night, he would not dream, or would dream only as all men do. He perceived the sounds and forms of the universe with a certain colorlessness: his absent son was being nurtured with these diminutions of his soul. His life's purpose was complete; the man persisted in a kind of ecstasy. After a time, which some narrators of his story prefer to compute in years and others in lustra, he was awakened one midnight by two boatmen; he could not see their faces, but they told him of a magic man in a temple of the North who could walk upon fire and not be burned. The magician suddenly remembered the words of the god. He recalled that, of all the creatures of the world, fire was the only one that knew his son was a phantom. This recollection, at first soothing, finally tormented him. He feared his son might meditate on his abnormal privilege and discover in some way that his condition was that of a mere image. Not to be a man, to be the projection of another man's dream, what a feeling of humiliation, of vertigo! All fathers are interested in the children they have procreated (they have permitted to exist) in mere confusion or pleasure; it was natural that the magician should fear for the future of that son, created in thought, limb by limb and feature by feature, in a thousand and one secret nights.

The end of his meditations was sudden, though it was foretold in certain signs. First (after a long drought) a faraway cloud on a hill, light and rapid as a bird; then, toward the south, the sky which had the rose color of the leopard's mouth; then the smoke which corroded the metallic nights; finally, the panicky flight of the animals. For what was happening had happened many centuries ago. The ruins of the fire god's sanctuary were destroyed by fire. In a birdless dawn the magician saw the concentric blaze close round the walls. For a moment, he thought of taking refuge in the river, but then he knew that death was coming to crown his old age and absolve him of his labors. He walked into the shreds of flame. But they did not bite into his flesh, they caressed him and engulfed him without heat or combustion. With relief, with humiliation, with terror, he understood that he too was a mere appearance, dreamt by another.

1940

Death and the Compass

For Mandie Molina Vedia
Translated by Donald A. Yates

Of the many problems which exercised the reckless discernment of Lönnrot, none was so strange—so rigorously strange, shall we say—as the periodic series of bloody events which culminated at the villa of Triste-le-Roy, amid the ceaseless aroma of the eucalypti. It is true that Erik Lönnrot failed to prevent the last murder, but that he foresaw it is indisputable. Neither did he guess the identity of Yarmolinsky's luckless assassin, but he did succeed in divining the secret morphology behind the fiendish series as well as the participation of Red Scharlach, whose other nickname is Scharlach the Dandy. That criminal (as countless others) had sworn on his honor to kill Lönnrot, but the latter could never be intimidated. Lönnrot believed himself a pure reasoner, an Auguste Dupin,* but there was something of the adventurer in him, and even a little of the gambler.

The first murder occurred in the Hôtel du Nord—that tall prism which dominates the estuary whose waters are the color of the desert. To that tower (which quite glaringly unites the hateful whiteness of a hospital, the numbered divisibility of a jail, and the general appearance of a bordello) there came on the third day of December the delegate from Podolsk to the Third Talmudic Congress, Doctor Marcel Yarmolinsky, a gray-bearded man with gray eyes. We shall never know whether the Hôtel du Nord pleased him; he accepted it with the ancient resignation which had allowed him to endure three years of war in the Carpathians and three thousand years of oppression and pogroms. He was given a room on Floor R, across from the suite which was occupied—not without splendor—by the Tetrarch of Galilee. Yarmolinsky supped, postponed until the following day an inspection of the unknown city, arranged in a *placard* his many books and few personal possessions, and before midnight extinguished his light. (Thus declared the Tetrarch's chauffeur who slept in the adjoining room.) On the fourth, at 11:03 A.M., the editor of the *Yidische Zaitung* put in a call to him; Doctor Yarmolinsky did not answer. He was found in his room, his face already a little dark, nearly nude beneath a large, anachronistic cape. He was lying

---

*Logician hero of "The Purloined Letter" and other detective stories by Edgar Allan Poe.—Ed.

not far from the door which opened on the hall; a deep knife wound had split his breast. A few hours later, in the same room amid journalists, photographers and policemen, Inspector Treviranus and Lönnrot were calmly discussing the problem.

"No need to look for a three-legged cat here," Treviranus was saying as he brandished an imperious cigar. "We all know that the Tetrarch of Galilee owns the finest sapphires in the world. Someone, intending to steal them, must have broken in here by mistake. Yarmolinsky got up; the robber had to kill him. How does it sound to you?"

"Possible, but not interesting," Lönnrot answered. "You'll reply that reality hasn't the least obligation to be interesting. And I'll answer you that reality may avoid that obligation but that hypotheses may not. In the hypothesis that you propose, chance intervenes copiously. Here we have a dead rabbi; I would prefer a purely rabbinical explanation, not the imaginary mischances of an imaginary robber."

Treviranus replied ill-humoredly:

"I'm not interested in rabbinical explanations. I am interested in capturing the man who stabbed this unknown person."

"Not so unknown," corrected Lönnrot. "Here are his complete works." He indicated in the wall-cupboard a row of tall books: a *Vindication of the Cabala; An Examination of the Philosophy of Robert Fludd;* a literal translation of the *Sepher Yezirah;* a *Biography of the Baal Shem;* a *History of the Hasidic Sect;* a monograph (in German) on the Tetragrammaton; another, on the divine nomenclature of the Pentateuch. The inspector regarded them with dread, almost with repulsion. Then he began to laugh.

"I'm a poor Christian," he said. "Carry off those musty volumes if you want; I don't have any time to waste on Jewish superstitions."

"Maybe the crime belongs to the history of Jewish superstitions," murmured Lönnrot.

"Like Christianity," the editor of the *Yidische Zaitung* ventured to add. He was myopic, an atheist and very shy.

No one answered him. One of the agents had found in the small typewriter a piece of paper on which was written the following unfinished sentence:

The first letter of the Name has been uttered

Lönnrot abstained from smiling. Suddenly become a bibliophile or Hebraist, he ordered a package made of the dead man's books and carried them off to his apartment. Indifferent to the police investigation, he dedicated himself to studying them. One large octavo volume revealed to him the teachings of Israel Baal Shem Tobh, founder of the sect of the Pious; another, the virtues and terrors of the Tetragrammaton, which is the unutterable name of God; another, the thesis that God has a secret name, in which is epitomized (as in the crystal sphere which the Persians ascribe to Alexander of Macedonia) his ninth attribute, eternity—that is to say, the immediate knowledge of all things that will be, which are and which have been in the universe. Tradition numbers ninety-nine names of God; the Hebraists attribute that imperfect number to magical fear of even numbers; the Hasidim reason that that hiatus indicates a hundredth name—the Absolute Name.

From this erudition Lönnrot was distracted, a few days later, by the appearance of the editor of the *Yidische Zaitung*. The latter wanted to talk about the murder; Lönnrot preferred to discuss the diverse names of God; the journalist declared, in three columns, that the investigator, Erik Lönnrot, had dedicated himself to studying the names of God in order to come across the name of the murderer. Lönnrot, accustomed to the simplifications of journalism, did not become indignant. One of those enterprising shopkeepers who have discovered that any given man is resigned to buying any given book published a popular edition of the *History of the Hasidic Sect*.

The second murder occurred on the evening of the third of January, in the most deserted and empty corner of the capital's western suburbs. Towards dawn, one of the gendarmes who patrol those solitudes on horseback saw a man in a poncho, lying prone in the shadow of an old paint shop. The harsh features seemed to be masked in blood; a deep knife wound had split his breast. On the wall, across the yellow and red diamonds, were some words written in chalk. The gendarme spelled them out ... That afternoon, Treviranus and Lönnrot headed for the remote scene of the crime. To the left and right of the automobile the city disintegrated; the firmament grew and houses were of less importance than a brick kiln or a poplar tree. They arrived at their miserable destination: an alley's end, with rose-colored walls which somehow seemed to reflect the extravagant sunset. The dead man had already been identified. He was Daniel Simon Azevedo, an individual of some fame in the old northern suburbs, who had risen from wagon driver to political tough, then degenerated to a thief and even an informer. (The singular style of his death seemed appropriate to them: Azevedo was the last representative of a generation of bandits who knew how to manipulate a dagger, but not a revolver.) The words in chalk were the following:

The second letter of the Name has been uttered

The third murder occurred on the night of the third of February. A little before one o'clock, the telephone in Inspector Treviranus' office rang. In avid secretiveness, a man with a guttural voice spoke; he said his name was Ginzberg (or Ginsburg) and that he was prepared to communicate, for reasonable remuneration, the events surrounding the two sacrifices of Azevedo and Yarmolinsky. A discordant sound of whistles and horns drowned out the informer's voice. Then, the connection was broken off. Without yet rejecting the possibility of a hoax (after all, it was carnival time), Treviranus found out that he had been called from the Liverpool House, a tavern on the rue de Toulon, that dingy street where side by side exist the cosmorama and the coffee shop, the bawdy house and the bible sellers. Treviranus spoke with the owner. The latter (Black Finnegan, an old Irish criminal who was immersed in, almost overcome by, respectability) told him that the last person to use the phone was a lodger, a certain Gryphius, who had just left with some friends. Treviranus went immediately to Liverpool House. The owner related the following. Eight days ago Gryphius had rented a room above the tavern. He was a sharp-featured man with a nebulous gray beard, and was shabbily dressed in black; Finnegan (who used the room for a purpose which Treviranus guessed) demanded a rent which was undoubtedly excessive; Gryphius paid the stipulated sum without hesitation. He almost never went out; he dined and lunched in his room; his face was scarcely known in the bar. On the night in question, he came downstairs to make a phone call from Finnegan's office. A closed cab stopped in front of the tavern. The driver didn't move from his seat; several patrons recalled that he was wearing a bear's mask. Two harlequins got out of the cab; they were of short stature and no one failed to observe that they were very drunk. With a tooting of horns, they burst into Finnegan's office; they embraced Gryphius, who appeared to recognize them but responded coldly; they exchanged a few words in Yiddish—he in a low, guttural voice, they in high-pitched, false voices—and then went up to the room. Within a quarter hour the three descended, very happy. Gryphius, staggering, seemed as drunk as the others. He walked—tall and dizzy—in the middle, between the masked harlequins. (One of the women at the bar remembered the yellow, red and green diamonds.) Twice he stumbled; twice he was caught and held by the harlequins. Moving off toward the inner harbor which enclosed a rectangular body of water, the three got into the cab and disappeared. From the footboard of the cab, the last of the harlequins scrawled an obscene figure and a sentence on one of the slates of the pier shed.

Treviranus saw the sentence. It was virtually predictable. It said:

The last of the letters of the Name has been uttered

Afterwards, he examined the small room of Gryphius-Ginzberg. On the floor there was a brusque star of blood; in the corners, traces of cigarettes of a Hungarian brand; in a cabinet, a book in Latin—the *Philologus Hebraeo-Graecus* (1739) of Leusden—with several manuscript notes. Treviranus looked it over with indignation and had Lönnrot located. The latter, without removing his hat, began to read while the inspector was interrogating the contradictory witnesses to the possible kidnapping. At four o'clock they left. Out on the twisted rue de Toulon, as they were treading on the dead serpentines of the dawn, Treviranus said:

"And what if all this business tonight were just a mock rehearsal?"

Erik Lönnrot smiled and, with all gravity, read a passage (which was underlined) from the thirty-third dissertation of the *Philologus: Dies Judacorum incipit ad solis occasu usque ad solis occasum diei sequentis.*

"This means," he added, " 'The Hebrew day begins at sundown and lasts until the following sundown.' "

The inspector attempted an irony.

"Is that fact the most valuable one you've come across tonight?"

"No. Even more valuable was a word that Ginzberg used."

The afternoon papers did not overlook the periodic disappearances. *La Cruz de la Espada* contrasted them with the admirable discipline and order of the last Hermetical Congress; Ernst Palast, in *El Mártir,* criticized "the intolerable delays in this clandestine and frugal pogrom, which has taken three months to murder three Jews"; the *Yidische Zaitung* rejected the horrible hypothesis of an anti-Semitic plot, "even though many penetrating intellects admit no other solution to the triple mystery"; the most illustrious gunman of the south, Dandy Red Scharlach, swore that in his district similar crimes could never occur, and he accused Inspector Franz Treviranus of culpable negligence.

On the night of March first, the inspector received an impressive-looking sealed envelope. He opened it; the envelope contained a letter signed "Baruch Spinoza" and a detailed plan of the city, obviously torn from a Baedeker. The letter prophesied that on the third of March there would not be a fourth murder, since the paint shop in the west, the tavern on the rue de Toulon and the Hôtel du Nord were "the perfect vertices of a mystic equilateral triangle"; the map demonstrated in red ink the regularity of the triangle. Treviranus read the *more geometrico* argument with resignation, and sent the letter and the map to Lönnrot—who, unquestionably, was deserving of such madnesses.

Erik Lönnrot studied them. The three locations were in fact equidistant. Symmetry in time (the third of December, the third of January, the third of February); symmetry in space as well . . . Suddenly, he felt as if he were on the point of solving the mystery. A set of calipers and a compass completed his quick intuition. He smiled, pronounced the word Tetragrammaton (of recent acquisition) and phoned the inspector. He said:

"Thank you for the equilateral triangle you sent me last night. It has enabled me to solve the problem. This Friday the criminals will be in jail, we may rest assured."

"Then they're not planning a fourth murder?"

"Precisely because they *are* planning a fourth murder we can rest assured."

Lönnrot hung up. One hour later he was traveling on one of the Southern Railway's trains, in the direction of the abandoned villa of Triste-le-Roy. To the south of the city of our story, flows a blind little river of muddy water, defamed by refuse and garbage. On the far side is an industrial suburb where, under the protection of a political boss from Barcelona, gunmen thrive. Lönnrot smiled at the thought that the most celebrated gunman of all—Red Scharlach—would have given a great deal to know of his clandestine visit. Azevedo had been an associate of Scharlach; Lönnrot considered the remote possibility that the fourth victim might be Scharlach himself. Then he rejected the idea . . . He had very nearly deciphered the problem; mere circumstances, reality (names, prison records, faces, judicial and penal proceedings) hardly interested him now. He wanted to travel a bit, he wanted to rest from three months of sedentary investigation. He reflected that the explanation of the murders was in an anonymous triangle and a dusty Greek word. The mystery appeared almost crystalline to him now; he was mortified to have dedicated a hundred days to it.

The train stopped at a silent loading station. Lönnrot got off. It was one of those deserted afternoons that seem like dawns. The air of the turbid, puddled plain was damp and cold. Lönnrot began walking along the countryside. He saw dogs, he saw a car on a siding, he saw the horizon, he saw a silver-colored horse drinking the crapulous water of a puddle. It was growing dark when he saw the rectangular belvedere of the villa of Triste-le-Roy, almost as tall as the black eucalypti which surrounded it. He thought that scarcely one dawning and one nightfall (an ancient splendor in the east and another in the west) separated him from the moment long desired by the seekers of the Name.

A rusty wrought-iron fence defined the irregular perimeter of the villa. The main gate was closed. Lönnrot, without much hope of getting in, circled the area. Once again before the insurmountable gate, he placed his hand between the bars almost mechanically and encountered the bolt. The creaking of the iron surprised him. With a laborious passivity the whole gate swung back.

Lönnrot advanced among the eucalypti treading on confused generations of rigid, broken leaves. Viewed from anear, the house of the villa of Triste-le-Roy abounded in pointless symmetries and in maniacal repetitions: to one Diana in a murky niche corresponded a second Diana in another niche; one balcony was reflected in another balcony; double stairways led to double balustrades. A two-faced Hermes projected a monstrous shadow. Lönnrot circled the house as he had the villa. He examined everything; beneath the level of the terrace he saw a narrow Venetian blind.

He pushed it; a few marble steps descended to a vault. Lönnrot, who had now perceived the architect's preferences, guessed that at the opposite wall there would be another stairway. He found it, ascended, raised his hands and opened the trap door.

A brilliant light led him to a window. He opened it: a yellow, rounded moon defined two silent fountains in the melancholy garden. Lönnrot explored the house. Through anterooms and galleries he passed to duplicate patios, and time after time to the same patio. He ascended the dusty stairs to circular antechambers; he was multiplied infinitely in opposing mirrors; he grew tired of opening or half-opening windows which revealed outside the same desolate garden from various heights and various angles; inside, only pieces of furniture wrapped in yellow dust sheets and chandeliers bound up in tarlatan. A bedroom detained him; in that bedroom, one single flower in a porcelain vase; at the first touch the ancient petals fell apart. On the second floor, on the top floor, the house seemed infinite and expanding. *The house is not this large,* he thought. *Other things are making it seem larger: the dim light, the symmetry, the mirrors, so many years, my unfamiliarity, the loneliness.*

By way of a spiral staircase he arrived at the oriel. The early evening moon shone through the diamonds of the window; they were yellow, red and green. An astonishing, dizzying recollection struck him.

Two men of short stature, robust and ferocious, threw themselves on him and disarmed him; another, very tall, saluted him gravely and said: "You are very kind. You have saved us a night and a day."

It was Red Scharlach. The men handcuffed Lönnrot. The latter at length recovered his voice.

"Scharlach, are you looking for the Secret Name?"

Scharlach remained standing, indifferent. He had not participated in the brief struggle, and he scarcely extended his hand to receive Lönnrot's revolver. He spoke; Lönnrot noted in his voice a fatigued triumph, a hatred the size of the universe, a sadness not less than that hatred.

"No," said Scharlach. "I am seeking something more ephemeral and perishable, I am seeking Erik Lönnrot. Three years ago, in a gambling house on the rue de Toulon, you arrested my brother and had him sent to jail. My men slipped me away in a coupé from the gun battle with a policeman's bullet in my stomach. Nine days and nine nights I lay in agony in this desolate, symmetrical villa; fever was demolishing me, and the odious two-faced Janus who watches the twilights and the dawns lent horror to my dreams and to my waking. I came to abominate my body, I came to sense that two eyes, two hands, two lungs are as monstrous as two faces. An Irishman tried to convert me to the faith of Jesus; he repeated to me the phrase of the *goyim:* All roads lead to Rome. At night my delirium nurtured itself on that metaphor; I felt that the world was a labyrinth, from which it was impossible to flee, for all roads, though they pretend to lead to the north or south, actually lead to Rome, which was also the quadrilateral jail where my brother was dying and the villa of Triste-le-Roy. On those nights I swore by the God who sees with two faces and by all the gods of fever and of the mirrors to weave a labyrinth around the man who had imprisoned my brother. I have woven it and it is firm: the ingredients are a dead heresiologist, a compass, an eighteenth-century sect, a Greek word, a dagger, the diamonds of a paint shop.

"The first term of the sequence was given to me by chance. I had planned with a few colleagues—among them Daniel Azevedo—the robbery of the Tetrarch's sapphires. Azevedo betrayed us: he got drunk with the money that we had advanced him and he undertook the job a day early. He got lost in the vastness of the hotel; around two in the morning he stumbled into Yarmolinsky's room. The latter, harassed by insomnia, had started to write. He was working on some notes, apparently, for an article on the Name of God; he had already written the words: *The first letter of the Name has been uttered.* Azevedo warned him to be silent; Yarmolinsky reached out his hand for the bell which would awaken the hotel's forces; Azevedo countered with a single stab in the chest. It was almost a reflex action; half a century of violence had taught him that the easiest and surest thing is to kill . . . Ten days later I learned through the *Yidische Zaitung* that you were seeking in Yarmolinsky's writings the key to his death. I read the *History of the Hasidic Sect;* I learned that the reverent fear of uttering the Name of God had given rise to the doctrine that that Name is all powerful and recondite. I discovered that some Hasidim, in search of that secret Name, had gone so far as to perform human sacrifices . . . I knew that you would make the conjecture that the Hasidim had sacrificed the rabbi; I set myself the task of justifying that conjecture.

"Marcel Yarmolinsky died on the night of December third; for the second 'sacrifice' I selected the night of January third. He died in the north; for the second 'sacrifice' a place in the west was suitable. Daniel Azevedo was the necessary victim. He deserved death; he was impulsive, a traitor; his apprehension could destroy the entire plan. One of us stabbed him; in order to link his corpse to the other one I wrote on the paint shop diamonds: *The second letter of the Name has been uttered.*

"The third murder was produced on the third of February. It was, as Treviranus guessed, a mere sham. I am Gryphius-Ginzberg-Ginsburg; I endured an interminable week (supplemented by a tenuous fake beard) in the perverse cubicle on the rue de Toulon, until my friends abducted me. From the footboard of the cab, one of them wrote on a post: *The last of the letters of the Name has been uttered.* That sentence revealed that the series of murders was *triple.* Thus the public understood it; I, nevertheless, interspersed repeated signs that would allow you, Erik Lönnrot, the reasoner, to understand that the series was quadruple. A portent in the north, others in the east and west, demand a fourth portent in the south; the Tetragrammaton—the name of God, JHVH—is made up of *four* letters; the harlequins and the paint shop sign suggested *four* points. In the manual of Leusden I underlined a certain passage: that passage manifests that Hebrews compute the day from sunset to sunset; that passage makes known that the deaths occurred on the *fourth* of each month. I sent the equilateral triangle to Treviranus. I foresaw that you would add the missing point. The point which would form a perfect rhomb, the point which fixes in advance where a punctual death awaits you. I have premeditated everything, Erik Lönnrot, in order to attract you to the solitudes of Triste-le-Roy."

Lönnrot avoided Scharlach's eyes. He looked at the trees and the sky subdivided into diamonds of turbid yellow, green and red. He felt faintly cold, and he felt, too, an impersonal—almost anonymous—sadness. It was already night; from the dusty garden came the futile cry of a bird. For the last time, Lönnrot considered the problem of the symmetrical and periodic deaths.

"In your labyrinth there are three lines too many," he said at last. "I know of one Greek labyrinth which is a single straight line. Along that line so many philosophers have lost themselves that a mere detective might well do so, too. Scharlach, when in some other incarnation you hunt me, pretend to commit (or do commit) a crime at A, then a second crime at B, eight kilometers from A, then a third crime at C, four kilometers from A and B, half-way between the two. Wait for me afterwards at D, two kilometers from A and C, again halfway between both. Kill me at D, as you are now going to kill me at Triste-le-Roy."

"The next time I kill you," replied Scharlach, "I promise you that labyrinth, consisting of a single line which is invisible and unceasing."

He moved back a few steps. Then, very carefully, he fired.

1942

Emma Zunz

Translated by Donald A. Yates

RETURNING HOME FROM the Tarbuch and Loewenthal textile mills on the 14th of January, 1922, Emma Zunz discovered in the rear of the entrance hall a letter, posted in Brazil, which informed her that her father had died. The stamp and the envelope deceived her at first; then the unfamiliar handwriting made her uneasy. Nine or ten lines tried to fill up the page; Emma read that Mr. Maier had taken by mistake a large dose of veronal and had died on the third of the month in the hospital of Bagé. A boardinghouse friend of her father had signed the letter, some Fein or Fain from Río Grande, with no way of knowing that he was addressing the deceased's daughter.

Emma dropped the paper. Her first impression was of a weak feeling in her stomach and in her knees; then of blind guilt, of unreality, of coldness, of fear; then she wished that it were already the next day. Immediately afterward she realized that that wish was futile because the death of her father was the only thing that had happened in the world, and it would go on happening endlessly. She picked up the piece of paper and went to her room. Furtively, she hid it in a drawer, as if somehow she already knew the ulterior facts. She had already begun to suspect them, perhaps; she had already become the person she would be.

In the growing darkness, Emma wept until the end of that day for the suicide of Manuel Maier, who in the old happy days was Emmanuel Zunz. She remembered summer vacations at a little farm near Gualeguay, she remembered (tried to remember) her mother, she remembered the little house at Lanús which had been auctioned off, she remembered the yellow lozenges of a window, she remembered the warrant for arrest, the ignominy, she remembered the poison-pen letters with the newspaper's account of "the cashier's embezzlement," she remembered (but this she never forgot) that her father, on the last night, had sworn to her that the thief was Loewenthal. Loewenthal, Aaron Loewenthal, formerly the manager of the factory and now one of the owners. Since 1916 Emma had guarded the secret. She had revealed it to no one, not even to her best friend, Elsa Urstein. Perhaps she was shunning profane incredulity; perhaps she believed that the secret was a link between herself and the absent parent. Loewenthal did not know that she knew; Emma Zunz derived from this slight fact a feeling of power.

She did not sleep that night and when the first light of dawn defined the rectangle of the window, her plan was already perfected. She tried to make the day, which seemed interminable to her, like any other. At the factory there were rumors of a strike. Emma declared herself, as usual, against all violence. At six o'clock, with work over, she went with Elsa to a women's club that had a gymnasium and a swimming pool. They signed their names; she had to repeat and spell out her first and her last name, she had to respond to the vulgar jokes that accompanied the medical examination. With Elsa and with the youngest of the Kronfuss girls she discussed what movie they would go to Sunday afternoon. Then they talked about boyfriends and no one expected Emma to speak. In April she would be nineteen years old, but men inspired in her, still, an almost pathological fear . . . Having returned home, she prepared a tapioca soup and a few vegetables, ate early, went to bed and forced herself to sleep. In this way, laborious and trivial, Friday the fifteenth, the day before, elapsed.

Impatience awoke her on Saturday. Impatience it was, not uneasiness, and the special relief of it being that day at last. No longer did she have to plan and imagine; within a few hours the simplicity of the facts would suffice. She read in *La Prensa* that the *Nordstjärnan,* out of Malmö, would sail that evening from Pier 3. She phoned Loewenthal, insinuated that she wanted to confide in him, without the other girls knowing, something pertaining to the strike; and she promised to stop by at his office at nightfall. Her voice trembled; the tremor was suitable to an informer. Nothing else of note happened that morning. Emma worked until twelve o'clock and then settled with Elsa and Perla Kronfuss the details of their Sunday stroll. She lay down after lunch and reviewed, with her eyes closed, the plan she had devised. She thought that the final step would be less horrible than the first and that it would doubtlessly afford her the taste of victory and justice. Suddenly, alarmed, she got up and ran to the dresser drawer. She opened it; beneath the picture of Milton Sills, where she had left it the night before, was Fain's letter. No one could have seen it; she began to read it and tore it up.

To relate with some reality the events of that afternoon would be difficult and perhaps unrighteous. One attribute of a hellish experience is unreality, an attribute that seems to allay its terrors and which aggravates them perhaps. How could one make credible an action which was scarcely believed in by the person who executed it, how to recover that brief chaos which today the memory of Emma Zunz repudiates and confuses? Emma lived in Almagro, on Liniers Street: we are certain that in the afternoon she went down to the waterfront. Perhaps on the infamous Paseo de Julio she saw herself multiplied in mirrors, revealed by lights and denuded by hungry eyes, but it is more reasonable to suppose that at first she wandered, unnoticed, through the indifferent portico . . . She entered two or three bars, noted the routine or technique of the other women. Finally she came across men from the *Nordstjärnan*. One of them, very young, she feared might inspire some tenderness in her and she chose instead another, perhaps shorter than she and coarse, in order that the purity of the horror might not be mitigated. The man led her to a door, then to a murky entrance hall and afterwards to a narrow stairway and then a vestibule (in which there was a window with lozenges identical to those in the house at Lanús) and then to a passageway and then to a door which was closed behind her. The arduous events are outside of time, either because the immediate past is as if disconnected from the future, or because the parts which form these events do not seem to be consecutive.

During that time outside of time, in that perplexing disorder of disconnected and atrocious sensations, did Emma Zunz think *once* about the dead man who motivated the sacrifice? It is my belief that she did think once, and in that moment she endangered her desperate undertaking. She thought (she was unable not to think) that her father had done to her mother the hideous thing that was being done to her now. She thought of it with weak amazement and took refuge, quickly, in vertigo. The man, a Swede or Finn, did not speak Spanish. He was a tool for Emma, as she was for him, but she served him for pleasure whereas he served her for justice.

When she was alone, Emma did not open her eyes immediately. On the little night table was the money that the man had left: Emma sat up and tore it to pieces as before she had torn the letter. Tearing money is an impiety, like throwing away bread; Emma repented the moment after she did it. An act of pride and on that day . . . Her fear was lost in the grief of her body, in her disgust. The grief and the nausea were chaining her, but Emma got up slowly and proceeded to dress herself. In the room there were no longer any bright colors; the last light of dusk was weakening. Emma was able to leave without anyone seeing her; at the corner she got on a Lacroze streetcar heading west. She selected, in keeping with her plan, the seat farthest toward the front, so that her face would not be seen. Perhaps it comforted her to verify in the insipid movement along the streets that what had happened had not contaminated things. She rode through the diminishing opaque suburbs, seeing them and forgetting them at the same instant, and got off on one of the side streets of Warnes. Paradoxically her fatigue was turning out to be a strength, since it obligated her to concentrate on the details of the adventure and concealed from her the background and the objective.

Aaron Loewenthal was to all persons a serious man, to his intimate friends a miser. He lived above the factory, alone. Situated in the barren outskirts of the town, he feared thieves; in the patio of the factory there was a large dog and in the drawer of his desk, everyone knew, a revolver. He had mourned with gravity, the year before, the unexpected death of his wife—a Gauss who had brought him a fine dowry—but money was his real passion. With intimate embarrassment, he knew himself to be less apt at earning it than at saving it. He was very religious; he believed he had a secret pact with God which exempted him from doing good in exchange for prayers and piety. Bald, fat, wearing the band of mourning, with smoked glasses and blond beard, he was standing next to the window awaiting the confidential report of worker Zunz.

He saw her push the iron gate (which he had left open for her) and cross the gloomy patio. He saw her make a little detour when the chained dog barked. Emma's lips were moving rapidly, like those of someone praying in a low voice; weary, they were repeating the sentence which Mr. Loewenthal would hear before dying.

Things did not happen as Emma Zunz had anticipated. Ever since the morning before she had imagined herself wielding the firm revolver, forcing the wretched creature to confess his wretched guilt and exposing the daring stratagem which would permit the Justice of God to triumph over human justice. (Not out of fear but because of being an instrument of Justice she did not want to be punished.) Then, one single shot in the center of his chest would seal Loewenthal's fate. But things did not happen that way.

In Aaron Loewenthal's presence, more than the urgency of avenging her father, Emma felt the need of inflicting punishment for the outrage she had suffered. She was unable not to kill him after that thorough dishonor. Nor did she have time for theatrics. Seated, timid, she made excuses to Loewenthal, she invoked (as a privilege of the informer) the obligation of loyalty, uttered a few names, inferred others and broke off as if fear had conquered her. She managed to have Loewenthal leave to get a glass of water for her. When the former, unconvinced by such a fuss but indulgent, returned from the dining room, Emma had already taken the heavy revolver out of the drawer. She squeezed the trigger twice. The large body collapsed as if the reports and the smoke had shattered it, the glass of water smashed, the face looked at her with amazement and anger, the mouth of the face swore at her in Spanish and Yiddish. The evil words did not slacken; Emma had to fire again. In the patio the chained dog broke out barking, and a gush of rude blood flowed from the obscene lips and soiled the beard and the clothing. Emma began the accusation she had prepared ("I have avenged my father and they will not be able to punish me . . ."), but she did not finish it, because Mr. Loewenthal had already died. She never knew if he managed to understand.

The straining barks reminded her that she could not, yet, rest. She disarranged the divan, unbuttoned the dead man's jacket, took off the bespattered glasses and left them on the filing cabinet. Then she picked up the telephone and repeated what she would repeat so many times again, with these and with other words: *Something incredible has happened . . . Mr. Loewenthal had me come over on the pretext of the strike . . . He abused me, I killed him . . .*

Actually, the story *was* incredible, but it impressed everyone because substantially it was true. True was Emma Zunz' tone, true was her shame, true was her hate. True also was the outrage she had suffered: only the circumstances were false, the time, and one or two proper names.

1949

Lydia Cabrera

b. 1900

LYDIA CABRERA WAS born in Havana on May 20, 1900, into a well-to-do family. As was the custom for women of her generation, her formal education did not go beyond secondary school. She developed an early interest in the visual arts and studied painting in Paris during the late 1920s. It was there that her childhood familiarity with Afro-Cuban folklore would flower during the 1930s. Cabrera's first collection of short stories, now considered a classic in Latin American literature, appeared first in French in 1936 and then in Spanish in 1940 as *Cuentos negros de Cuba* (Black tales from Cuba). Over the next fifty years, Cabrera would devote her research and writing to an exploration of Cuba's rich oral African literature. Among her best known works are *El monte* (1954; The mountain), a study of Afro-Cuban religion, and *Refranes de negros viejos* (1955; Proverbs from old black folk). She has lived in Miami since the early 1960s and has continued to publish steadily.

The Hill Called Mambiala

Translated by Elizabeth Millet

IT WAS NO secret in town that Serapio Trebejos, a black man, was ready for anything—except to work for his living.

For him there were always enough excuses for not working; his avocations were more important. And because of his graceful way of speaking and his talent for playing the guitar, in the end it was hard to refuse him anything, most of all because it seemed as if he wasn't asking for anything. A few cents for a cheap cigar and a drop of brandy, whatever was left over from dinner, and from time to time, some old and well-worn clothes—because it wasn't possible to walk about simply naked.

He lived with his family in a meager shack not owned or leased by anyone. The poor shack was about to tumble down once and for all; in a strong gust of wind or a threatening storm it held up precariously. It stood in front of the hill known as The Hill of Mambiala, outside the town, where the road twists and descends like a reptile down to the coast, in between the palm trees.

From charity, blessed be God, and without too many problems, they had been able to eat most of the time: he, his wife, and their children—two big-bellied black girls with their kinky hair tangled and full of lice, dirty, lazy, always tumbled across an old lop-sided cot, and now at a marriageable age; and two black long-limbed boys, ragged, wild and both without a job, a trade, or the will to work. All in all, boys who could not be relied upon for anything. But there came a very bad time—very bad, worse than anyone had thought possible, and food became scarce for everybody . . .

No one would help the black man Serapio. . . .

Nobody remembered ever seeing him cutting sugar cane or clearing a piece of land—not even planting a sweet potato!

Now he wandered all in vain, improvising ballads, playing the guitar, and holding out his sombrero full of holes and cockroaches . . .

"Why don't you work, Serapio? No more free soup, lazy man!"

And the good women of the house, lovers of justice, said:

"Don't let him in the door! Tell him that whatever's left over today is for the chickens."

"I'm sorry, brother, come back another day . . ."

This is how he and his offspring began to feel the pangs of hunger.

The Hill of Mambiala, not so far away, was a light downy green color, round as an orange and its top was covered with pumpkin vines. A patch of pumpkin vines without pumpkins. It was well known, those vines just did not bear fruit.

It was some days now that the black man and his family had lain down to sleep without so much as a mouthful. That morning, which happened to be a Palm Sunday, Serapio woke up from dreaming that he was inside a pumpkin like an unborn baby inside its mother's womb. With all his teeth fully grown, he bit into the soft flesh of the pumpkin, which caused her to jump up and down and run around yelling: "Help! Police! Save me!"—they were tickling her to death, she was going crazy . . .

"Is this a sign from heaven?" wondered the black man, crossing himself. "Oh, if only today on the Hill of Mambiala I could meet such a lady pumpkin!"

And, after telling his dream to the family, feeling much better as he did so, he climbed up to the top of the hill, and for a long time he eagerly searched about the area. Leaves, and stalks, and more leaves! In the whole thick, twisted, and dense patch, there wasn't a single meager little pumpkin—and he hadn't left out so much as an inch of ground in his search. Looking and looking, twelve o'clock came and went: the hour that other men were sitting down to eat their lunch.

Serapio wept, he implored God and Mambiala to help him. He patiently went on looking, leaf by leaf, stem by stem, in the silent pumpkin patch.

> Give me one, Mambiala, Mambiala
> Oh, Lord, Mambiala!
> Me poor, Mambiala,
> Oh, Lord, Mambiala!

"I'm dying of hunger, Mambiala, Mambiala!"

He was now exhausted, but before giving up his last hope, he got down on his knees and raised his arms up to heaven. He remembered a picture of a miracle he had once seen and he began to chant loudly up to the heavens.

The heavens did not pay him the slightest bit of attention. Not even one single pumpkin rained down upon his head. In the heat of his anguish he fell flat on his stomach. After weeping all the tears out onto the ground that his eyes could hold, he got up to go home, but just then he caught sight of something next to him on the ground. A little pot of red clay, in whose edges the sun shone like liquid gold. The most graceful and young pot that had ever come out of the hands of a potter. She was so nice, that he suddenly felt happy and wanted to caress her. He spoke to her as if it were completely natural that she would understand him, and even more natural that she would console him.

"Oh! How pretty and round and new you are! Who brought you here? Some poor wretched man like me, looking for a pumpkin?"

And, sighing, he asked her, "What's your name, fat little black one?"

The little pot, moving softly on her hips, replied very coquettishly,

"My name is the Little Good Cooking Pot."

"The hunger must be making me imagine this nonsense," thought

Serapio. "What did you say your name was? Is it you who is speaking, or is it me who is speaking for both of us, one sane and one crazy, and both starving?"

"The Little Good Cooking Pot."

"Well, cook me something!"

The little pot made a flourish in the air. She spread out a beautifully white tablecloth for herself upon the grass, and with elegant silverware (silver spoons and silver forks) she served up an exquisite lunch for the poor man, who did not know how to use any utensils other than his fingers, but who ate until he couldn't touch one more mouthful, and drank till the Hill of Mambiala began to sway from side to side . . .

And so the Hill of Mambiala lifted itself off the earth; it rose up like a balloon that went softly higher and higher into the deep blue. The black man held on tightly to the scraggly vines so he wouldn't fall, and fell deep asleep . . .

When the sun began to weaken, the man returned home with the little pot underneath his arm.

The members of his family ravenously awaited him. They had hardly seen him before they all began to yell: "The pumpkin! The pumpkin!" He replied by making a strange gesture, a gesture they had never seen before, but when they saw him coming closer with no pumpkin in his arms they knew it was bad news. Dismay came over the faces of those unlucky people, who had had little more than sugar-water and hope in the miracle of Mambiala all day, and they all accused him of eating the pumpkin by himself. All by himself, taking advantage of them when they couldn't see him!

Only the mother, the long and lean old woman who was indifferent to everything, did not move a muscle or seem to be excited. She sat stiffly upon her stool; hunger had turned her into wood, or maybe she had always been made of wood—thus was Mama Tecla. She never spoke. If by chance she did, it was in a jumbled confusion of words: she would grunt to herself or give short and unintelligible answers to some being who was only visible to her and was always bothering her with useless questions. They understood each other very well, however, and what she probably mumbled to this creature, looking at it with contempt, impatience, and a cigar butt hanging from her barely moving lips, was:

"You don't have to tell me anything: I already know it all."

Most of the time, the old woman who sat like an object in the corner, so silent and stiff and miserable, only seemed to be expressing in her abstraction, intensely . . . nothing.

And nobody paid her any attention. By now it was quite a while since anyone had remembered to pass her—if anything remained—the leftovers of their daily grub. When they did pass her something, the long dry fingers of Mama Tecla would roll up the leftovers into a ball and she would swallow it mechanically, not making an effort to chew or taste it. She did this with an indifference that reached the height of scorn.

"Go out and invite the neighbors—Yes sir, to stuff themselves full with us tonight!," ordered the black man, revealing the pot with pride, but one of his daughters, who had the mumps, said,

"Stuff themselves with what? With mice? This is all we need, did you hear him? My father has gone crazy!"

And not even one of his children obeyed him. Serapio himself had to go out and invite all the black people of the town and round up, where and when he could, some planks of wood and two donkeys.

Some came to laugh, others came out of sheer curiosity. The guests arrived without delay. When many of them saw the table as they came up the road, all set but empty of anything to eat and with the little pot, also empty, in the center of the table, they were offended and wanted to leave immediately without even waiting for an explanation, good people that they were.

It took a lot of effort for Serapio to keep them together . . .

"This is a feast for a lizard," said Cesáreo Bonaches, a lame tinker who had a good sense of humor. "Why don't we just open up our mouths to all this fresh air!"

Then Serapio, his voice full of sweetness, turned to the little pot upon the table, and making a *moforivale,** he asked it:

"What is your name?"

"The Little Good Cooking Pot."

"Well, cook something for these people like you know how, pretty one."

And no sooner had the people recovered from their amazement, but the little pot had set and covered the table with the most succulent and wonderful dishes. What chickens! What stuffed turkeys, what goat stew! Hams, sausages, roast pig, vegetables, fruits, and all kinds of sweets. All served excellently, and without end. And the whole town stuffed itself. There wasn't anyone who didn't get drunk from the fountain of delicious wine that flowed without end from the bottom of every glass.

*Gesture of reverence made by those of the *lucumí* religion to their gods, called *Orichas.*—Author.

And everybody had to dance all night, all the next day and evening, too.

The feast went on just as splendidly hour after hour . . . And so Serapio, once a beggar, suddenly became the well-loved benefactor of the entire neighborhood. They called him Don Serapio—even his close friends did so, without noticing. And when he heard this title, the black man felt—as his stomach grew fatter (and worthy of a gold watch chain or an enormous diamond), that something new was entering into his soul and speaking to him in a mysterious language not unlike the one in which Mama Tecla would mumble, forever sitting stiffly upon her stool, gazing impassively at everything around her, her eyes holding that same hard, fixed look as always.

Finally the news became widespread and people heard about it in the five parts of the world. They wrote about it in the newspapers, and even the Pope himself became concerned from the evidence of this miracle and quickly sent out an encyclical to the pumpkins, forbidding them to work any more miracles without his consent.

Shortly the poor Hill of Mambiala was made bald by the feet of many pilgrims.

However, it's a rare thing when the luck that suddenly falls on a humble man does not come hand in hand with his destruction as well. . . .

For the rich people came to eat with Serapio, and over dessert one of them, whose beard was as black as shoes of patent leather, said:

"I'll give you ten large and good pieces of land, already sown with sugar cane, for your pot."

"No, sir," replied Serapio, "she has plenty of sugar cane, pan sugar and sugar-cane syrup, and all that is sweet . . ."

"I," said another grand gentleman, belching elegantly, "would give you one of my coffee plantations."

"I," said the owner of a Shipping Company, a very honorable slave-trader, "would give you my schooner called *Gaviota*—in all the seas, there is no ship so beautiful or with such a cargo of ebony like hers. . . ."

And in the midst of all these extravagantly rich men, there was one millionaire—a money lender—named Don Cayetano, Marquis of Zarralarraga, who in order not to lose the opportunity of making a profit would sell all his hair, his teeth, and the fat and bones of his dead family. Making calculations and more calculations within his rock-like brain as he ate, he finally spoke:

"I," said Zarralarraga, picturing a monopoly of the world's food, "will offer you . . . not one penny more! . . . One million pesos for The Good Cooking Pot!"

When the black man heard "one million pesos," he went running off in search of a notary and in a little while he returned, dragging one by the coat-tails. Right then and there they drew up the bill of sale: at the bottom of the document, under a round sun-shaped seal which looked like a fried egg, stamped and crossed by a ribbon, Zarralarraga penned his illustrious name in thick letters, finishing off with a period and a triple-curved flourish underneath the ribbon.

"Now you sign Don Serapio."

"It's just that I don't know how to write," said the black man, realizing this for the first time in his life, "and now that I think about it, I don't know how to read, either . . ."

"It doesn't matter. We are among gentlemen!"

And it so happened that the document was null. That very night, the Marquis of Zarralarraga slipped on the peel of a mango while stepping down from his carriage and broke the pot; and the black man Serapio (who had by now seen himself wearing a top hat and tails and diamond rings set with three stones on every finger, not to mention gold caps on every tooth, and riding in a carriage by day, and sleeping in a featherbed at night), remained as miserably poor as the day he was born.

During the course of the next few days, now very bitter ones—well, the memory of this great loss was still quite recent—Serapio awoke one morning with his stomach as taut as a thread. He looked once more toward the Hill of Mambiala . . .

"Who knows," Serapio said to his daughters (the daughters who might have been able to wear silk dresses but who were now barefoot, in tattered rags which never failed to reveal their behinds) "who knows, if Mambiala might not be sympathetic, and provide us another miracle! Anyway, if I don't find another pot, maybe I'll find a pumpkin."

He went up to the hill—but there was no pumpkin patch now. Just a few sorry weeds among the stones.

> Oh, Lord Mambiala!
> Mambiala, Let it come, Mambiala.
> Me poor, Mambiala,
> Oh, Lord, Mambiala!

"I'm dying of hunger, Mambiala, Mambiala!" And he repeated his whining plea with very little hope, when suddenly the big toe of his right foot stubbed itself on a cane that seemed to be lying on the ground. A cane made out of the hide of a manatee.

"What's your name?" He immediately asked the cane, balancing it in his hand and grinning ecstatically.

"My name is Señor Manatee, The Just Distributor," answered the cane, with the growly voice of a bully who has few friends . . .

"Well, give me my share, Señor Manatee!"

Right away Manatee jumped out of his hands—very eager to obey his wishes—and Bam! Zam! Bam!—he smashed him and beat him up . . . and he would have finished him off, if the black man, after being knocked halfway down the Hill of Mambiala by its sure blows, had not cried out between the thumps, spitting out a piece of his tongue and three teeth:

"Tha-a-t's e-nough, Señor Manatee!"

Señor Manatee suddenly stopped in mid-air and calmly placed himself at Serapio's side, awaiting further orders very patiently.

"What am I going to do now?" wondered the black man, very perplexed, counting the bumps on his head. "This Señor Manatee . . . I don't know if it would be wise to introduce him to the family . . . But—on the other hand—they certainly deserve it! When I brought The Good Cooking Pot home, everyone stuffed themselves like pigs; neither I nor she refused anyone anything, so isn't it fair for them to share in the beating, too?"

And, down by the main road, the whole family was waiting impatiently. They had already invited all the neighbors and friends. They were so sure in their hearts that their father wouldn't come back empty-handed!

"The pot, the pot!" They all yelled when they saw him coming, walking in a strange way that none of them had ever seen before.

"Do we have guests for dinner?"

"Yes, some."

"Go and tell the Mayor, the Judge, the Priest, the Notary, and all the officials! Go and tell that Marquis of Zarralarraga, who bought the pot from me. Ask everyone! There will be enough for all! And, daughter . . . ask the doctor and the undertaker, too!"

They knew right then that Serapio had come back with another miracle from Mambiala—which proved beyond a doubt that God will protect a bum more than once, and that there is no need to ever give up hope, but to follow this example and be patient.

They set up, just as he had ordered, a long table by the road, while a crowd of people assembled who were anxious to see Serapio's new miracle.

The extravagantly rich and the officials presented themselves first. All were green with envy as they took their seats. Zarralarraga sat at the head of the table.

The rest of the crowd clustered themselves about the table excitedly, promising themselves a banquet, with a dance to follow all night long. Serapio once again heard himself called Don Serapio, amidst many smiles and flatteries.

("But it is not a pot . . . ahem . . . they say it is a cane," an old woman kept repeating—and huddling in her shawl, she returned home, having remembered that she had left some beans on the fire and that they might burn.)

Finally Serapio shouted, "Attention!" He put Señor Manatee on the table. "Nobody move."

"Papa, I want some ham!"

"Papa, chicken!" demanded the daughters.

Then there was a silence of wide-open eyes, of held breath.

Serapio drew away from the table as far as he could.

He climbed up a tree. No one had lifted their eyes off of the cane. Hidden up in the branches, his voice trembling a little, Serapio said: "To the one who is on the table . . . What is your name?"

"Señor Manatee, The Just Distributor."

"Well give, Señor Manatee, give justly."

Zam! ZamBamZam! Bam!

The punishment began. Smashes and crashes! Manatee the basher. . . . All that could be heard were the sounds of smashes and crashes resounding everywhere at once. Quickly and drily Manatee hit each and every one of the surprised heads, instantly causing fiery stars to explode around all of them. In less than one second the blows had swept over the heap of people in a great whirlwind; the luckier ones escaped by the skin of their teeth, carrying off the bruised remains that the feast had left them with.

The blows fell a bit harder on the backs of the officials. As soon as Manatee had delivered one blow upon someone who was in the center of the confusion he attacked another who was farther away and trying to crawl for his life. They ended up piled one on top of another in a heap with their flesh exposed bloodily like ripe pomegranates, and all their bones broken. And Serapio, who sat in the branches shaking them contentedly like his predecessor the ape, urged Señor Manatee on. . . .

"Really hard on the Mayor, Señor Manatee, for all the fines he imposes on the people! Hard, harder on the head of the moneylender! And as for the Policeman . . . Get him on the bunions!"

Señor Manatee left all the authorities flat on their backs and went into the shack where the children of the black man were hiding, huddled about the imperturbable Mama Tecla. As each whack was distributed by Señor Manatee upon the family, Mama Tecla repeated to that other one, her invisible friend, opening her terrible white eyes a little wider:

"I already know it; I already know!"

The shack realized that this was the right moment to collapse.

When Serapio saw that everyone lay lifeless: the Marquis of Zarralarraga, his mouth monstrously twisted and his nose turned into an eggplant; one eye dripping down like a tear . . . the rocklike head now a mass of broken bones and brains . . . his four children in little pieces . . . the old woman dead, still sitting stiffly upon her stool—and even still he could hear the glug-glug sound of the blood dripping down onto the ground, which sucked it in. When Serapio saw all this, he picked up his cane and started away from town. . . .

"We have gone a little too far, Señor Manatee!"

He wandered the whole night without destination, leaning upon the cane, and being led by the cane.

"Oh, Mambiala, what a splendid present you have given me! I didn't ask for that much, Mambiala, Mambiala! A poor man like me, who never meant harm to come to anyone. . . . What a way to go through life . . . by hurting others! What is left for me now? I have power, if I want it. . . . But not one, not one of those leeches is left to bleed me!"

The dawn arrived; the birds broke the silence by beginning their song in the dewy trees. He found himself seated by a well that gave off its reserve of freshness, its odor of secret water, of damp stone untouched by the sun. He looked inside the well and the water made him a sign.

"Yes," said Serapio, "It's best to rest a little!"

He dropped the cane and then threw himself into the well.

This is the well of Yaguajay.

The black women knew the story. They told it to the children, who drawn by fear, wanted to throw stones into the silence of the well. To put their faces over the water, and spit into it. To look, to look and never be tired of looking into the Soul of the Well; at the Drowned One, whom they never saw but who saw them, from his deep hiding place.

In the night the Drowned One woke everyone up, making the frogs in the well sing within the empty sockets of his eyes. The people walked down to the well in their sleep, drawn by the intense mystery—and their delicious fear—to look at him, and with the toss of another stone they would break the black mirror, their pupils wide as plates. To spit, leaning dangerously over in the dark, into the irresistible and tranquil presence. The

Yaguajay Well at night! The Drowned One would then rise up in the deep still water, scaling the silent walls.

A noiseless splash dissolved the fallen stars, and all of the Drowned One rose up in two unfolded desperate hands, with the piercing smell of mint. The black women had seen the hands; the women who never went near the well after dark. Too late to be saved, too late for their cries to be heard. Alone in the dream of the well. As cold and as hard as the stones, the hands reached over the mouth of the well and pulled the sleepwalkers down into the terrifying deepness of untold secrets.

1948

Lino Novás Calvo

1905–1983

LINO NOVÁS CALVO was born in Galicia, Spain, in 1905. Hoping to save him from the oppressive poverty that afflicted the family, his mother sent him to Cuba when he was seven years old to live with some relatives. Like many Spanish immigrants in Cuba during the early part of the century, Novás Calvo had no formal education and had no choice but to support himself through menial jobs from an early age, including driving a cab. He published his first poem in 1927 in the prestigious *Revista de Avance,* and over the next few years would become a well-respected young talent among Havana's literary circles. He worked as a foreign correspondent in Spain during the 1930s and traveled in France and Germany; during the 1940s and 1950s, he worked in Cuba as a journalist, teacher, and translator and continued to write and publish his stories. He became an exile again in 1963 and taught at Syracuse University for several years before his death in 1983.

Perhaps because of his immigrant roots, Novás Calvo's language is distinctly Cuban. His major characters are often alienated and marginalized, portraying the anguish of the lower classes. His innovative narrative techniques and his use of colloquial language set him apart from his contemporaries and gave him a unique place in Cuban literature. Among his major works are *La luna nona y otros cuentos* (1942; The ninth moon and other stories) and *Cayo Canas* (1946; Key Canas). Although published in 1942, "The Dark Night of Ramón Yendía" was written in 1933 and takes place in Havana during the general strike that preceded the toppling of dictator Gerardo Machado.

The Dark Night of Ramón Yendía

Translated by Raymond Sayers

RAMÓN YENDÍA AWOKE from a troubled sleep aching in every muscle. Worn out, he had slumped down over the wheel while the car was still moving, scraping the curb that separated the street from the vacant lot. On the left side a row of new houses huddled symmetrically together. Some were still unfinished; others were occupied by small businessmen and prosperous working men who had not yet found their place in the community and were therefore not too aggressive. Either by instinct or by chance, Ramón had come here to rest. He had spent four days away from home, sleeping in his taxi in different places. One night he had stayed at the taxi stand right in front of the Parados Bar, and it was there that his troubles had started. He had been afraid, but he had made an effort to control himself and to prove to himself that he could face the situation. He did not want to flee, for he knew in a way that if you fled you were sure to be pursued—unless, of course, you had someone to protect you. Every minute of these four days had been like a death sentence he had seen coming, taking shape like a thick cloud, growing claws. Ramón could not escape, he knew that, but perhaps he might remain, hiding or just waiting. After every earthquake someone is always left to tell the tale. It is a terrifying gamble, but then, life itself is a kind of gamble. Still, on the second night he went out into the outskirts of the city and parked next to a wall; the following night he drove up in front of the house of a revolutionary he knew, though the man probably did not know him. "Maybe he'll want to ride in my cab," he thought. If the man did, then perhaps he might be able to weather the storm unnoticed. Somehow he felt that the storm had to come and that it would pass. His regular customers had already taken off; therefore there was something serious in the wind.

Having had no experience in these struggles, Ramón felt almost as if he had fallen into a maelstrom. He had been driving a cab for three years, and his first daughter was born four years ago—now there were three of them, all girls and not one healthy. His wife did what she could. She left the little one in a cradle tied with ribbons while she went to work in a factory sewing hatbands.

All through these four days he had only been able to slip into their house twice. They still lived on the Calle de Cuarteles in one room. The

55

back door opened on the patio, the front door on the street. Estela had
been longing for a little home of their own, even if it was only a shack.
They could have gotten one in the new development for a down payment
of only one hundred pesos. They would have been able to save the money
if their eldest, the boy, had not fallen sick and died in spite of their
desperate efforts to save him. Now that Ramón had a good cab, which he
rented for three pesos a day, they were beginning to get on their feet again.
He also longed for a car of his own, even if it were only a Ford. He had
some good regular fares, and he stayed at the wheel up to fifteen hours a
day. But then besides his own family, he had to look out for the amazingly
fertile Balbina, who had had eight children by three different men. Everything was hard. The cab drank gasoline like water. It was a six-cylinder
job, but he did not have the patience to wait his turn in the stand. Now,
four days before, he had rented a new car from a different garage. He was
a nervous man with big brown eyes, who was quick to catch on. Sometimes, even when there was no actual signal, he could see things coming.
The other drivers laughed at him and called him a spiritualist.

On the night of the 6th he put his car away early and did not go back
to the garage the next day. On the 8th he went to another garage, the
Palanca, and hired a newer car. None of his usual fares was in the street
any more. They, too, must have sensed the impending storm. Every day
for a year he had been driving them, and when all is said and done, they
were all right, at least to him. Their voices were warm and human, and
they seemed to believe in what they were doing. They were not gunmen;
their mission was to get information and nothing else. And Ramón had
helped them out; he had placed himself at their service.

Now, today, the morning of the 12th, his premonitions were more
urgent, like something out of a painful dream. Until three o'clock in the
morning he had been cruising the streets or waiting outside of dance halls
or cabarets. He had not had a bad day; in fact, as far as that goes, there
had been nothing unusual about it. Before turning in he had stopped
beside a lamppost near the Capitol and counted his take, which amounted
to six pesos and change. Just then he felt that he was being stared at hard
by a passerby, a young fellow who looked like a college student and who
had one hand in his jacket pocket. Ramón decided to go home with the
money; he made a detour and stopped a block away from the house. He
walked up the side street, crossed the patio, and entered cautiously. He
turned on the fine flashlight that one of his regular customers had given
him, and played it as though he were a burglar or a policeman instead of
a fugitive. Not that anything as yet implied that he was a fugitive, he just

sensed it. He did not dare to switch on the electricity lest he make a target of himself, and he felt his way in. He turned the flashlight on the beds. In one of the cots, two of the girls, the twins, were sleeping naked, cheek to cheek on top of the sheet, with their open hands over their shoulders. In the second cot slept Estela and the baby; the empty one was his. No one awoke. Estela had on a nightgown, and her head was between her hands, which were turned palms up. In spite of all she had gone through, she was still beautiful. She was young; she had a delicate nose, large eyes, heavy hair, a prominent chin, thick, well-formed lips, and a large, sensual mouth. As he stopped for a moment to gaze at her, Ramón could visualize her healthy, slightly protruding row of teeth, her honey-colored eyes, and her lively glance. Then he put the money on the table where his dinner was waiting for him and went out. There was nobody near the automobile. Everything seemed normal except that there were too many cars moving too fast and the lights were on in several houses. That was all—but it was enough!

On his return trip he passed police headquarters. There seemed to be an unusual amount of activity going on inside, and as he went by he thought the two guards on duty moved their guns nervously when they heard his car. He turned into the first street on the right without stopping to think whether it was a one-way street. He stopped at the next corner, in doubt about which way to go; his thoughts had turned back several years, and old scenes flashed before his eyes as if on a movie screen. In those days some sort of revolutionary spirit had taken hold of him; he couldn't say why, for he had never been able to examine his feelings coldly and analytically. Perhaps he had merely caught it from the air, for he did not read much and he did not belong to any group from which he might have absorbed any basic principles or which might have helped him to clarify his own ideas. Twelve years before, he had come with his brothers and sisters from the country. His father had lost his savings when the bank crashed, and had disappeared into the swamps with his head held high and his body as stiff as a corpse. (Nobody had ever seen him since.) He had caught it without warning; it was in the air. The girls had not yet been born, and the little boy was strong and handsome. Ramón did not find business too bad, for he was lucky at picking up steady customers; perhaps it was because he was a good driver; he knew when to speed and when to go slow.

And that's how things were. Almost every day he picked up three or four young fellows, sometimes together and sometimes alone. He had not yet found out who they were; he only knew that they were revolutionaries and they had money to spend. Being a revolutionary was a virtue, for the word recalled the country's struggles for independence, and since childhood he had heard it constantly from people of all classes. It was the national bona fide currency. Therefore it was all right. Things were not so bad at home, and his customers were fond of him, for he seemed to them to be reliable. They would talk to him and gradually he caught their tone, their language, and their enthusiasm. He talked like them at the taxi stand, in the garage—in fact, almost everybody was beginning to talk the same way. There still did not seem to be much danger in it, and a fellow was not afraid to speak his mind and even to pay an occasional brief call late at night. Sometimes he served as a courier, driving his empty car from one place to another. They paid him regularly, and the pay was not bad. After all, Ramón was one of them.

Then the tide turned. Justino, the boy, got sick. Estela was pregnant and irritable. Then came the twins, hard going, and perhaps even doubt. Ramón could get excited and carried away, but he lacked real conviction. He saw that being a revolutionary was not all smooth sailing. One night—a night like this, at the beginning of August, near morning—two men hailed him. He realized at once that something was up. Perhaps they were plainclothesmen. Others had hailed him in the same way and then, when they were in the car, had said: "Police headquarters." When they reached the station he would discover that he had been charged with cruising, going through a red light, or speeding, or some such thing. Naturally, it was against the law, but the union would bail him out, and sometimes a judge was good-natured enough to let him off without fining him. These two men were not paying passengers, either; they also said: "Police headquarters," but this time, when he got there, he was given different treatment.

He stood it the first time. They took him into a bare room with the cement floor and walls splotched with blood, and they slapped him, punched him, kicked him. There wasn't an insult or foul word that they didn't throw at him; their language besmirched everything he loved; and they threatened that his wife would get hers, too. He took it all. Then, to his surprise, they took him to the front desk, and the lieutenant let him go. He got into his car and somehow managed to drive it to the garage. He did not go home that night, for his lips were cut and he was spitting blood. He could say that he had had a collision; that was the excuse the police told him to give. No, thanks; he was not going to bring home to his wife any more trouble. During those days his best customers were in hiding, and his day's take did not amount to more than two pesos. He slept in the garage that night. Early the next morning he went home and told his wife that he had been out all night with a customer who said he would pay him later. One of the girls was sick; the mother thought she was teething, but he was afraid that it was something else, for she cried all the time and was as thin as a rail.

During the days that followed he did not see any of his old customers, and he had the impression that eyes were watching him from all sides. In the course of those twenty-four hours he got two tickets, and the next day three. The fourth day he was taken back to the police station and beaten again, but this time worse. Then they let him go, but they assigned another cabby he knew to keep an eye on him and put him on the right track. He was a slippery fellow who worked at night, picking up fares in front of hotels and cabarets or waiting in taxi stands. He began his job with kid gloves; then gradually he began to put it into Ramón's head that politicians were out for themselves and looked out for nobody but number one. He told him some stories, and to Ramón the little room he lived in began to appear more and more gloomy and his family more anemic and pitiful. He struggled with himself before he gave in, but the other man's arguments were convincing. He told him that after all it was just a case of one politician fighting another. Didn't "they" have enough money to pay him? They all began in the same way, and they ended up by forgetting the people who had helped them up in the world. No, Ramón was a fool if he didn't switch sides. Naturally, he could continue to drive his regular customers, for he was only asked to follow certain instructions and get certain information.

That was the why and wherefore of it all. He felt himself cornered and he gave in. They would wipe the slate clean and help him out. That was when Estela, trying to get the children back to health, began to dream about owning her own little wooden house, and he about driving his own cab. The doctor said the children needed fresh air and good food. It was always the same old story. Every worker's child needs fresh air and good food, but perhaps his would get it. After all, Ramón was human; unlike some other people, he had warm blood in his veins, and so he yielded for the sake of his family and for his own sake, too. And suppose he hadn't? Could he have let himself go on being arrested and beaten up? Could he have let Estela and the children die? He began to rationalize, for he knew that he was not doing the right thing, and it worried him so that he had to use all his willpower to go through with it. He calmed himself by concentrating on the goals that he had in mind. Perhaps he had done wrong, but his motives were good. Should he have refused and let himself be wiped out?

From then on he hadn't had a peaceful moment. He lost weight, he became more nervous and gloomy, and he had to make a strenuous effort to hide from his wife the drama that was gnawing at him from within. He knew that some of the men he had informed on were in jail and that one had perhaps even been murdered. When he thought about it, his only consolation was that he was poorer than anyone else; all the others, at least, had relatives and friends who could do something for them and would never forget them. But there was nobody to lend him a hand. He could depend only upon himself, himself alone. If the day came when he did not take home his three pesos, his family would not eat; if he did not pay his fee every day, he would lose his car; if he got sick, he would not even be able to get into the hospital. So it was only right and human for him to take care of himself, no matter who had to suffer for it. He was always having to recall these arguments to quiet his conscience, but deep down inside he carried his own accusation, which tortured and pursued him. Every day his spirits sank lower, and he felt that sooner or later something was going to snap. The atmosphere was getting more oppressive; his best customers had disappeared, and he suspected that the others had begun to distrust him. In fact, he was even afraid that he might be assaulted and he began to go about armed, feeling that he was engaged in the struggle. He always kept his Colt within reach; the feel of it had a quieting effect upon his nerves.

Finally he began to feel that he was being deserted by the very men who had got him into this—the other driver and the two or three plainclothesmen. They had enough to do to take care of themselves, and besides he was not much use to them any more. All the revolutionaries' doors were closed to him, and he felt paralyzed, as though he could not go forward or backward. After some months of this tension, he felt that he could not endure it much longer. When he saw the storm gathering, breaking, and spreading, he had a sensation of relief. "Let's get it over with," he said, and he waited.

But soon this feeling of relief, which had been caused by the changed situation, gave way to a new kind of anxiety. He had the impression now that he was surrounded, cut off, blockaded even; he knew that somewhere, sometime, he was being sought for by eyes he might never even have seen, eyes that were perhaps just awaiting a more favorable opportunity that would soon come. Then the situation would be the same as that first time he had been taken to headquarters, only just the opposite; and this time it would take a more violent and decisive form. It would be the end—that's all. If they had found him out—he thought they had—and if the "new ones" won—and he knew they were winning—then there was no way out.

There was only one thing to do: lie low and wait—or get the drop on them and defend himself.

Both solutions were bad. Now, while he was trying to make up his mind where to go, he wondered whether there might not be a third possibility. He had imagination, but he had no faith in the images he conjured up. Still, he had to make up his mind one way or other. They wouldn't do anything to Estela; she was not to blame. The worst that could happen would be that she would have to face worse poverty, the children might die, maybe she would, too. . . . But if he saved himself, he would come back for her some day. Could he save himself?

He thought so. He started the car and let it roll slowly, though he did not know exactly where he was going. He thought he would take it to the garage and from there he would get to the country on foot or somehow. In Nuevitas there were still people who would remember him, or at least his father. They might give him some help, hide him, and let him wait. But then it suddenly occurred to him that there was sure to be a general uprising and that to appear in a little town would only be a sure way of attracting more attention, and that town was not revolutionary-minded. He had only a few friends there, as poor as he, whereas here in Havana at least there were plenty of people, plenty of houses. He would move to another garage! And if he could only move into a different house! That was what had been in his mind when he had gone over to that row of houses opposite the vacant lot, where they were building, but then he had suddenly felt utterly exhausted, and had fallen asleep before the automobile had quite stopped.

And now he was waking up on this August morning, when all hell was popping. Ramón realized that there was nothing he could do any more. Two men with revolvers at their belts were going into one of the seemingly empty houses. At the same time another man appeared at one of the frameless windows, and when the others who were downstairs motioned to him, he rushed down. He, too, was armed. Ramón, who had gotten out of the car, had his head under the hood and was pretending to fix the motor. He did not know any of them, but they might know him. The three men, however, went by briskly and triumphantly up the street. In normal circumstances they would hardly have dared to act like that, for Ramón was sure that they were revolutionaries and that they were going after someone. They were not workers like him; they were well dressed, though at the moment coatless, and they looked well fed. It was their fight, a fight among the upper classes. Why had he been dragged into it, first by one side and then by the other? Still, that's how it was, and now there was no way out. First the old gang had been going to get rid of him, and now the new one was going to finish him off. That was a fact.

Well, perhaps it was, and yet he still had a flicker of hope, though he did not know exactly why. At any rate, he was not going to give up his taxi for a while, and he was not going to put it in the garage. He still had enough money for eight gallons of gas. His first thought was to explore the roads running out of the city, but when he reached the highway he could see that in Aguadulce it was being patrolled. He turned at the first corner and dived back into the heart of the city.

There was excitement everywhere. The whole town was on strike, and the streets were full of people and cars crowded with civilians and soldiers. They were shouting, cheering, leaping about, and brandishing their pistols. Ramón put down the flag of his meter, but it was no use. Four respectable-looking men rushed out of San Joaquín and into his car, ordering him to take them to the Cerro. At Tejas he saw a man struggling to get away from some others who had seized him and who were being egged on by the watching crowd, both men and women. Ramón took advantage of an opening in the mob to try to keep on going, but someone glanced into the car, and a group of men began to follow him, shooting on the run. One of the bullets went through the back window and out through the windshield. Ramón stopped and his passengers jumped out of the car and began to run madly through the side streets, pursued by several youths. Among them there were some who were little more than children—one of them must have been about fifteen—but they were firing large revolvers. Ramón pulled over to the curb, thinking: "Now they are going to come for me," but nobody seemed to pay any attention to him. Some excited bystanders came up to him to ask where he had picked up his passengers, and when he had told them the truth, they ran off toward San Joaquín Street. He even gave them the number of the house the men had come out of, but perhaps they did not live there; most likely they had spent the previous night hiding in one of the stairways. Who could tell what would happen now to the people who lived there? Everybody was openly armed; everybody was looking for someone to shoot at.

Once more Ramón started the car and went back to the same place, saying to himself, almost aloud: "I'll lose myself among them, and they'll think I'm one of them. That should throw them off the track." After all, he had been one of them. But then he wondered whether he could keep his nerve. He looked at himself in the rear view mirror and saw that he was pale and unshaved like a fugitive. At a time like this his face alone would arouse suspicion. But then as he was passing Cuatrocaminos, he saw another group of men running by with guns in their hands; some of them were as bearded and as grimy as he. Doubtless they were men who had been hiding these last months or who had been freed from jail. He might give the same impression; at any rate no one would take him for a person who had been on the payroll of the fallen government. He kept on moving. A few blocks farther along he ran into a mob that was frantically chasing a lone man. He was zigzagging madly down the street, hurling handfuls of bills at his pursuers, who did not stop to pick them up, but stepped on them and kept on following him, shooting as they went. Ramón stopped and waited with interest to see what the outcome would be. Finally the man, who was already wounded and had been leaving a trail of blood behind him, fell on his face a few steps from where Ramón had parked. On seeing that he had fallen, one of his pursuers went over to Ramón with his revolver in his hand and ordered him to give him a can of gasoline. Ramón obeyed, siphoning it from the tank with a tube. Seizing the can, the others sprinkled the wounded man, who was still writhing, while a third set fire to him. Ramón turned his back on the scene.

The streets were full of civilians and soldiers. Ramón started his car again. A few yards farther on, some armed youths piled into it, and kept him driving them around for hours without any apparent objective. Sometimes they would get out, force their way into a house, and come out again. As they passed the garage to which his car belonged, he noticed that it had been broken into. He stopped and asked to have the tank filled. Seeing that the car was full of armed youths, the attendant did as he was asked, and Ramón drove off with his passengers without bothering to pay. An hour later the young men had him stop in front of a small restaurant and invited him to eat with them.

It was past noon. Ramón sat down at the table with the strangers. It surprised him that not one of them had bothered to ask him a single question; apparently they took it for granted that he was one of them, that as an ordinary taxi driver he could be nothing else. While they ate, the young men talked mysteriously and with great excitement. They ate fast and went out into the street, apparently forgetting all about him, for instead of getting into the cab again, they went off down the street and disappeared into the crowd, which was thicker in this zone than anywhere else. They were in the very heart of the city. Ramón got in behind the wheel and sat for a while, wondering what he should do. He felt tired; he had gone so long without eating that his stomach no longer seemed to want food. And yet his fatigue could not outweigh his anxiety. Now he was fully conscious of being in a world to which he did not belong and in which, perhaps, there was no place for him. It would do him no good to seek new friends now; nobody would even recognize a man with whom he had just committed a murder a couple of hours ago unless they had been friends previously. In a few hours those youths he had been driving would not recognize him. Everybody seemed to be looking too high or too low; nobody was staring at eye level. And yet, he thought, there might be an advantage in that, for the people seemed to be possessed of a mysterious, frenzied sense of well-being which would perhaps prevent them from keeping close control of things.

Ramón came out of this daydream to see that a man was staring at him insistently from the opposite sidewalk. The man was watching him with a cold, attentive gaze whose meaning he could not understand, but he was sure that there was something behind it. Making an effort to overcome his nervousness, he got out of the car and as calmly and as naturally as possible pretended to look for something in the motor. He got in again, stepped on the starter without giving it gas, trying to give the impression that there was something wrong with the car (and that was what he was worried about), and then started off with a series of jerks. The man pulled a scrap of paper out of his pocket and jotted down the number of the license. Perhaps he was not sure. Ramón's may have seemed to him one of those faces we do not like, yet cannot recall at the moment exactly where we have seen them before. Otherwise, Ramón was sure, the man would have done something right then and there. He took for granted that his fate had been decided, mentally at least, somewhere, by people he did not know. To escape from the whirlpool seemed completely impossible; he did not even dare think of trying, for the mere attempt would have aroused suspicion. If there was any salvation, it was at the very heart of the maelstrom.

There was no driving down these streets. The whole city had poured into them. Ramón turned into a cross street and stopped when he arrived at the corner of the Prado, for it seemed a place where he would be inconspicuous. To keep people from trying to hire him, he let the air out of a tire and jacked up the wheel. Then he opened his toolbox and began to poke around in the motor. He took off the top and unscrewed the carburetor and a valve. Then he took out the other valves and began to clean them. He noticed that they were full of carbon, and when he got to the carburetor, he saw that it was dirty and almost clogged up. No wonder the car jerked and rattled. The work calmed his nerves a bit. He did not look at anybody or anything except the car, and therefore nobody looked at him. He had taken off his jacket, and in the trunk he discovered an old pair of mechanic's overalls that might almost have been put there on purpose. He put them on and smudged his face with grease. Then, climbing into his seat, he looked at himself in the mirror as he stepped on the starter. He thought it would be hard for anyone to recognize him the way he looked unless they scrutinized him very closely and knew whom they were looking for. Still, some of his features were hard to forget. He had large brown eyes with lids somewhat drawn together at the corners. Above one of his high cheekbones there was a small scar, and the curious line of his lips made him look as though he was on the verge of smiling—a wry smile. "Rabbit-laugh" they called him in the garage. All in all, his features made a strong impression on people. It had never occurred to him that this might be of any importance.

He got out of the car and went on tinkering with it. He took out the battery, cleaned the terminals, and put it back again. By the time he had reassembled everything, it was getting late in the afternoon. Those hours had passed less disagreeably than any other time since the beginning of the strike. The work had quieted his nerves, and the car was running better than ever before. Checking the four tires, Ramón saw that they were new; he had oil and gasoline. Before starting he took the revolver out of the pocket of the front door and examined it; it was a new Colt; with it he had a box of bullets. He took out those in the drum and snapped the trigger six times to make sure it was working right. When he had closed it again, he noticed that two or three boys were watching him enviously. Any one of them would have given his eyeteeth for a gun like it. The revolutionaries seemed to them the luckiest beings in the world. And they would be thinking that Ramón was one.

The car started again. Without knowing how he got there, Ramón soon found himself a block away from his home. He stopped. He felt an irresistible impulse to run in, to pay them a little visit; but at that moment he saw a huge crowd coming down the cross street. They were bearing trophies and shouting cheers and threats. The trophies were scraps of curtains, bedcovers, pictures, a telephone receiver, vases. . . . Ramón did not wait to see any more, but dived into the nearest grocery and turned his back on the crowd. When the people had passed, he raised the hood again and said to one of the children who came over to watch: "Go to Number 12 on that street and tell whoever you see to come over here for a moment." The child charged off, happy to have been noticed, and was back in a couple of minutes to say that there was nobody home. "They must have gone over to Balbina's," Ramón thought. "Estela must have realized"—as much as to say: "Estela knows that I am a dead man and has gone to consult with Balbina about how she's to look after the kids."

Once more he started the automobile. He went aimlessly along the same street as far as the Avenida de las Misiones, and there he turned off toward the sea. But he turned back at once, afraid of straying too far from the downtown area. He felt that as soon as he got to a solitary spot he would be assaulted, and there would be no witness to what happened. But what good were witnesses any more? None at all; but Ramón did not want to die, to be murdered, without someone around to tell the tale. It did not matter if they could not come to his aid; the deed would at least be engraved on their eyes, in their memories, and in a way it would stand as an accusation. Once at his house a crazy relative of his wife's had said: "Murder will out." She could not have been very crazy if she was able to say such deep things.

The sun was setting when he got downtown again. He moved slowly through parks and boulevards crowded with shouting, running people, and officers and soldiers fraternizing in a tremendous sense of triumph. All the cars were in motion; people and vehicles moved around in whirlpools from which strong currents of vengeance emanated. He heard shots high in the air; everybody had bloodthirsty eyes, everybody was hunting something. That was what frightened him most: in everybody's eyes he could see the hunting instinct. The slightest pretext, the slightest justification, would have been enough to unleash the rage he saw in every eye. As night fell, the movements of the crowds seemed to take on a new objective and a definite aim. There were groups that marched in brisk time, cutting like tanks through the others, which were shapeless and yielding. Ramón saw at once that these were like-minded comrades who, in the midst of the excitement and confusion, felt they had a self-assigned mission to accomplish.

These last few days he had often wondered what had become of Servando, the driver who had started him off as a traitor. He had stopped going to the taxi stand; he had left his car, which was his own, in the garage, and Ramón knew nothing about him. Now Ramón was parked in the very stand that used to be Servando's. Cruising about aimlessly, he had stopped there, though he could not have said why or how. He had seldom stopped there in the past. A big wagon appeared along the street where the trolley ran. It was apparently loaded with sacks of sugar; the lone carter was driving a team of old, worn-out mules. As it passed in front of the taxi stand, a group of eight or ten youths came out of a doorway and, going over to the driver, forced him to pull up. They began to throw the sacks on the pavement; after they had unloaded a number of them, three men climbed out from under the rest. The three men leaped to the pavement and shot off in the direction of the Prado. One managed to reach the first group of people and disappear; the second turned down the next street, closely followed by some of the youths, who were firing point-blank at him; Ramón did not have time to see the end. The third dropped right where he was. He had hardly touched the sidewalk, making for the doorway, when he straightened up suddenly, spun about on his heels, and toppled over. Looking out of the car window just as the man turned around, Ramón saw that his face was a mask of terror. It was Servando.

By then it had become completely dark. The people had begun to drift away, and there remained only the few who seemed to be going somewhere. Ramón at a glance could distinguish between the two kinds of people: those who were going somewhere and those who seemed to have no place to go. The latter withdrew early, leaving the streets to the others. "Now there's only them and us left," Ramón thought. Still he lingered for a while in the stand. He was the only one there; now he no longer dared to move away, for the center of the city was all open, while the streets were lined with dark doorways and sinister corners. The die was cast, he thought. Servando had fallen first, and now it was his turn, for his offense was the same. These maddened people were in no mood for explanations: they would not ask what his motives had been; they would only ask whether he was Ramón Yendía. The ghosts of the men he had betrayed would soon rise up to haunt him.

His train of thought was interrupted by the sight of a lone pedestrian who had stopped on the corner and was looking at him suspiciously. Servando's body had already been dragged away, and there was no longer any activity in the place where the car was parked. The pedestrian crossed the street diagonally, passing the car and looking at Ramón out of the corner of his eye as he went by. As he stepped up on the sidewalk, his face was illuminated by the light inside the building, where some factory hands were moving spools of paper. Ramón recognized the face instantly. It was that of one of his earliest (and less important) customers. He had been among the first to disappear when Ramón turned informer. Bad luck, undoubtedly. And now he was the first to turn up again. He would be followed by the others who were still alive. They would surround him. Perhaps they were already waiting for him at the street intersections he would have to cross. They had him cornered, like a runaway slave whose roads of escape have been cut off, and soon they would set the hounds on him.

Which hounds? The one that had stared at him as he passed must have been one of them, he was sure. A few moments later another man—a stranger, this time—passed and also stared hard at him. Ramón realized now that the executioners had arrived and that the execution ground would be that two-block rectangle. In his mind's eye he could see them posted, gun in hand, on the six corners. What were they waiting for?

This thought spurred him to action. He would not stay there. He would not accept death without a fight, huddled behind the wheel. At least he would run, fighting with what strength he had left. Who knows—life is full of surprises and the guy who fights has luck on his side.

Once he had made the decision, he stepped on the starter and took off in second. Thinking only of his driving, he moved down the first block at a good clip. The mounting speed and the hum of the motor brought him a sudden feeling of complete relief. His anguished thinking was over; a sense of action took its place. The danger, the torment, the foreboding disappeared, leaving only one thing: the determination to run the gauntlet of his enemies and win out. As he approached the intersection where he supposed they would be waiting, he drove with one hand. In the other he held the revolver at the level of the window. But to his surprise no one bothered him, no one was waiting for him. He kept on a little farther along the street with the trolley tracks, and then slowed down. There were few people on the sidewalks, and they seemed to pay no attention to him. No one, not even his probable executioners, would believe that a condemned man could be at liberty and driving an automobile. Still, those men had looked at him meaningfully, and one of them definitely had a score to settle with him. Why hadn't he attacked him right then and there? Perhaps because he was not a killer; very likely he was not made of that kind of stuff. There are men who can't do it, no matter what they feel. There are some who can't even give the order. This man must have gone off with the information, and the other probably had nothing to do with Ramón.

Ramón pulled up beside a lamppost in the park. As he looked up toward an illuminated sign, he happened to see a clock. Time had passed too fast. Absorbed in his own drama, he had not felt it go by, and now it was nine. Now there was no one on the street except those who had something to do. You could see it by the way they acted and walked, but no one paid any special attention to him, though it seemed that everyone was hiding or at least betraying a certain amount of suspicion. Of all the cars that were moving about the city, his was the most conspicuous. He reflected that if it were parked, it would be likely to attract still more attention.

Then began a slow, painful drive. It seemed to Ramón that these were the last two hours of his life, and that very soon, perhaps before daybreak, everything that his eyes could see and his ears could hear would have disappeared, dissolved into eternal nothingness as if nothing had ever existed in the world, as if he himself, Ramón Yendía, had never been born, as if all that he had loved, suffered, and enjoyed had never had any reality. And the scenes of his life began to flash before him in pictures, as on a screen, clear, sharp, and exact, neither hurrying nor lingering. Present reality itself took on a meaning that it had never had; it was the reality of a dream. In it he saw many things at the same time, and still they never ran together or became confused. Past, present, people, things, feelings—everything was sharp, transparent, and definite. And yet all passed in a kind of procession from which no detail was omitted. The streets were fairly empty, and not a traffic policeman was to be seen. As Ramón drove, the car might have been moving on rails or floating in the air. Without knowing why, he went to all the places most closely connected with his life. First he passed the house where he and his two brothers and two sisters had spent their first night in the city, Balbina's home. Then the little factory where Balbina worked, and from there to the house where his elder sister, Lenaida—what could have become of her?—had lived with the Spaniard. After that he drove past the house of the Chinese who had married his sister Zoila, and, forgetting that the city limits might be policed, he reached the outskirts—the little wooden shack where the baby had died. He had met Estela in that neighborhood, first at a dance and then behind the place where they had the cockfights. Where the dance hall had been, there was now a factory; a watchman with a rifle stood at the door. Nobody bothered Ramón as he drove by. In fact, the soldiers who were guarding the exit from the city let him pass, once they had checked to see there was no one else in the car. On his way back, they did not even search it. Once more he passed the familiar places—the theaters, the movies, the nightclubs, the brothels, all those places where he had taken people looking for a good time. It had never occurred to him to think that life really had so many charms. Could it be on account of these charms that men fought and killed one another? And yet they were not satisfied; they always wanted more; they wanted to rise, to stand out above the crowd, to dream, to have power, to command, to be, to rule, to possess. They wanted to rise, trampling on others, just for the sake of rising and not merely in order to enjoy such things as music, women, wine, leisure, flattery, service, fine food, health—health!

This thought suddenly brought him out of his reverie. His car was moving along as though driving itself. There were no obstacles or stops; no one crossed the road; furthermore, he had been driving for five years, and now he could have kept it up all day long through the heaviest, most nerve-racking traffic, without having to think once about what he was doing; he could spend hour after hour musing and dreaming, letting his fancy wander, and still observe all the traffic regulations. Now it was easier. Then, suddenly, he began to concentrate all his thoughts on one thing: his wife and his children. It was for them, after all, that he had done what he had done, that he was where he was now. Where was he? He realized that he was just going by police headquarters, the place where he had been "persuaded" to change sides. Without noticing it, he had passed within a block of his house, and now he was going up Montserrate Street. At the door there was a cluster of soldiers and civilians, and there was evidently a lot going on inside. He braked a little to come to another decision: he still wanted to go home and see whether Estela had come back and how the children were. He would leave the car a short way off; right around the corner, opposite Palacio, was a good place.

Before he reached the corner where he planned to turn, a car sped by, almost scraping his mudguard. A face peered out of the window. It was like a powder flash. The face had appeared only for an instant, and it had been barely visible by the light of a street lamp, but that was more than enough. Ramón tried to go straight ahead and went into second at once, but before he could do so, the other car, which was newer and faster, had cut him off. Ramón then moved it into reverse, made a sharp turn, and took off at full speed in the direction of the sea.

And that's how the chase began. The other car, which was one of the latest models, started after him with the same fury. Two other new, fast cars started at once in support of the first, taking short cuts through different streets, disregarding the one-way arrows. Ramón had recognized that face, but before he had even been able to start off, two bullets had whizzed by his ears. It was strange, but he was not afraid; no one had ever before shot at him from such close range, and yet what he felt was not fear. Nor did he even feel distressed. That meeting had suddenly dissipated the terrible anxiety that had been oppressing him. His bursting brain, which had been pulled in a thousand directions, tortured by a thousand wires, began to work lucidly and with a single purpose. Like the aviator engaged in single combat at an altitude of a thousand feet, he had only one objective: to overcome his enemies, even if it was only by escaping. Before he reached the sea, the first Ford had caught up with him; they had managed to keep him within range and directly ahead of them. The three or four occupants at once opened fire with rifles and revolvers, but none of the bullets hit either the tires or the driver. One of them just grazed his skull; he had crouched down instinctively. As he emerged into the avenue, he pulled out the choke, turned the car rapidly, and gradually gave it all the gas he could. Then he took his foot off the brake and concentrated completely on the wheel and the accelerator.

The other car kept tailing him. Seeing the two of them turning in the distance, another of the pursuers turned in order to head off Ramón a few blocks farther down on the Paseo del Malecón, but Ramón turned right instantly and went up the Avenida de las Misiones. Although he did not have time to think it out, he knew that he had the advantage on the turns. He had always been outstanding in the races for his skill on sharp curves. He would let up on the gas entering the curve and then suddenly, coming out of it, he would give it all he had. Besides, he was a condemned man, fleeing for his life, and the dangers involved in speeding were of small consequence. His first pursuer also turned quickly and fell in behind, determined not to lose sight of him. Then the race began through the downtown streets. On reaching the Parque Central, Ramón shot like an arrow into the old city, where the narrowness of the streets gave him the advantage. Besides, in that labyrinth which he had covered a thousand times he was able to maneuver continually and throw the other cars off the track. Of course, Ramón did not have time to figure all this out. He, the man who had been so absorbed in thought, had suddenly burst into action under the guidance of a hidden being within him who had taken control. Seeing that he was going down Obispo, one of the other cars tried to take a shortcut through a side street on the assumption that he would turn to the right. The reasoning was correct, for two or three blocks farther down, Ramón turned right on a cross street. Hearing him coming, the other car attempted to block the way, but Ramón was speeding so fast that the other went up on the sidewalk and ran head on into a wooden door, bursting into a brothel. That left him out of the race, at least for the time being.

The other two continued in hot pursuit without yielding an inch. Only by turning continually could Ramón manage to keep out of their line of fire. They saw him for a moment from far off and began shooting, but he had just arrived at an intersection, and he turned quickly. The tires shrieked along the asphalt. Sometimes he took his foot off the accelerator for a moment, at other times he stepped on it hard, heedless of the danger. Even at a distance people realized that it was a race and got out of the way. One man climbed a lamppost like a cat the moment Ramón emerged into the Parque Cristo and—to quote the man—"turned like lightning"—in the direction of Muralla Street. Somehow or other the third pursuing car also foresaw that Ramón would try to come out near the Terminal and sent two or three other cars to cut off that exit. But before Ramón got there, that mysterious being who was now guiding him made him turn about. He went down San Isidro at full speed, turned into the Alameda de Paula, went up Oficios, then along Tacón and came out at the Avenida del Malecón. Now he had another idea, and it was not to avoid the shots of his pursuers in narrow streets. It had suddenly occurred to him that if he got into the open country he could jump out of the car, leave it in motion, and flee through the hills.

But he could not get out into the hills by driving along the wide streets where he would be an easy target, so he turned at once toward the heart of the city, and then, going uptown from there, he started to look for a way out. Now he was being followed by more than two cars, which, however, were still unable to overcome their initial handicap. Their advantage lay in their weapons and numerical superiority, and in the fact that if one ran out of gasoline, the others could still keep on going. Ramón, on the other hand, could not stop to fill his tank; perhaps that was why he made up his mind to flee to the hills.

After weaving in and out of the uptown streets for some minutes, he decided to make a break for it. The moment had come when he would have to go through some wide street for a fairly long stretch. It was a risk he would have to run. His first plan was to go down the Avenida de Carlos Tercero in the direction of Zapata, past the cemetery, and then race down beyond the river. But before actually starting on this route, a strange idea came to him out of nowhere: he would not flee into the country, but would go as far as the hospital, run the car against a lamppost, and then enter the hospital to have his wounds bandaged. If he did not have a wound by then, he would inflict one on himself. Maybe his pursuers would not follow him so far, but would seek him instead among the houses where they found the auto. At the same time he thought that perhaps when day came he would find some way out. He did not know exactly how or what, but in some vague, fuzzy way he still hoped to find it. Naturally, he was not sure whether the hospital was not also in the hands of those who were now his enemies.

Having worked out his plan, he decided to put it into effect at once. In one second he visualized the exact spot where he would crash his car, and the speed that he would have to be going at in order to put it out of commission and yet escape with his life. The thought of the hospital came to him purely by accident. Passing a street corner where he had run over a child years before, he remembered that he had taken him to the hospital; it had been one of the most agonizing moments of his life. While he was waiting for the doctor to operate, he had turned so pale, his face had become so distorted, and his eyes had taken on such a terrified expression that another doctor had taken one look at him and ordered some medicine for him which he did not recognize. After that they had taken him into a room full of strange white machines and examined his heart and asked him a lot of questions. To their surprise, Ramón was not ill, nor had he suffered any attack; his conscience was responsible for the expression on his face. The doctors themselves had asked the mother of the child, who, fortunately, did not die, not to be too hard on Ramón in her accusations. She was a very poor woman, and she did not even lodge a complaint; after that Ramón used to go to see the child when he could and bring him little presents. He had always remembered the doctors' attention as one of the happiest experiences of his life. And now in this moment of supreme peril, when he had put his whole being into this struggle to save himself, he thought about those doctors or others like them as his possible protectors.

So he made a supreme effort to reach the hospital. As he was still in the heart of the uptown section of the city, he would have to cross a wide square before he could reach the place where he hoped to crash the car. Veering continually, cutting sharply, and turning on two wheels, he finally managed to approach his goal, but just as he was about to emerge into the broad avenue, he saw that two cars were drawn up across the street ahead of him. They were probably parked there. Ramón put on the brake as slowly as possible, mounted one of the sidewalks, and made a U-turn. The ones in front began to shoot at him; one of the bullets pierced his left wrist, but he felt very little more pain than if it had been a pinprick. As he turned, he observed that his relentless pursuer was coming toward him like a torpedo and shooting as he came. The bullets hit the car, but none managed to put it out of commission. Ramón gave it all the gas he had and drove straight at the other. For a moment a fatal collision seemed inevitable; the pursuer saw Ramón's car coming toward him and jammed on the brakes just before turning off on the next-to-the-last intersection. Without reducing his speed, Ramón turned into the same street through a hail of bullets. The pursuer lost a few seconds before he could regain full speed, but Ramón had been hit by another bullet, this time right on the temple. It had scraped the skin, like a plowshare turning up the grass cover of the earth. It did not hurt, but the blood forced him to close one eye, which began to smart. And so, blind in one eye, with one wrist perforated, bleeding profusely, he continued the race. He kept up his speed, more determined than ever to reach the hospital. Once more he headed in that direction, but this time by a different route. With the slight advantage that he had gained, he was able to reach the Calle de San Lázaro; turning into it, he pushed the accelerator down to the floorboard and shot off in a straight line.

He was blocked again. From three cars that had been drawn up across one of the last intersections came a hail of bullets, but the shooting had begun too soon, and he had time to turn to the right and get out of the line of fire. But by now the first pursuer had been able to regain the time he had lost, and was almost on top of him.

Ramón was now headed toward the city along the wide Avenida del Maine. He had lost considerable blood, and with it, no doubt, some of the energy and mental alertness that made it possible for him to continue that uneven duel. He began to feel faint; his hand was trembling on the wheel. The car kept on down the middle of the avenue, but no longer as steadily as before. His pursuers noticed what was happening. For a moment he would reduce his speed as if he was going to stop, and then he would hurtle forward at full speed. Furthermore, he was no longer traveling at a steady pace. Sometimes he would veer one way, sometimes the other, as if his steering gear was twisted. Three more cars caught up with the first pursuer. The quarry was losing speed. Now they had him!

Still fearing a trick, they did not close in at once. Surely there was someone else in the car besides the driver. If not, what were they following him for? One of the men in the first car assured the others that when the chase had begun he had seen a man throw himself to the floor of the taxi. Yet no one had answered their shots; there was only that crazy, desperately fleeing driver. Then he himself must be guilty; otherwise why expose himself to such danger? They followed him, no longer shooting, but keeping their distance. It was obvious that the pursued man was losing speed and control. Sometimes he appeared to be getting ready to stop once and for all, but then he would move ahead in a series of jerks. Now they had him within range not only of their rifles, but of their pistols too. They gradually crept closer! With what strength he had left, Ramón once more reached the Avenida de las Misiones, and then for no apparent reason turned back toward the city. He kept coming back to the spot where both his home and police headquarters were located and where the pursuit had begun. His pursuers guessed that he was trying to make it to headquarters. All they could think of now was not to lose the man who, they supposed, was in the back seat. In order to make his escape impossible, the car on the left and the car on the right drew up almost alongside Ramón, while the one in the middle approached from behind.

Opposite the Palacio, Ramón's car almost stopped, but then it moved forward again briefly, as if in the tow of an invisible force. The others kept their distance, approaching slowly. Once more Ramón stopped, this time in the very spot from which he had set out.

The lights were still on in headquarters, and people were going in and out; the air seemed filled with a distant noise, a noise filtered and deadened through a dense felt wall. The different voices were merged into a single even, dying murmur. Ramón turned his eyes toward the building, whose inner lights were bursting from the windows. His head dropped over his left shoulder, went limp, and sank on his chest. And still there was that smothered, dying noise far away, very far away. . . .

The other three cars stopped side by side in the middle of the street. Several armed men jumped out; others came out of police headquarters and surrounded Ramón's car. One opened the front door, and the driver tumbled out over the running board with his feet still on the pedals. At the same time others threw open the rear doors and searched the inside with their flashlights. They looked at each other in amazement. There was nobody there! Then one of the leaders bent over the driver, who was still lying with his body twisted, his head hanging, and his eyes closed. He flashed the light on him, looked at him slowly; he put out the light and reflected for a moment as though trying to recall something. Then once more he shone the light on the face and once more stopped to think. Everybody around him was silent, awaiting an explanation. The man said: "Does anybody know him?"

Nobody knew him. More men came out of headquarters. The body, still warm, was taken out of the car and carried inside. And in the electric light they were able to distinguish his features clearly. They were not ordinary features. Anybody who had ever known him would have recognized him. But no one recognized him. The first man who had shot at him was called in.

"What did you see in the car?" the policeman on duty asked. "I'm sure I saw a man; he looked out of the window and then he hid. Then I looked at the driver, and he tried to get away at once. That's why I followed him, and when we were out a ways he returned the fire."

They searched the car, but there was no gun. Ramón had not fired; most likely someone in one of the houses had done it. In fact, his revolver had been stolen from the pocket of the door, perhaps in the taxi stand while he was watching one of the men who was staring at him so intently. No one had seen anything else. The only testimony was that of the fellow who thought he had seen a man in the back seat. But why had the driver fled? He was only an ordinary hacker, obviously of no importance at all.

They looked at his license, they inquired of the Secret Police and the Justice Department. They could not find his name in any of the files. Meanwhile the body was there, lying on a table. They had taken for granted that he was dead, though he was really only in a state of shock due to loss of blood. But in two hours his body was rigid and cold. His address was on his license; a policeman went to his house, woke Estela and asked her some questions, but got nothing. The terrified, trembling woman could give them no information. She was living in the greatest poverty; it was impossible that a government agent could have been so badly paid.

All who had taken part in the pursuit were now standing perplexed around the body. Why the race, the pursuit, the victim? No one could throw any light on anything. If there had been a passenger, he could never have jumped out of the car. There had been no opportunity, for he had never been traveling slowly enough, and they had never lost sight of him. As far as the driver was concerned, they had not been able to get to the bottom of things even in the garage. Everybody regarded him as a nice guy; nobody had ever heard that he had any political connections. (Obviously they did not consider him very important, for the only person who had known anything about him was his boss, the other driver, and he had been silenced forever. He had left no written evidence, for he carried everything in his head.) Finally, near dawn, there appeared a little old man in uniform who had once been a policeman and was now a clerk. He shouldered the others aside and stood staring thoughtfully at the corpse. Then he looked around while he stroked his long, tobacco-stained mustache.

"Why did you kill this one?" he asked. "He is one of your own men. I remember him. I don't know who he is or what his name is, but quite a while ago I saw him brought in here and beaten up. They said he was a revolutionary. And he must have been one of the best. They took him in there two or three times, and they beat him black and blue, but they couldn't get a word out of him. Then he never came back."

They looked at each other. The old man turned around, once more shouldered his way through the crowd, and went back to his work, bowed by the weight of years and experience.

1942

Juan Carlos Onetti

b. 1909

JUAN CARLOS ONETTI was born in Montevideo on July 1, 1909. He dropped out of high school and worked at various odd jobs before becoming a writer for the Reuters Agency, first in Montevideo and then in Buenos Aires, where he lived between 1941 and 1955 and published most of his works. Onetti returned to his native country in 1957, becoming director of the Municipal Libraries of Montevideo. In 1975, he was forced into exile by Uruguay's military government, and lived in Spain for several years. During the 1960s Onetti gained recognition as one of the major forerunners of the Boom in Latin American literature. Although he has written many short stories, he is better known to English-language readers for his novels *La vida breve* (1950; *A Brief Life,* 1976) and *El astillero* (1961; *The Shipyard,* 1968). Both novels are daringly experimental in terms of narrative technique, and have influenced such writers as Julio Cortázar and Guillermo Cabrera Infante.

The Image of Misfortune

for Dorothea Muhr—forgotten dog of happiness
Translated by Daniel Balderston

1

At dusk, despite the high wind, I was in shirtsleeves, leaning on the rail of the hotel porch, alone. The light made the shadow of my head reach as far as the edge of the sandy trail through the bushes that links the highway and the beach with the cluster of houses.

The girl appeared, pedaling along the road, only to be immediately lost from sight behind the A-frame cabin, vacant but still adorned with the sign in black letters above the mailbox. It was impossible for me not to look at the sign at least once a day; though lashed by rain, siestas, and the sea wind, it showed a proud face and a lasting glow, and stated: "My Rest."

A moment later the girl appeared again along the sandy margin surrounded by thickets. She held her body erect on the seat, moving her legs at a slow, easy pace, her legs wrapped with calm arrogance in thick gray wool socks, tickled by the pine needles. Her knees were amazingly round and mature considering the age of the rest of her body.

She braked the bicycle right beside the shadow of my head, and her right foot, seeking balance, released the pedal and came to rest in the short dead grass, all brown now, on the shadow of my body. All at once she pulled the hair from her forehead and looked at me. She was wearing a dark sweater and a pink skirt. She looked at me calmly and attentively as if her brown hand, pulling the hair away from her eyes, were sufficient to hide her examination of me.

I calculated there were sixty feet between us and less than thirty years. Leaning on my forearms I held her gaze, changing the position of the pipe in my mouth, looking steadily toward her and her heavy bicycle, the colors of her thin body set against a backdrop of a landscape of trees and sheep sinking into the calm of the evening.

Suddenly sad and irritated, I looked at the smile the girl offered my exhaustion, her hair stiff and messy, her thin curved nose moving as she breathed, the childish angle at which her eyes had been stuck onto her face (which had nothing to do by now with her age, which had been formed once and for all and would remain that way until death), the excessive space left for the sclerotic membrane lining the eye. I looked at the glow of sweat and fatigue gathered together by the last or perhaps first light of sunset, covering and highlighting the coming darkness.

The girl laid her bicycle gently down on the bushes and looked at me again, her hands touching her hips, the thumbs sunk below the waist of her skirt. I don't know if she was wearing a belt; that summer all the girls were using wide belts. Then she looked around. Now she was facing sideways, her hands joined behind her back, without breasts as yet, still breathing with an odd shortness of breath, her face turned toward the spot in the afternoon where the sun would set.

Suddenly she sat down on the grass, took off her sandals, and shook them; one at a time she held her bare feet in her hands, rubbing the short toes and moving them in the air. Over her broad shoulders I watched her shake her dirty reddish feet. I saw her stretch out her legs, take out a comb and a mirror from the large monogrammed pocket on the lap of her skirt. She carelessly combed her hair, almost without looking at me.

She put her sandals back on and got up, then stood for a moment banging on the pedals with swift kicks. Repeating a sharp quick movement, she turned toward me, standing alone by the porch railing, still as ever, looking at her. The smell of honeysuckle was starting; the light from the hotel bar made pale splotches of light on the grass, the areas of sand, and the round driveway that circled the terrace.

It was as if we had seen each other before, as if we knew each other, as if we had fond memories. She looked at me with a defiant expression while her face slipped off into the meager light; she looked at me with the defiance of her whole scornful body, of the shiny metal of the bicycle, of the landscape with the A-frame cabin and the privet hedges and the young eucalyptus with milky trunks. For a moment that's all there was; everything that surrounded her became a part of her and her absurd pose. She climbed back on her bicycle and pedaled off beyond the hydrangeas, behind the empty benches painted blue, ever more quickly through the lines of cars in front of the hotel.

2

I emptied my pipe and watched the sun dying through the trees. I already knew what she was, perhaps too well. But I didn't want to name her. I thought of what was awaiting me in the hotel room around dinnertime. I tried measuring my past and my guilt with the rod I had just discovered: the profile of the thin girl looking toward the horizon, her brief, impossible age, the pink feet a hand had hit and squeezed.

By the door of my room, I found an envelope from the management with the biweekly bill. When I picked it up, I caught myself bending over to smell the honeysuckles' perfume barely floating in the room, feeling expectant and sad, without any new reason I could point to. I lit a match so as to reread the framed *Avis aux passagers* on the door, then lit my pipe again. For several minutes I stood there, washing my hands, playing with the soap; I looked at myself in the mirror above the washstand in almost total darkness, until I could pick out my thin, badly shaven, white face, perhaps the only white face among the guests in the hotel. It was my face; all the changes of the last few months had no real importance. I realized that the custom of playing with the soap had begun when Julian died, perhaps the very night of the wake.

I went back to the bedroom and opened the suitcase, after pushing it out from under the bed with my foot. It was a stupid ritual, but a ritual; however, perhaps it would be better for everyone if I stuck faithfully to this form of madness until using it up or getting used up myself. Without looking, I sorted things out, separated clothes and two little books, and found the folded newspaper at last. I knew the story by heart; it was the fairest, the most profoundly mistaken, and the most respectful of any of the ones published. I pulled the armchair up to the light and began not reading, just looking at, the big black headline across the top of the page, now starting to fade: FUGITIVE TREASURER KILLS SELF. Underneath was the picture, the gray spots forming the face of a man looking at the world with an expression of astonishment, his mouth almost smiling under a mustache that slanted down at the edges. I remembered the sterility of having thought about the girl, a few minutes earlier, as if she might be the beginning of some melody that would resound elsewhere. This place, my place, was a private world, narrow, irreplaceable. No friendship, presence, or dialogue could find a place there, apart from that ghost with the listless mustache. Sometimes he allowed me to choose between Julian and the Fugitive Treasurer.

Anyone would admit the possibility of having influence on, or of doing something for, one's younger brother. But Julian was—or had been until a few days more than a month before—a little more than five years older than I was. Nonetheless, I should write nonetheless. I may have been born, and continued to live, to spoil his condition as an only child; I may have forced him, by means of my fantasies, my aloofness, and my scant sense of responsibility, to turn into the man he became: first into the poor devil proud of his promotion, then into a thief. Also, of course, into the other, into the relatively young dead man we all looked at but whom only I could recognize as my brother.

What has he left me? A row of crime novels, some childhood memories, clothes I cannot use because they are too tight and too short. And the photo in the newspaper beneath the long headline. I looked down on his acceptance of life. I knew he was a bachelor for lack of spirit. How many times would I pass, almost always by chance, in front of the barbershop where he went for a shave every day. His humility irritated me and it was hard for me to believe in it. I was aware of the fact that a woman visited him punctually every Friday. He was very affable, incapable of bothering anyone, and from the time he was thirty, his clothes gave off the smell of an old man. A smell that cannot be defined, that comes from God knows where. When he doubted something, his mouth formed the same grimace as our mother's. Had circumstances been different he would never have been my friend; I would never have chosen him or accepted him as that. Words are pretty, or try to be, when they point toward an explanation. From the first, all these words are useless, at odds with one another. He was my brother.

Arturo whistled in the garden, jumped over the railing, and came straight into the room, dressed in a bathrobe, shaking sand from his hair as he crossed toward the bathroom. I saw him rinse in the shower and hid the newspaper between my leg and the back of the chair. But I heard him shout: "The ghost, same as always."

I did not answer and once again lit my pipe. Arturo came out of the bathroom whistling and closed the door on the night. Sprawled on the bed, he put on his underwear and then continued dressing.

"And my belly keeps growing," he said. "I barely had any lunch, swam out to the breakwater. Result: my belly keeps growing. I would have bet anything that of all the men I know, this wouldn't have happened to you. Yet it happens, and happens hard. About a month ago, right?"

"Yes. Twenty-eight days."

"You've even counted," Arturo continued. "You know me well. I say it without any disrespect. Twenty-eight days since that wretch shot himself, and you—you, no less—go on playing with feelings of remorse. Like some hysterical spinster. Because not even all spinsters would behave like this. It's unbelievable."

He sat on the edge of the bed drying his feet and putting on his socks.

"Yes," I said. "If he shot himself, he was apparently none too happy. Not so happy, at least, as you are at this moment."

"It's maddening," Arturo went on. "As if you had killed him. And don't ask me again . . ." He stopped for a moment to look at himself in the mirror, "Don't ask me again whether in one of the seventeen dimensions you are guilty of the fact that your brother shot himself."

He lit a cigarette and lay down on the bed. I stood up, put a pillow over the rapidly yellowing newspaper, and began walking around in the heat of the room.

"As I told you, I'm leaving tonight," Arturo said. "What do you intend to do?"

"I don't know," I answered softly, with some feeling of indifference. "For the moment I'll stay here. The summer will last for a while yet."

I heard Arturo sigh and listened as his sigh turned into a whistle of impatience. He got up, throwing his cigarette in the toilet.

"It so happens that my moral duty is to kick you a few times and take you with me. You know that everything is different there. When you get very drunk, on toward dawn, completely distracted, then it will be all over."

I shrugged my shoulders, just my left shoulder, and recognized a gesture that Julian and I had inherited, not chosen.

"I'm telling you again," Arturo said, poking a handkerchief in his lapel pocket. "I'm telling you, insisting over and over, with a bit of anger and with the respect I mentioned earlier. Did you tell your unfortunate brother to shoot himself to escape from the trap? Did you tell him to buy Chilean pesos and change them into liras and then turn the liras into francs and the francs into Swedish crowns and the crowns into dollars and the dollars into pounds and the pounds into yellow silk slips? No, don't shake your head. Cain in the depths of the cave. I want a yes or a no. Although I don't really need an answer. Did you advise him (which is all that matters) to steal? Never. You're incapable of that. I told you so, many times. And you'll never know whether that's a compliment or a reproach. You didn't tell him to steal. And so?"

I sat down on the armchair again.

"We already talked about all that so many times. Are you leaving tonight?"

"Sure, on the bus at nine something. I have five days off and have no intention of spending them getting healthier and healthier only to waste it all right afterward on the office."

Arturo chose a tie and began knotting it.

"It's just that it doesn't make sense," he said once more in front of the mirror. "I admit that I too have shut myself in with a ghost one time or another. The experiment always turned out badly. But with your own brother, the way you're doing now . . . A ghost with a wiry mustache. Never. The ghost isn't your brother, that much we know. But now it's the ghost of nothingness, that's all. This time it came from misfortune. It was the treasurer of a cooperative who wore the mustache of a Russian general."

"Won't you be serious for this one last time?" I said in a low voice. I wasn't asking him for anything: I just wanted to keep my promise, and even today I don't know to whom, or even what promise.

"The last time," said Arturo.

"I see the reason well enough. I didn't tell him, didn't make the least suggestion, that he should use the Cooperative's money for the currency exchange business. But one night, just to encourage him or so his life would be a little less boring, I explained to him that there were things that could be done in this world to make money and spend it, something other than picking up a check at the end of the month . . ."

"I know," Arturo said, sitting down on the bed with a yawn. "I swam too hard; I'm not up for such things anymore. But it was the last day. I know the whole story. Now explain to me—and I would like to remind you that the summer is coming to an end—what good can you hope to do by staying shut in up here? Explain to me why it's your fault if the other guy did something stupid."

"Something is my fault," I mumbled with my eyes half-closed, my head resting on the armchair; my words were sluggish and choppy. "It's my fault that I was enthusiastic, that I lied maybe. It's my fault that I spoke for the first time to Julian of something we cannot define, something we call the world. It's my fault that I made him feel, though I can't say believe, that if he took risks that thing I called the world would be his."

"And so what," Arturo said, looking at his hair in the mirror at the far end of the room. "Brother. All of that is just complicated idiocy. Well, life is also just complicated idiocy. One of these days this phase of yours will pass; when that happens come visit me. Now get dressed and let's go have a drink before dinner. I have to leave early. But, before I forget, I want to leave you with one last argument. Maybe it will be good for something."

He touched my shoulder and looked me in the eye.

"Listen," he said. "In the middle of all this happy complicated idiocy, did your brother Julian use the money properly, did he use it in exact accordance with the silly things you had told him?"

"Him?" I asked with surprise, getting up. "Please. When he came to see me, it was already too late. At first, I'm almost certain, he made good buys. But he got frightened right away and did unbelievable things. I know few of the details. It was something like a combination of bonds and foreign currency, of casinos with racehorses."

"You see?" Arturo said, nodding his head. "A certificate of irresponsibility. I give you five minutes to get dressed and meditate on that. I'll wait for you in the bar."

3

We had a drink while Arturo tried to find a woman's picture in his wallet.

"It's not here," he said finally. "I lost it. The picture, not the woman. I wanted to show it to you because there was something unique about her that few people saw. And before you went crazy you understood such things."

And, I thought, there were memories of childhood that would surge up and become clear in the next days, weeks, or months. There was also the deceitful, perhaps deliberate, deformation of memory. In the best possible case, it was a choice I had not made. I would see the two of us, in a moment of recollection or in nightmares, dressed in ridiculous clothes, playing in a damp garden, or hitting one another in a bedroom. He was older but weaker. He was tolerant and kind, had accepted the burden of my faults, lied sweetly about the marks my blows had made on his face, about a broken cup, about coming home late. It was strange that it all had not yet begun during the month of fall vacation at the beach; perhaps, without meaning to, I was holding back the torrent with the newspaper articles and the evocation of the last two nights. During one of them Julian was alive, on the next he was dead. The second night was of no importance, and all the interpretations of it had been mistaken.

It was his wake; they had just hung his jaw back on his head; the bandage around his head grew old and yellow before dawn. I was very busy offering drinks and comparing the similarity of the regrets. As he was five years older than I, Julian had turned forty some time before. He had never asked life for anything of importance, or perhaps only for this: that he be left in peace. As in childhood, he came and went, asking permission. His residence on earth, unsurprising but long, stretched out by me, had not been any use to him, not even to become known. All the whispering and listless people, drinking coffee or whiskey, agreed to judge and feel sorry for the suicide as a sort of mistake. Because with a good lawyer, after a couple of years in jail . . . And besides, everyone found the ending out of proportion and grotesque in relation to the crime as they understood it. I thanked them and nodded; afterward I wandered around the hall and the kitchen, carrying drinks or empty glasses. Without any information to help me, I was trying to imagine what the cheap tart who visited Julian every Friday or every Monday (days when there were few clients) must be thinking. I pondered the invisible, never revealed truth of their relationship. I asked myself what her judgment would be, attributing an impossible degree of intelligence to her. She who each day endured the fact of being a prostitute, what could she think about Julian, who accepted the idea that he was a thief for a few weeks but who could not, as she could, endure the idea that the fools who inhabit and form the world might learn of his slip? But she did not come at any point during the night, or at least I did not recognize a face, an insolence, a perfume, a meekness that could be identified as hers.

Without stirring from the bar stool, Arturo had bought the bus ticket and seat reservation—9:45.

"There's time to spare. I can't find the picture. Today there's no use talking anymore. Bartender, another round."

I already said that the night of the wake was of no importance. The one before was much briefer and more difficult. Julian could have waited for me in the hallway of the apartment. But he was already thinking about the police and chose to wander around in the rain until light appeared in my window. He was soaked—he was born to use an umbrella and this time he had forgotten it—and he sneezed various times, begging pardon, joking, before sitting down next to the electric heater, before using my house. All of Montevideo knew the story of the Cooperative, and at least half of the newspaper readers desired, absentmindedly, that nothing more be discovered about the treasurer.

But Julian had not waited an hour and a half in the rain to see me, to say goodbye with words announcing the suicide. We had a few drinks. He accepted the alcohol without display, without resistance: "Now in any case . . ." he mumbled, laughing almost, shrugging one shoulder.

Nonetheless, he had come to say goodbye to me in his own way. Memory was unavoidable: thoughts of our parents, of the now demolished house and garden of our childhood.

He moistened his long mustache and said worriedly, "It's strange. I always thought you knew and I didn't. Since I was a child. And I don't think it's a problem of character or intelligence. It's something else. There are people who instinctively find their way in the world. You do and I don't. I always lacked the necessary faith." He stroked his unshaven jawbones. "But neither is it a case of my having had to adjust to deformities or vices. There was no handicap, or at least I never knew of one."

He stopped and emptied his glass. When he raised his head—the head I have been looking at on the front page of a newspaper every day for the last month—he showed me his healthy, tobacco-stained teeth.

"But," he continued as he stood up, "your strategy was very good. You should teach it to someone else. The failure is not yours."

"Sometimes it works out and other times it doesn't," I said. "You can't go out in this rain. You can stay on here forever, as long as you want."

He leaned on the back of the armchair and was making fun of me without looking at me.

"In this rain. Forever. As long as you want." He came up to me and grasped my arm. "Forgive me. There will be trouble. There is always trouble."

He had already gone. He was bidding me farewell with his presence, cowering as always, with his generous, well-trimmed mustache, with a reference to everything dead and dissolved which the blood tie could (can) revive for a couple of minutes at a time.

Arturo was speaking of swindles at the races. He looked at his watch and asked the bartender for a last drink. "But with a little more gin, please," he said.

Then, not listening to him, I caught myself linking my dead brother with the girl on the bicycle. I didn't want to remember his childhood or his passive goodness, nothing in fact except his impoverished smile, his body's meek posture during our final conversation (if I could give that name to what I allowed to happen between us when he came to my apartment, soaked to the skin, to say goodbye to me in his own way).

I knew nothing about the girl on the bicycle. But then, all of a sudden, while Arturo was speaking of Ever Perdomo or the poor promotion of tourism, I felt my throat penetrated by a whiff of the old, unfair, almost always mistaken feeling of pity. What was clear was that I loved her and wanted to protect her. I could not guess from what or against what. Angry, I sought to save her from herself and from all danger. I had seen her unsure of herself and defiant; I had seen her face turn into a haughty image of misfortune. Such an image might last but is usually crushed in a premature way, out of all proportion. My brother had paid for his excess of simplicity. In the case of the girl—whom I might never see again—the debts were different. But, by very different paths, both of them coincided in their anxious approach to death, to the definitive experience. Julian, by inertia; she, the girl on the bicycle, by trying to do everything in a great hurry.

"But," Arturo said, "even if they show you that all the races are fixed, you go on betting just the same. Hey, now it looks to me like it's going to rain."

"For sure," I answered, and we went into the dining room. I saw her right away.

She was near a window, breathing in the stormy air of the night, with a lock of dark, wind-ruffled hair hanging down over her eyes and forehead, and areas of light freckles—now, beneath the unbearable fluorescent light of the dining room—on her cheeks and nose, while her childish, watery eyes absentmindedly looked at the shadow of the sky or at the mouths of her table companions, with strong, thin bare arms reaching out from under what could be considered a yellow evening gown, a hand over each shoulder.

An old man was sitting next to her and was talking to a woman sitting across the table, a young woman whose fleshy white back faced us, a wild rose in her hair above one ear. And when she moved, the little white circle of the flower would cover the girl's absent profile, then would uncover it again. When the woman laughed, tossing her head toward the shiny skin on her back, the girl's face would be left alone against the night.

While talking with Arturo, I looked at the table, trying to guess the origin of her secret, the sensation that she was something extraordinary. I wanted to remain quiet forever beside the girl and take charge of her life. I saw her smoke as she drank her coffee, her eyes now fixed on the old man's slow mouth. Suddenly she looked at me as she had earlier on the path, with the same calm, defiant eyes, accustomed to contemplating or imagining disdain. With an inexplicable feeling of desperation, I felt the girl's eyes on me, pulling mine in the direction of the long noble young head, then escaping from the tangible secret only to plunge into the stormy night, to conquer the intensity of the sky and scatter it, impose it on the young face that observed me, still and expressionless. The face which let flow the sweetness and adolescent modesty of scarlet freckled cheeks in the direction of my serious and exhausted grown man's face, for no purpose, unconsciously.

Arturo smiled, smoking.

"Et tu, Brute?" he asked.

"What?"

"The girl on the bicycle, the girl in the window. If I didn't have to leave at this very moment . . ."

"I don't understand."

"That one, the one in the yellow dress. Hadn't you seen her before?"

"Once. This afternoon, from the porch. Before you came back from the beach."

"Love at first sight," Arturo agreed. "Intact youth, scarred experience. It is a pretty story. But, I must confess, there is someone who tells it better. Wait."

The waiter came up to clear the plates and the fruit bowl. "Coffee?" he asked. He was small, with a dark monkey face.

"OK," Arturo smiled, "what passes for coffee. They also say 'miss' to the girl in yellow by the window. My friend is very curious; he wants to know something about the girl's nocturnal excursions."

I unbuttoned my jacket and sought out the girl's eyes. But her face had turned to one side, and the old man's black sleeve cut diagonally across the yellow dress. Right then the hairdo of the woman with the flower leaned forward, covering the freckled face. All that was left of the girl was a bit of her dark brown hair, metallic-looking at the top of her head where the light was reflected. I remembered the magic of her lips and her glance; *magic* is a word I cannot explain, which I use now because I have no other choice, not the slightest possibility of substituting another one.

"Nothing bad," Arturo continued with the matter. "The gentleman, my friend, is interested in cycling. Tell me, what happens at night when daddy and mommy, if that's who they are, are asleep?"

The waiter rocked back and forth smiling, the empty fruit bowl raised to shoulder height.

"That's right," he said finally. "Everybody knows. At midnight the young lady rides off on her bicycle; sometimes she goes to the woods, other times to the dunes." He had managed to look serious, repeating without malice: "What else can I tell you? I don't know anything else, no matter what anyone says. I never watched. That she returns with her hair mussed up and without makeup. That one night I was on duty and I ran into her and she put ten pesos in my hand. The English fellows who are staying at the Atlantic talk a lot. But I won't say anything because I didn't see it."

Arturo laughed, patting the waiter's leg.

"There you have it," he said, as if he had scored a victory.

"Excuse me," I asked the waiter. "How old do you think she is?"

"The young lady?"

"Sometimes, this afternoon, she seems like a child to me; now she seems older."

"This much I know for certain, sir," the waiter said. "According to the register she is fifteen. Her birthday was a few days ago. So, two cups of coffee?" He leaned over before leaving.

I tried to smile at Arturo's merry look; at the corner of the tablecloth, my hand trembled as it held the pipe.

"In any case," Arturo said, "whether it works out or not, it is a more interesting program than living shut up with a ghost with a mustache."

When she got up from the table, the girl turned to look at me again, from a higher angle now, one hand still wrapped in the napkin—for a moment, while the air from the window tossed the stiff hair on her forehead—and I stopped believing what the waiter had said and what Arturo accepted as the truth.

In the hallway, carrying his suitcase, his overcoat over his arm, Arturo patted me on the shoulder.

"One more week and we'll see one another again. I'll go to the Jauja and meet you at a table savoring the flower of knowledge. Well, happy cycling."

He went out into the garden and then toward the group of cars parked across from the terrace. When Arturo had crossed the lighted area, I lit my pipe, leaned on the railing, and smelled the air. The storm seemed far-off. I went back to the bedroom and lay there, sprawled on the bed, listening to the music that wafted in endlessly from the hotel dining room, where perhaps they had already started dancing. I held the warmth of my pipe in my hand and went slipping into a heavy dream of a grimy, airless world where I had been condemned to go forward, with enormous effort and no desire to do so, my mouth open, toward an entrance where the intense light of the morning was shining indifferently, always out of reach.

I woke up in a sweat and went to sit down again in the armchair. Neither Julian nor the memories of childhood had appeared in the nightmare. I left the dream forgotten on the bed, inhaled the air that was blowing in the window from the storm, pulled the paper out from under my body and looked at the headline, smelled the heavy, hot smell of a woman. Almost without moving, I saw Julian's faded picture. I dropped the paper, turned out the bedroom light, and jumped over the railing onto the soft earth of the garden. The wind was making thick zigzags and wrapped around my waist. I decided to cross the lawn as far as the patch of sand where the girl had been sitting that afternoon. Her gray socks riddled by the pine needles, then their bare feet in her hands, the skinny buttocks flattened on the ground. The woods were off to my left, the dunes to the right; everything was black and the wind struck my face. I heard steps and immediately saw the luminous smile of the waiter, the monkey face next to my shoulder.

"Bad luck," the waiter said. "She's gone."

I felt like striking him but quickly calmed my hands, scratching at the pockets of my raincoat. I stood panting, facing the noise of the sea, still, my eyes half-closed. "What you can do is wait for her when she comes back. If you give her a good scare . . ."

I slowly unbuttoned the raincoat without turning around; I took a bill out of my pants pocket and gave it to the waiter. I waited until the sound of his footsteps disappeared in the direction of the hotel. Then I bent my head down—my feet held firm on the spongy ground and the grass where she had sat—sunken in that memory (the girl's body and movements in the seemingly so distant afternoon), protected from myself and my past by an indestructible aura of belief and hope without object, breathing the hot air where everything was forgotten.

4

I saw her all of a sudden, under the excessive autumn moon. She was walking by herself along the shore, dodging the rocks and the bright puddles that were growing ever larger, pushing her bicycle, no longer wearing the comical yellow dress, with tight pants and a sailor's jacket on instead. I had never seen her wear those clothes, and her body and footsteps had not had time to become familiar to me. But I recognized her immediately and crossed the beach almost in a straight line toward her.

"Night," I said.

A while later she turned to look me in the eye; she stopped and turned her bicycle toward the water. She looked at me attentively for a time, and there was already something solitary and helpless about her when I greeted her again. This time she answered me. On the deserted beach her voice shrieked like a bird. It was an unpleasant and alien voice, utterly separate from her, from the beautiful face, so sad and thin; it was as if she had just learned a language, some dialogue in a foreign language. I reached out to hold the bicycle. Now I was looking at the moon and she was protected by the shadow.

"Where were you going," I said, then added: "Baby."

"Nowhere in particular," her strange voice uttered laboriously.

I thought of the waiter, of the English boys at the Atlantic; I thought of everything I had lost forever, through no fault of my own, without anyone consulting me.

"They say . . ." I said. The weather had changed: it was no longer cold or windy. Helping the girl hold up the bicycle in the sand beside the pounding sea, I had a sensation of solitude that no one had ever allowed me to feel before: solitude, peace, and trust.

"If you don't have anything better to do, they say that very nearby there is a boat that's been turned into a bar and restaurant."

The hard voice repeated with mysterious joy, "They say that very nearby there is a boat that's been turned into a bar and restaurant."

I heard her struggle with her shortness of breath; after a rest she added, "No, I don't have anything to do. Is that an invitation? And like this, with these clothes on?"

"Yes. Like that."

When she turned away I saw her smile; she was not making fun of me, she seemed happy and unaccustomed to happiness.

"You were at the next table with your friend. Your friend left this evening. But one of my tires burst as soon as I left the hotel."

She irritated me with her recollection of Arturo; I took the handlebar from her, and we began walking along the shore toward the boat.

Two or three times I spoke some idle phrase, but she didn't answer. The heat and air of a storm were increasing again. I felt the girl growing sad at my side; I spied her firm steps, the resolute erectness of her body, the boyish buttocks hugged by the ordinary trousers.

The boat was there, pointed toward land, all its lights off.

"There is no boat, no party," I said. "I beg your pardon for having made you walk all this way for nothing."

She had stopped to look at the tilted freighter under the moon. She stayed like that for a while, her hands behind her back as if she were alone, as if she had forgotten about me and the bicycle. The moon was going down toward the watery horizon or was coming up from there. All of a sudden the girl turned and came toward me; I did not let the bicycle fall. She took my face in her rough hands and moved it until it was facing the moon.

"What?" she said hoarsely. "You spoke. Once more."

I could hardly see her but I remembered her. I remembered many other things for which she could serve effortlessly as a symbol. I had begun to love her, and sadness was beginning to leave her and fall on me.

"Nothing," I said. "There's no boat, no party."

"No party," she repeated. I glimpsed a smile in the darkness, white and brief as the foam of the little waves that lapped a few yards down the beach. She suddenly kissed me; she knew how to kiss and I felt her warm face damp with tears. But I did not release the bicycle.

"There's no party," she said again, now with lowered head, smelling my chest. The voice was more confused, almost guttural. "I had to see your face." Once again she raised it toward the moon. "I had to know that I was not mistaken. Does that make sense?"

"Yes," I lied; then she took the bicycle from my hands, climbed on, and made a large circle on the wet sand.

When she came around next to me, she rested a hand on the back of my neck, and we returned toward the hotel. We avoided the rocks and made a detour toward the woods. It was not her doing, or mine. She stopped next to the first pine trees and let the bicycle drop.

"Your face. Once more. I don't want you to get angry with me," she begged.

I obediently looked toward the moon, toward the first clouds that were appearing in the sky.

"Something," she said in her strange voice. "I want you to say something. Anything."

She put her hand on my chest and stood on tiptoe to bring her girlish eyes nearer my mouth.

"I love you. And it's no good. It's just another kind of misfortune," I said after a while, speaking with almost the same slowness as she did.

Then the girl mumbled "poor thing" as if she were my mother, with her strange voice, now tender and protective, and we began to go crazy with kisses. We helped one another undress her to the extent necessary, and I suddenly had two things I did not deserve: her face shaped by weeping and happiness beneath the moon and the disconcerting certainty that she had never been penetrated before.

We sat down near the hotel on the dampness of the rocks. The moon was covered up. She began throwing pebbles; sometimes they fell in the water with a loud sound, other times they barely went beyond her feet. She did not seem to notice.

My story was grave and definitive. I told it with a serious masculine voice, resolving furiously to tell the truth, unconcerned whether she believed it or not.

All the facts had just lost their meaning; from now on they could only have the meaning she desired to give them. I spoke, of course, of my dead brother. However, since that night, the girl had turned into the central theme of my story, even going back in time to become a principal obsession in the previous days. From time to time I heard her move and tell me yes with her strange malformed voice. It was also necessary to refer to the years that separated us, to feel excessively sad about it, to feign a disconsolate belief in the power of the word *impossible,* to display a certain degree of discouragement in the face of the inevitable struggles. I did not want to ask her any questions; her affirmatives, not always uttered during the right pauses, did not demand confessions. There was no doubt that the girl had freed me from Julian and from many other failures and complications that Julian's death represented or had brought to the surface; there was no doubt that I, since a half hour earlier, needed her and would continue to need her.

I accompanied her almost to the hotel door, and we parted without telling each other our names. As she drew away I thought I noticed that the two bicycle tires were full of air. Perhaps she had lied to me about that, but nothing mattered any more. I didn't even see her go into the hotel; just the same, I went into the shadow parallel to the hallway outside my room; I continued laboriously toward the dunes, wanting to think of nothing, at last, and to wait for the storm.

I walked along the dunes and then, already some distance away, returned toward the eucalyptus grove. I walked slowly through the trees, between the twisting wind and its cry, beneath thunderclaps threatening to rise up from the invisible horizon, closing my eyes against the stinging sand that was blowing in my face. Everything was dark and—as I had to repeat several times afterward—I saw no bicycle lamp, were anyone to use one on the beach, nor did I see the burning cigarette tip of anyone walking or resting on the sand, seated on the dry leaves, leaning against a trunk, with legs drawn up, tired, damp, happy. That was the way I was, and although I did not know how to pray, I wandered around giving thanks, refusing to accept the way things were, incredulous.

I finally reached the end of the trees, a hundred yards from the sea, just opposite the dunes. I felt cuts on my hands and stopped to suck on them. I walked toward the noise of the surf until I felt the damp sand of the shore underfoot. I did not see, I repeat once more, I saw no light, no movement in the shadow; I heard no voice breaking or deforming the wind.

I left the shore and began climbing up and sliding down the dunes, slipping on the cold sand that trickled into my shoes, pushing aside the bushes with my legs, almost running, angry and with a sort of joy that had pursued me for years and was now within reach, excited as if I would never be able to stop, laughing in the midst of the windy night, running up and down the little peaks, falling to my knees and relaxing my body until I could breathe without pain, my face turned toward the storm that was coming off the water. Afterward it was as if all of my discouragement and renunciation had given me chase; for hours I looked, unenthusiastically, for the path that would take me back to the hotel. Then I encountered the waiter and I repeated the act of not speaking to him, of putting ten pesos in his hand. The man smiled and I was so tired that I thought he had understood, that all of the world understood and for all time.

Half-dressed, I fell back to sleep on my bed as if on the sand, listening to the storm that had finally decided to break, knocked by the thunderclaps, sinking thirstily into the angry noise of the rain.

5

I had just finished shaving when I heard fingers knocking on the glass of the door that opened onto the porch. It was very early; I knew that the nails of those fingers were long and painted fiery colors. Still carrying my towel, I opened the door. It was unavoidable: there she was.

Her hair was dyed blond and perhaps it had been blond when she was twenty. She wore a tailor-made herringbone suit that the years and the frequent washings made cling to her body. She carried a green umbrella with an ivory handle that had perhaps never been opened. Of the three things, I had guessed at two of them—correctly, to be sure—in the course of my brother's life and of his wake.

"Betty," she said as she turned around, with the best smile she could put on.

I pretended that I had never seen her, that I did not know who she was. It was just a sort of compliment, a twisted form of tact that no longer interested me.

I thought, this was, and will never again be, the woman whose blurry image I saw behind the dirty windows of a neighborhood cafe, touching Julian's fingers during the long prologues to the Fridays or Mondays.

"Excuse me," she said, "for coming so far to bother you and at this time of day. Especially at these moments when you, the best of Julian's siblings . . . Even now, I swear to you, I cannot accept that he is dead."

The light of the morning made her look older; she must have looked different in Julian's apartment, even in the cafe. To the end, I had been Julian's only sibling, not the best or the worst. She was old and it seemed easy to soothe her. I too, despite everything I had seen and heard, despite the memory of the night before on the beach, had not fully accepted Julian's death. It was only when I raised my head and held out my arm to ask her into my room that I discovered that she was wearing a hat and that she decorated it with fresh violets surrounded by ivy leaves.

"Call me Betty," she said, choosing to sit on the armchair where I hid the newspaper, the picture, the headline, the sordid (yet not utterly sordid) article. "But it was a matter of life or death."

No trace remained of the storm, and the night might well not have happened. I looked at the sun in the window, the yellowish splotch that was heading for the rug. Nonetheless it was certain that I felt different, that I breathed the air with eagerness, that I felt like walking and smiling, that indifference—and also cruelty—seemed to me possible forms of virtue. But all of that was confused and I could only understand it a bit later.

I drew my chair up near the armchair and offered my excuses to the woman, to that outmoded form of slovenliness and unhappiness. I took out the newspaper, struck several matches, and let the burning paper dance out over the porch rail.

"Poor Julian," she said behind me.

I went back to the center of the room, lit my pipe, and sat down on the bed. I suddenly discovered that I was happy and tried to calculate how many years separated me from the last time I had felt happiness. The smoke of the pipe irritated my eyes. I lowered it to my knees and sat there happily, looking at the trash there on the armchair, the mistreated filth that lay half-conscious in the fresh morning.

"Poor Julian," I repeated. "I said it many times during the wake and afterward. Now I'm fed up, enough is enough. I was waiting for you during the wake and you didn't come. But, please understand, thanks to the anticipation I knew what you were like; I could have met you on the street and recognized you."

She observed me, disconcerted, and smiled again. "Yes, I think I understand."

She was not very old, though far from my age or Julian's. But our lives had been very different, and what was lying there on the armchair was nothing but fat, a wrinkled baby face, suffering, veiled rancor, the grease of life stuck forever to her cheeks, to the corners of her mouth, to the wrinkled dark circles under her eyes. I felt like hitting her and throwing her out. But I sat there quietly, began smoking again and speaking to her with a sweet voice.

"Betty. You gave me permission to call you Betty. You said it was a matter of life or death. Julian is dead, out of the picture. What is it then, who else?"

She sprawled back on the armchair covered in faded cretonne, on a cover with hideous huge flowers, and sat there looking at me as if at a possible client: with the inevitable quota of hatred and calculation.

"Who dies now?" I insisted. "You or me?"

She relaxed her body and was preparing a touching expression. I looked at her, admitted that she could be convincing, and not just to Julian. Behind her the autumn morning stretched without a cloud, the little offering of glory to mankind. The woman, Betty, twisted her mouth and composed a bitter smile.

"Who?" she said, speaking in the direction of the announcement on the door. "You and me."

"I don't think so; the business is just beginning."

"There are IOUs with his signature and no money to back them up, and they're coming into court now. And there is the mortgage on my house, the only thing I possess. Julian assured me that it was no more than an offer, but the house, my little house, is mortgaged. And it has to be paid off right away. If we want to save something from the disaster. Or if we want to save ourselves."

By the violets on her hat and the sweat on her face, I had foreseen that it was inevitable that sooner or later on this sunny morning I would listen to some such phrase.

"Yes," I said, "you may be right, maybe we have to join together and do something."

For many years I had not derived so much pleasure from a lie, from sham and iniquity. But I had turned young again and didn't owe any explanations even to myself.

"I don't know," I said cautiously, "how much you know about my guilt, about my part in Julian's death. In any case, I can assure you that I never advised him to mortgage your house, your little house. But I am going to tell you everything. I was with Julian about three months ago: one brother eating in a restaurant with his older brother. And it was a matter of brothers who did not see one another more than once a year. I think it was somebody's birthday—his, our dead mother's. I don't remember and it isn't important. The date, whatever it was, seemed to dishearten him. I spoke to him about speculation, about some exchange of foreign currency, but I never told him to steal money from the Cooperative."

She had let the time go by with the help of a sigh and stretched her high heels toward the rectangular patch of sun on the carpet. She waited for me to look at her and then smiled once again; now she looked as if it was somebody's birthday—Julian's or my mother's. She was tenderness and patience, wanted to help me get through without stumbling.

"Kid," she mumbled, her head leaning on one shoulder, the smile brandished against the limit of tolerance. "Three months ago?" she snorted while raising her shoulders. "Kid, Julian was stealing from the Cooperative for the last five years. Or four. I remember. You spoke to him, dear, about some deal with dollars, right? I don't know whose birthday it was that night. And I'm not being disrespectful. But Julian told me the whole story and I couldn't stop laughing hysterically. He didn't even think about the dollar deal, whether it was a good idea or not. He stole and bet on the horses. For the last five years, since before I met him."

"Five years," I repeated, chewing on my pipe. I got up and went over to the window. There was still water on the weeds and the sand. The fresh air had nothing to do with us or with anybody.

In some hotel room upstairs, the girl must have been sleeping peacefully, sprawled out, beginning to stir amid the insistent desperation of dreams and hot sheets. I imagined her and kept on loving her, loving her breathing, her smell, the references I imagined to the memory of the previous night, to me, that might fit into her morning slumber. I returned heavily to the window and looked without revulsion or pity at what destiny had located in the armchair of my hotel room. She was arranging the lapels of the tailored jacket, which was perhaps not herringbone after all; she smiled at the empty air, waited for me to return, for my voice. I felt old, with little strength left. Perhaps the obscure dog of happiness was licking my knees, my hands; perhaps it was something else altogether: that I was old and tired. But, in any case, I felt the need to let time pass, to light the pipe again, to play with the flame of the match, with its sputtering.

"As far as I'm concerned," I said, "everything's fine. It's true that Julian did not use a revolver to make you sign a mortgage application. And I never signed an IOU. If he forged the signature and was able to live that way for five years—I think you said five—then you had quite something, you both had something. I look at you, think about you, and it doesn't matter to me at all that they take away your house or bury you in jail. I never signed an IOU for Julian. Unfortunately for you, Betty—and the name does not seem particularly apt to me, I don't think it fits you—no danger or threats will work for you. We cannot be partners in anything, and that is always a sad thing. I think it's especially sad for women. I would be very grateful to you if you left right away, if you made no fuss, Betty."

I went outside and continued insulting her in a low voice, searching for defects in the wondrous autumn morning. Very far away, I heard the apathetic cursing she directed at my back. I heard, almost immediately, a door slamming. A blue Ford appeared near the cluster of houses.

I was small and all of that seemed undeserved to me, organized by the poor uncertain imagination of a child. Since adolescence I had always displayed my defects; I was always right, inclined to converse and argue without reserve or silence. Julian, on the other hand—and I began to feel sympathy and some very different form of pity for him—had deceived us all for many years. This Julian I had only become acquainted with after his death was laughing softly at me ever since he began to confess the truth, exhibiting his mustache and his smile in the coffin. Maybe he was still laughing at all of us a month after his death. But it was useless for me to invent rancor or disillusionment.

Above all, I was irritated by the memory of our last conversation, by the gratuitous nature of his lies, and could not understand why he had come to visit me, considering all the risks, to lie for one last time. For, though Betty provoked only my pity or contempt, I believed her story and felt sure of the unending filth of life.

The blue Ford sputtered its way up the hill, behind the cabin with the red roof; it left the road and crossed parallel to the porch until reaching the hotel door. I saw a policeman get out in a faded summer uniform and an extraordinarily tall, thin man in a suit with thick stripes on it and also a young blond man dressed in gray, no hat, smiling at every phrase, holding a cigarette to his mouth between two long fingers.

The hotel manager went slowly down the staircase and approached them, while the waiter from the night before came out from behind a column on the stairs in shirtsleeves, his dark brown hair shining. They all spoke with few gestures, almost without moving the position of their feet. The manager took a handkerchief from the inner pocket of his jacket, wiped his lips with it, and put it back, only to pull it out again a few seconds later with a rapid movement, squeeze it, and rub his mouth with it. I went inside to confirm that the woman had gone; when I came out on the porch again, paying attention to my own movements, to the lethargy with which I wanted to live, to assume each pose as if trying to caress everything that my hands had made, I felt happy in the morning air, felt that other days might be waiting for me somewhere.

I saw that the waiter was looking at the ground and that the four other men had raised their heads and that their faces revealed an absentminded observation of me. The young blond man tossed away his cigarette; then I began to part my lips into a smile and, nodding my head, greeted the manager, and just after, before he could answer, before he could bow, staring up at the porch, wiping his mouth with the handkerchief, I raised a hand and repeated my greeting. Then I went back to my room to finish getting dressed.

I passed quickly through the dining room, watching the guests have breakfast, and then decided to have a gin, just one, at the bar; I bought cigarettes and went down the stairs to the group that was waiting at the bottom. The manager greeted me again, and I noticed that his jaw was trembling a little. I uttered a few words and heard them talking; the young blond man came up to me and touched my arm. They were all in silence, and the blond and I looked at each other and smiled. I offered him a cigarette, and he lit it without taking his eyes off my face; then he stepped three steps back and looked at me again. Perhaps he had never seen the face of a happy man; such was my case also. He turned his back on me, walked over to the first tree in the garden, and leaned there beside some man. All of that had some meaning, and without understanding, I found I agreed and nodded my head in assent. Then the very tall man said: "Shall we go to the beach in the car?"

I walked forward and got in the front seat. The tall man and the blond sat down in the back seat. The policeman slowly got into the driver's seat and started the car. Right away we were riding quickly through the calm morning; I could smell the cigarette the young man was smoking, could feel the silence and stillness of the other man, the will at work in that silence and stillness. When we got to the beach, the car stopped by a pile of gray rocks that separated the road from the sand. We got out, crossed the rock wall, and went down toward the sea. I walked beside the blond youth.

We stopped by the shore. The four of us were silent, our ties whipped by the wind. We lit cigarettes once more.

"The weather seems uncertain," I said.

"Shall we go?" the young blond answered.

The tall man in the striped suit stretched out one arm until he touched the young man's chest and said in a thick voice: "Notice. From here to the dunes. Two blocks. No more, no less."

The other nodded in silence, shrugging his shoulders as if it were of no importance. He smiled again and looked at me.

"Let's go," I said, starting to walk toward the car. When I was about to get in, the tall man stopped me.

"No," he said. "It's over there, on the other side."

In front of us there was a shed made of bricks stained with the dampness. It had a corrugated tin roof and dark letters painted above the door. We waited while the policeman came back with a key. I turned to see the midday sun close at hand over the beach; the policeman took off the open lock, and we all went into the shadow and the unexpected cold. The rafters were a shiny black, softly painted with tar, and bits of burlap were hanging from the ceiling. When we walked in the gray twilight, I felt the shed grow bigger as every step moved us farther from the long table made of sawhorses in the middle of the room. I saw the form stretched out, wondering who teaches the dead the posture of death. There was a little puddle of water on the ground, dripping from one corner of the table. A barefoot man, his shirt open to his ruddy chest, came up, clearing his throat, and put one hand on a corner of the plank table, his short index finger covered instantly by the shiny water that had not yet dripped off. The tall man stretched out one arm and, pulling on the canvas, uncovered the face that was lying on the planks. I looked at the air, at the man's striped arm, still stretched out against the light of the door, holding the ringed edge of the canvas. I looked once more at the bareheaded blond and made a sad grimace.

"Look at this," the tall man said.

Then, little by little, I saw that the girl's face was bent backward, that it looked as if the head—purple, with spots of a reddish purple atop a more delicate bluish purple—would roll away at any moment were anyone to speak too loudly, were anyone to step hard on the floor, were time simply to pass.

From the back, invisible to me, someone was beginning to recite in a hoarse common voice, as if speaking to me. Who else?

"The hands and feet, the skin whitened a bit and folded at the edges of the fingers and toes, also exhibit a small amount of sand and mud under the nails. There is no wound or scarring on the hands. On the arms, particularly on the forearms near the wrists, there are various superimposed ecchymoses on the transversal, the results of violent pressure on the upper limbs."

I didn't know who it was, I didn't have any desire to ask questions. I had the lone defense, I repeated to myself, of silence. Silence for us. I went closer to the table and touched the stubborn bones of the forehead. Perhaps the five men were waiting for something more, and I was prepared for anything.

The idiot, back at the end of the shed, was now listing in his vulgar voice: "The face is stained with a bluish bloodlike liquid that has flowed out of her mouth and nose. After having washed her carefully, we recognize extensive flaying and ecchymosis and the marks of teeth sunken into the flesh. Two similar marks exist below the right eye, the lower lid of which is deeply bruised. Besides marks of violence obviously made while the subject was still alive, on the face numerous contusions are visible on the skin, scoring, without redness or ecchymosis, a simple drying of the skin produced by the rubbing of the body on the sand. There is a clot of blood on either side of the larynx. The tegumenta have begun to decay, but vestiges of contusions or ecchymosis are visible in them. The interior of the trachea and of the bronchial tube contains a small amount of a cloudy (though not foamy) dark liquid mixed with sand."

It was a good answer; everything was lost. I leaned over to kiss her forehead and then, out of pity and love, the reddish liquid that was bubbling out of her lips.

But the head with its stiff hair, the squat nose, the dark mouth stretched in the shape of a sickle, the edges pointing down, limp, dripping, remained there without moving, the size of the head unchanging in the dark air smelling of bilge, as if harder each time my eyes passed over cheekbones and forehead and chin that refused to hang open. They, the tall man and the blond, spoke to me one after another, as if they were playing a game, banging away with the same question. Then the tall man let go of the canvas, sprang up, and shook me by the lapels. But he didn't believe in what he was doing—it was enough to look at his round eyes—and when

I smiled at him out of fatigue, he quickly showed me his teeth and with hatred opened his hand.

"I understand, I guess, that you have a daughter. Don't worry: I will sign whatever you want without even reading it. The funny part is that you have made a mistake. But that doesn't matter. Nothing, not even this, really matters."

I paused before the violent light of the sun and asked the tall man in a proper voice, "I may be overly curious and I beg pardon—do you believe in God?"

"I will answer, of course," the giant said, "but first, if you don't mind, and not for the record of the proceedings, just, as in your case, out of simple curiosity . . . Did you know that the girl was deaf?"

We had stopped halfway between the renewed summery heat and the cool shade of the shed.

"Deaf?" I asked. "I was indeed with her last night. She never seemed deaf to me. But that's neither here nor there. I asked you a question; you promised to answer it."

The lips were too thin to call the grimace the giant made a smile. He looked at me again without disdain, with sad surprise, and crossed himself.

1960

María Luisa Bombal

1910–1980

BORN IN VIÑA DEL MAR, Chile, on June 8, 1910, María Luisa Bombal moved to Paris with her family at the age of twelve and lived there until 1931. She received a degree in French literature from the Sorbonne and also became involved in the performing arts. She moved to Buenos Aires in 1933 and participated in the literary gatherings of Victoria Ocampo (editor of the influential journal *Sur*). Bombal's novels, *La última niebla* (1935; *House of Mist,* 1947) and *La amortajada* (1938; *The Shrouded Woman,* 1948) have influenced later generations of women writers in Latin America. Her lyricism and individual voice are also evident in her short stories, translated and collected in the volume *New Islands* (1982), from which the title story has been selected.

New Islands

Translated by Richard and Lucia Cunningham

ALL NIGHT LONG a howling wind had raged across the pampa. Now and then it would slip inside the house through cracks in the doors and window frames, sending ripples through the mosquito netting. Each time this happened, Yolanda would turn on the light, which flickered, held for a moment, and then faded out again. At dawn, when her brother Federico came into the room, she lay on her left shoulder, breathing with difficulty, moaning in her sleep.

"Yolanda! Yolanda!"

She sat up like a shot. In order to see Federico, she parted her long black hair and tossed it over her shoulders.

"Were you dreaming?" he asked.

"Oh, yes—horrible dreams."

"Why must you always sleep in that position? It's bad for your heart."

"I know, I know. What time is it? And where are you off to so early in all this wind?"

"The lakes. It seems another island has emerged. That makes four so far. Some people from La Figura hacienda have come to see them. So we'll be having guests later. I wanted to let you know before I left."

Without shifting her position, Yolanda regarded her brother: a thin, white-haired man whose tightfitting riding boots lent him an air of youth. Men—how absurd they were! Always in motion, forever willing to take an interest in everything. Upon retiring for the night, they demand to be awakened at daybreak. If they go to a fireplace, they remain standing, ready to run to the other end of the room—ready always to escape, to flee toward the futile. And they cough and smoke, speak loud as if they feared silence—indeed, as if tranquillity were a mortal enemy.

"It's all right, Federico."

"So long, then."

The door slams; Federico's spurs jingle on the tile floor in the corridor. Yolanda closes her eyes once more and, delicately, using elaborate care, sinks back onto the pillows on her left shoulder, curling herself as usual into that position which Federico claims is so damaging to one's heart. Breathing heavily, she sighs, falling suddenly into one of her disturbing dreams—dreams from which, morning after morning, she wakes pale and exhausted, as if she had been battling insomnia throughout the entire night.

The visitors from La Figura hacienda, meanwhile, had reached the grassy bank where the lakes began. Daylight was spreading across the water, unfurling over the landscape like a fire. Out there against the horizon, barely visible under the cloudy sky, were the new islands: still smoking from the fiery effort that had lifted them from who knows what stratified depths.

"Four, four new islands!" the people shouted.

The wind did not subside until nightfall, by which time the men were returning from hunting.

Do, re, mi, fa, sol, la, ti, do . . . Do, re, mi, fa, sol, la, ti, do . . .

The notes rise and fall, rise and fall like round, limpid crystal bubbles carried on the wind from the house, now flattened in the distance, to burst over the hunters like solemn, regulated raindrops.

Do, re, mi, fa, sol, la, ti, do . . .

It's Yolanda practicing, Sylvester says to himself. He pauses a moment to shift the carbine slung on his left shoulder, his heavy body trembling slightly.

Among the bushes bordering the lawn there are white flowers that appear touched by frost. Juan Manuel bends over to examine one.

"Don't touch them," Sylvester warns. "They turn yellow. They're Yolanda's camellias," he adds with a smile.

That humble smile which does not suit him, thinks Juan Manuel. As soon as he relaxes his proud countenance, you see how old he is.

The house is in total darkness, but the notes continue to flow regularly: Do, re, mi, fa, sol, la, ti, do . . . Do, re, mi, fa, sol, la, ti, do . . .

"Have you met my sister Yolanda, Juan Manuel?"

On Federico's question, the woman sitting in shadow at the piano gives the stranger her hand, withdrawing it immediately. She then rises, so slowly that she seems to grow upright, uncoiling like a beautiful snake. Very tall, she is extremely slender. Juan Manuel follows her with his eyes as she quickly and quietly turns on the lamps.

She is exactly like her name, thinks Juan Manuel. Pale, angular, and a bit savage. And there is something odd about her that I cannot place. But of course, he realizes as she glides through the door and disappears—her feet are too small. How strange that she can support such a long body on such tiny feet.

How dull this dinner among men, Juan Manuel decides. Among ten hunters thwarted by the wind who gulp down their food without a single manly deed to boast about. And Yolanda, he reflects, why doesn't she preside over the table now that Federico's wife is in Buenos Aires? What an extraordinary figure she makes! Ugly? Pretty? Fragile, that's it, very fragile. And that dark and brilliant gaze of hers—aggressive yet hunted . . . Whom does she look like? What does she resemble?

Juan Manuel lifts his glass, staring at the wine. Across from him sits Sylvester, who is drinking heavily and talking and laughing in a loud voice. He seems desperate.

The hunters stir the coals with a scoop and tongs, scattering ashes over the multiple fiery eyes which refuse to close—this the final act in a long and boring evening.

And now suddenly the grass and the trees in the garden begin to shiver in the cold night breeze. Large insects beat their wings against the lantern illuminating the long open corridor. Leaning on Juan Manuel, Sylvester staggers toward his room, his feet slipping on the tiles that shine with vapor as if they had just been washed. His footsteps send frogs scurrying off to hide timidly in dark corners.

The iron grilles slamming shut across the doors seem in the silence of the night to echo the useless volley of shots fired by the hunters. Sylvester throws his heavy body on the bed and buries his emaciated face in his hands. His sighs irritate Juan Manuel—he who always detested sharing a room with anyone, let alone with a drunkard who moans.

"Oh, Juan Manuel, Juan Manuel . . ."

"What's the matter, Don Sylvester? You don't feel well?"

"Oh, my boy—who could know, who could know! . . ."

"Know what, Don Sylvester?"

"This," said the old man, taking his wallet from his jacket and handing it to Juan Manuel. "Look for the letter. Read it. Yes, a letter. That one, yes. Read it and tell me if you understand it."

An elongated, wavering handwriting flows like smoke across the yellowed, wrinkled pages: *Sylvester, I cannot marry you. Believe me, I have thought it over at great length. It isn't possible, it just isn't. Nevertheless, I love you, Sylvester, I love you and I suffer. But I cannot. Forget me. In vain I ask myself what might save me. A son, perhaps, a child whose sweet weight I could feel inside me forever. Forever! Not to see him grow, separated from me! Myself attached forever to that tiny heart, possessed always by that presence! I weep, Sylvester, I weep; and I cannot explain myself.—Yolanda.*

"I don't understand," Juan Manuel whispers uneasily.

"I have been trying for thirty years to understand," said Sylvester. "I loved her. You cannot know how much I loved her. No one loves like that any more, Juan Manuel . . . One night, two weeks before we were to be married, she sent me this letter. Afterwards she refused to offer any explanation, and I was never permitted to see her alone. I waited, telling myself that time would solve everything. I am still waiting."

Juan Manuel seemed confused. "Was it the mother, Don Sylvester? Was she also named Yolanda?"

"What? I am speaking of the one and only Yolanda, who tonight has again rejected me. This evening when I saw her, I said to myself: Maybe now that so many years have passed, Yolanda will at long last give me an explanation. But, as usual, she left the room. Sometimes, you know, Federico tries to talk to her about all this. But she starts trembling and runs away, as always . . ."

The far-off chugging of a train can now be heard. The steady insistent clacking seems to increase Juan Manuel's uneasiness.

"Yolanda was your fiancée, Don Sylvester?"

"Yes, my fiancée . . . my fiancée . . ."

Juan Manuel stares coldly at Sylvester's disoriented gestures, his swollen, sixty-year-old body so disastrously preserved. Don Sylvester, his father's old friend, and Yolanda's fiancé.

"Then she is not a young girl, Don Sylvester?"

Sylvester laughs stupidly.

"How old is she?" Juan Manuel inquires.

Sylvester rubs his forehead, eyes closed, trying to count. "Let's see, at that time I was twenty . . . no, twenty-three . . ."

But Juan Manuel hardly listens, momentarily relieved by a consoling reflection: What does age matter when one is so prodigiously young!

"Therefore she must be . . ."

Sylvester's words dissolve in a hacking cough. And again Juan Manuel feels a resurgence of the anxiety that holds him attentive to the secret Sylvester is drunkenly unraveling. And that train in the distance, coming closer now, its regular rhythm as laden with suspense as a drum roll—like a threat not yet become reality. The muffled, monotonous pounding unnerves him, growing louder and louder until, like one seeking escape, he goes to the window, pushes it open, and bends into the night. The headlights of the express glare across the immense plain like malevolent eyes.

"Damned train!" he grumbles. "When will it pass?"

Sylvester comes over to lean beside him, breathing deep as he gestures toward the two shimmering lights.

"It just left Lobos," he explains. "It generally takes half an hour to go by here."

She is fragile and her feet are too small for her height.

"How old is she, Don Sylvester?"

"I don't remember. I'll tell you tomorrow."

But why? Juan Manuel asks himself. Why this preoccupation with a woman I have seen only once in my life? Do I desire her? The train. Oh, that monotonous hissing monster advancing slowly, inexorably across the pampa! What's wrong with me? It must be that I am tired, he thinks, closing the window.

Meanwhile, she is at one end of the garden, leaning against the fence overlooking the hill as if she were bending over the rail of a ship anchored on the prairie. In the sky, a single motionless star: a large red star that seems about to shake loose from its orbit and spin off into infinite space. Juan Manuel stands beside her at the fence, gazing, too, at the pampa now submerged in the dark saturnine twilight. He speaks. What does he say?

He whispers words of destiny in her ear. And now he takes her in his arms. And now the arms around her waist tremble, slide lower, caressing her gently. And she tosses, struggles, gripping the wooden rail to better resist. And then she wakes to find herself clutching the sheets, sobbing deep in her throat.

For a long time she weeps without moving, listening to the house quaver. The mirror moves slightly. A withered camellia blossom falls from a vase, dropping on the carpet with the soft thick sound of ripe fruit.

She waits for the train to go by and then, listening to its receding sonic boom, she drifts back to sleep, lying on her left shoulder.

In the morning the wind has resumed its fierce race across the pampa. But this day the hunters are in no mood to waste their ammunition in a gale. Instead, they launch two boats, bound for those new islands afloat on the horizon, rising from a cloud of foam and wheeling birds.

They land proudly, boisterously, carbines on their shoulders as they leap to shore, only to discover an oppressive, foul-smelling atmosphere that stops them in their tracks. After a brief pause they advance, stepping in amazement on slimy weeds that seem to be oozing from the hot and shifting soil. They stagger on amid spirals of sea gulls that swoop around them, flashing by their faces and screeching as they dip and rise. At one point, Juan Manuel lurches as the edge of a wing flails his chest.

And still they advance, crushing under their boots frenzied silver fish stranded by the tide. Farther on, they find more strange vegetation: low bushes of pink coral, which they struggle for some time to uproot, pulling and pulling until their hands bleed.

The sea gulls cluster round them in ever-tightening spirals. Low, running clouds skim by overhead, weaving a vertiginous pattern of shadows. The fumes rising from the earth grow more dense by the moment. Everything boils, shakes violently, trembles. The hunters cannot see; can hardly breathe. Disheartened and afraid, they flee to their boats, return in silence to the mainland.

All afternoon they sat around a bonfire, chatting with the peons who periodically fed the flames with eucalyptus branches, waiting for the wind to abate. But again, as if to exasperate them, the wind did not die down until dusk.

Do, re, mi, fa, sol, la, ti, do . . . Once again, that methodical scale drifts toward them from the house. Juan Manuel pricks up his ears.

Do, re, mi, fa, sol, la, ti, do . . . Do, re, mi, fa, sol, la, ti, do . . . Do, re, mi, fa . . . Do, re, mi, fa . . . —the piano insists. And those notes repeated over and over beat against Juan Manuel's heart, striking where the sea gull's wing had wounded him that morning. Without knowing why, he gets to his feet and starts walking toward that music chiming endlessly through the trees like a summons.

As he reaches the camellia bushes, the piano suddenly falls silent. He enters the darkened drawing room almost at a run, sees logs burning in the fireplace, the piano open . . . But where is Yolanda?

At the far end of the garden she leans against the fence, as if resting on the rail of a ship anchored on the pampa. And now she trembles, hearing the rustle of the lowermost pine-tree branches being brushed aside by someone coming up cautiously behind her. If only it were Juan Manuel!

She slowly turns her head. It is him, in the flesh this time. Oh, his dark, golden complexion in the gray twilight! Golden as though he were enveloped by a sunray. Joining her at the fence, he, too, stares out across the pampa. Frogs begin to sing in the irrigation ditches; and it is as if night were being ushered in by thousands of crystal bells.

Now he looks at her and smiles. Oh, his fine white teeth! They must be cold and hard like tiny chips of ice. And that warm virile odor he gives off, piercing her with pleasure. How sad to resist such pleasure, to shun that circle formed by this strong, beautiful man and his shadow!

"Yolanda," he murmurs.

She feels upon hearing her name that a sudden intimacy exists between them. How marvelous that he called her by name! It would seem that now they are linked by a long and passionate past. Not sharing a past—that was what held them apart and inhibited them.

"All night long I dreamed of you, Juan Manuel, all night long . . ."

He embraces her; she does not reject him. But she obliges his arm to remain chastely around her waist.

"Someone is calling me," she says abruptly, moving out of his embrace and running off. The pine branches she hastily brushes aside rebound with a snap in Juan Manuel's face, scratching his cheek. Disconcerted by a woman for the first time in his life, he runs after her.

She is dressed in white. Only now, as she goes over to her brother to light his pipe—gravely and meticulously, as if performing a trifling daily ritual—only now does he notice that she is wearing a long gown. She has put it on to dine with them. Then Juan Manuel remembers the mud on his boots and rushes to his room to clean them.

On his return to the drawing room, he finds Yolanda seated on a sofa in front of the fireplace. The dancing flames alternately lighten and darken her black eyes. With her arms crossed behind her neck, she is long and slender like a sword, or like . . . like what? In vain Juan Manuel searches for the proper simile.

"Dinner is served," the maid announces.

As Yolanda rises, her flame-lightened pupils are suddenly extinguished. And going past Juan Manuel, she casts those opaque black eyes on him, the sheer tulle sleeve of her dress grazing his chest like a wing. And in that instant the simile comes to him.

"Now I know what you look like," he whispers. "A sea gull."

Uttering a strange, hoarse cry, Yolanda collapses on the carpet. Momentarily stunned, the others now rush to her side, pick her up, carry her unconscious form to the sofa. Federico sends the maid scurrying for water. Turning angrily to Juan Manuel, he asks: "What did you say to her? What did you *say?"*

"I told her . . ." Juan Manuel begins; then lapses into silence, feeling a sudden stab of guilt—fearing, without knowing why, to reveal a secret which is not his.

Yolanda, meanwhile, comes to. Sighing, she presses her heart with both hands, as if recovering from a fright. She half sits up, then stretches out on her left shoulder.

"No," Federico protests, "not on your heart. It's bad for you."

She gives him a weak smile, whispers as she waves him away: "I know, I know. Now please leave me alone."

And there is such sad vehemence, such weariness in her gesture, that everyone moves off into the next room without objecting—everyone except Juan Manuel, who remains standing beside the fireplace.

Pale and motionless, Yolanda sleeps, or pretends to sleep, while Juan Manuel, a silent sentinel, waits anxiously for a sign—be it to stay or go.

At daybreak on this third morning the hunters gather once more at the edge of the lakes, which today at last are calm. Mute, they contemplate the smooth surface of the water, shocked into silence by the vista on that distant gray horizon.

For the new islands have vanished.

Again they launch boats, Juan Manuel setting off alone in a dinghy. He rows determinedly, skirting the old islands, which teem with wildlife, refusing to be tempted like his companions by the lashing sound of wings, of cooing and small sharp cries—the old islands, where things rattle and crack like rattan splitting, where the banks are covered with oozy moving flowers spread out like a bed of slime. Soon Juan Manuel is lost in the distance, a receding silhouette rowing a zigzagging course in search of the exact spot where only yesterday they had landed to explore the four new islands. Where was the first one? Here. No, there. No, rather, here. He leans over the water to look for it, though he knows that his eyes could never see the muddy bottom, where, after its vertiginous plunge, the island sank into silt and algae.

Within the circle of a nearby whirlpool something soft and transparent floats: a small jellyfish. Plucking it from the water in his handkerchief, Juan Manuel ties the four corners of the cloth over it like a pouch.

The day is drawing to a close when Yolanda brings her horse to a halt at the base of the hill and opens the gate for the returning hunters. Setting off again, she rides on ahead to the house, the skirt of her tweed riding habit brushing the bushes. And Juan Manuel notes that, though she is mounted in the old-fashioned way, sitting genteelly sidesaddle, with her hair streaming around her face she looks like an Amazon huntress. The light is fading fast, giving way to a dusky bluish spectrum. A chorus of long-tailed magpies croaks by overhead before fluttering down on the naked branches of the now ashen forest.

Juan Manuel suddenly recalls a painting that still hangs in the corridor of his old hacienda in Adrogué: a tall, pensive Amazon equestrienne who, having surrendered to her horse's will, seems to wander lost and disheartened among dry leaves at dusk. The picture is entitled "Autumn," or "Sadness"—he does not remember which.

On the night table in his room he finds a letter from his mother. *Since you are not here, I will take the orchid for Elsa tomorrow,* she writes. Tomorrow. That is today, he realizes. Today, then, is the fifth anniversary of his wife's death. Five years already. Her name was Elsa. He had never grown accustomed to the fact that she had such a lovely name. "And your name is *Elsa,*" he would say as he embraced her, as if that alone were a miracle more breathtaking even than her fair beauty and placid smile. Elsa! The perfection of her features! Her translucent complexion, under which ran veins that seemed the fine blue strokes of a master watercolorist. So many years of love! And then that deadly disease. Like a piercing knife comes the memory of that night when, covering her face with her hands to ward off his kiss, she had cried: "I don't want you to see me like this, so ugly . . . not even after death. You must cover my face with orchids. You have to promise me . . ."

But Juan Manuel does not want to begin thinking of all that. Desolate, he tosses the letter on the night table without reading further.

The same serene twilight suffusing the pampa washes over Buenos Aires, inundating in steel blue the stones and the air and the mist-covered trees in Recoleta Square.

Juan Manuel's mother walks confidently through a labyrinth of narrow streets. Never has she lost her way in this intricate city, for as a child her parents taught her how to find her bearings in any quarter. And here is their dwelling—the small cold crypt where parents, grandparents, and so many ancestors rest. So many in such a narrow chamber! If only it were true that each of them sleeps alone with his past and his present, isolated yet side by side! But no, that isn't possible. She lays her spray of orchids on the ground, rummaging through her purse for the key. Then, before the altar, she makes the sign of the cross and checks that the candelabra are well polished, that the white altar cloth is well starched. She sighs and descends into the crypt, holding nervously on to the bronze railing. An oil lamp hangs from the low ceiling, its flame mirrored in the black marble floor and shining on the bronze rings of the various compartments arranged sequentially by date. Here all is order and solemn indifference.

Outside, the drizzle starts up again. The raindrops rebound audibly on the concrete streets. But here everything seems remote: the rain, the city, the obligations that await her at home. And now she sighs again, going over to the smallest and newest compartment, and places the orchids at the head of the casket—where Elsa's face reposes. Poor Juan Manuel, she thinks.

She tries unsuccessfully to feel sadness for her daughter-in-law's fate. But that rancor she admits only to the priest persists in her heart, despite the dozens of rosaries and the multiple short prayers her confessor orders her to recite as penance.

She stares hard at the casket, wishing her eyes could pierce the metal liner, wanting to see, to know, to verify . . . Dead for five years! She was so fragile. Perhaps the plain gold ring has already slipped off her frivolous crumbling fingers, fallen into that dusty hole that was once her bosom. Maybe so. But is she dead? No. She has won in spite of everything. One never dies entirely, that is the truth. That strong dark little boy who continues their line, the grandson who has become her only reason for living, has the blue and candid eyes of Elsa.

At three o'clock in the morning Juan Manuel finally resolves to abandon the armchair beside the fireplace where, nearly stupefied by the heat of the flames, he has been smoking and drinking listlessly for hours. He hops over the dogs asleep in the doorway and starts down the long, open corridor. He feels lazy and tired, very tired. Last night Sylvester, he thinks, and tonight me. I am completely drunk.

Sylvester is asleep. He must have dropped off unexpectedly, because the lamp on the night table is still lit.

His mother's letter lies where he left it, still half open. A long postscript scribbled by his son brings a brief smile to his lips. He tries to decipher the winding infantile handwriting through blurred eyes: *Papá. Grandma says I can write to you here. I have learned three more words from the new geography book you gave me. And I am going to write the words and the definitions from memory.*

Aerolite: Name given to pieces of minerals that fall from outer space to the earth's surface. Aerolites are planetary fragments that float in space and . . .

"Aiee!" Juan Manuel moans to himself, staggering as he shakes his head to blot out the definition, those evocative, dazzling words that blind him as though a thousand tiny suns were bursting in front of his eyes.

Hurricane: Violent swirling wind made up of various opposing air masses that form whirlwinds . . .

"That boy!" Juan Manuel groans. And he feels chilled to the bone, while a tremendous roaring pounds his brain like icy waves pounding a beach.

Halo: Luminous circle that sometimes surrounds the moon.

A light mist seeping through the open window obscures his vision, a blue mist that enfolds him softly. "Halo," he murmurs. An immense tenderness comes over him. Yolanda! If only he could see her, talk to her!

If only he could stand at her bedroom door and listen to her breathing.

Everyone, everything is asleep. How many doors he had to open, some by force, as he crept across the east wing of that old hacienda, hooding the lamp flame with his cupped hand! How many empty, dusty rooms where furniture lay piled in the corners, and how many others in which, as he passed by, unrecognizable people sighed and turned under the sheets!

He had chosen the way of ghosts and murderers.

And now that he has his ear against Yolanda's door, all he can hear is the beating of his own heart.

A piece of furniture must, no doubt, block the door from the inside; a very light piece of furniture, since he shoves it aside with little effort. Who is moaning? Juan Manuel turns up the lamp; the room at first seems to spin, then becomes quiet and orderly as his eyes adjust.

He sees a narrow bed veiled by mosquito netting where Yolanda sleeps on her left side, her dark curly hair covering her face like a latticework of luxuriant vines. She moans, caught in some nightmare. Juan Manuel sets the lamp on the floor, parts the mosquito netting, and takes her hand. She clutches his fingers as he helps her to rise from the pillows, to escape from the dream and the weight of that monstrous hair which must have pinned her down in those dark regions of sleep.

She opens her eyes at last, sighs with relief, and whispers: "Thank you."

"Thank you," she repeats, fixing him with her somnambulant eyes. "Oh, it was awful!" she explains. "I was in a horrible place. In a park I often visit in my sleep. A park. Giant plants. Ferns tall as trees. And silence . . . I don't know how to describe it . . . Silence as green as chloroform . . . and suddenly, beneath the silence, a low buzzing sound, growing louder, coming nearer . . . Death, it is death. And then I tried to escape, to wake up. Because if I did not wake up, if death ever found me in that park, I would be doomed to stay forever, don't you think?"

Juan Manuel makes no reply, fearing to shatter this intimacy with the sound of his voice.

Taking a deep breath, Yolanda continues. "They say that in sleep we return to those places where we lived in a prior existence. I, too, sometimes return to a certain Creole house. A room, a patio, a room, another patio with a fountain in the center. I go there and . . ."

She falls silent and looks at him.

The moment he feared so much has come. The moment when, lucid at last and free from terror, she asks herself how and why this man is sitting on the edge of her bed. He waits, resigned for the imperious "Out of here!" and that solemn gesture with which women are reported to show one the door in instances like this.

But no. Yolanda puts her head on his chest, pressing against his heart.

Astonished, Juan Manuel does not move. Oh, that delicate temple and the smell of flowering honeysuckle coming from those locks of hair pressed against his lips! He remains motionless for a long time. Motionless, tender, full of wonder—as if an unexpected and priceless treasure had fallen into his arms by accident.

Yolanda! His embrace tightens, pressing her to him. But she cries out—a brief, husky, strange cry—and grabs his arms. They struggle, Juan Manuel entangling himself in her thick, sweet-scented hair. He grapples until he is able to seize her by the neck, and then he brutally throws her down on her back.

Gasping, she tosses her head from side to side, weeping as Juan Manuel kisses her mouth and caresses one of her breasts, small and hard like the camellias she cultivates. So many tears. Running silently down her cheeks, so many tears. Falling on the pillow like hot watery pearls, dropping into the hollow of his hand still gripping her neck.

Ashamed, his passion ebbing, Juan Manuel relaxes his embrace.

"Do you hate me, Yolanda?"

She is silent, inert.

"Shall I stay?"

Closing her eyes, she whispers: "No, please go."

The wooden floorboards creak as he crosses to the lamp and goes to the door, leaving Yolanda submerged in shadow.

On the fourth day, a fine mist shrouds the pampa in a white cottony silence that muffles and shortens the sound of the hunters' guns out on the islands and blinds the frightened storks planing in to seek sanctuary on the lake.

And Yolanda—what is she doing? Juan Manuel wonders. What is she doing while he drags his mudheavy boots through the reeds, killing birds without reason or passion? Maybe she is in the orchard looking for the last strawberries, or pulling up the first radishes: *One must grasp the leaves tight and take them with a single pull, tearing them out of the dark earth like tiny red hearts.* Or it may be that she is in the house, standing on a stool by an open cupboard, the maid handing her a stack of freshly ironed sheets which she will carefully arrange in even piles. And if she were waiting at the window for his return? Anything is possible with a woman like Yolanda, such a strange woman, one who resembles a . . . But he checks himself, afraid of hurting her in his thoughts.

Twilight again. The hunter gazes across the shadowy pampa, trying to locate the hill and the house. A distant light blinks on amid the fog, pointing the way like a miniature lighthouse.

He drags his boat up the bank and starts across the grassland toward the light. On the way he puts to flight a few head of grazing cattle, their hair twisted into curls by the damp breath of the fog. He leaps barbed-wire fences, the fog clinging to the points like fleece. He sidesteps the thick clumps of thistle that glisten silvery and phosphorescent in the darkness.

Reaching the gate, he crosses the park and goes past the camellias in the garden to a certain window, where he wipes the pane free of fog and then stands transfixed as before his eyes a fairy tale unfolds.

Yolanda is standing naked in the bathroom, absorbed in the contemplation of her right shoulder.

Her right shoulder—on which something light and flexible looms, drooping down to cover a small portion of her back. A wing, or rather, the beginning of a wing. Or more exactly, the stump of a wing. A small atrophied member which she now strokes carefully, as if dreading the touch.

The rest of her body is exactly as he had imagined: slender, proud, and white.

A hallucination, Juan Manuel thinks to himself as he drives crazily, his hands shaking on the steering wheel, along the highway. The long walk, the fog, the weariness, and this state of anxiety I've been living in for the last few days have all combined to make me see what does not exist. Should I go back? But how would I explain my abrupt departure? Don't think about it until you get to Buenos Aires. That's the best thing to do.

By the time he reaches the suburbs of the city, a fine powdery mist coats the windshield. The windshield wipers click like nickel swords, tic-tac, tic-tac, back and forth with a regularity as implacable as his anguish.

He crosses Buenos Aires, dark and deserted in the light shower which bursts into heavy rain as he opens the gate and starts up the walk to his house.

"What's the matter?" his mother asks. "Why have you come back at this hour?"

"My son?"

"Sleeping. It's eleven o'clock, Juan Manuel."

"I want to see him. Good night, Mother."

The old woman shrugs her shoulders and pads off to her room wrapped in a long robe. No, she will never grow accustomed to her son's whims. He is very bright, a fine lawyer; but she would have preferred him less talented and more conventional, like everyone else's sons.

Juan Manuel goes into his son's bedroom and turns on the light. Curled up next to the wall, his head covered by the sheets, the boy resembles a ball of white twine. Uncovering him, Juan Manuel thinks: He sleeps like an untamed little animal. In spite of the fact that he is nine years old, and notwithstanding his meticulous grandmother.

"Billy, wake up."

The boy sits up in bed, blinks his eyes, and grants his father a sleepy smile.

"I brought you a gift, Billy."

The boy stretches out his hand. Searching through his pockets, Juan Manuel takes out the handkerchief tied into a pouch and hands it to his son. Billy unties the knots and spreads the handkerchief open. Finding nothing, he looks up at his father with a trusting expression, waiting for an explanation.

"It was a kind of flower, Billy—a magnificent jellyfish, I swear. I fished it from the lake for you . . . and it has disappeared . . ."

The boy thinks for a moment and then cries triumphantly: "No, Papa, it didn't disappear; it *melted*. Because jellyfish are made out of water, just water. I learned it in the geography book you gave me."

Outside, the rain lashes the great leaves of the palm tree in the corner of their garden, its shiny-as-patent-leather branches thrashing against the walls.

"You're right, Billy. It melted."

"But . . . jellyfish live in the sea, Papa. How did they get to the lakes?"

"I don't know, son," says Juan Manuel, suddenly tired of the conversation, his mind whirling.

Maybe I should telephone Yolanda, he thinks. Everything might seem less vague, less dreadful if I could hear her voice—which, like all other voices under similar circumstances, would simply sound distant, a bit surprised by an unexpected call.

He covers Billy and arranges the pillows. Then he goes back down the solemn staircase in that huge house, so cold and ugly in the rain and lightning. The telephone hangs in the hall—another of his mother's inspirations. As he unhooks the small tube-like receiver, a flash of lightning illuminates the front windows from top to bottom. He asks the operator for a number, and while he waits, the deafening thunderclap rolls over the sleeping city like a train roaring through his living room.

And my call, he thinks, now races through the wires under the rain. Now it is passing through Rivadavia with its line of darkened streetlights, and now it is zooming by the suburbs with their muddy flooding pathways, taking now to the freeway and flying along that straight and lonely road until, by now surely, it reaches the vast pampa with its occasional small villages, going like a bullet now across provincial cities where the asphalt glistens like water under the moonlight, and now perhaps shooting out into open country, alone in the rain again, hurtling past a closed railway station, and then dashing across the pasture to the hill, along the poplar-lined drive to dive into the house. And now it rings insistently, echoing and reechoing in the large deserted drawing room, where the wooden floors creak and the roof leaks in one corner.

The ringing resounds for a long time, vibrating hoarsely in Juan Manuel's ear, echoing sharply in the empty drawing room while he waits anxiously. Then someone suddenly lifts the receiver at the other end. But before the voice can say a word, Juan Manuel slams the receiver onto its hook.

Thinking: If I had said, "I can't go through with it, Yolanda. I've thought it out, believe me. It just isn't possible." If I had at least confirmed my doubts about that horror. But I'm afraid to know the truth.

He climbs the staircase slowly.

There was something more cruel, more punishing than death, after all. And he had believed that death was the final mystery, the ultimate suffering!

Death—that blind alley!

While he grew older, Elsa would remain eternally young, preserved forever at age thirty-three as on the day she departed from this life. And the day would come when Billy would be older than his mother, when he would know more of the world than she.

Think of it: Elsa's hands become dust, yet her very gestures perpetuated in her letters, in the sweater she knitted for him; and those luminous irises of her now empty eyes still shining with life in her photographs . . . Elsa erased, fixed in the earth but yet living in their memory and still part of their everyday life as though her spirit kept growing and could react even to things she once ignored.

Nevertheless, Juan Manuel now knows that there is a condition far more cruel and incomprehensible than any of death's little corollaries, for he has perceived a new mystery: a suffering consisting of amazement and fear.

The light from Billy's bedroom throws a shaft into the dark corridor, inviting him to enter once more in hope of finding his son still awake. But Billy is asleep, and so Juan Manuel looks around the room for something to distract himself and thereby ease his anguish. He goes to Billy's desk and turns the pages of the new geography book. *History of the Earth . . . The Sidereal Phase of the Earth . . . Life in the Paleozoic Era . . .*

And then he reads: *How beautiful must this silent landscape have been in which giant lycopodiums and equisetums raised themselves to such a height, and where mammoth ferns swayed like trees in the humid air . . .*

What landscape is this? he wonders. I cannot have seen it before, surely. Why, then, does it seem so familiar? He turns the page, reading at random: *. . . In any case, it is during the Carboniferous Period when swarms of flying insects appear over the now arborescent regions. During the Late Carboniferous there were insects which possessed three pairs of wings. The most*

remarkable insects of this Period were very large, similar in shape to our
present-day dragonflies but much bigger, having a wingspan of sixty-five
centimeters . . .

Yolanda's dreams, he realizes. The sweet and terrible secret of her shoulder. Perhaps this was where the explanation of the mystery lay.

But Juan Manuel feels incapable of soaring into the intricate galleries of Nature in order to arrive at the mystery's origin. He fears losing his way in that wild world with its disorderly and poorly mapped pathways, strewn with an unsystematic confusion of clues; fears falling into some dark abyss that no amount of logic will lead him out of. And abandoning Yolanda once more, he closes the book, turns off the light, and leaves the room.

1939

Virgilio Piñera

1912–1979

ONE OF CUBA'S most original writers, Virgilio Piñera was born in Cárdenas, Cuba, on August 4, 1912. Between 1937 and 1949, he studied philosophy and literature at the University of Havana, became involved with the prestigious literary journal *Orígenes,* headed by José Lezama Lima, and started writing poetry and drama. In 1950, relentless poverty and dissatisfaction with Cuba's cultural and political situation drove Piñera to try his luck in Buenos Aires. It was there that he gained the admiration of Jorge Luis Borges and José Bianco with the publication of his short-story collection *Cuentos fríos* (1956; *Cold Tales,* 1988). Piñera returned to his native country after the Cuban Revolution and was part of the literary elite until 1961, when he was arrested for "political and moral crimes." Although he was soon freed, Piñera was marginalized by the regime for his homosexuality. He lived in Cuba until his death in 1979, but his works from that period were published in Spain. Among his plays, representative of the "theater of cruelty," the best known are *Electra Garrigó* (1943; Electra Garrigó), *Aire frío* (1958; *Cold Air,* 1985); and *Una caja de zapatos vacía* (1968; An empty shoebox). Piñera's third and last novel, *Presiones y diamantes* (1967; Pressures and diamonds), a phantasmagoric exercise in science fiction, has been interpreted as a skillfully veiled critique of oppression and totalitarianism. In his short stories, Piñera combines everyday situations and speech with a grotesque, horrifying vision of reality. One of his recurring obsessions is the theme of the double, which he explored in his first novel, *La carne de René* (1943; René's meat) and in several of his short stories. His characters are alienated, absurd creatures, whose anguished sense of irony distances them from the horror of their circumstances.

The Philanthropist

Translated by Mark Schafer

I

Had the secretary of Coco, the great banker, not been in love . . .

This sounds like the beginning of a sentimental story. How edifying for the author and the reader that the story obligingly continues:

. . . Eduardo would still be an unhappy employee in the Ministry of War. But love works miracles. Coco received Eduardo at last, listened to his troubles, made him a partner in his business, married him to his secretary, and everyone was happy.

It isn't the author's fault that Coco totally rewrites the traditional *dénouement*. Certainly, love works miracles, and one of them is to see Eduardo forcing Coco's door. Unhappy lovers! They don't realize they are sealing their own fate. Coco is just about to throw the untimely man out. Because untimely he is, and in a big way: Eduardo has entered the office just as Coco is placing his dentures on a green cloth. Coco blushes, Eduardo coughs, the secretary blanches. . . . Coco points to the door, the secretary disappears, but Eduardo—growing more Eduardo—takes the set of dentures and puts it in Coco's hands. He has broken the ice.

Why did Eduardo have that impulse? Had he followed his fiancée, he would not have fallen into Coco's clutches. The fact is that Eduardo wanted to triumph at all costs. As soon as Coco had his teeth in again, he opened his mouth and the drama began:

"I'm listening, young man. . . ."

Eduardo did not need to be coaxed. Not knowing when to speak up and when to shut his mouth, he was, up to this point, a failure. But now things were very different; he wouldn't let the opportunity pass; he would speak opportunely. Having recently turned thirty, he was truly in love for the first time in his life. He could not get married soon enough, but, as is always the case, money, damn it. . . . Oh, damned money, the cause of Eduardo's ruin! But don't think that Eduardo and money. . . . No, that's not the trouble; our hero's calculations with the cold cash were always quite modest. At this very moment he was about to ask for a lousy thousand dollars. For poor Eduardo, however, this seemed a fabulous sum. For this reason, he went on and on: he was hauling every topic for discussion concerning money onto the carpet. He mixed these topics with those of integrity, and, to make the mixture even more solid, he stuck in

120

those topics relating to success. A witness to this horrifying scene would have wondered with fascination what Coco was waiting for before throwing this ill-timed man out into the street headfirst. But, with good reason, the old banker seemed, with an imploring look in his eyes, to be asking Eduardo to expound on his foolish explanation, to dissect his petition, and even to speak on matters unrelated to the interview.

That was how Eduardo, without meaning to do so, fulfilled Coco's wishes. Since Coco was not saying yes or no to his words, our hero went on from the thousand dollars to the Red Socks' victory over the White Socks . . . and this discourse on sports mysteriously led him to describe—in abundant detail—Sultan's new kennel. . . .

Coco opened his mouth precisely at this moment, and since he opened his mouth as Eduardo closed his, Coco "swallowed" Eduardo.

"Well, then, a thousand dollars. . . ."

"A thousand . . ." Eduardo said, passing slowly through Coco's esophagus.

"I demand it be a million."

Eduardo felt faint. Had he heard correctly? The figure was so unfamiliar! His ear was not trained for certain metallic sounds. They were deafening.

"Excuse me, sir, I said a thousand dollars."

"And I said a million," thundered Coco.

Eduardo was getting visibly ill. Without a doubt, Coco was throwing him a rope. Nevertheless, a rope is a rather peculiar thing for a beggar. Oh, he hadn't fallen for it! A plutocrat's bad joke, a rather cruel way of denying him a thousand dollars. He was tempted to send him about his business; the old man deserved to be given a piece of his mind. Nevertheless, hope—more credulous than the man himself—prevented such an outburst.

"I can't accept such a sum, sir. I could never pay it all back."

"All you need to do is ask me for it," Coco replied.

"Ask you for it! I can do that, but. . . ."

Coco interrupted him with a paternal gesture; that is, patted him encouragingly on the back.

"Ask for it in writing. . . . Ask me for the million in writing."

"I insist, sir; I'm sorry, sir . . . I can't accept. How would I pay it back?"

"Who's talking about paying anything back?" Coco shouted. "Who's talking about that? I'm giving you a million as a gift, I'm giving it to you as a gift. . . ."

Eduardo, caught in the claws of the absurd, resorted to pat phrases:

"You have a charitable soul."

Coco doubled over with laughter. The word "soul" in particular reduced him to a state of uncontrollable hilarity. He added mysteriously:

"Fortify your hands, not your soul. . . ."

Eduardo became confused again. What was Coco getting at? The thought of being put on passed through his mind. He quickly dismissed this idea. Behind the humor, he could perceive a tragic game. He looked at his hands: first one, then the other. Why would he have to fortify them? Was it symbolic in some way? He thought it wise to leave; one more step and he would land right in Coco's belly.

"I don't understand a thing," and Eduardo was on the verge of bursting into tears.

"You'll understand it all." Coco made himself comfortable. "Have a little patience. I am a man of few words, but the occasion demands all the words I have uttered during my long life. I am seventy years old. It can be said quickly, and yet. . . . Let's say: seventy, eighty, a hundred years. . . . What's that? Smoke, nothing but smoke. Barely time to catch the trolley. . . . And despite all this, seventy years is a rather tiresome joke. We agree with the street philosophers: something at once short and very long. I'm not going to get sentimental about my age, but—my God!—it's my age that brings me directly to this explanation. Believe me: seventy years are as vast and as passionate as an interplanetary voyage."

Eduardo felt it necessary to flatter the old man:

"Still, you have the satisfaction of a job well done."

Coco looked at him the way one looks at a rat. That is, with the tips of his shoes. He proceeded:

"How has the voyage been? Quite boring. From home to work, from work, home again. It's enough to kill a person. And then, I drained the cup of pleasure. There are people who roundly hate me for my yacht, for my villa on the beach, for my cabin in the woods, for my women. . . . They should also pity me. I used up those things; my money won't buy them any longer. Unfortunately, I don't believe in the great beyond, and far less, of course, in the great here-and-now. Each man for himself. I've never done anything else in my whole life. They will say that I lack the fiber of a saint. Too bad. It isn't in me to resolve the contradiction between my lack of saintliness and my hundred million. I am prepared to give even the last penny away. To do it, yes, not as a saint, but as Coco. What does society expect from a banker with a hundred million, with seventy years pressing down on his shoulders? Why, that the banker become a philanthropist. This is my situation; I shouldn't escape the law of nature. I don't feel that

I could hold off the practice of philanthropy one minute longer. I don't have a wife, I don't have children; I'm forced by indisposition to live ascetically. I don't want to die and have my money placed in the hands of organized philanthropy. This is the undismissible thought that has kept me awake for months. But happily, Eduardo," and he wrapped Eduardo in a loving gaze, "you offer me the solution. You have my eternal gratitude."

As if propelled by a spring, Eduardo leaped from the chair. He naïvely thought that the old man's last words put the whole affair back on a plane of normality.

"The gratitude is mutual," he whispered.

"Don't kid yourself," Coco said coolly. "I'm the only grateful one in all of this. As for you, you will probably curse me."

"I don't understand. . . ."

"You'll understand very soon. Isn't it true that you have knocked down my door to ask for a loan? Didn't you ask for a thousand dollars? Isn't it true that I have offered you a million? Isn't it true that I have demanded that you request this sum in writing?"

"Very true," Eduardo exclaimed, hurt by Coco's tone of voice. "So true that I'll make the request in writing right this minute. May I have some paper?" And he took out his fountain pen.

"Here you are," and Coco put one of his business cards in Eduardo's hands.

"What!" Eduardo shouted. "What! Sir, this is a rather tiresome joke!"

"I never joke about money. That card is more than enough for what I'm going to dictate to you. Are you ready?"

"I'm sorry. A strange way to close a deal. It looks like child's play. But if it pleases you that much, begin."

In the middle of a deathly silence, Coco's voice, terribly confident, uttered:

"Coco. . . . Now a colon. Ready? *I want a million."*

"Is that all? Eduardo said. "This scrap of paper is enough for you! Do I sign it?"

"You will sign when you finish."

"But my dear sir, it's finished already. It's so short you can write it out in a second."

"That's true," Coco said, "but the money will be yours if you write it out one million times."

If the offer of a million is a heavy blow for someone who has asked for a thousand, how does one characterize Coco's cruel demand? And how

does one describe its effect? At that moment, our hero was turned into a cataclysm: the worlds of moral humiliation colliding with the worlds of stupor combined with the worlds of greed and with the naïve worlds of calculation. The visible effect of this collision was localized in his skin and eyes. Eduardo got gooseflesh—copying something a million times makes one think of an immortality one doesn't possess—while his eyes, popping out of their sockets, expressed wild greed. Then, since reason was foundering, since the brain was madly combining fabulous figures, Eduardo said:
"Madness!"

"Madnesses like that one are the only kind that interest me. Philanthropy for its own sake is meaningless. Always the same thing: bequeathing dowries to a hundred marriageable maidens, patronizing painters and poets, establishing asylums. . . . I detest imitations. I want to be an original philanthropist. The classic philanthropists elicit the love of their *protégés;* I want to elicit their hate. A happy partnership of philanthropy and cruelty. Don't you think?"

Eduardo wasn't listening. Coco didn't take it badly. He knew that Eduardo was multiplying and dividing. . . . The greatest excitement for a human being takes the form of money. Eduardo, who didn't escape this law, exclaimed:

"I don't see how to win this money writing the phrase you just dictated to me one million times. The rest of the years of my life wouldn't be enough."

"Time is conquered by hard work," said Coco impertinently. "The number of years will decrease the more times you write the phrase each day. But let's allow the numbers to speak for themselves; out of the infinite combinations that can be made on the basis of time and numbers, I will explain four to you. First tell me: how old are you?"

"I just turned thirty," Eduardo said in a melancholy voice.

"All right then, given those thirty years, the aforementioned four combinations are feasible. I've said 'feasible,' but the first combination isn't so feasible. I don't see how a man of your age could reach a safe harbor after so many years of sailing. Bah! Let's forgo symbolism and speak the concise language of numbers! If you write *Coco: I want a million* fifty times a day, it would take you twenty thousand days to complete a million. Okay now, twenty thousand days is less than fifty-five years, six months and twenty days. I don't believe this solution appeals to you. Besides the many years you would have to be my prisoner (we will talk about this at the proper time), you would see your strength decreasing perceptibly, your pulse would grow increasingly unsteady, your vision would decline, and above all, my friend, your spirit . . . your spirit that can move mountains would become a sticky, soft thing; tears would come continually to your eyes; helplessness, frustration, hate, loathing for yourself would be the terrible deities attending to your solitary existence. Although you would still have vengeance. . . ." Coco saw Eduardo's glassy eyes brighten. "Yes, my dear sir, you would still have vengeance. You could pass your sentence on to another aspirant to the one million. It would be a pleasure of the gods. But there remains something even more discouraging: supposing you passed the test, triumphant, supposing that with one hand helping the other, you wrote the final *Coco: I want a million,* of what use would it be? At the age of eighty-five, you could only look forward to a magnificent mausoleum. Obviously, this solution doesn't suit you."

"No," Eduardo repeated in a funereal tone of voice, "it doesn't suit me."

"The second solution," Coco continued, "though problematic, would allow you the pleasures of senility. Sad pleasures, I admit; nevertheless, it's an age that, it is said, has its charms. In short, I leave it to you to choose. I understand that you might be eager to know how many years you would spend writing. It's a quite simple calculation, which, because of your emotional state, surprise, and growing hatred, you are unable to do at the moment. In this case, it is a matter of doubling the work. That is, if you write *Coco: I want a million* one hundred times a day, it would take you ten thousand days to finish the one million copies. Can you tell me how many years, months, and days you would spend asking me for the money?"

"Never!" Eduardo shouted. "I will never accept that solution! It's just as atrocious as the first."

"Nearly as atrocious," Coco said as he rapidly multiplied and divided. "Or to be more precise: half the atrocity. It would take you twenty-six years, nine months, and ten days."

"For God's sake, put yourself in my place," Eduardo pleaded. "Would you want to spend whole years copying one stupid phrase?"

"I must admit I would not."

"Well then. . . ." Eduardo clenched his fists. "Remember the commandment: do unto others. . . ."

"With a hundred million, one has the luxury of ignoring commandments. I do unto others what I would not want done unto me. I want, for example, that you spend years locked up, copying stupid phrases."

"I can refuse!" Eduardo cried out. "You'd be left with your schemes. . . ."

"I hold time to be sacred," Coco said. "Let's not lose any time on tangents. Are you interested in hearing a third solution?"

Here, Eduardo did what anyone caught in the middle would do:

"I'll listen to it out of curiosity, but I'm not committing myself."

"Let's examine the third option," Coco said simply, knowing the ropes. "Hold on tight, because now we're leaping into the abyss. Soon you'll see how we pass over dozens of years at fantastic speeds. It is blessed, sacrosanct work that allows us to conquer time. This superhuman force will never be praised highly enough. It will be work that allows you to make that million without seeing yourself turned into a doddering old man. You will emerge triumphant from the test, and scarcely a single silver thread will pepper your black hair. Good looks, physical vigor, and spirit—above all, spirit. . . . You come to rest in such a beautiful harbor in only two thousand days, Eduardo; only two thousand days writing *Coco: I want a million!* Don't think I'm trying to trick you. You know now that the emotion incited by such intense pleasure prevents you from calculating accurately. Nevertheless, the numbers will never deceive us. If you write the phrase five hundred times a day, it will only take you two thousand days. And do you know how long that is? Spirit, courage, perseverance, Eduardo! Five miserable years, six months, and twenty days."

Eduardo almost became happy. This reduction in time had the power to revive him. He could already see himself with the million in his pocket. He asked:

"Didn't you speak of a fourth solution? It must be more advantageous."

"You're catching on," Coco responded. "We're trying to reduce the amount of time. Write *Coco: I want a million* one thousand times a day, and in two years, nine months, and ten days you'll have the cash in your pocket."

"Where's the hitch?" Eduardo exclaimed, surprised at the relative ease of the trial.

"There isn't any hitch," Coco said. "I play clean. But you shouldn't trust your enthusiasm. After you've adjusted, it's quite easy to live in hell, but until then. . . ."

"Are you finished yet?" Eduardo said with a defiant look on his face. "Have you told me everything, or is there more?"

"That's it," Coco said with a cheerful look on his face.

"Then keep your hell—swallow it whole, and cook up a nice sauce out of your millions to make it taste better. . . . So you thought you had me in your clutches? You made your calculations: I have a hundred million.

Needy man looking for a thousand dollars. I'll offer him a million. He won't be able to resist the temptation. I'll impose a very high price. Every dollar he earns will turn into a wrinkle, a groan, a bitterness. His sentence will serve to brighten my final days. It's enough to make you die laughing."

". . . laughing," Coco repeated, and indeed he laughed.

"There's no lack of people who can provide me with a thousand dollars," Eduardo said.

"Why, of course!" said Coco "some provide a thousand; others, a million. I, for example. . . ."

Eduardo pretended not to hear. He continued:

"With a thousand dollars, borrowed according to established procedures, I will arrive at my goal."

"In any event," Coco said, "remember I am at your service."

"Be aware that we are seeing each other for the first and last time. I will stand on my own two feet. And, for starters, I'm going to actually stand up. This proves I have freedom of movement."

II

Anxious to finish as soon as possible, Eduardo had chosen the fourth solution. According to his calculations, it wouldn't take him more than four hours a day. Writing the phrase five times a minute, he would write it for the one thousandth time in exactly three hours and twenty minutes. So, since Coco wasn't setting any limits on his writing, Eduardo could double and even triple his output if he approached the task diligently. That's what he did from the first day. He applied himself to the task with ardor; exhausted but happy, he finished his third thousand at midnight. He had divided his time as follows: the first thousand, from nine to twelve-twenty in the afternoon; the second thousand, from three to six-twenty in the evening; the third thousand, from nine to twelve-twenty at night.

Eduardo's urgency was justified for many reasons. First and foremost: by voluntarily making himself Coco's prisoner, he was required to spend his days and nights in the cramped space of a prison cell. The banker proved to be unyielding on this point. Eduardo's arguments, based on the physical and moral health of the prisoner, had no effect on Coco. He had his reasons for putting Eduardo behind bars. If the aspirant to the million did not have the counterweight of humiliation, he would lose himself in his task; tempted by other stimulants, he would cease copying the request with the necessary regularity and end up by abandoning the enterprise. Eduardo had pleaded in vain for a few hours of freedom to attend to his personal affairs. Coco replied that his only personal affair was to write.

For better or worse, Eduardo was convinced. True, he wouldn't be spared captivity, but he was going to reduce it. "I'll be his prisoner for about a year. I'm going to show that old man that I have more guts than it took him to make a hundred million. And on close inspection, my situation is not so unattractive: I'm not a common criminal or a crook whose offense is known throughout society. No one in the world except Coco and María knows where I am. Meanwhile, I continue writing, and one fine day the dictator will be in for a surprise."

(First letter from Eduardo to María)
"My dear María: I feel like a fish in water. . . . Everything is quite different from what we imagined. I have let a month pass without writing to you so I could offer you a detailed description of my physical and spiritual condition. Well, I feel magnificent. Seeing that your love and my ardent desire to beat that scoundrel both sustain me in this undertaking, I can assure you that I feel strong enough to get all his millions. You remember our fear about the possibility of failure? You were thinking very correctly that the uniformity of such a life would reduce my capacity to work, that the number of times my hand could put that ridiculous phrase on paper would gradually decrease. Well, my beloved María, a month has passed; thirty days have gone straight into the grave of time, and your beloved Eduardo has written *Coco: I want a million* ninety thousand times. Are you happy? Don't you feel proud of your Eduardo? Think that in little more than a year we will own that tidy sum. Think what one can do with a million: you will have jewelry and dresses and, most important, you won't have to look at Coco's face—that alone is worth money in the bank. We will show that bitter old man that good triumphs in the end. Without a doubt, he is an evil spirit; he comes every day and, under the pretext of encouraging me in the enterprise, tells me of his terrible doubts concerning my triumph. Only yesterday, he wore himself out repeating that one shouldn't put the horse before the carriage (you know how the old man loves metaphoric language), that a good captain doesn't force his ship, that a bird in the hand is worth two in the bush. . . . But I don't let his chats affect me and cheerfully continue with my work. I should tell you, though, that it would be dangerous to add a fourth shift. You're not going to believe it: writing the same phrase three thousand times a day demands a great deal of concentration. If you let yourself go mechanically, you end

up making a mistake in the text—not to mention worse things; for example, being surprised by words unrelated to the undertaking, which have mysteriously slipped into the writing. Of course, Coco allows erasures and even ink blots, for, as a philosopher would say, he seeks content, not form. Which is not to say that erasures and ink blots conspire with Coco in this race against time. Because I shouldn't hide anything from you, I'll tell you that in the month just passed, I made two hundred and twenty-four errors, which equal approximately ten hours. That is why I must be cautious, not hazard the fourth thousand. The worst thing in work like this is improvisation; it can lead to fatal results. Nevertheless, don't be alarmed by insignificant slip-ups. I expect in this second month now beginning that the emotions of the neophyte will give way to the confidence of the initiate. I say this in Coco's pompous style so that your pretty face might light up with laughter. A thousand kisses, your Eduardo."

One stifling hot afternoon, Eduardo went up to the roof to stretch his legs. He was feeling very depressed. The writing was proceeding full steam ahead (he was nearly approaching half a million), but inside, something was warning him that he was reaching the limit of his powers. The first alarm was signaled by food. At that point, after five months of voluntary confinement, it was very difficult for him to swallow solids. The fact was that he was full—full of the sinister phrase that, like a cancer, was slowly invading his organs. His stomach felt so stuffed and upset by those *Coco: I want a million*s, that he watched with horror as mealtimes approached. Sometimes he threw up or, unable to do that, would experience horrible retching. Coco, who continued to visit him daily, never tired of advising Eduardo to reduce his workload. On this point Eduardo would not accept advice. He took to heart the saying: "Win, or die in the attempt. . . ."

Something of supreme importance revealed itself to him concerning his mental integrity: Coco was not his worst enemy. At most, Coco symbolized the humiliation that one man imposes on another. True, the humiliated man might find a crack in the iron armor of humiliation. For the time being, Eduardo was defending himself with contempt. But how does one defend oneself against writing?

"Step by step," Eduardo thought. But he would have to decide on the pace of those steps. Very slow, it would mean long years of captivity; very short, it would sap his strength until he abandoned the ordeal. Mithridates, king of Pontus, would swallow small doses of poison. One fine day, the poison found its own image in Mithridates' stomach. In contrast, Eduardo was arguing in vain against writing: mistakes came with increasing frequency, the letters came out of the pencil in knotted confusion, as if the phrase, composed of five words, were composed of millions of words. One day, he was surprised by a string of disconnected words resembling automatic writing. It was as if that damned phrase had the power to make his mind come unhinged. Eduardo, struggling to escape the mental prison these words embodied, was falling into other larger prisons of excessive phrases containing no sense whatsoever and with a bewitching power capable of plunging him into complete mental abjection. It was very possible that Eduardo would avoid writing, that he would get up one ill-fated day without the necessary enthusiasm and—like a classic prisoner—would start training a mouse or teaching a bird to sing. . . .

It was with such dark thoughts that he had gone up to the roof that afternoon to take his customary walk. He barely responded at all to the guard's greeting. Walking quickly, he headed for the overhang at the back of the rooftop. He flung himself down like a dog and began to swat away imaginary flies. Finally, he stopped moving his hands and lay there drowsily. How surprised he was to hear a child's voice mixed with a mature authoritarian one! He opened his eyes. Like someone coming out of a nightmare, he took the two people standing a few feet away for the last traces of his terrible dream. They were a beautiful boy about five years old and a young woman who seemed to be his mother. Pointing at the man lying on the roof, she put her mouth to the boy's ear and whispered a few words to him. The boy fixed his timid eyes on Eduardo and began to laugh. Eduardo was just about to greet the woman when the boy, hugging her legs, babbled to him:

"I'm writing the same thing you are. . . ."

All hell broke loose. Reason, don't flounder, world, don't come apart, equilibrium, don't break! Have we heard correctly? Did you say that, or is the feverish mind now hearing everything through the filter of writing?

But the boy, implacable and innocent, repeated:

"I'm writing the same thing you are. . . ."

Eduardo fixed his eyes on the woman as he clasped the boy to his breast. The woman was already opening her mouth when the boy, escaping from Eduardo's arms, shouted:

"Coco: I want a million. . . ."

Eventually, everything was cleared up. Things are always clarified in the end, in spite of the atrocious confusion they cause at the time. Because the mother (she was, in fact, the boy's mother), one more person asking for money, had asked Coco. Only a hundred dollars. An insignificant sum. A sum out of line with Coco's grandeur. How could one think, how could one imagine that Coco might accept, that Coco might stoop so low, that Coco might bother. . . ! But she—what else could she do? The poor woman would have found it difficult to count beyond one hundred. And then . . . those erroneous calculations of the needy: if I ask for a lot it will be denied; if I ask for a little, the money purse will open. Finally, humility—real or feigned: one has to crawl, lick, bless, lower oneself. . . .

But with Coco such arguments failed. It was impossible to come to such an original philanthropist with humble petitions. So he shook his head in disgust. The poor woman interpreted the gesture according to the laws of humility and silently recriminated herself for having said one hundred when she should have said fifty. Perhaps, she thought, fifty is the figure that will make Coco nod his head in approval. And she was already opening her mouth to correct the figure when Coco said:

"I offer you one hundred thousand. . . ."

At this, there was no commotion, no worlds coming together, no abysses opening; here calculation didn't join with stupor, nor did humiliation extend its arm to greed. The woman simply didn't understand, and since she didn't understand, she put on the expression of someone who doesn't understand a foreign language. Coco hastened to explain. It was useless for him to show a hundred-dollar bill and explain that a thousand like this one comprised the amount he was offering. Nevertheless, something clicked, for her eyes grew brighter. Coco, with patience worthy (according to him) of a better cause, took out a roll of bills, broke the tape, and arranged ten groups of one hundred on the table. He asked the woman to count them.

"One thousand dollars," she said after a while.

"Let's suppose," Coco added in a kindergarten teacher's voice, "that there are a thousand hundred-dollar bills on this table. How many dollars would that be?"

"One hundred thousand," the woman said, and this time she was on the verge of choking as she brought the rags of misery together with the robes of calculation for the first time.

"Well, they're yours," Coco said, "I'm giving them to you as a gift."

And, since at this point the petitioner follows Eduardo, we spare the reader the torture of repetition. Of course, she would make herself a voluntary prisoner. "For her son," Coco said. "She was prepared to make any sacrifice for her little orphaned son." And how strange life is, how it writes *awry* when it should write *right;* how life, at once foolish and wise, surprises us with its decisions, and how its whims disconcert us!

"Son. . . . A little son," Coco said with the devilish gleam in his eyes that writers portray. "So the lady has a little son. . . ."

"Only five years old, sir; a lovely boy, an innocent boy who has had the tremendous misfortune of losing his father."

"Orphan . . . adoptive parent . . . one hundred thousand . . . five years . . . philanthropist . . ." Coco sputtered.

A poor person, even when he hears unconnected phrases like the ones Coco just uttered, is not entitled to explanations. Consequently, the mother put on an expression of blind adoration. She began to drool when Coco added:

"Your son will copy *Coco:* etc., etc."

(Second letter from Eduardo to María)

"My dear María: yesterday I completed the first year of my voluntary imprisonment. I know that you're going to get depressed with this business about 'my first year.' I see in your face the question: Are you thinking of remaining in Coco's fortress forever? I must tell you that I have well-founded fears. Don't think that I've come upon such devastating evidence all of a sudden. I refer you to my first letter. In it, I was displaying the first symptoms, giving the first warning signals. It's significant that I didn't write you again. You've found out about me through Coco's cold, official reports. Although he suspects part of the truth and even imagines how close I am to quitting, he talks to you constantly about 'the fine progress of my affairs.' He's deceiving you when he says that my release is only days away; he's deceiving you when he assures you that just a few more *Coco: I want a million*s will be the signal for us to be instantly swimming in cash. He repeats to me, point by point, his conversations with you; with a masterly hand, he paints your face flooded with happiness before such a bright future. Then he'll leave you to plummet suddenly into the abysses of desperation, then bring you to the dark realization that you'll be his secretary forever.

"Don't think that I'm satisfied with pathetic phrases. I am only speaking the facts. About a week ago, he appeared very mysteriously in my cell. He was coming, he said, to apologize for missing that night's visit. Such a remark surprised me. He loved to torture me with his interminable talks about the possibilities of victory or defeat.

"At first, I didn't suspect anything out of the ordinary. On the contrary, he seemed to be enjoying one of his brilliant days. Seeing him smiling so much, I asked him if he had made a good business deal. 'I just made a million,' he replied, rubbing his hands together. And he added: 'I'm going to get paid. Now you know why we can't talk tonight.'

"It seemed only appropriate for me to punch him. These small acts of revenge don't solve anything, but are all that we slaves can allow ourselves. I told him that this million would look very meager next to his hundred million. His response left me cold as ice: 'At my age, it would be childish to exceed that figure. On the other hand, to decrease it would be catastrophic. When I say that I've earned a million, I mean to say that I could have lost that much. Do you realize how ridiculous it would be for me to reduce my fortune to ninety-nine million?'

"My darling, I swear I felt all was lost; it put a knot in my throat. I thought he was telling me that my case was closed, that the million I had defended so jealously was slipping through my fingers. At last, I could speak. In a faltering voice, I begged him not to judge the trial over; that although I had been writing rather slowly of late, I wasn't giving up the million on that account. He smiled, gave me several affectionate slaps on the back, told me not to get alarmed, that I hadn't lost yet, that what he had said didn't have anything to do with my case, that he was referring to José. . . .

"You will feel this blow in your heart as intensely as I felt it reverberating in mine. A wisely calculated blow. That there was a José, living as a voluntary prisoner like me, didn't surprise me. The young prisoner was enough of a surprise for me. Furthermore, it's logical that Coco might have many voluntary prisoners. The wisely calculated blow was not telling me that one of his prisoners had failed in his writing. What demolished me in one blow was that he had put José ahead of me. This José, he told me, had also tried to make *his* million. It was a particularly painful situation. He was within inches of triumph. He had succeeded in writing *Coco: I want a million* eight hundred thousand times but stopped there, his head filled with fog. Like the shipwrecked man who, after swimming for miles, finds himself a few strokes away from the coast, struggles bravely and is finally overcome by the waves, José had struggled fruitlessly with the writing. Coco gave me a detailed account of this struggle: according to him, José suffered two great periods of depression, separated by a brief interval of furious graphomania. The first depression was characterized by mental and physiological saturation; he couldn't ingest any food. Why continue . . . I'm familiar with each phase of the hateful process. And of course, I am most familiar with the brief attack of graphomania. Coco told me that during such an interval José had, in a matter of ten days, written the odious phrase fifty thousand times. Dear María, when I had my attack (not yet a week ago), I wrote the phrase eighty thousand times.

" 'Then,' Coco told me, 'then the fog enveloped José. His second depression took the form of complete powerlessness, an unconditional surrender before the task of writing.' And he added that, like the madman who spends the day consumed by a preoccupation, José spent his days monotonously intoning: *Coco: I want a million.* "

As one might expect, Eduardo was defeated. Now five years have passed, and the bitter taste of the familiar phrase remains forever in his mouth. After having "earned" thousands of theoretical dollars, he must content himself with the one hundred actual dollars that Coco allots him monthly. That is to say that Eduardo is one of many lowly employees in the powerful banking organization *Coco and Co.* He has this job, the humble position of assistant cashier, thanks to his beloved María. She had the good sense to throw herself at the philanthropist's feet.

Millions pass through Eduardo's hands, millions that must, at six in the evening (when the bank closes) be scrupulously tallied. Nothing easier! The electronic machine adds them up and writes them down in a fraction of a second. Of course, Eduardo is quite careful to stop it in time. Otherwise, it would continue to add hundreds of millions with conspicuous ease.

1957

The One Who Came
to Save Me

Translated by Mark Schafer

I ALWAYS HAD one great fear: not knowing when I would die. My wife claimed it was my father's fault; my mother was dying, he set me in front of her and made me kiss her. I was ten years old at the time and we all know the business about how the specter of death leaves a profound impression on children. . . . I'm not saying the assertion is wrong, but my case is different. What my wife doesn't know is that I saw a man executed, and saw it purely by accident. Unusual justice: two men tied a noose around another man's neck in the bathroom of a movie theater and slit his throat. How did I see? I was in a stall taking a shit, and they couldn't see me; they were at the urinals. I was calmly taking a shit and all of a sudden I heard: "But you're not going to kill me. . . ." I looked through the grating and saw a knife slitting a throat, torrents of blood; I heard a scream, and feet running away at full speed. When the police arrived at the scene of the crime, they found me unconscious, nearly dead, in what they call "a state of shock." For a month, I hung between life and death.

Now don't think that thereafter I would be afraid of having my throat slit. Well, think that if you want, it's your prerogative. If someone sees a man's throat being slit, it's logical he would think the same thing could happen to him too, but it's also logical to think it highly unlikely that the damned coincidence of fate—or whatever—would assign him the same luck as the man whose throat they slit in the bathroom of the movie theater.

No, that was not my fear. The fear I felt at the very moment they slit the guy's throat could be expressed in these words: When will it happen? Imagine an eighty-year-old man, quite ready to face death; I think the single thought in his mind can only be to wonder: Will this be the night . . . ? Will it be tomorrow . . . ? Will it be three in the morning the day after . . . ? Will it be right now, while I'm thinking it will be the day after at three in the morning . . . ? Knowing and feeling that his remaining time is quite short, he figures his calculations of the "fatal hour" are precise enough, but at the same time, the impotence he experiences as he tries to determine "the moment" reduces his calculations to nothing. On the other hand, the guy murdered in the bathroom knew at once when his time would come. The moment he uttered the words "But you're not going to kill me . . . ," he knew his time had come. Between his desperate exclamation and the hand that guided the knife to slit his throat, he knew the exact moment of his death. That is, if, for example, the exclamation was uttered at four minutes and five seconds past nine in the evening, and his throat was slit at four minutes eight seconds past nine, he knew the time of his death precisely three seconds beforehand.

On the other hand, lying here on the bed alone (my wife died last year and anyway, I don't know how that poor woman would be able to help me with this business about the moment of my death), I am racking what little brains I have left. It's well known that when one is ninety years old as I am, like the traveler, one is dependent on the clock, with the difference that the traveler knows what time it is and the ninety year old does not. But let's not get ahead of ourselves.

When the guy had his throat slit in the bathroom, I was only twenty years old. Being "full of life" in those days and, moreover, seeing life stretch ahead of me almost like an eternity, that bloody picture and that distressing question were soon erased. When you're full of life, you only have time to live and be alive. You feel alive and say: "How healthy I am. I exude health from all my pores, I could eat an ox, copulate five times a day, work twenty hours straight without tiring . . ." and at that moment one can't conceive of what it means to die and to be dying. When I got married at twenty-two, my wife, observing my passion, said to me one night: "Will you be the same with me when you're an old man?" And I replied: "What's an old man? You think you know?"

Of course, she didn't know either. And since neither she nor I could, at the time, imagine an old man, well, we started laughing, and then we made love like crazy.

But soon after turning fifty, I began to see a glimmering of what it meant to be an old man and I also began to think about this business of the moment of death. . . . Of course I kept on living, but at the same time, I was beginning to die, and a sickly, ravenous curiosity was forcing me to face the fatal moment. Since I had to die, at least knowing at what moment my death would occur, the way I know, for example, the precise moment I brush my teeth. . . .

And as I grew older, this thought became more and more obsessive until it was what we call a fixation. When I was in my early seventies, I—unexpectedly—took my first plane trip. I received a cablegram from the wife of my only brother informing me that he was dying. So I took the plane. Two hours into the flight we encountered bad weather. The plane was a feather in the storm; it was everything they say about planes in the middle of a tempest: passengers filled with terror, the comings and going of the stewardesses, objects falling to the floor, screams of women and children mixed with the Lord's Prayer and Hail Marys—in short, that *memento mori* that is all the more *memento* at an altitude of forty thousand feet.

"Thank God," I said to myself. "Thank God that for the first time I'm approaching a certain precision concerning the moment of my death. At least on this plane in danger of being dashed to pieces, I can already start calculating the moment. Ten, fifteen, thirty-eight minutes . . . ? It doesn't matter. I'm close and you, death, will not be able to surprise me."

I confess that I rejoiced wildly. Not for an instant did it occur to me to pray, review my life, make an act of contrition, or (that simple physiological function) vomit. No, I was only attentive to the imminent crash of the plane so I might know, as we were dashed to pieces, that this was the moment of my death.

Once the danger had passed, a passenger said to me: "Listen, I was watching you while we were falling, and you looked as if nothing was wrong." I smiled, didn't answer her; she, anguish still showing on her face, was unaware of "my anguish," which for once in my life had been transformed at forty thousand feet into a state of grace comparable to that of the most illustrious saints of the Church.

But it isn't every day one finds oneself at an altitude of forty thousand feet in a plane whipped by storm winds—the only paradise glimpsed during my long life. On the contrary, we each inhabit the hell we ourselves create: its walls are of thought, its roof terrors, and its windows abysses. . . . And within, one freezes over a low flame, that is, one's life seeps out amidst flames that adopt unusual forms: "at what hour," "a Tuesday or a Saturday," "in the fall or in the spring. . . ."

And I freeze myself and burn myself more and more. I've become a worn-out exhibit from a museum of teratology and at the same time, the very picture of malnutrition. I'm sure it's not blood but pus that runs through my veins; my scabs—festering, purplish—and my bones seems to have conferred a very different anatomy on my body. My hip bones, like a river, have overflown their banks; my collarbone (as I lose my flesh) is like an anchor hanging over the side of a ship; the occipital bone makes my head look like a coconut bashed in with a sledgehammer.

In spite of this, the stuff in my head continues thinking, and thinking its *idée fixe;* right now, at this very instant, stretched out on the bed in my bedroom, with death hovering overhead, with death, who might be that photograph of my dead father, who looks at me and says: "I'm going to surprise you, you'll never know, you're watching me but you don't know when I'll deal you the blow. . . ."

In response, I looked more intently at the photograph of my father and said to him: "You won't have your way. I'll know the moment you make a move, and before you do, I'll shout: 'Now's the time!' and you'll have to admit defeat." And just at that moment, that moment that shares reality and anomaly, I heard footsteps that were also part of that same reality and unreality. I turned my eyes from the photograph and unconsciously focused them on the closet mirror facing my bed. In it, I saw reflected the face of a young man—only his face, since the rest of his body was hidden from my sight by a folding screen placed between the foot of the bed and the mirror. But I didn't pay much attention to him—something that would have been unthinkable had I been a younger man; I mean, at the age when you're truly alive and the unexpected presence of a stranger in your bedroom would elicit anything from surprise to terror. But at my age, and in the state of languor in which I found myself, a stranger and his face were just a part of the reality-unreality you must tolerate. That is, the stranger and his face were either another among the many objects that populate my bedroom, or among the many ghosts that populate my head. So I turned my eyes again to the photograph of my father, and when I looked back at the mirror, the stranger's face had disappeared. I looked once more at the photograph and thought I noticed that my father's face was angry; that is, my father's face inasmuch as it was his, but with a face that was also not his, but rather, looked as if it were made up like a character out of a tragedy. Who knows. . . . On this boundary between reality and unreality, everything is possible, and, more importantly, everything occurs and doesn't occur. At that point, I closed my eyes and began to say aloud: now, now. . . . Suddenly I heard the sound of footsteps very near the head of my bed. I opened my eyes and there in front of me was the stranger, his body a mile high. I thought: "Bah, the same as the one in the mirror . . ." and I looked again at the photograph of my father. But something told me to look again at the stranger. I didn't disobey my inner voice and looked at him. Now he wielded a knife and was slowly bending over as I watched him intently. Then I understood that this stranger was the one who was coming to save me. I knew several seconds beforehand the exact moment of my death. When the knife sank into my jugular vein, I looked at my savior and said to him, through torrents of blood: "Thank you for coming."

1967

Julio Cortázar

1914–1984

KNOWN FOR HIS beautifully constructed narratives of the uncanny, Julio Cortázar was born in Brussels, Belgium on August 26, 1914. He studied at the University of Buenos Aires and held several positions in Argentina as a teacher and translator between 1937 and 1945. Cortázar lived in Paris from the early 1950s until his death in 1984, pursuing a full-time career as a writer and working as a freelance translator for UNESCO. (He is also the Spanish translator of works by Edgar Allan Poe, André Gide, and Marguerite Yourcenar, among others.) Cortázar's short stories from the 1950s show already his mastery of the genre and develop fully the kinds of themes that would obsess him for the rest of his life: the presence of the bizarre and the fantastic in everyday situations and the duality of the human psyche. Among the better known collections from this period are: *Bestiario* (1951; Bestiary); *Final del juego* (1956; End of the game), and *Las armas secretas* (1959; Secret weapons). Fifteen stories from these three collections appear in English translation in *Blow-Up and Other Stories* (1967). (The script for Michaelangelo Antonioni's 1966 film, *Blow-Up,* was adapted from the title story.) With *Rayuela* (1963; *Hopscotch,* 1966), a portrayal of bohemian Argentine expatriates living in Paris, Cortázar's reputation as a novelist of international stature was firmly established. One of the most representative works of the Latin American literary Boom, *Hopscotch* is a challenging experimental work. Some critics have argued that it radically changed the future trend of Latin American literature, revolutionizing readers' perceptions of the process of reading itself. Cortázar would continue to push the limits of fiction with such works as *Todos los fuegos el fuego* (1966; *All the Fires the Fire, and Other Stories,* 1973); *62: Modelo para armar* (1968; *62: A Model Kit,* 1972); and *Libro de Manuel* (1973; *A Manual for Manuel,* 1978).

139

Bestiary

Translated by Paul Blackburn

BETWEEN THE LAST spoonful of rice pudding with milk (very little cinnamon, a shame) and the goodnight kisses before going up to bed, there was a tinkling in the telephone room and Isabel hung around until Inés came from answering it and said something into their mother's ear. They looked at one another, then both of them looked at Isabel who was thinking about the broken birdcage and the long division problems and briefly of old lady Lucera being angry because she'd pushed her doorbell on the way back from school. She wasn't all that worried, Inés and her mother were looking as if they were gazing past her somewhere, almost taking her as an excuse; but they were looking at her.

"I don't like the idea of her going, believe you me," Inés said. "Not so much because of the tiger, after all they're very careful in that respect. But it's such a depressing house and only that boy to play with her . . ."

"I don't like the idea either," her mother said, and Isabel knew, as if she were on a toboggan, that they were going to send her to the Funes' for the summer. She flung herself into the news, into the great green wave, the Funes', the Funes', sure they were going to send her. They didn't like it, but it was convenient. Delicate lungs, Mar del Plata so very expensive, difficult to manage such a spoiled child, stupid, the way she always acted up with that wonderful Miss Tania, a restless sleeper, toys underfoot everyplace, questions, buttons to be sewn back on, filthy knees. She felt afraid, delighted, smell of the willow trees and the *u* in Funes was getting mixed in with the rice pudding, so late to be still up, and get up to bed, right now.

Lying there, the light out, covered with kisses and rueful glances from Inés and their mother, not fully decided but already decided in spite of everything to send her. She was enjoying beforehand the drive up in the phaeton, the first breakfast, the happiness of Nino, hunter of cockroaches, Nino the toad, Nino the fish (a memory of three years before, Nino showing her some small cutouts he'd glued in an album and telling her gravely, "This-is-a-toad, and THIS is-a-fish"). Now Nino in the park waiting for her with the butterfly net, and also Rema's soft hands—she saw them coming out of the darkness, she had her eyes open and instead of Nino's face—zap!—Rema's hands, the Funes' younger daughter. "Aunt Rema loves me a lot," and Nino's eyes got large and wet, she saw Nino again disjointedly floating in the dim light of the bedroom, looking at her contentedly. Nino the fish. Falling asleep wanting the week to be over that same night, and the goodbyes, the train, the last half-mile in the phaeton, the gate, the eucalyptus trees along the road leading up to the house. Just before falling asleep, she had a moment of terror when she imagined that she was maybe dreaming. Stretching out all at once, her feet hit the brass bars at the foot of the bed, they hurt through the covers, and she heard her mother and Inés talking in the big dining room, baggage, see the doctor about those pimples, cod-liver oil and concentrate of witch hazel. It wasn't a dream, it wasn't a dream.

It wasn't a dream. They took her down to Constitution Station one windy morning, small flags blowing from the pushcarts in the plaza, a piece of pie in the railroad station restaurant, and the enormous entrance to platform 14. Between Inés and her mother they kissed her so much that her face felt like it'd been walked on, soft and smelly, rouge and Coty powder, wet around the mouth, a squeamish feeling of filth that the wind eradicated with one large smack. She wasn't afraid to travel alone because she was a big girl, with nothing less than twenty pesos in her pocketbook, Sansinena Co., Frozen Meats a sweetish stink seeping in the window, the railroad trestle over the yellow brook and Isabel already back to normal from having had to have that crying spell at the station, happy, dead with fear, active, using fully the seat by the window, almost the only traveler in that portion of the coach from which one could examine all the different places and see oneself in the small mirrors. She thought once or twice of her mother, of Inés—they'd already be on the 97 car, leaving Constitution—she read no smoking, spitting is forbidden by law, seating capacity 42 passengers, they were passing through Banfield at top speed, vavooom! country more country more country intermingled with the taste of Milky Way and the menthol drops. Inés had reminded her that she would be working on the green wool in such a way that Isabel packed the knitting into the most inaccessible part of the suitcase, poor Inés, and what a stupid idea.

At the station she was a little bit worried because if the phaeton . . . But there it was, with don Nicanor very red and respectful, yes miss, this miss, that miss, was the trip fine, was her mother as well as ever, of course it had rained— Oh the swinging motion of the phaeton to get her back into the whole aquarium of her previous visit to Los Horneros. Everything smaller, more crystalline and pink, without the tiger then, don Nicanor with fewer white hairs, barely three years ago, Nino a toad, Nino a fish, and Rema's hands which made you want to cry and feel them on your head forever, a caress like death almost and pastries with vanilla cream, the two best things on earth.

They gave her a room upstairs all to herself, the loveliest room. A grownup's room (Nino's idea, all black curls and eyes, handsome in his blue overalls; in the afternoon, of course, Luis made him dress up, his slate-grey suit and a red tie) and inside, another tiny room with an enormous wild cardinal. The bathroom was two doors away (but inside doors through the rooms so that you could go without checking beforehand where the tiger was), full of spigots and metal things, though they did not fool Isabel easily, you could tell it was a country bathroom, things were not as perfect as in a city bath. And it smelled old, the second morning she found a waterbug taking a walk in the washbasin. She barely touched it, it rolled itself into a timid ball and disappeared down the gurgling drain.

Dear mama, I'm writing to— They were eating in the dining room with the chandelier because it was cooler. The Kid was complaining every minute about the heat. Luis said nothing, but every once in a while you could see the sweat break out on his forehead or his chin. Only Rema was restful, she passed the plates slowly and always as if the meal were a birthday party, a little solemnly and impressively. (Isabel was secretly studying her way of carving and of ordering the servants.) For the most part, Luis was always reading, fist to brow, and the book leaning against a siphon. Rema touched his arm before passing him a plate, and the Kid would interrupt him once in a while to call him philosopher. It hurt Isabel that Luis might be a philosopher, not because of that, but because of the Kid, that he had an excuse then to joke and call him that.

They ate like this: Luis at the head of the table, Rema and Nino on one side, the Kid and Isabel on the other, so that there was an adult at the end and a child and a grownup at either side. When Nino wanted to tell her something serious, he'd give her a kick on the shin with his shoe. Once Isabel yelled and the Kid got angry and said she was badly brought up. Rema looked at her continuously until Isabel was comforted by the gaze and the potato soup.

Mama, before you go in to eat it's like all the rest of the time, you have to look and see if— Almost always it was Rema who went to see if they could go into the dining room with the crystal chandelier. The second day she came to the big living room and said they would have to wait. It was a long time before a farmhand came to tell them that the tiger was in the clover garden, then Rema took the children's hands and everyone went in to eat. The fried potatoes were pretty dry that morning, though only Nino and the Kid complained.

You told me I was not supposed to go around making— Because Rema seemed to hold off all questions with her terse sweetness. The setup worked so well that it was unnecessary to worry about the business of the rooms. It was an absolutely enormous house, and at worst, there was only one room they couldn't go into; never more than one, so it didn't matter. Isabel was as used to it as Nino, after a couple of days. From morning until evening they played in the grove of willows, and if they couldn't play in the willow grove, there was always the clover garden, the park with its hammocks, and the edge of the brook. It was the same in the house, they had their bedrooms, the hall down the center, the library downstairs (except one Thursday when they couldn't go into the library) and the dining room with the chandelier. They couldn't go into Luis' study because Luis was reading all the time, once in a while he would call to his son and give him picture books; but Nino always took them out, they went to the living room or to the front garden to look at them. They never went into the Kid's study because they were afraid he would throw a tantrum. Rema told them that it was better that way, she said it as though she were warning them; they'd already learned how to read her silences.

After all's said, it was a sad life. Isabel wondered one night why the Funes' had invited her for the summer. She wasn't old enough to understand that it was for Nino not for her, a summer plaything to keep Nino happy. She only managed to see the sadness of the house, that Rema seemed always tired, that it hardly ever rained and that, nonetheless, things had that air of being damp and abandoned. After a few days she got used to the rules of the house and the not-difficult discipline of that summer at Los Horneros. Nino was beginning to learn to use the microscope Luis had given him; they spent a magnificent week growing insects in a trough with stagnant water and lily pads, putting drops on the glass slide to look at the microbes. "They're mosquito larvae, you're not going to see microbes with that microscope," Luis told them, his smile somewhat pained and distant. They could never believe that that wriggling horror was not a microbe. Rema brought them a kaleidoscope which she kept in her wardrobe, but they still preferred detecting microbes and counting their legs. Isabel carried a notebook and kept notations of their experiments, she combined biology with chemistry and putting together a medicine chest. They made the medicine chest in Nino's room after ransacking the whole house to get things for it. Isabel told Luis, "We want some of everything: things." Luis gave them Andreu lozenges, pink cotton, a test tube. The Kid came across with a rubber bag and a bottle of green pills with the label worn off. Rema came to see the medicine chest, read the inventory in the notebook, and told them that they were learning a lot of useful things. It occurred to her or to Nino (who always got excited and wanted to show off in front of Rema) to assemble an herbarium. As it was possible that morning to go down to the clover garden, they went about collecting samples and by nightfall they had both their bedroom floors filled with leaves and flowers on bits of paper, there was hardly room to step. Before going to bed, Isabel noted: "Leaf #74: green, heart-shaped, with brown spots." It annoyed her a little that almost all the leaves were green, nearly all smooth, and nearly all lanceolate.

The day they went out ant-hunting she saw the farmhands. She knew the foreman and the head groom because they brought reports to the house. But these other younger hands stood there against the side of the sheds with an air of siesta, yawning once in a while and watching the kids play. One of them asked Nino, "Why'ya collectin' all them bugs?" and tapped him on top of his head with all the curls, using two fingers. Isabel would have liked Nino to lose his temper, to show that he was the boss's son. They already had the bottle crawling with ants and on the bank of the brook they ran across a bug with an enormous hard shell and stuck him in the bottle too, to see what would happen. The idea of an ant-farm they'd gotten out of *The Treasure of Youth,* and Luis loaned them a big, deep glass tank. As they left, both of them carrying it off, Isabel heard him say to Rema, "Better this way, they'll be quiet in the house." Also it seemed to her that Rema sighed. Before dropping off to sleep, when faces appear in the darkness, she remembered again the Kid going out onto the porch for a smoke, thin, humming to himself, saw Rema who was bringing him out coffee and he made a mistake taking the cup so clumsily that he caught Rema's fingers while trying to get the cup, Isabel had seen from the dining room Rema pulling her hand back and the Kid was barely able to keep the cup from falling and laughed at the tangle. Black ants better than the red ones: bigger, more ferocious. Afterward let loose a pile of red ones, watch the war from outside the glass, all very safe. Except they didn't fight. Made two anthills, one in each corner of the glass tank. They consoled one another by studying the distinctive habits, a special notebook for each kind of ant. But almost sure they would fight, look through the glass at war without quarter, and just one notebook.

Rema didn't like to spy on them, she passed by the bedrooms some-times and would see them with the ant-farm beside the window, impas-sioned and important. Nino was particularly good at pointing out imme-diately any new galleries, and Isabel enlarged the diagram traced in ink on double pages. On Luis' advice they collected black ants only, and the ant-farm was already enormous, the ants appeared to be furious and worked until nightfall, excavating and moving earth with a thousand methods and maneuvers, the careful rubbing of feelers and feet, abrupt fits of fury or vehemence, concentrations and dispersals for no apparent rea-son. Isabel no longer knew what to take notes on, little by little she put the notebook aside and hours would pass in studying and forgetting what had been discovered. Nino began to want to go back to the garden, he men-tioned the hammocks and the colts. Isabel was somewhat contemptuous of him for that. The ant-farm was worth the whole of Los Horneros, and it gave her immense pleasure to think that the ants came and went without fear of any tiger, sometimes she tried to imagine a tiny little tiger like an eraser, roaming the galleries of the ant-farm; maybe that was why the dispersals and concentrations. And now she liked to rehearse the real world in the one of glass, now that she felt a little like a prisoner, now that she was forbidden to go down to the dining room until Rema said so.

She pushed her nose against one of the glass sides, promptly all atten-tion because she liked for them to look at her; she heard Rema stop in the doorway, just silent, looking at her. She heard those things with such a sharp brightness when it was Rema.

"You're alone here? Why?"

"Nino went off to the hammocks. This big one must be a queen, she's huge."

Rema's apron was reflected in the glass. Isabel saw one of her hands slightly raised, with the reflection it looked as if it were inside the ant-farm; suddenly she thought about the same hand offering a cup of coffee to the Kid, but now there were ants running along her fingers, ants instead of the cup and the Kid's hand pressing the fingertips.

"Take your hand out, Rema," she asked.

"My hand?"

"Now it's all right. The reflection was scaring the ants."

"Ah. It's all right in the dining room now, you can go down."

"Later. Is the Kid mad at you, Rema?"

The hand moved across the glass like a bird through a window. It looked to Isabel as though the ants were really scared this time, that they ran from the reflection. You couldn't see anything now, Rema had left, she went down the hall as if she were escaping something. Isabel felt afraid of the question herself, a dull fear, made no sense, maybe it wasn't the question but seeing Rema run off that way, or the once-more-clear empty glass where the galleries emptied out and twisted like twitching fingers inside the soil.

It was siesta one afternoon, watermelon, handball against the wall which overlooked the brook, and Nino was terrific, catching shots that looked impossible and climbing up to the roof on a vine to get the ball loose where it was caught between two tiles. A son of one of the farmhands came out from beside the willows and played with them, but he was slow and clumsy and shots got away from him. Isabel could smell the terebinth leaves and at one moment, returning with a backhand an insidious low shot of Nino's, she felt the summer's happiness very deep inside her. For the first time she understood her being at Los Horneros, the vacation, Nino. She thought of the ant-farm up there and it was an oozy dead thing, a horror of legs trying to get out, false air, poisonous. She hit the ball angrily, happily, she bit off a piece of a terebinth leaf with her teeth, bitter, she spit it out in disgust, happy for the first time really, and at last, under the sun in the country.

The window glass fell like hail. It was in the Kid's study. They saw him rise in his shirtsleeves and the broad black eyeglasses.

"Filthy pains-in-the-ass!"

The little peon fled. Nino set himself alongside Isabel, she felt him shaking with the same wind as the willows.

"We didn't mean to do it, uncle."

"Honest, Kid, we didn't mean to do it."

He wasn't there any longer.

She had asked Rema to take away the ant-farm and Rema promised her. After, chatting while she helped her hang up her clothes and get into her pajamas, they forgot. When Rema put out the light, Isabel felt the presence of the ants, Rema went down the hall to say goodnight to Nino who was still crying and repentant, but she didn't have the nerve to call her back again. Rema would have thought that she was just a baby. She decided to go to sleep immediately, and was wider awake than ever. When the moment came when there were faces in the darkness, she saw her mother and Inés looking at one another and smiling like accomplices and pulling on gloves of phosphorescent yellow. She saw Nino weeping, her mother and Inés with the gloves on that now were violet hairdos that twirled and twirled round their heads, Nino with enormous vacant eyes—maybe from having cried too much—and thought that now she would see Rema and Luis, she wanted to see them, she didn't want to see the Kid, but she saw the Kid without his glasses with the same tight face that he'd had when he began hitting Nino and Nino fell backwards until he was against the wall and looked at him as though expecting that would finish it, and the Kid continued to whack back and forth across his face with a loose soft slap that sounded moist, until Rema intruded herself in front of Nino and the Kid laughed, his face almost touching Rema's, and then they heard Luis returning and saying from a distance that now they could go into the dining room. Everything had happened so fast because Nino had been there and Rema had come to tell them not to leave the living room until Luis found out what room the tiger was in and she stayed there with them watching the game of checkers. Nino won and Rema praised him, then Nino was so happy that he put his arms around her waist and wanted to kiss her. Rema had bent down, laughing, and Nino kissed her on the nose and eyes, the two of them laughing and Isabel also, they were so happy playing. They didn't see the Kid coming, when he got up to them he grabbed Nino, jerked at him, said something about the ball breaking the window in his room and started to hit him, he looked at Rema while he hit him, he seemed furious with Rema and she defied him with her eyes for a moment. Terrified, Isabel saw her face up to him, then she stepped in between to protect Nino. The whole evening meal was a deceit, a lie, Luis thought that Nino was crying from having taken a tumble, the Kid looked at Rema as if to order her to shut up, Isabel saw him now with his hard, handsome mouth, very red lips; in the dimness they were even more scarlet, she could see his teeth, barely revealed, glittering. A puffed cloud emerged from his teeth, a green triangle, Isabel blinked her eyes to wipe out the images and Inés and her mother appeared again with their yellow gloves; she gazed at them for a moment, then thought of the ant-farm: that was there and you couldn't see it; the yellow gloves were not there and she saw them instead as if in bright sunlight. It seemed almost curious to her, she couldn't make the ant-farm come out, instead she felt it as a kind of weight there, a chunk of thick, live space. She felt it so strongly that she reached about for the matches, the night-lamp. The ant-farm leaped from the nothingness, wrapped in shifting shadow. Isabel lifted the lamp and came closer. Poor ants, they were going to think that the sun was up. When she could see one of the sides, she was frightened; the ants had been working in all that blackness. She watched them swarm up and down, in silence, so visible, palpable. They were working away inside there as though they had not yet lost their hope of getting out.

It was almost always the foreman who kept them advised of the tiger's movements; Luis had the greatest confidence in him, and since he passed almost the whole day working in his study, he neither emerged nor let those who came down from the next floor move about until don Roberto sent in his report. But they had to rely on one another also. Busy with the household chores inside, Rema knew exactly what was happening upstairs and down. At other times, it was the children who brought the news to the Kid or to Luis. Not that they'd seen anything, just that don Roberto had run into them outside, indicated the tiger's whereabouts to them, and they came back in to pass it on. They believed Nino without question, Isabel less, she was new and might make a mistake. Later, though, since she always went about with Nino stuck to her skirt, they finally believed both of them equally. That was in the morning and afternoon; at night it was the Kid who went out to check and see that the dogs were tied up or that no live coals had been left close to the houses. Isabel noticed that he carried the revolver and sometimes a stick with a silver handle.

She hadn't wanted to ask Rema about it because Rema clearly found it something so obvious and necessary; to pester her would have meant looking stupid, and she treasured her pride before another woman. Nino was easy, he talked straight. Everything clear and obvious when he explained it. Only at night, if she wanted to reconstruct that clarity and obviousness, Isabel noticed that the important reasons were still missing. She learned quickly what was really important: if you wanted to leave the house, or go down to the dining room, to Luis' study, or to the library, find out first. "You have to trust don Roberto," Rema had said. Her and Nino as well. She hardly ever asked Luis because he hardly ever knew. The Kid, who always knew, she never asked. And so it was always easy, the life organized itself for Isabel with a few more obligations as far as her movements went, and a few less when it came to clothes, meals, the time to go to bed. A real summer, the way it should be all year round.

. . . *see you soon. They're all fine. I have an ant-farm with Nino and we play and are making a very large herbarium. Rema sends her kisses, she is fine. I think she's sad, the same as Luis who is very nice. I think that Luis has some trouble although he studies all the time. Rema gave me some lovely colored handkerchiefs, Inés is going to like them. Mama, it's nice here and I'm enjoying myself with Nino and don Roberto, he's the foreman and tells us when we can go out and where, one afternoon he was almost wrong and sent us to the edge of the brook, when a farmhand came to tell us no, you should have seen how awful don Roberto felt and then Rema, she picked Nino up and was kissing him, and she squeezed me so hard. Luis was going about saying that the house was not for children, and Nino asked him who the children were, and everybody laughed, even the Kid laughed. Don Roberto is the foreman.*

If you come to get me you could stay a few days and be with Rema and cheer her up. I think that she . . .

But to tell her mother that Rema cried at night, that she'd heard her crying going down the hall, staggering a little, stop at Nino's door, continue, go downstairs (she must have been drying her eyes) and Luis' voice in the distance: "What's the matter, Rema? Aren't you well?", a silence, the whole house like an enormous ear, then a murmur and Luis' voice again: "He's a bastard, a miserable bastard . . ." almost as though he were coldly confirming a fact, making a connection, a fate.

. . . is a little ill, it would do her good if you came and kept her company. I have to show you the herbarium and some stones from the brook the farmhands brought me. Tell Inés . . .

It was the kind of night she liked, insects, damp, reheated bread, and custard with Greek raisins. The dogs barked constantly from the edge of the brook, and an enormous praying mantis flew in and landed on the mantelpiece and Nino went to fetch the magnifying glass; they trapped it with a wide-mouthed glass and poked at it to make it show the color of its wings.

"Throw that bug away," Rema pleaded. "They make me so squeamish."

"It's a good specimen," Luis admitted. "Look how he follows my hand with his eyes. The only insect that can turn its head."

"What a goddamned night," the Kid said from behind his newspaper.

Isabel would have liked to cut the mantis' head off, a good snip with the scissors, and see what would happen.

"Leave it in the glass," she asked Nino. "Tomorrow we can put it in the ant-farm and study it."

It got hotter, by ten-thirty you couldn't breathe. The children stayed with Rema in the inside dining room, the men were in their studies. Nino was the first to say that he was getting sleepy.

"Go on up by yourself, I'll come see you later. Everything is all right upstairs." And Rema took him about the waist with that expression he liked so well.

"Tell us a story, Aunt Rema?"

"Another night."

They were down there alone, with the mantis which looked at them. Luis came to say his goodnights to them, muttering something about the hour that children ought to go to bed; Rema smiled at him when she kissed him.

"Growly bear," she said, and Isabel, bent over the mantis' glass, thought that she'd never seen Rema kissing the Kid or a praying mantis that was so so green. She moved the glass a little and the mantis grew frantic. Rema came over to tell her to go to bed.

"Throw that bug away, it's horrible."

"Rema, tomorrow."

She asked her to come up and say goodnight to her. The Kid had the door of his study left partly open and was pacing up and down in his shirtsleeves, the collar open. He whistled to her as she passed.

"I'm going to bed, Kid."

"Listen to me: tell Rema to make me a nice cold lemonade and bring it to me here. Then you go right up to your room."

Of course she was going to go up to her room, she didn't see why he had to tell her to. She went back to the dining room to tell Rema, she saw her hesitate.

"Don't go upstairs yet. I'm going to make the lemonade and you take it down yourself."

"He said for you . . ."

"Please."

Isabel sat down at the side of the table. Please. There were clouds of insects whirling under the carbide lamp, she would have stayed there for hours looking at nothing, repeating: Please, please. Rema, Rema. How she loved her, and that unhappy voice, bottomless, without any possible reason, the voice of sadness itself. Please. Rema, Rema . . . A feverish heat reached her face, a wish to throw herself at Rema's feet, to let Rema pick her up in her arms, a wish to die looking at her and Rema be sorry for her, pass her cool, delicate fingers through her hair, over the eyelids . . .

Now she was holding out a green tumbler full of ice and sliced lemons.

"Take it to him."

"Rema . . ."

Rema seemed to tremble, she turned her back on the table so that she shouldn't see her eyes.

"I'll throw the mantis out right now, Rema."

One sleeps poorly in the viscous heat and all that buzzing of mosquitoes. Twice she was on the point of getting up, to go out into the hall or to go to the bathroom to put cold water on her face and wrists. But she could hear someone walking, downstairs, someone was going from one side of the dining room to the other, came to the bottom of the stairway, turned around ... They weren't the confused, long steps of Luis' walk, nor was it Rema's. How warm the Kid had felt that night, how he'd drunk the lemonade in great gulps. Isabel saw him drinking the tumblerful, his hands holding the green tumbler, the yellow discs wheeling in the water under the lamp; but at the same time she was sure the Kid had never drunk the lemonade, that he was still staring at the glass she had brought him, over to the table, like someone looking at some kind of infinite naughtiness. She didn't want to think about the Kid's smile, his going to the door as though he were about to go into the dining room for a look, his slow turning back.

"She was supposed to bring it to me. You, I told you to go up to your room."

And the only thing that came to her mind was a very idiot answer: "It's good and cold, Kid."

And the tumbler, green as the praying mantis.

Nino was the first one up, it was his idea that they go down to the brook to look for snails. Isabel had hardly slept at all, she remembered rooms full of flowers, tinkling bells, hospital corridors, sisters of charity, thermometers in jars of bichlorate, scenes from her first communion, Inés, the broken bicycle, the restaurant in the railroad station, the gypsy costume when she had been eight. Among all this, like a delicate breeze between the pages of an album, she found herself wide awake, thinking of things that were not flowers, bells, hospital corridors. She got out of bed grudgingly, washed her face hard, especially the ears. Nino said that it was ten o'clock and that the tiger was in the music room, so that they could go down to the brook right away. They went downstairs together, hardly saying good morning to Luis and the Kid who were both reading with their doors open. You could find the snails mostly on the bank nearest the wheatfields. Nino moved along blaming Isabel for her distraction, said she was no kind of friend at all and wasn't helping form the collection. She saw him suddenly as so childish, such a little boy with his snails and his leaves.

She came back first, when they raised the flag at the house for lunch. Don Roberto came from his inspection and Isabel asked him the same question as always. Then Nino was coming up slowly, carrying the box of snails and the rakes; Isabel helped him put the rakes away on the porch and they went in together. Rema was standing there, white and silent. Nino put a blue snail into her hand.

"The nicest one, for you."

The Kid was eating already, the newspaper beside him, there was hardly enough room for Isabel to rest her arm. Luis was the last to come from his room, contented as he always was at noon. They ate, Nino was talking about the snails, the snail eggs in the reeds, the collection itself, the sizes and the colors. He was going to kill them by himself, it hurt Isabel to do it, they'd put them to dry on a zinc sheet. After the coffee came and Luis looked at them with the usual question, Isabel got up first to look for don Roberto, even though don Roberto had already told her before. She made the round of the porch and when she came in again, Rema and Nino had their heads together over the snail box, it was like a family photograph, only Luis looked up at her and she said, "It's in the Kid's study," and stayed watching how the Kid shrugged his shoulders, annoyed, and Rema who touched a snail with a fingertip, so delicately that her finger even seemed part snail. Afterwards, Rema got up to go look for more sugar, and Isabel tailed along behind her babbling until they came back in laughing from a joke they'd shared in the pantry. When Luis said he had no tobacco and ordered Nino to look in his study, Isabel challenged him that she'd find the cigarettes first and they went out together. Nino won, they came back in running and pushing, they almost bumped into the Kid going to the library to read his newspaper, complaining because he couldn't use his study. Isabel came over to look at the snails, and Luis waiting for her to light his cigarette as always saw that she was lost, studying the snails which were beginning to ooze out slowly and move about, looking at Rema suddenly, but dropping her like a flash, captivated by the snails, so much so that she didn't move at the Kid's first scream, they were all running and she was still standing over the snails as if she did not hear the Kid's new choked cry, Luis beating against the library door, don Roberto coming in with the dogs, the Kid's moans amid the furious barking of the dogs, and Luis saying over and over again, "But if it was in his study! She said it was in his own study!", bent over the snails willowy as fingers, like Rema's fingers maybe, or it was Rema's hand on her shoulder, made her raise her head to look at her, to stand looking at her for an eternity, broken by her ferocious sob into Rema's skirt, her unsettled happiness, and Rema running her hand over her hair, quieting her with a soft squeeze of her fingers and a murmuring against her ear, a stuttering as of gratitude, as of an unnameable acquiescence.

1951

Secret Weapons

Translated by Paul Blackburn

STRANGE HOW PEOPLE are under the impression that making a bed is exactly the same as making a bed, that to shake hands is always the same as shaking hands, that opening a can of sardines is to open the same can of sardines *ad infinitum*. "But everything's an exception," Pierre is thinking, smoothing out the worn blue bedspread heavy-handedly. "Yesterday it rained, today there was sun, yesterday I was gloomy, today Michèle is coming. The only invariable is that I'll never get this bed to look decent." Not important, women enjoy disorder in a bachelor's room, they can smile (mother shining out from every tooth), they fix the curtains, change the location of a chair or flowerpot, say to put this table where there isn't any light wouldn't occur to anyone but you. Michèle will probably say things like that, walk about touching and moving books and lamps, and he'll let her, stretched out on the bed or humped down into the old sofa, watching her through a wreath of Gauloise smoke, and wanting her.

"Six o'clock, the critical hour," Pierre thinks. The golden hour when the whole neighborhood of Saint-Sulpice begins to alter, ready itself for the night. Soon the girls will begin to emerge from the notary's office, Madame Lenôtre's husband will thump his leg up the stairs, the sisters' voices on the sixth floor will be audible, they're inseparable when the hour arrives to buy a fresh loaf of bread and the paper. Michèle can't be much longer, unless she gets lost or hangs around in the streets on the way, she has this extraordinary capacity to stop any place and take herself a trip through the small particular worlds of the shop windows. Afterward, she will tell him about: a stuffed bear that winds up, a Couperin record, a bronze chain with a blue stone, Stendhal's complete works, the summer fashions. Completely understandable reasons for arriving a bit late. Another Gauloise, then, another shot of cognac. Now he feels like listening to some MacOrlan songs, feeling around absently among the piles of papers and notebooks. I'll bet Roland or Babette borrowed the record; they ought to tell somebody when they're taking something. Why doesn't Michèle get here? He sits on the edge of the bed and wrinkles the bedspread. Oh great, now he'll have to pull it from one side to the other, back, the damned edge of the pillow'll stick out. He smells strongly of tobacco, Michèle's going to wrinkle her nose and tell him he smells strongly of tobacco. Hundreds and hundreds of Gauloises smoked up on hundreds and hundreds of days: his thesis, a few girlfriends, two liver attacks, novels, boredom. Hundreds and hundreds of Gauloises? He's always surprised to find himself hung up over trifles, stressing the importance of details. He remembers old neckties he threw into the garbage ten years ago, the color of a stamp from the Belgian Congo, his prize from a whole childhood of collecting stamps. As if at the back of his head he kept an exact memory of how many cigarettes he'd smoked in his life, how each one had tasted, at what moment he'd set the match to it, where he'd thrown the butt away. Maybe the absurd numbers that appear sometimes in his dreams are the top of the iceberg of this implacable accounting. "But then God exists," Pierre thinks. The mirror on the wardrobe gives him back his smile, obliging him as usual to recompose his face, to throw back the mop of black hair that Michèle is always threatening to cut off. Why doesn't Michèle get here? "Because she doesn't want to come to my room," Pierre thinks. But to have the power to cut off the forelock someday, she'll have to come to his room and lie down on his bed. Delilah pays a high price, you don't get to a man's hair for less than that. Pierre tells himself that he's stupid for having thought that Michèle doesn't want to come to his room. He thinks it soundlessly, as if from far off. Thought at times seems to have to make its way through countless barriers, to resolve itself, to make itself known. It's idiotic to have imagined that Michèle doesn't want to come up to his room. If she isn't here it's because she's standing absorbed in front of a hardware or some other kind of store window, captivated by a tiny porcelain seal or a Tsao-Wu-Ki print. He seems to see her there, and at the same time he notices that he's imagining a double-barreled shotgun, just as he's inhaling the cigarette smoke and feels as though he's been pardoned for having done something stupid. There's nothing strange about a double-barreled shotgun, but what could a double-barreled shotgun and that feeling of missing something, what could you do with it at this hour and in his room? He doesn't like this time of day when everything turns lilac, grey. He reaches his arm out lazily to turn on the table lamp. Why doesn't Michèle get here? Too late for her to come now, useless to go on waiting for her. Really, he'll have to believe that she doesn't want to come to his room. Well, what the hell. No tragedy; have another cognac, a novel that's been started, go down and eat something at Leon's. Women won't be any different, in Enghien or Paris, young or full-blown. His theory about exceptional cases begins to fall down, the little mouse retreats before she enters the trap. What trap? One day or the next, before or after . . . He's been waiting for her since five o'clock, even if she wasn't supposed to arrive before six; he smoothed out the blue coverlet especially for her, he scrambled up on a chair feather duster in hand to detach an insignificant cobweb that wasn't hurting anybody. And it would be completely natural for her to be stepping down from the bus that very moment at Saint-Sulpice, drawing nearer his house, stopping in front of the store windows or looking at pigeons in the square. There's no reason she shouldn't want to come up to his room. Of course, there's no reason either to think of a double-barreled shotgun, or to decide that right this moment Michaux would make better reading than Graham Greene. Instant choices always bother Pierre. Impossible that everything be gratuitous, that mere chance decides for Greene against Michaux, or Michaux against Enghien, I mean, against Greene. Including confusing a place-name like Enghien with a writer like Greene . . . "It can't all be that absurd," Pierre thinks, throwing away his cigarette. "And if she doesn't come it's because something's happened; it has nothing to do with the two of us."

He goes down into the street and waits in the doorway for a bit. He sees the lights go on in the square. There's almost no one at Leon's where he sits down at an outside table and orders a beer. From where he's sitting he can still see the entranceway to his house, so if . . . Leon's talking about the Tour de France bicycle race; Nicole and her girlfriend arrive, the florist with the husky voice. The beer is ice-cold, he ought to order some sausages. In the doorway to his house the concierge's kid is playing, jumping up and down on one foot. When he gets tired he starts jumping on the other foot, not moving from the door.

"What nonsense," Michèle says. "Why shouldn't I want to go to your place, when we'd agreed on it?"

Edmond brings the eleven o'clock coffee. There's almost no one there at that hour of the morning, and Edmond dawdles beside the table so as to make some remarks about the Tour de France. Then Michèle explains what happened, what Pierre should have assumed. Her mother's frequent fainting spells, papa gets alarmed and telephones the office, grabbing a taxi home and it turns out to be nothing, a little dizziness. It's not the first time all this has happened, but you'd have to be Pierre to . . .

"I'm glad she's better now," Pierre says, feeling foolish.

He puts one hand on top of Michèle's. Michèle puts her other hand on top of Pierre's. Pierre puts his other hand on top of Michèle's. Michèle pulls her hand out from underneath and lays it on top. Pierre pulls his hand out from under and places it on hers. Michèle pulls her hand out from the bottom and presses the palm against Pierre's nose.

"Cold as a little dog's."

Pierre admits that the temperature of his nose is an insoluble enigma. "Dope," says Michèle, summing up the situation.

Pierre kisses her on the forehead, kisses her hair. As she ducks her head, he takes her chin and tilts it to make her look at him before he kisses her on the mouth. He kisses her once, twice. She smells fresh, like the shadow under trees. *Im wunderschönen Monat Mai,* he hears the melody distinctly. He wonders vaguely at remembering the words so well that make total sense to him only when translated. But he likes the tune, the words sound so well against Michèle's hair, against her wet mouth. *Im wunderschönen Monat Mai, als . . .*

Michèle's hand digs into his shoulder, her nails bite into him.

"You're hurting me," she says, pushing him off, running her fingers over her lips.

Pierre sees the marks of his teeth on the edge of her lip. He pets her cheek and kisses her again, lightly. Is Michèle angry? No, she's not. When, when are they ever going to find themselves alone? It's hard for him to understand, Michèle's explanations seem to have to do with something else. Set on the idea of her coming some day to his place, that she's going to climb five flights and come into his room, he doesn't follow that suddenly everything's solved, that Michèle's parents are going down to the farm for two weeks. Let them, all the better, because then Michèle . . . Then it hits him all at once, he sits staring at her. Michèle laughs.

"You're going to be alone at your house for fifteen days?"

"You're a dope," says Michèle. She sticks one finger out and draws invisible stars, rhomboids, gentle spirals. Of course her mother is counting on faithful Babette to stay those two weeks with her, there've been so many robberies and muggings in the suburbs. But Babette will stay in Paris as long as they want.

Pierre doesn't know the summerhouse, though he's imagined it so often that it's as though he were already in it, he goes with Michèle into a small parlor crowded with antiquated furniture, he goes up a staircase, his fingers grazing the glass ball on the banister post at the bottom. He doesn't know why he doesn't like the house, he'd rather go out into the garden, though it's hard to believe that such a small cottage would have a garden. It costs him effort to sweep away the image, to find that he's happy, that he's in the café with Michèle, that the house will be different from the one he imagines, which would depress him somewhat with its furniture and its faded carpets. "I'll have to get the motorcycle from Xavier," Pierre thinks. He'll come here to meet Michèle and they'll be in Clamart in half an hour, they'll have two weekends for excursions, I'll have to get a thermos jug and buy some Nescafé.

"Is there a glass ball at the bottom of the staircase in your house?"

"No," Michèle says, "you're confusing it with . . ."

She breaks off suddenly, as if she had something bothering her in her throat. Slumped on the stool, his head back against the tall mirror with which Edmond tries to multiply the number of tables in his café, Pierre acknowledges vaguely that Michèle is like a cat or an anonymous portrait. He's known her such a short time, maybe she finds him difficult to understand too. For one thing, just to be in love never needs an explanation, you don't have to have friends in common or to share political opinions to be in love. You always begin by thinking that there's no mystery, no matter who, it's so easy to get information: Michèle Duvernois, age twenty-four, chestnut-colored hair, grey eyes, office worker. And she also knows: Pierre Jolivet, age twenty-three, blond hair . . . But tomorrow he'll go to her home with her, half an hour's ride they'll be in Enghien. "Oh, fuck Enghien," Pierre thinks, brushing the name away as if it were a fly. They'll have fifteen days to be together, and there's a garden at the house, likely very different from the one he imagines, he'll have to ask Michèle what the garden's like, but Michèle is calling Edmond, it's after eleven-thirty, and the manager'll give her the fish-eye if he catches her coming back late.

"Stay a little longer," Pierre says. "Here come Roland and Babette. It's unbelievable how we can never be alone in this café."

"Alone?" Michèle says. "But we came here to meet them."

"I know, but even so."

Michèle shrugs, and Pierre knows that she understands and that she's sorry, too, at bottom, that friends have to put in such a punctual appearance. Babette and Roland have their usual air of quiet happiness that irritates him this time and makes him impatient. They are on the other side, sheltered by a breakwater of time; their angers and dissatisfactions belong to the world, to politics or art, not to themselves ever or to their deep relationship. Saved by force of habit, though, by the automatic gesture. Everything smooth, ironed out, numbered and filed away. Happy little pigs, poor kids, and good friends. He's on the point of not shaking the hand Roland reaches out to him, swallows his saliva, looks him in the eye, then puts a grip on his fingers as if he wanted to break them. Roland laughs and sits down opposite them; he's got the schedule from some cinematheque, they can't miss the show on Monday. "Happy piglets," Pierre gnaws away at it. All right, I'm being an idiot and unjust. But a Pudovkin film, oh come on, couldn't he look around and find something new?

"New?" Babette teases. "Something new. You're such an old man, Pierre."

No reason to not want to shake Roland's hand.

"And she had on that orange blouse and it looked so good on her," Michèle's talking.

Roland offers his pack of Gauloises around and orders coffee. No reason to not want to shake Roland's hand.

"Yes, she's a bright girl," Babette is saying.

Roland looks at Pierre and winks. Tranquil, no problems. Absolutely no problems, placid little pig. Pierre loathes their tranquillity, that Michèle can sit there talking about an orange blouse, as far from him as ever. He has nothing in common with them, he was the last one to come into their crowd, they barely tolerate him.

As she talks (it's about shoes now), Michèle runs a finger along the edge of her lips. He can't even kiss her nicely, he hurt her and Michèle is remembering. And everybody hurts him, winks at him, smiles at him, likes him very much. It's like a weight on his chest, a need to get up and go, to be alone in his room wondering why Michèle hasn't arrived, why Babette and Roland took a record without telling him.

Michèle takes one look at the clock and jumps up. They set the date for the cinematheque, Pierre pays for the coffee. He feels better, he'd like to talk a little more with Roland and Babette, says goodbye to them affectionately. Nice piglets, good friends of Michèle's.

Roland watches them going off, going into the street full of sun. He drinks his coffee slowly.

"I wonder," Roland says.

"Me too," says Babette.

"Why not, after all?"

"Sure, why not. But it would be the first time since then."

"It's about time Michèle did something with her life," Roland says. "And if you ask me, she's very much in love."

"They're both very much in love."

Roland looks thoughtful.

He's made a date with Xavier at a café in the place Saint-Michel, but he gets there much too early. He orders beer and leafs through the newspaper; he doesn't remember too clearly what he's done since he left Michèle at the door to her office. These last few months are as confused as a morning that isn't over yet and is already a mixture of fake memories, mistakes. In that remote life of his, the only absolute certainty is that he's been as close as possible to Michèle, waiting and being aware that he's not content with that, that everything's vaguely surprising, that he knows nothing about Michèle, absolutely nothing, really (she has grey eyes, five fingers on each hand, is unmarried, combs her hair like a little girl), absolutely nothing really. Well, if you know nothing about Michèle, all you have to do is not see her for a bit for the emptiness to turn into a dense, unpleasant thicket; she's afraid of you, you disgust her, at times she rejects you at the deepest moment of a kiss, she doesn't want to go to bed with you, she's horribly afraid of something, just this morning she pushed you away violently (and how lovely she was, that she crushed up against you when it was time to say goodbye, that she'd arranged everything to meet you tomorrow and go out together to her place at Enghien) and you left tooth-marks on her mouth, you were kissing her and you bit her and she bitched, she ran her fingers across her mouth and complained, not angry, just a little surprised, *als alle Knospen sprangen,* you were singing Schumann inside, you sonofabitch, you were singing while you bit her on the mouth and now you remember, besides you were going up the staircase, yes, climbing the steps, your hand grazing the glass ball on the banister post at the bottom, but Michèle had said later that there was no glass ball at her house.

Pierre slides down the bench, looking for his cigarettes. After all, Michèle does not know much about him either, she's not at all inquisitive, though she has that attentive and serious way of listening when he unburdens himself, an ability to share any given moment in life, oh anything, a cat coming out of a garage door, a storm on the Cité, a leaf of clover, a Gerry Mulligan record. Attentive, eager, and serious at the same time, listening as easily as being listened to. As though from meeting to meeting, from one conversation to the next, they've drifted into the solitude of a couple lost in the crowd, some politics, novels shared, going to the movies, kissing more passionately each time, letting his hand run down her throat and touch her breasts lightly, repeating the endless question without an answer. It's raining, let's get under that doorway; the sun's burning down on our heads, we'll go into that bookstore, tomorrow I'll introduce you to Babette, she's an old friend of mine, you'll like her. And it turns out that Babette's boyfriend is an old buddy of Xavier's who is Pierre's best friend, and the circle will start to close, sometimes at Babette and Roland's place, sometimes at Xavier's consultation room, or at night in the cafés of the Latin Quarter. Pierre will be grateful, without knowing why, that Babette and Roland are such close friends of Michèle's and that it feels as though they are protecting her discreetly without any particular reason for Michèle's needing protecting. In that group nobody talks much about the others; they like the larger subjects, politics or trials, and more than anything else to exchange satisfied looks, pass cigarettes around, sit in cafés and live their lives feeling that they're surrounded by friends. He'd been lucky that they'd accepted him and let him in; they're not easy to make friends with, and they know all the ways of discouraging newcomers. "I like them," Pierre thinks to himself, and finishes the rest of his beer. Maybe they think that he's already Michèle's lover, at least Xavier must think so; it would never occur to him that Michèle would have been able to hold him off all this time, without any definite reason, only hold him off and go on seeing him, going out together, talking or letting him talk. You can get used to some weird things, get to think that the mystery will explain itself and that you end up living inside the mystery, accepting the unacceptable, saying goodbye on street corners or in cafés when everything could be so simple, a staircase with a glass ball at the bottom of the banister, that leads to the meeting, to the very truth. But Michèle said that there isn't any glass ball.

Tall and scraggly, Xavier brings along his regular working face. He talks about some experiments, of biology as a provocation toward skepticism. He looks at his tobacco-stained middle finger. Pierre asks him:

"Does it ever happen to you, all at once thinking about things completely different from what you've been thinking?"

"Completely different is a working hypothesis, that's all," Xavier says.

"I feel pretty weird these days. Maybe you ought to give me something, you know, some kind of objectifier."

"Objectifier?" Xavier says. "There's no such thing, old buddy."

"I think too much about myself," Pierre says. "It's stupid."

"And Michèle, doesn't she objectify you?"

"Right, yesterday it so happened that . . ."

He hears himself talking, sees Xavier looking at him, sees Xavier's reflection in the mirror, the back of Xavier's neck, sees himself talking to Xavier (but why do I have to think there's a glass ball at the bottom of the banister), and from time to time notices how Xavier's head moves, a professional gesture that looks ridiculous outside a consulting room when the doctor doesn't have on the white coat that sets him on another level and confers other powers.

"Enghien," Xavier says. "Don't bother about it. I'm always confusing Le Mans with Menton. Probably due to one of your schoolteachers back in your childhood."

Im wunderschönen Monat Mai, Pierre's memory hums.

"If you aren't sleeping well, let me know, I'll give you something," Xavier says. "In any case, these fifteen days in heaven should settle you,

I'm sure of that. There's nothing like sharing a pillow, it clarifies ideas marvelously; sometimes it even gets rid of them, which is very restful."

Maybe if he worked harder, if he tired himself out more, maybe he should paint his room or make the trek to the university on foot instead of taking the bus. If he had to earn the seventy thousand francs his parents sent him every month. Leaning on the railing at Pont Neuf, he watches the barges going by underneath and feels the summer sun beating on his neck and shoulders. A bunch of girls laughing and playing, he can hear a horse trotting; a redheaded cyclist cruises past the girls with a long-drawn-out whistle, they laugh even harder, and it's as if the dry leaves were coming up to meet his face and were eating it in one single horrible black bite.

Pierre rubs his eyes, straightens up slowly. There'd not been any words, not even a vision; something between the two, an image decomposed into so many words like dry leaves on the ground (that came up to hit him smack in the face). He notices that his right hand is shaking against the railing of the bridge. He makes a fist, fights to control its trembling. Xavier will already be too far away, useless to run after him, add one more illustration to this senseless catalogue. "Dry leaves," Xavier would say, "there are no dry leaves on Pont Neuf." As if he didn't know that there were no dry leaves on Pont Neuf, that the dry leaves are at Enghien.

Now I'm going to think about you, sweetheart, only about you all night. I'm going to think only about you, it's the only way I'm conscious of myself, to hold you in the center of myself like a tree there, to loosen myself little by little from the trunk, which sustains me and guides me, to float cautiously around you, testing the air with each leaf (green, we are green, I myself and you yourself, trunk full of sap, and green leaves: green, green), without being away from you, not letting the other thing come between you and me, distract me from you, deprive me for a single second of realizing that tonight is swinging towards, into, dawn, and that there on the other side, where you live and are asleep, when it will be night again we'll arrive together and go into your house, we'll go up the porch steps, turn on the lights, pet the dog, drink coffee, we'll look for a long time at one another before I take you in my arms (hold you in the center of myself like a tree) and carry you to the stairs (but there's no glass ball at all) and we begin to go up, climb, the door's locked, but I have the key in my pocket . . .

Pierre jumps out of bed and sticks his head under the cold-water tap in the bathroom. Think only about you, but how can it be that what he's thinking is a dark, stifled desire in which Michèle is no longer Michèle (hold you in the center of myself like a tree), where he can't manage to feel her in his arms as he ascends the stairs, because he's hardly taken the first step, has seen the glass ball and is alone, he's going up the stairs alone and Michèle is upstairs, locked in, she's behind the door not knowing that he has another key in his pocket and that he's on his way up.

He dries his face, throws the window open all the way on the early morning freshness. A drunk is conducting a friendly monologue in the street, swaying as though he were floating in water as thick as paste. He's humming, going and coming back and forth, completing a sort of suspenseful and ceremonial dance in the grey light that bites into the cobblestones, the locked-up doors, little by little. *Als alle Knospen sprangen,* the words draw themselves onto Pierre's dry lips, they adhere onto the humming down in the street which has nothing to do with the melody, they come like the rest of it, they adhere to life for a moment and then there's something like bitter anxiety, holes that tip over to show through pieces that hook onto anything else, a double-barreled shotgun, a mattress of dry leaves, the drunk dancing a kind of stately pavane, with curtsies that turn into tatters and stumblings and vaguely mumbled words.

The cycle roars out the length of the rue d'Alésia. Pierre feels Michèle's fingers grab his waist tighter every time they pass a bus close or swing around a corner. When a red light stops them, he throws his head back and waits for a caress, a kiss on the hair.

"I'm not afraid any more," Michèle says. "You ride it very well. You have to take the next right, now."

The summerhouse is lost among dozens of houses that look much the same on a hill just beyond Clamart. The word "summerhouse" for Pierre sounds like a hideaway, an assurance that everything will be quiet and isolated, that it'll have a garden with wicker chairs and, at night, maybe a firefly.

"Do you have fireflies in your garden?"

"I don't think so. You've got such odd ideas."

It's hard to talk on the motorcycle, you have to concentrate on the traffic, and Pierre's tired, he got only a few hours of sleep toward morning. He'll have to remember to take the pills Xavier gave him, but of course he won't remember, and besides, who'll need them? He throws his head back, and grumbles when Michèle is slow in kissing him, Michèle laughs and runs her hand through his hair. "Just cut out the nonsense," Xavier had said, clearly disconcerted. Of course it'll pass, two tablets before bedtime, glass of water. How does Michèle sleep?

"Michèle, how do you sleep?"

"Very well," Michèle says. "Sometimes I have nightmares like anyone else."

Right. Like anyone else, except that when she wakes up, she knows she's left the dream back there, without getting it mixed up with the street noises, friends' faces, something that infiltrates the most innocent occupations (but Xavier said that everything'd be all right, two tablets), she'd sleep with her face buried in the pillow, legs drawn up a little, light breathing, now he's going to see her like that, hold her sleeping like that against his body, listening to her breathe, defenseless, naked, when he holds her down by the hair with one hand, and the yellow light, red light, stop.

He brakes so violently that Michèle screams and then sits very quietly in back, as if she were ashamed of having screamed. One foot on the ground, Pierre twists his head around and grins at someone not Michèle, and stays lost in the air, smiling. He knows that the light's going to turn green, there's a truck and a car behind the motorcycle, green light, a truck and a car behind the cycle, someone begins to lean on the horn, twice, three times.

"What's the matter with you?" Michèle says.

The driver of the car, as he passes them, hurls an insult at him and Pierre pulls out slowly. Where were we, he was going to see her as she is, naked and defenseless. We said that, we had gotten to the exact moment when he was seeing her sleep defenseless and naked, that is to say, there's no reason to imagine, even for a moment, that it's going to be necessary to . . . Right, I heard you, first to the left and then left again. There? That slate roof? There are pines, hey great, what a nice house you have, garden, pines, and your folks gone off to the farm, I can hardly believe it, Michèle, something like this is almost unbelievable.

Bobby, who's met them with a loud volley of barks, saves face by sniffing conscientiously at Pierre's pants as he's pushing the motorcycle up to the porch. Michèle's already gone into the house, raises the blinds, goes back to get Pierre, who's looking at the walls and finding that none of this resembles what he had imagined.

"There ought to be three steps here," Pierre says. "And this living room, but of course . . . Don't pay any attention to me, one always figures on something other than . . . even the details, the furniture. Ever happen to you?"

"Sure, at times," Michèle says. "Pierre, I'm hungry. No, Pierre, now listen, be good and help me out; we'll have to cook up something."

"Sweetheart."

"Open that window, let the sun in. Just stay steady, Bobby will think that you're . . ."

"Michèle . . ."

"No, now let me go up and change. Take off your jacket if you want, there are drinks in that cabinet. I don't know anything about liquor."

He sees her run off, climb the stairs, disappear around the landing. There are drinks in the cabinet, she doesn't know anything about that. The living room is wide and dark, Pierre's hand caresses the newel post at the bottom of the banister. Michèle told him, but it's like an irrational disappointment, all right, there's no glass ball then.

Michèle comes down in old slacks and an unlikely blouse.

"You look like a mushroom," Pierre says with that tenderness every man shows toward a woman wearing clothes much too big for her. "Aren't you going to show me the house?"

"If you want," Michèle says. "Didn't you find the drinks? Wait, never mind, you're helpless."

They take their glasses into the living room and sit on the sofa facing the half-open window. Bobby leaps about hoping for attention, then lies down on the rug and watches them.

"He took to you right away," Michèle says, licking the rim of her glass. "You like my house?"

"No. It's gloomy, middle class, and stuffed with abominable furniture. But you're here, with those terrible pants on."

He caresses her throat, pulls her against him, kisses her on the mouth. They kiss each other on the mouth, the heat of Michèle's hand burns into Pierre, they kiss one another on the mouth, they slide down a little, but Michèle moans and tries to untangle herself, murmurs something he doesn't get. Confusedly, he thinks that the most difficult will be to cover her mouth, he doesn't want her to pass out. He lets go of her abruptly, looks at his hands as if they weren't his own, hearing Michèle's quick breathing, Bobby's muted growling from the rug.

"You're going to drive me out of my head," Pierre says, and the extravagance of the words is less painful than what has just happened. A compulsion, an irresistible desire to cover her mouth so that she won't pass out. He stretches out his hand and strokes Michèle's cheek from a distance, he agrees to everything, to eat whatever there is, yes, he'll have to choose the wine, that it's very hot next to the window.

Michèle has her own way of eating, mixing the cheese with the anchovies in oil, the salad and bits of crabmeat. Pierre drinks white wine, looks at her and smiles. If he married her, he'd drink his white wine at that table every day, and he'd look at her and smile.

"It's curious," Pierre says. "We've never mentioned the war years."

"The less we talk . . ." says Michèle, cleaning up her plate.

"I know, but memories come back sometimes. For me it wasn't too bad, after all, we were children then. Like an endless vacation, totally absurd, and almost fun."

"It was no vacation for me," Michèle says. "It rained all the time."

"Rained?"

"Here," she says, touching her forehead. "In front of my eyes, behind my eyes. Everything was damp, everything felt damp and sweaty."

"Did you live in this house?"

"At the beginning, yes. Later, during the occupation, they took me down to my aunt and uncle's in Enghien."

Pierre doesn't see that the match is burning down between his fingers, his mouth opens, he jerks his hand and swears. Michèle smiles, happy to be able to change the subject. When she gets up to fetch the fruit, Pierre lights the cigarette and inhales as if he were suffocating, but it's already passed, everything has an explanation if you look for it, Michèle must have mentioned Enghien lots of times during their talks at the café, those phrases which seem insignificant and are quickly forgotten, and later turn out to be the subjects of a dream or a fantasy. A peach, yes, thank you, but peeled. Ah, terribly sorry, but women have always peeled his peaches, and no reason for Michèle to be an exception.

"Women. If they peeled your peaches for you, they were as stupid as I am. You'd be better off grinding the coffee."

"Then you lived in Enghien," Pierre says, watching Michèle's hands with the vague distaste that watching a fruit being peeled always gives him. "What did your old man do during the war?"

"Oh, nothing much, we just lived, hoping that it would all be over soon."

"The Germans didn't bother you at all?"

"No," Michèle says, turning the peach with her wet fingers.

"It's the first time you've mentioned to me that you lived in Enghien."

"I don't like to talk about those days," Michèle says.

"But you must have talked about it once," Pierre says argumentatively. "I don't know how I knew, but I knew you lived in Enghien."

The peach falls onto the plate and pieces of the skin stick to its flesh. Michèle cleans the peach with a knife and Pierre feels the distaste again, starts grinding the coffee as hard as he can. Why doesn't she say something? She looks like she's suffering, busy cleaning the horrible runny peach. Why doesn't she talk? She's full of words, all you have to do is look at her hands, or the nervous flutter of her eyelids that turns into a kind of tic sometimes, all of one side of her face rises slightly, then goes back, he remembers once on a bench in the Luxembourg gardens, he noticed that the tic always coincides with a moment of uneasiness or a silence.

Michèle is preparing the coffee, her back to Pierre, who uses the butt of one cigarette to light another. They go back into the living room, carrying the porcelain cups with the blue design on them. The smell of the coffee makes them feel better, they look at one another, surprised by the period of silence and what went before it; they exchange a few casual words, looking at one another and smiling, they drink the coffee distract-edly, the way you drink love potions that tie you forever. Michèle has partly closed the shutters and a warm, greenish light filters in from the garden and wraps around them like the cigarette smoke and the cognac that Pierre is sipping, lost in a mild loneliness. Bobby is sleeping on the rug, trembling and sighing.

"He dreams all the time," Michèle says. "Sometimes he barks and wakes up all at once, then looks at all of us as if he'd just been in great pain. And he's not much more than a puppy . . ."

The pleasure of being there, of feeling so good in that moment, just to close the eyes and sigh, like Bobby, to run his hand through his hair, once, twice, feeling the hand in his hair almost as though it were not his own, the delicate tickle as it touched the back of his neck, relaxed. When he opens his eyes he sees Michèle's face, her mouth half open, her face white as a sheet. He looks at her, not understanding, a cognac glass is rolling across the rug. Pierre is standing in front of the mirror, he sort of likes it, his hair parted in the middle like a silent-film star. Why does Michèle have to cry. She isn't crying, but hands over the face always means someone's crying. He pulls them apart roughly, kisses her on the neck, searches for her mouth. Words are born, his, hers, like little animals looking for one another, a meeting prolonged with caresses, the smell of siesta, the house empty, the stairway waiting with a glass ball on the newel post, bottom of the banister. Pierre would like to lift Michèle into the air, run upstairs, he has the key in his pocket, he'll go into the bedroom, stretch himself out upon her, feel her shiver, begin sluggishly to undo ties, buttons, but there isn't any glass ball on the newel post, it's all far off and horrible, Michèle there beside him, so far away and weeping, her face crying between the wet hands, her body that breathes and is afraid and rejects him.

Falling to his knees, he puts his head in Michèle's lap. Hours pass, a minute or two goes by, time is something filled with whips and spittle.

Michèle's fingers caress Pierre's hair, and he sees her face again, a smile peeping through, Michèle's fingers are combing his hair, it sort of hurts him when she pushes his hair back, then she bends over and kisses him and smiles.

"You gave me a scare, it seemed to me for a minute that . . . Oh, I'm so stupid, but you were . . . you looked different."

"Who did you see?"

"Nobody," Michèle answers.

Pierre crouches down, waiting, now there's something, like a door swinging, ready to open. Michèle breathes deeply, something like a swimmer waiting for the starter's gun.

"I was frightened because . . . I don't know, you made me think of that . . ."

It swings, the door swings open, the swimmer, she's waiting for the shot to dive in. Time stretches like a piece of rubber, then Pierre reaches out his arms and imprisons Michèle, raises himself to her and kisses her passionately, his hands reaching under her blouse to find her breasts, to hear her moan, he moans too kissing her, come, come on now, trying to pick her up (there are fifteen stairs and the door's on the right), hearing Michèle's moan, her useless protest, he stands up holding her in his arms, he can't wait any longer, now, right this minute, it won't do her any good to try to grasp the glass ball or the banister (but there isn't any glass ball at the banister), all the same he has to carry her upstairs and then like a bitch, all of him is a single knot of muscle, like the bitch that she is, she'll learn, oh Michèle, oh my love, don't cry like that, don't be sad, love, don't let me fall again into that black pit, how could I have thought that, don't cry Michèle.

"Put me down," Michèle says in a low voice, struggling to get loose. She has finally pushed him away, looks at him for a moment as if he were someone else and runs out of the living room, closes the kitchen door, a key turns in the lock, Bobby is barking in the garden.

The mirror shows Pierre a smooth, expressionless face, arms hanging like rags, a shirttail outside the trousers. He rearranges his clothes mechanically, still looking at himself in his reflection. His throat is so tight that the brandy burns his mouth, refuses to go down, so he forces himself and drinks directly from the bottle, swallowing interminably. Bobby has stopped barking, there's a silence of siesta about the place, the light grows greener and greener in the house. A cigarette between his too-dry lips, he goes out onto the porch, down into the garden, walks past the motorcycle and toward the back. There's an odor of bees buzzing, of a mattress of pine needles, and now Bobby has begun to bark among the trees, is barking at him, has suddenly started to growl and bark without coming too close, but each time a bit closer, and barking at him.

The rock catches him in the middle of his back; Bobby lets out a howl and runs off, begins to bark again from a safe distance. Pierre takes aim slowly and lands one on a back leg. Bobby hides in the underbrush. "I have to find some place to think," Pierre tells himself. "I have to find a place to hide and think right now." His shoulder slides down the trunk of a pine, he lowers himself slowly. Michèle is watching him from the kitchen window. She must have seen me throwing stones at the dog, she's looking at me as though she didn't see me, she's watching me and not crying, she's not saying anything, she looks so alone at the window, I have to go to her and be nice, I want to be good, I want to take her hand and kiss her fingers, each finger, skin so soft.

"What are we playing, Michèle?"

"I hope you didn't injure him."

"I threw a stone just to scare him. He acted like he didn't know me, same as you."

"Don't talk nonsense."

"And you, don't lock doors with keys."

Michèle lets him in, accepts without resisting the arm he takes her around the waist with. The living room is darker, you can almost not see the bottom of the stairs.

"Forgive me," Pierre says. "I can't explain it to you, it's so stupid."

Michèle picks up the brandy glass from the floor and corks the bottle of cognac. It's getting hotter all the time, as though the house were breathing heavily through their mouths. A handkerchief that smells of moss wipes the sweat off Pierre's forehead. Oh Michèle, how can we go on like this, not talking to one another, not trying to figure this thing out that breaks us up every time we start . . . Yes, sweet, I'll sit beside you, I won't be stupid, I'll kiss you, lose myself in your hair, your throat, and you'll understand that there's no reason . . . yes, you'll understand that when I want to take you in my arms and carry you with me, go up to your bedroom, I don't want to hurt you, your head leaning on my shoulder . . .

"No, Pierre, no. Not today, love, please."

"Michèle, Michèle . . ."

"Please."

"Why, tell me why?"

"I don't know, forgive me . . . Don't blame yourself, it's all my fault. But we have time, so much time . . ."

"Let's not wait any more, Michèle, now."

"No, Pierre, not today."

"But you promised me," Pierre says feeling stupid. "We came out here . . . After all this time, waiting so long so that you'd love me a little . . . I don't know what I'm saying, it all comes out so dirty when I say . . ."

"If you could forgive me, if I . . ."

"How can I forgive you when you don't talk, I hardly know you? What's there to forgive?"

Bobby growls out on the porch. Their clothes are stuck to them with the heat, the tick-tock of the clock sticks to them, the hair sticks to Michèle's forehead, she's slumped down on the sofa looking at Pierre.

"I don't know you very well either, but that's not it, you're going to think I'm crazy."

Bobby growls again.

"Years ago . . ." Michèle says, and closes her eyes. "We were living in Enghien, I already told you that. I think I mentioned that we were living in Enghien. Don't look at me like that."

"I'm not looking at you," Pierre says.

"Yes you are, it hurts."

But that's not so, how can he hurt her by hanging on her words, unmoving, waiting for her to go on, watching her lips barely move, now it's going to happen, she's going to join her hands and beg, a flower of delight opening while she pleads, wrestling and weeping in his arms, a damp flower that's opening, the pleasure of feeling her struggling in vain . . . Bobby comes in, dragging himself over to a corner to lie down. "Don't look at me like that," Michèle just said, and Pierre answered, "I'm not looking at you," and then she said yes, it hurt, someone looking at her like that, but she can't go on because Pierre's standing up now looking at Bobby, looking at himself in the mirror, runs his hand down his face, breathes with a long moan, a whistle that keeps going, and suddenly falls on his knees against the sofa and buries his face in his hands, shaking and panting, trying to pull off the images that stick to his face like a spiderweb, like dry leaves that stick to his drenched face.

"Oh Pierre," Michèle says in a whisper of a voice.

His sobbing comes out from between his fingers that cannot hold it back, fills the air with a clumsy texture, obstinate, starts again and keeps up.

"Pierre, Pierre," Michèle says. "Why, love, why."

She caresses his hair slowly, reaches him his handkerchief with its moldy smell.

"I'm a goddamn idiot, forgive me. You . . . you were t-telling me that . . ."

He gets up, he sinks onto the other end of the sofa. He hasn't noticed that Michèle has swung back to it again suddenly, she's looking at him again as she did before he ran away. He repeats, "You were . . . you were telling me," with great effort, his throat's tight, and what's that, Bobby is growling again, Michèle's on her feet, retreating step by step without turning, looking at him and walking backwards, what's that, why is that now, why is she leaving, why. The door slamming leaves him indifferent. He smiles, sees his smile in the mirror, smiles again, *als alle Knospen sprangen,* he hums, his lips compressed, there's a silence, the click of a telephone being taken off the hook, buzzing sound of the dialing, one letter, another letter, the first number, the second. Pierre stumbles, tells himself vaguely that he should go explain himself to Michèle, but he's already out the door next to the motorcycle, Bobby growling on the porch, the house rattles violently with the sound of the starter, first, up the street, second, under the sun.

"Babette, it was the same voice. And then I realized that . . ."

"Nonsense," Babette answers. "If I were out there I think I'd give you a good hiding."

"Pierre's gone."

"It's about the best thing he could have done."

"Babette, if you could come out here."

"For what? Sure, I'll come, but it's idiotic."

"He was stuttering, Babette, I swear to you . . . It's not my imagination, I already told you before that . . . It was as if again . . . Come right away, I can't explain like this on the telephone . . . Now I just heard the cycle taking off and I feel awful, how can he understand what's happening with me, poor thing, but he's acting crazy himself, Babette, it's so strange."

"I thought you'd gotten over that whole business," Babette says in a very indifferent voice. "After all, Pierre's not foolish, he'll understand. I thought he'd known already for some time."

"I was going to tell him, I wanted to tell him and then . . . Babette, I swear he was stuttering, and before, before . . ."

"You told me that already, but you're exaggerating. Roland combs his hair anyway he wants to sometimes, and you don't get him confused with anyone else, what the hell."

"And now he's left," Michèle repeats dully.

"He'll be back," Babette says. "All right, cook up something tasty for Roland, he's getting hungrier and hungrier every day."

"You're ruining my reputation," Roland says from the doorway. "What's wrong with Michèle?"

"Let's go," Babette says. "Let's go right away."

The world is steered by a little rubber tube that fits in the hand; turning just a little to the right, all the trees become a single tree spread out at the side of the road; then turn the slightest bit to the left, the green giant splits into hundreds of aspens that race backwards, the towers carrying the high-tension wires move forward with a leisurely motion, one at a time, the march is a cheerful cadence, even words can get into it, tags of images, nothing to do with what you see along the road, the rubber tube turns to the right, the sound gets louder and louder, a wire of sound extends itself unbearably, but there's no more thinking now, it's all machine, body set onto the machine and the wind against the face like forgetfulness, Corbeil, Arpajon, Linas-Montlhéry, the aspen trees again, bus dispatcher's sentry shack, the light turning more violet, cool air that rushes into your half-open mouth, slower now, take a right at this crossroad, Paris 18 kilometers, *Cinzano,* Paris 17 kilometers. "I haven't killed myself," Pierre thinks, swinging slowly into the road on the left. "It's incredible, I haven't killed myself." Exhaustion weighs him down, like a passenger leaning on his shoulders, something that gets softer and more necessary every minute. "I think she'll forgive me," Pierre thinks. "We're both so absurd, it's necessary that she understand, that she understand, that she understand, you don't know anything until you've made love together, I want her hair in my hands, her body, I want her, I want her . . ." The woods start at the roadside, dry leaves invade the highway, drawn out by the wind. Pierre looks at the leaves the motorcycle is eating up and whipping back; the rubber tube starts to turn to the right again, a little more, more. And suddenly it's the glass ball that gleams faintly at the bottom of the stairs. Don't have to leave the motorcycle too far from the house, but Bobby will start barking so you have to hide the bike in the trees and go up on foot with the last of the daylight, go into the living room looking for Michèle, who will be there, but Michèle's not sitting on the sofa, there's only the cognac bottle and some used glasses, the kitchen door is wide open and a reddish light's coming in through there, the sun that's setting at the bottom of the garden, and just silence, so the best thing to do is head for the stairs, steering yourself by the glass ball that's shining, or they're Bobby's eyes, he's stretched out on the bottom step with his hair bristling, growling a bit, it's not hard to step up over Bobby, to climb the stairs carefully so they won't creak and Michèle won't get scared, door half-open, the door shouldn't be half-open and he not have the key in his pocket, but if the door is ajar he won't need the key now, it feels good to run his hands through his hair walking toward the door, you go in leaning on your right foot lightly, lightly edging the door that opens soundlessly, and Michèle sitting at the side of the bed looks up and sees him, puts her hands to her mouth, looks like she's going to scream (but why isn't her hair loose, why doesn't she have the pale blue nightgown on, she's wearing trousers now and looks older), and then Michèle smiles, sighs, stands up and stretches out her arms to him, says, "Pierre, Pierre," instead of wringing her hands and begging and fighting him off, she says his name and is waiting for him, she looks at him and trembles as if out of happiness or shyness, like the double-crossing bitch that she is, as if he could see her in spite of the mattress of dry leaves that again cover his face and that he tears away with both hands while Michèle steps backward, trips on the edge of the bed, looks behind her desperately, screams, screams, all the pleasure that rises and drenches him, screams, like this, her hair between his fingers, like this, I don't care if you beg, like this then, you bitch, just like this.

"For God's sake, that business is more than gone and forgotten," Roland says, taking a turn at top speed.

"I thought so too. Almost seven years. And it has to pop up just now . . ."

"You're mistaken there," Roland says. "If there was any time it was going to pop up it's now, given that it's absurd, it's really very logical. Even I . . . you know, sometimes I dream about all that. The way we killed that guy, you don't forget things like that very easy. Anyway, you couldn't handle things any better in those days," Roland says, pushing the gas pedal to the floor.

"She doesn't know a thing," Babette says. "Just that they killed him shortly afterwards. It was right to tell her at least that much."

"I guess. But it didn't seem right to him at all. I remember his face when we pulled him out of the car in the middle of the woods, he knew immediately he was a goner. He was brave, sure."

"It's always easier to be brave than to be a man," Babette says. "To force himself on a child who . . . When I think that I had to fight to keep Michèle from killing herself. Those first nights . . . It doesn't surprise me that she's feeling the same thing again now, it's almost natural."

The car enters the street on which the house is located, doing seventy.

"Yeah, he was a pig," Roland says. "The pure Aryan, that's the way they saw it, those days. Naturally, he asked for a cigarette, the complete ceremony. Also, he wanted to know why we were going to liquidate him, we explained it to him, boy, we certainly explained it to him. When I dream about him, it's that moment especially, his disdainful air of surprise, the almost elegant way of stuttering. I remember how he fell, his face blasted to bits among the dry leaves."

"Don't go on, please," Babette says.

"He had it coming, besides, we didn't have any other weapons. A shotgun properly used . . . It's on the left, down there at the bottom?"

"Yes, on the left."

"I hope there's some cognac," Roland says, coming down hard on the brake.

1959

The Southern
Thruway

Translated by Suzanne Jill Levine

*Sweltering motorists do not seem to have
a history . . . As a reality a traffic jam is
impressive, but it doesn't say much.*

—*Arrigo Benedetti,* L'Espresso, *Rome, 6.21.64*

AT FIRST THE girl in the Dauphine had insisted on keeping track of the
time, but the engineer in the Peugeot 404 didn't care anymore. Anyone
could look at his watch, but it was as if that time strapped to your right
wrist or the beep beep on the radio were measuring something else—the
time of those who haven't made the blunder of trying to return to Paris
on the southern thruway on a Sunday afternoon and, just past Fontaine-
bleau, have had to slow down to a crawl, stop, six rows of cars on either
side (everyone knows that on Sundays both sides of the thruway are
reserved for those returning to the capital), start the engine, move three
yards, stop, talk with the two nuns in the 2CV on the right, look in the
rear-view mirror at the pale man driving the Caravelle, ironically envy the
birdlike contentment of the couple in the Peugeot 203 (behind the girl's
Dauphine) playing with their little girl, joking, and eating cheese, or suffer
the exasperated outbursts of the two boys in the Simca, in front of the
Peugeot 404, and even get out at the stops to explore, not wandering off
too far (no one knows when the cars up front will start moving again, and
you have to run back so that those behind you won't begin their battle of
horn blasts and curses), and thus move up along a Taunus in front of the
girl's Dauphine—she is still watching the time—and exchange a few dis-
couraged or mocking words with the two men traveling with the little
blond boy, whose great joy at this particular moment is running his toy car
over the seats and the rear ledge of the Taunus, or to dare and move up
just a bit, since it doesn't seem the cars up ahead will budge very soon, and
observe with some pity the elderly couple in the ID Citroën that looks like
a big purple bathtub with the little old man and woman swimming around
inside, he resting his arms on the wheel with an air of resigned fatigue, she
nibbling on an apple, fastidious rather than hungry.

The translator wishes to thank Roberto González Echevarría for his collaboration in
the translation of this story.

By the fourth time he had seen all that, done all that, the engineer decided not to leave his car again and to just wait for the police to somehow dissolve the bottleneck. The August heat mingled with the tire-level temperature and made immobility increasingly irritating. All was gasoline fumes, screechy screams from the boys in the Simca, the sun's glare bouncing off glass and chrome frames, and to top it off, the contradictory sensation of being trapped in a jungle of cars made to run. The engineer's 404 occupied the second lane on the right, counting from the median, which meant that he had four cars on his right and seven on his left, although, in fact, he could see distinctly only the eight cars surrounding him and their occupants, whom he was already tired of observing. He had chatted with them all, except for the boys in the Simca, whom he disliked. Between stops the situation had been discussed down to the smallest detail, and the general impression was that, up to Corbeil-Essonnes, they would move more or less slowly, but that between Corbeil and Juvisy things would pick up once the helicopters and motorcycle police managed to break up the worst of the bottleneck. No one doubted that a serious accident had taken place in the area, which could be the only explanation for such an incredible delay. And with that, the government, taxes, road conditions, one topic after another, three yards, another commonplace, five yards, a sententious phrase or a restrained curse.

The two little nuns in the 2CV wanted so much to get to Milly-la-Forêt before eight because they were bringing a basket of greens for the cook. The couple in the Peugeot 203 were particularly interested in not missing the games on television at nine-thirty; the girl in the Dauphine had told the engineer that she didn't care if she got to Paris a little late, she was complaining only as a matter of principle because she thought it was a crime to subject thousands of people to the discomforts of a camel caravan. In the last few hours (it must have been around five, but the heat was unbearable) they had moved about fifty yards according to the engineer's calculations, but one of the men from the Taunus who had come to talk, bringing his little boy with him, pointed ironically to the top of a solitary plane tree, and the girl in the Dauphine remembered that this plane (if it wasn't a chestnut) had been in line with her car for such a long time that she would no longer bother looking at her watch, since all calculations were useless.

Night would never come; the sun's vibrations on the highway and cars pushed vertigo to the edge of nausea. Dark glasses, handkerchiefs moistened with cologne pressed against foreheads, the measures improvised to protect oneself from screaming reflections or from the foul breath expelled by exhaust pipes at every start, were being organized, perfected, and were the object of reflection and commentary. The engineer got out again to stretch his legs, exchanged a few words with the couple (who looked like farmers) traveling in the Ariane in front of the nun's 2CV. Behind the 2CV was a Volkswagen with a soldier and a girl who looked like newlyweds. The third line toward the edge of the road no longer interested him because he would have had to go dangerously far from the 404; he could distinguish colors, shapes, Mercedes Benz, ID, Lancia, Skoda, Morris Minor, the whole catalog. To the left, on the opposite side of the road, an unreachable jungle of Renaults, Anglias, Peugeots, Porsches, Volvos. It was so monotonous that finally, after chatting with the two men in the Taunus and unsuccessfully trying to exchange views with the solitary driver of the Caravelle, there was nothing better to do than to go back to the 404 and pick up the same conversation about the time, distances, and the movies with the girl in the Dauphine.

Sometimes a stranger would appear, someone coming from the opposite side of the road or from the outside lanes on the right, who would slip between cars to bring some news, probably false, relayed from car to car along the hot miles. The stranger would savor the impact of his news, the slamming of doors as passengers rushed back to comment on the events; but after a while a horn, or an engine starting up, would drive the stranger away, zigzagging through the cars, rushing to get into his and away from the justified anger of the others. And so, all afternoon, they heard about the crash of a Floride and a 2CV near Corbeil—three dead and one child wounded; the double collision of a Fiat 1500 and a Renault station wagon, which in turn smashed into an Austin full of English tourists; the overturning of an Orly airport bus, teeming with passengers from the Copenhagen flight. The engineer was sure that almost everything was false, although something awful must have happened near Corbeil or even near Paris itself to have paralyzed traffic to such an extent. The farmers in the Ariane, who had a farm near Montereau and knew the region well, told them about another Sunday when traffic had been at a standstill for five hours, but even that much time seemed ludicrous now that the sun, going down on the left side of the road, poured a last avalanche of orange jelly into each car, making metals boil and clouding vision, the treetops behind them never completely disappearing, the shadow barely seen in the distance up ahead never getting near enough so that you could feel the line of cars was moving, even if only a little, even if you had to start and then slam on the brakes and never leave first gear; the dejection of again going from first to neutral, brake, hand brake, stop, and the same thing time and time again.

At one point, tired of inactivity, the engineer decided to take advantage of a particularly endless stop to make a tour of the lanes on the left and, leaving the Dauphine behind he found a DKW, another 2CV, a Fiat 600, and he stopped by a De Soto to chat with an astonished tourist from Washington, D.C. who barely understood French, but had to be at the Place de l'Opéra at eight sharp, you understand, my wife will be awfully anxious, damn it, and they were talking about things in general when a traveling salesman type emerged from the DKW to tell them that someone had come by before saying that a Piper Cub had crashed in the middle of the highway, several dead. The American couldn't give a damn about the Piper Cub, likewise the engineer who, hearing a chorus of horns, rushed back to the 404, passing on the news as he went to the men in the Taunus and the couple in the 203. He saved a more detailed account for the girl in the Dauphine as the cars moved a few slow yards. (Now the Dauphine was slightly behind in relation to the 404, later it would be the opposite; actually, the twelve rows moved as a block, as if an invisible traffic cop at the end of the highway were ordering them to advance in unison, not letting anyone get ahead.) A Piper Cub, Miss, is a small touring plane. Oh. Some nerve crashing right on the thruway on a Sunday afternoon! Really. If only it weren't so hot in these damn cars, if those trees to the right were finally behind us, if the last number in the odometer were finally to fall into its little black hole instead of hanging by its tail, endlessly.

At one point (night was softly falling, the horizon of car tops was turning purple), a big white butterfly landed on the Dauphine's windshield, and the girl and the engineer admired its wings, spread in brief and perfect suspension while it rested; then with acute nostalgia, they watched it fly away over the Taunus and the old couple's ID, head toward the Simca, where a hunter's hand tried vainly to catch it, wing amiably over the Ariane, where the two farmers seemed to be eating something, and finally disappear to the right. At dusk, the line of cars made a first big move of about forty yards; when the engineer looked absently at the odometer, one half of the six had vanished, and the seven was beginning to move down. Almost everybody listened to the radio, and the boys in the Simca had theirs at full blast, singing along with a twist, rocking the car with their gyrations; the nuns were saying their rosaries; the little boy in the Taunus had fallen asleep with his face against the window, the toy car still in his hand. At one point (it was nighttime now), some strangers came with more news, as contradictory as the news already forgotten. It wasn't a Piper, but a glider flown by a general's daughter. It was true that a Renault van had smashed into an Austin, not in Juvisy though, but practically at the gates of Paris. One of the strangers explained to the couple in the 203 that the pavement had caved in around Igny, and five cars had overturned when their front wheels got caught in the cracks. The idea of a natural catastrophe spread all the way to the engineer, who shrugged without a comment. Later, thinking of those first few hours of darkness when they had begun to breathe more easily, he remembered that, at one point, he had stuck his arm out of his window to tap on the Dauphine and wake up the girl; she had fallen asleep, oblivious to a new advance. It was perhaps already midnight when one of the nuns timidly offered him a ham sandwich, assuming that he was hungry. The engineer accepted it (although, in fact, he felt nauseous) and asked if he could share it with the girl in the Dauphine, who accepted and voraciously ate the sandwich and a chocolate bar she got from the traveling salesman in the DKW, her neighbor to the left. A lot of people had stepped out of the stuffy cars, because again it had been hours since the last advance; thirst was prevalent, the bottles of lemonade and even the wine on board were already exhausted. The first to complain was the little girl in the 203, and the soldier and the engineer left their cars to go with her father to get water. In front of the Simca, where the radio seemed to provide ample nourishment, the engineer found a Beaulieu occupied by an older woman with nervous eyes. No, she didn't have any water, but she could give him some candy for the little girl. The couple in the ID consulted each other briefly before the old woman pulled a small can of fruit juice out of her bag. The engineer expressed his gratitude and asked if they were hungry, or if he could be of any service; the old man shook his head, but the old lady seemed to accept his offer silently. Later, the girl from the Dauphine and the engineer explored the rows on the left, without going too far; they came back with a few pastries and gave them to the old lady in the ID, just in time to run back to their own cars under a shower of horn blasts.

Aside from those quick jaunts, there was so little to do that the hours began to blend together, becoming one in the memory; at one point, the engineer thought of striking that day from his appointments book and had to keep from laughing out loud, but later, when the nuns, the men in the Taunus, and the girl in the Dauphine began to make contradictory calculations, he realized it would have been better to keep track of time. The local radio stations stopped transmitting for the day, and only the traveling salesman had a short-wave radio, which insisted on reporting exclusively on the stockmarket. Around three, it seemed as if a tacit agreement had been reached, and the line didn't move until dawn. The boys in the Simca pulled out inflatable beds and laid down by their car; the engineer lowered the back of the front seat of the 404 and offered the cushions to the nuns, who refused them; before lying down for a while, the engineer thought of the girl in the Dauphine, who was still at the wheel, and, pretending it didn't make any difference to him, offered to switch cars with her until dawn, but she refused, claiming that she could sleep fine in any position. For a while, you could hear the boy in the Taunus cry; he was lying on the back seat and probably suffering from the heat. The nuns were still praying when the engineer laid down on the seat and began falling asleep, but his sleep was too close to wakefulness, and he finally awoke sweaty and nervous, not realizing at first where he was. Sitting up straight, he began to perceive confused movements outside, a gliding of shadows between the cars, and then he saw a black bulk disappear toward the edge of the highway; he guessed why, and later he, too, left his car to relieve himself at the edge of the road; there were no hedges or trees, only the starless black fields, something that looked like an abstract wall fencing off the white strip of asphalt with its motionless river of cars. He almost bumped into the farmer from the Ariane, who mumbled something unintelligible; the smell of gasoline over the road now mingled with the more acid presence of man, and the engineer hurried back to his car as soon as he could. The girl in the Dauphine slept leaning on the steering wheel, a lock of hair in her eyes. Before climbing into the 404, the engineer amused himself by watching her shadow, divining the curve of her slightly puckered lips. On the other side, smoking silently, the man in the DKW was also watching the girl sleep.

In the morning they moved a little, enough to give them hope that by afternoon the route to Paris would open up. At nine, a stranger brought good news: The cracks on the road had been filled, and traffic would soon be back to normal. The boys in the Simca turned on the radio, and one of them climbed on top of the car singing and shouting. The engineer told himself that the news was as false as last night's and that the stranger had taken advantage of the group's happiness to ask for and get an orange from the couple in the Ariane. Later another stranger came and tried the same trick, but got nothing. The heat was beginning to rise, and the people preferred to stay in their own cars and wait for the good news to come true. At noon, the little girl in the 203 began crying again, and the girl in the Dauphine went to play with her and made friends with her parents. The 203's had no luck: On the right they had the silent man in the Caravelle, oblivious to everything happening around them, and from their left they had to endure the verbose indignation of the driver of the Floride, for whom the bottleneck was a personal affront. When the little girl complained of thirst again, the engineer decided to talk to the couple in the Ariane, convinced that there were many provisions in that car. To his surprise, the farmers were very friendly; they realized that in a situation like this it was necessary to help one another, and they thought that if someone took charge of the group (the woman made a circular gesture with her hand, encompassing the dozen cars surrounding them), they would have enough to get them to Paris. The idea of appointing himself organizer bothered him, and he chose to call the men from the Taunus for a meeting with the couple in the Ariane. A while later, the rest of the group was consulted one by one. The young soldier in the Volkswagen agreed immediately, and the couple in the 203 offered the few provisions they had left. (The girl in the Dauphine had gotten a glass of pomegranate juice for the little girl, who was now laughing and playing.) One of the Taunus men who went to consult with the boys in the Simca received only mocking consent; the pale man in the Caravelle said it made no difference to him, they could do whatever they wanted. The old couple in the ID and the lady in the Beaulieu reacted with visible joy, as if they felt more protected now. The drivers of the Floride and DKW made no comment, and the American looked at them astonished, saying something about God's will. The engineer found it easy to nominate one of the Taunus men, in whom he had instinctive confidence, as coordinator of all activities. No one would have to go hungry for the time being, but they needed water; the leader, whom the boys in the Simca called Taunus for fun, asked the engineer, the soldier, and one of the boys to explore the zone of highway around them, offering food in exchange for beverages. Taunus, who evidently knew how to command, figured that they should obtain supplies for a maximum of a day and a half, taking the most pessimistic view. In the nun's 2CV and the farmer's Ariane there were enough supplies for such a period of time and, if the explorers returned with water, all problems would be solved. But only the soldier returned with a full flask, and its owner had demanded food for two people in exchange. The engineer failed to find anyone who could give him water, but his trip allowed him to observe that beyond his group other cells were being organized and were facing similar problems; at a given moment, the driver of an Alfa Romeo refused to speak to him, referring him to the leader of his group five cars behind. Later, the boy from the Simca came back without any water, but Taunus figured they already had enough water for the two children, the old lady in the ID, and the rest of the women. The engineer was telling the girl in the Dauphine about his trip around the periphery (it was one in the afternoon, and the sun kept them in their cars), when she interrupted him with a gesture and pointed to the Simca. In two leaps the engineer reached the car and grabbed the elbow of the boy sprawled in the seat and drinking in great gulps from a flask he had brought back hidden in his jacket. To the boy's angry gesture the engineer responded by increasing the pressure on his arm; the other boy got out of the car and jumped on the engineer, who took two steps back and waited for him, almost with pity. The soldier was already running toward them, and the nuns' shrieks alerted Taunus and his companion. Taunus listened to what had happened, approached the boy with the flask, and slapped him twice. Sobbing, the boy screamed and protested, while the other grumbled without daring to intervene. The engineer took the flask away and gave it to Taunus. Horns began to blare, and everyone returned to his car, but to no avail, since the line moved barely five yards.

At siesta time, under a sun that was even stronger than the day before, one of the nuns took off her coif, and her companion doused her temples with cologne. The women improvised their Samaritan activities little by little, moving from one car to the next, taking care of the children to allow the men more freedom. No one complained, but the jokes were strained, always based on the same word plays, in snobbish skepticism. The greatest humiliation for the girl in the Dauphine and the engineer was to feel sweaty and dirty; the farmers' absolute indifference to the odor that emanated from their armpits moved them to pity. Toward dusk, the engineer looked casually into the rear-view mirror and found, as always, the pale face and tense features of the driver of the Caravelle who, like the fat driver of the Floride, had remained aloof from all the activities. He thought that his features had become sharper and wondered if he were sick. But later on, when he went to talk with the soldier and his wife, he had a chance to look at him more closely and told himself that the man was not sick, that it was something else, a separation, to give it a name. The soldier in the Volkswagen later told him that his wife was afraid of that silent man who never left the wheel and seemed to sleep awake. Conjectures arose; a folklore was created to fight against inactivity. The children in the Taunus and the 203 had become friends, quarreled, and later made up; their parents visited each other, and once in a while the girl in the Dauphine went to see how the old lady in the ID and the woman in the Beaulieu were doing. At dusk, when some gusts of wind swept through, and the sun went behind the clouds in the west, the people were happy, thinking it would get cooler. A few drops fell, coinciding with an extraordinary advance of almost 100 yards; far away, lightning glowed, and it got even hotter. There was so much electricity in the atmosphere that Taunus, with an instinct the engineer silently admired, left the group alone until night, as if he sensed the possible consequences of the heat and fatigue. At eight, the women took charge of distributing the food; it had been decided that the farmer's Ariane should be the general warehouse and the nun's 2CV a supplementary depot. Taunus had gone in person to confer with the leaders of the four or five neighboring groups; later, with the help of the soldier and the man in the 203, he took an amount of food to the other groups and returned with more water and some wine. It was decided that the boys in the Simca would yield their inflatable beds to the old lady in the ID and the woman in the Beaulieu; the girl in the Dauphine also brought them two plaid blankets, and the engineer offered his car, which he mockingly called the "sleeping car," to whomever might need it. To his surprise, the girl in the Dauphine accepted the offer and that night shared the 404 cushions with one of the nuns; the other nun went to sleep in the 203 with the little girl and her mother, while the husband spent the night on the pavement wrapped in a blanket. The engineer was not sleepy and played dice with Taunus and his mate; at one point, the farmer in the Ariane joined them, and they talked about politics and drank a few shots of brandy that the farmer had turned over to Taunus that morning. The night wasn't bad; it had cooled down, and a few stars shone between the clouds.

Toward morning, they were overcome by sleep, that need to feel covered which came with the half-light of dawn. While Taunus slept beside the boy in the back seat, his friend and the engineer rested up front. Between two images of a dream, the engineer thought he heard screams in the distance and saw a vague glow; the leader of another group came to tell them that thirty cars ahead there had been the beginnings of a fire in an Estafette—someone had tried to boil vegetables on the sly. Taunus joked about the incident as he went from car to car to find out how they had spent the night, but everyone got his message. That morning, the line began to move very early, and there was an excited rush to pick up mattresses and blankets, but, since the same was probably happening all over, almost no one was impatient or blew his horn. Toward noon, they had moved more than fifty yards, and the shadow of a forest could be seen to the right of the highway. They envied those lucky people who at that moment could go to the shoulder of the road and enjoy the shade; maybe there was a brook or a faucet with running water. The girl in the Dauphine closed her eyes and thought of a shower falling down her neck and back, running down her legs; the engineer, observing her out of the corner of his eye, saw two tears streaming down her cheeks.

Taunus, who had moved up to the ID, came back to get the younger women to tend the old lady, who wasn't feeling well. The leader of the third group to the rear had a doctor among his men, and the soldier rushed to get him. The engineer, who had followed with ironical benevolence the efforts the boys in the Simca had been making to be forgiven, thought it was time to give them their chance. With the pieces of a tent the boys covered the windows of the 404, and the "sleeping car" became an ambulance where the old lady could sleep in relative darkness. Her husband lay down beside her, and everyone left them alone with the doctor. Later, the nuns attended to the old lady, who felt much better, and the engineer spent the afternoon as best he could, visiting other cars and resting in Taunus' when the sun bore down too hard; he had to run only three times to his car, where the old couple seemed to sleep, to move it up with the line to the next stop. Night came without their having made it to the forest.

Toward two in the morning, the temperature dropped, and those who had blankets were glad to bundle up. Since the line couldn't move until morning (it was something you felt in the air, that came from the horizon of motionless cars in the night), the engineer sat down to smoke with Taunus and to chat with the farmer in the Ariane and the soldier. Taunus' calculations no longer corresponded to reality, and he said so frankly; something would have to be done in the morning to get more provisions and water. The soldier went to get the leaders of the neighboring groups, who were not sleeping either, and they discussed the problem quietly so as not to wake up the women. The leaders had spoken with the leaders of faraway groups, in a radius of about eighty or 100 cars, and they were sure that the situation was analogous everywhere. The farmer knew the region well and proposed that two or three men from each group go out at dawn to buy provisions from the neighboring farms, while Taunus appointed drivers for the cars left unattended during the expedition. The idea was good, and it was not difficult to collect money from those present; it was decided that the farmer, the soldier, and Taunus' friend would go together, taking all the paper bags, string bags, and flasks available. The other leaders went back to their groups to organize similar expeditions and, at dawn, the situation was explained to the women, and the necessary preparations were made, so that the line could keep moving. The girl in the Dauphine told the engineer that the old lady felt better already and insisted on going back to her ID; at eight, the doctor came and saw no reason why the couple shouldn't return to their car. In any case, Taunus decided that the 404 would be the official ambulance; for fun the boys made a banner with a red cross and put it on the antenna. For a while now, people preferred to leave their cars as little as possible; the temperature continued to drop, and at noon, showers began to fall with lightning in the distance. The farmer's wife rushed to gather water with a funnel and a plastic pitcher, to the special amusement of the boys in the Simca. Watching all this, leaning on his wheel with a book in front of him that he wasn't too interested in, the engineer wondered why the expeditionaries were taking so long; later, Taunus discreetly called him over to his car and, when they got in, told him they had failed. Taunus' friend gave details: The farms were either abandoned or the people refused to sell to them, alleging regulations forbidding the sale to private individuals and suspecting that they were inspectors taking advantage of the circumstances to test them. In spite of everything, they had been able to bring back a small amount of water and some provisions, perhaps stolen by the soldier, who was grinning and not going into details. Of course, the bottleneck couldn't last much longer, but the food they had wasn't the best for the children or the old lady. The doctor, who came around four-thirty to see the sick woman, made a gesture of weariness and exasperation and told Taunus that the same thing was happening in all the neighboring groups. The radio had spoken about emergency measures being taken to clear up the thruway, but aside from a helicopter that appeared briefly at dusk, there was no action to be seen. At any rate, the heat was gradually tapering off, and people seemed to be waiting for night to cover up in their blankets and erase a few more hours of waiting in their sleep. From his car the engineer listened to the conversation between the girl in the Dauphine and the traveling salesman in the DKW, who was telling her jokes that made her laugh halfheartedly. He was surprised to see the lady from the Beaulieu, who never left her car, and got out to see if she needed something, but she only wanted the latest news and went over to talk with the nuns. A nameless tedium weighed upon them at nightfall; people expected more from sleep than from the always contradictory or unfounded news. Taunus' friend discreetly went to get the engineer, the soldier, and the man in the 203. Taunus informed them that the man in the Floride had just deserted; one of the boys in the Simca had seen the car empty and after a while started looking for the man just to kill time. No one knew the fat man in the Floride well. He had complained a lot the first day, but had turned out to be as silent as the driver of the Caravelle. When at five in the morning there was no longer any doubt that Floride, as the boys in the Simca got a kick out of calling him, had deserted, taking a handbag with him and leaving behind another filled with shirts and underwear, Taunus decided that one of the boys would take charge of the abandoned car so as not to immobilize the lane. They were all vaguely annoyed by this desertion in the dark and wondered how far Floride could have gotten in his flight through the fields. Aside from this, it seemed to be the night for big decisions; lying on the seat cushion of his 404, the engineer seemed to hear a moan, but he figured it was coming from the soldier and his wife, which, after all, was understandable in the middle of the night and under such circumstances. But then he thought better and lifted the canvas that covered the rear window; by the light of one of the few stars shining, he saw the ever-present windshield of the Caravelle a yard and a half away, and behind it, as if glued to the glass and slightly slanted, the man's convulsed face. Quietly, he got out the left side so as not to wake up the nuns and approached the Caravelle. Then he looked for Taunus, and the soldier went to get the doctor. Obviously, the man had committed suicide by taking some kind of poison; a few lines scrawled in pencil in his appointments book were enough, plus the letter addressed to one Yvette, someone who had left him in Vierzon. Fortunately, the habit of sleeping in the cars was well established (the nights were so cold now that no one would have thought of staying outside), and few were bothered by others slipping between the cars toward the edges of the thruway to relieve themselves. Taunus called a war council, and the doctor agreed with his proposal. To leave the body on the edge of the road would mean to subject those coming behind to an at least painful surprise; to carry him further out into the fields could provoke a violent reaction from the villagers who, the night before, had threatened and beaten up a boy from another group, out looking for food. The farmer in the Ariane and the traveling salesman had what was needed to hermetically seal the Caravelle's trunk. The girl in the Dauphine joined them just as they were beginning their task, and hung on to the engineer's arm. He quietly explained what had happened and returned her, a little calmer, to her car. Taunus and his men had put the body in the trunk, and the traveling salesman worked with tubes of glue and Scotch tape by the light of the soldier's lantern. Since the woman in the 203 could drive, Taunus decided that her husband would take over the Caravelle, which was on the 203's right; so, in the morning, the little girl in the 203 discovered that her daddy had another car and played for hours at switching cars and putting some of her toys in the Caravelle.

For the first time, it felt cold during the day, and no one thought of taking off his coat. The girl in the Dauphine and the nuns made an inventory of coats available in the group. There were a few sweaters that turned up unexpectedly in the cars, or in some suitcase, a few blankets, a light overcoat or two. A list of priorities was drawn up, and the coats were distributed. Water was again scarce, and Taunus sent three of his men, including the engineer, to try to establish contact with the villagers. While impossible to say why, outside resistance was total. It was enough to step out of the thruway's boundaries for stones to come raining in from somewhere. In the middle of the night, someone threw a sickle that hit the top of the DKW and fell beside the Dauphine. The traveling salesman turned very pale and didn't move from his car, but the American in the De Soto (who was not in Taunus' group, but was appreciated by everyone for his guffaws and good humor) came running, twirled the sickle around and hurled it back with everything he had, shouting curse words. But Taunus did not think it wise to increase the hostility; perhaps it was still possible to make a trip for water.

Nobody kept track anymore of how much they had moved in that day or days; the girl in the Dauphine thought that it was between eighty and two hundred yards; the engineer was not as optimistic, but amused himself by prolonging and confusing his neighbor's calculations, interested in stealing her away from the traveling salesman, who was courting her in his professional manner. That same afternoon, the boy in charge of the Floride came to tell Taunus that a Ford Mercury was offering water at a good price. Taunus refused, but at nightfall one of the nuns asked the engineer for a drink of water for the old lady in the ID, who was suffering in silence, still holding her husband's hand, and being tended alternately by the nuns and the girl in the Dauphine. There was half a bottle of water left, and the women assigned it to the old lady and the woman in the Beaulieu. That same night Taunus paid out of his own pocket for two bottles of water; the Ford Mercury promised to get more the next day, at double the price.

It was difficult to get together and talk, because it was so cold that no one would leave his car except for very pressing reasons. The batteries were beginning to run down, and they couldn't keep the heaters running all the time, so Taunus decided to reserve the two best equipped cars for the sick, should the situation arise. Wrapped in blankets (the boys in the Simca had ripped off the inside covers of their car to make coats and hats for themselves, and others started to imitate them), everyone tried his best to open doors as little as possible to preserve the heat. On one of those freezing nights the engineer heard the girl in the Dauphine sobbing softly. Quietly he opened her door and groped for her in the dark until he felt a wet cheek. Almost without resistance, she let herself be drawn to the 404; the engineer helped her lie down on the back seat, covered her with his only blanket, and then with his overcoat. Darkness was thicker in the ambulance car, its windows covered with the tent's canvas. At one point, the engineer pulled down the two sun visors and hung his shirt and a sweater from them to shut the car off completely. Toward dawn, she whispered in his ear that before starting to cry she thought she saw in the distance, on the right, the lights of a city.

Maybe it was a city, but in the morning mist you couldn't see more than twenty yards away. Curiously, the line moved a lot more that day, perhaps two or three hundred yards. This coincided with new radio flashes. (Hardly anyone listened anymore, with the exception of Taunus, who felt it was his duty to keep up.) The announcers talked emphatically about exceptional measures that would clear the thruway and referred to the weary toil of highway patrolmen and police forces. Suddenly, one of the nuns became delirious. As her companion looked on terrified, and the girl in the Dauphine dabbed her temples with what was left of the cologne, the nun spoke of Armageddon, the Ninth Day, the chain of cinnabar. The doctor came much later, making his way through the snow that had been falling since noon and that was gradually walling the cars in. He regretted the lack of sedatives and advised them to put the nun in a car with good heating. Taunus put her in his own car, and the little boy moved to the Caravelle with his little girl friend from the 203; they played with their toy cars and had a lot of fun, because they were the only ones who didn't go hungry. That day and the following days, it snowed almost continuously, and when the line moved up a few yards, the snow that had accumulated between cars had to be removed by improvised means.

No one would have conceived of being surprised at the way they were getting provisions and water. The only thing Taunus could do was administer the common fund and get as much as possible out of trades. The Ford Mercury and a Porsche came every night to traffic with food; Taunus and the engineer were in charge of distributing it according to the physical state of each one. Incredibly, the old lady in the ID was surviving, although sunken in a stupor that the women diligently fought off. The lady in the Beaulieu, who had been fainting and feeling nauseous a few days before, had recovered with the cold weather and was now one of the most active in helping the nun take care of her companion, still weak and a bit lost. The soldier's wife and 203's were in charge of the two children; the traveling salesman in the DKW, perhaps to console himself for losing Dauphine to the engineer, spent hours telling stories to the children. At night, the groups entered another life, secret and private; doors would open or close to let a frozen figure in or out; no one looked at the others; eyes were as blind as darkness itself. Some kind of happiness endured here and there under dirty blankets, in hands with overgrown fingernails, in bodies smelling of unchanged clothes and of days cramped inside. The girl in the Dauphine had not been mistaken—a city sparkled in the distance, and they were approaching it slowly. In the afternoons, one of the boys in the Simca would climb to the top of the car, relentless lookout wrapped in pieces of seat covers and green burlap. Tired of exploring the futile horizon, he'd look for the thousandth time at the cars surrounding him; somewhat enviously he'd discover Dauphine in 404's car, a hand caressing a neck, the end of a kiss. To play a joke on them, now that he had regained 404's friendship, he'd yell that the line was about to move. Dauphine would have to leave 404 and go to her car, but after a while she'd come back looking for warmth, and the boy in the Simca would have liked so much to bring a girl from another group to his car, but it was unthinkable with this cold and hunger, not to mention that the group up front was openly hostile to Taunus' because of some story about a can of condensed milk, and except for official transactions with Ford Mercury and Porsche, there was no possible contact with other groups. Then the boy in the Simca would sigh unhappily and continue his lookout until the snow and the cold forced him trembling back into his car.

But the cold began to give way and, after a period of rains and winds that enervated a few spirits and increased food supply difficulties, came some cool sunny days when it was again possible to leave your car, pay visits, restore relations with neighboring groups. The leaders had discussed the situation, and peace was finally made with the group ahead. Ford Mercury's sudden disappearance was much talked about, although no one knew what could have happened to him. But Porsche kept coming and controlling the black market. Water and some preserves were never completely lacking, but the group's funds were diminishing, and Taunus and the engineer asked themselves what would happen the day when there was no more money to give Porsche. The possibility of an ambush was brought up, of taking him prisoner and forcing him to reveal the source of his supplies; but the line had advanced a good stretch, and the leaders preferred to wait some more and avoid the risk of ruining it all by a hasty decision. The engineer, who had given into an almost pleasant indifference, was momentarily stunned by the timid news from the girl in the Dauphine, but later he understood that nothing could be done to avoid it, and the idea of having a child by her seemed as natural as the nightly distribution of supplies or the secret trips to the edge of the thruway. Nor could the death of the old lady in the ID surprise anyone. Again it was necessary to work at night, to console her husband, who just couldn't understand, and to keep him company. A fight broke out between the two groups up ahead, and Taunus had to act as mediator and tentatively solve the disagreement. Anything would happen at any moment, without prearranged schedules; the most important thing began when nobody expected it anymore, and the least responsible was the first to find out. Standing on the roof of the Simca, the elated lookout had the impression that the horizon had changed (it was dusk; the meager, level light of a yellowish sun was slipping away) and that something unbelievable was happening five hundred, three hundred, two hundred and fifty yards away. He shouted it to 404, and 404 said something to Dauphine, and she dashed to her car, when Taunus, the soldier, and the farmer were already running, and from the roof of the Simca the boy was pointing ahead and endlessly repeating the news as if to convince himself that what he was seeing was true. Then they heard the rumble, as if a heavy but uncontrollable migratory wave were awakening from a long slumber and testing its strength. Taunus yelled at them to get back to their cars; the Beaulieu, the ID, the Fiat 600, and the De Soto started moving at once. Now the 2CV, the Taunus, the Simca, and the Ariane were beginning to move, and the boy in the Simca, proud of what was to him something of a personal triumph, turned to the 404 and waved his arm, while the 404, the Dauphine, the 2CV, and the DKW in turn started moving. But it all hinged on how long this was going to last, 404 thought almost routinely, as he kept pace with Dauphine and smiled encouragement to her. Behind them, the Volkswagen, the Caravelle, the 203, and the Floride started moving slowly, a stretch in first gear, then second, forever second, but already without having to clutch, as so many times before, with the foot firmly on the accelerator, waiting to move on to third. 404, reaching out to touch Dauphine's hand, barely grazed her fingertips, saw on her face a smile of incredulous hope, and thought that they would make it to Paris and take a bath, go somewhere together, to her house or his to take a bath, eat, bathe endlessly and eat and drink, and that later there would be furniture, a bedroom with furniture and a bathroom with shaving cream to really shave, and toilets, food and toilets and sheets, Paris was a toilet and two sheets and hot water running down his chest and legs, and a nail clipper, and white wine, they would drink white wine before kissing and smell each other's lavender water and cologne before really making love with the lights on, between clean sheets, and bathing again just for fun, to make love and bathe and drink and go to the barber shop, go into the bathroom, caress the sheets and caress each other between the sheets and make love among the suds and lavender water and toothbrushes, before beginning to think about what they were going to do, about the child and all the problems and the future, and all that as long as they didn't stop, just as long as the rows kept on moving, even though you couldn't go to third yet, just moving like that, in second, but moving. With his bumper touching the Simca, 404 leaned back, felt the speed picking up, felt that it was possible to accelerate without bumping into the Simca and that the Simca could accelerate without fear of crashing into Beaulieu, and that behind came the Caravelle and that they all accelerated more and more, and that it was O.K. to move on to third without forcing the engine, and the pace became even, and they all accelerated even more, and 404 looked around with surprise and tenderness, searching for Dauphine's eyes. But, naturally, speeding up like that the lanes could no longer stay parallel. Dauphine had moved almost a yard ahead of 404, and he saw her neck and barely her profile just as she was turning to look at him with surprise, noticing that the 404 was falling further behind. 404 calmed her down with a smile and accelerated abruptly, but he had to brake almost immediately, because he was about to bump the Simca; he blew the horn, and the boy looked at him in the rear-view mirror and made a gesture of helplessness, pointing to the Beaulieu, which was up against him. The Dauphine was three yards ahead, level with the Simca, and the little girl in the 203, now alongside the 404, waved her arms and showed him her doll. A red blot on his right confused 404; instead of the nuns' 2CV or the soldier's Volkswagen, he saw an unknown Chevrolet, and almost immediately the Chevrolet moved ahead followed by a Lancia and a Renault 8. To his left, an ID was gaining on him yard by yard, but before its place was taken by a 403, 404 was still able to make out up ahead the 203 that was already blocking Dauphine. The group was falling apart; it didn't exist anymore. Taunus had to be at least twenty yards away, followed by Dauphine; at the same time, the third row on the left was falling behind since, instead of the traveling salesman's DKW, 404 could see only the rear end of an old black van, perhaps a Citroën or a Peugeot. The cars were in third, gaining or losing ground according to the pace of their lane, and on the side of the thruway trees and some houses in the thick mist and dusk sped by. Later, it was the red lights they all turned on, following the example of those ahead, the night that suddenly closed in on them. From time to time, horns blew, speedometer needles climbed more and more, some lanes were going at forty-five miles an hour, others at forty, some at thirty-five. 404 still hoped that with the gaining and losing of ground he would again catch up with Dauphine, but each minute that slipped by convinced him that it was useless, that the group had dissolved irrevocably, that the everyday meetings would never take place again, the few rituals, the war councils in Taunus' car, Dauphine's caresses in the quiet of night, the children's laughter as they played with their little cars, the nun's face as she said her rosary. When the Simca's brake lights came on, 404 slowed down with an absurd feeling of hope, and as soon as he put on the handbrake he bolted out and ran ahead. Outside of the Simca and the Beaulieu (the Caravelle would be behind him, but he didn't care), he didn't recognize any cars; through strange windows faces he'd never seen before stared at him in surprise and perhaps even outrage. Horns began to blare, and 404 had to go back to his car; the boy in the Simca made a friendly gesture, pointing with encouragement toward Paris. The line got moving again, slowly for a few minutes, and later as if the thruway were completely free. On 404's left was a Taunus, and for a second 404 had the impression that the group was coming together again, that everything was returning to order, that it would be possible to move ahead without destroying anything. But it was a green Taunus, and there was a woman with dark glasses at the wheel who looked straight ahead. There was nothing to do but give in to the pace, adapt mechanically to the speed of the cars around, and not think. His leather jacket must still be in the soldier's Volkswagen. Taunus had the novel he had been reading the first few days. An almost empty bottle of lavender water was in the nuns' 2CV. And he had, there where he touched it at times with his right hand, the teddy bear Dauphine had given him as a pet. He clung absurdly to the idea that at nine-thirty the food would be distributed and the sick would have to be visited, the situation would have to be examined with Taunus and the farmer in the Ariane; then it would be night, Dauphine sneaking into his car, stars or clouds, life. Yes, it had to be like that. All that couldn't have ended forever. Maybe the soldier would get some water, which had been scarce the last few hours; at any rate, you could always count on Porsche, as long as you paid his price. And on the car's antenna the red-cross flag waved madly, and you moved at fifty-five miles an hour toward the lights that kept growing, not knowing why all this hurry, why this mad race in the night among unknown cars, where no one knew anything about the others, where everyone looked straight ahead, only ahead.

1966

Augusto Roa Bastos

b. 1917

AUGUSTO ROA BASTOS was born in Guaira, Paraguay, on June 13, 1917, and was educated in the capital city of Asunción. He started his writing career as a journalist and was a correspondent in Europe and Africa during World War II. He lived in exile in Argentina and France between 1947 and 1989, when he returned to his native country. Roa Bastos taught for many years at the University of Toulouse and received several literary prizes for his work, among them a Guggenheim Award (1970) and the coveted Cervantes Prize for Literature (1989). He is best known to English-language readers for his monumental novel on dictatorship, *Yo el supremo* (1974; *I, the Supreme,* 1986). The following story, selected from the collection *El trueno entre las hojas* (1953; Thunder among the leaves), deals with the social injustice and political turmoil that have dominated Paraguay's history since the bloody wars of the late nineteenth century.

The Prisoner

Translated by Gustavo Pellón

THE SHOTS ANSWERED one another intermittently in the cold wintry night. They formed a wavering and indecisive line around the hut. Between long anxious pauses, they advanced and retreated along the edge of the forest and the marshes adjacent to the riverbank, like the mesh of a net which cautiously but implacably closes. The echo of the shots went bouncing through thin acoustic layers in the air which broke as they gave way. From the duration of the echo, it was possible to calculate the diameter of the dragnet. Taking the hut as the center, it was perhaps about four or five kilometers long. But that square league of terrain, tracked and scouted in every direction, was practically without boundaries. The same thing was happening everywhere.

The popular uprising refused to die out completely. Unaware that it had already been cheated of its triumph, it stubbornly continued to raise hopes, with its threadbare guerrillas, in the swamps, in the thickets, in the razed villages.

It was when it ended, more than during the fighting itself, that hatred wrote its most heinous pages. The factional struggle degenerated into a brutal orgy of vengeance. The fate of whole families was sealed by the color of the partisan badge worn by the father or the brothers. The tragic storm devastated everything it could. It was the cyclical blood rite. The carnivorous aboriginal deities had once more revealed their fiery eyes through the foliage; in them men were reflected like the shadows of an old primeval dream. And the green stone jaws were grinding up those fleeing shadows. A cry in the night, the screech of an owl impossible to locate, the hiss of a snake in the tall grass erected walls which the fugitives did not dare to cross. They were boxed into a sinister funnel, trapped between the automatic rifles and the Mausers at their backs and the waves of hallucinatory terror that stalked their flight. Some chose to face the government patrols, and end it, once and for all.

The burned-out hut in the middle of the thicket was an appropriate setting for the things that were happening. It was a mournful and, at the same time, a peaceful sight—a scene whose effectiveness resided in its innocence ripped to shreds. Violence itself had not finished its work. It had not been able to erase certain small details in which the memory of another time still survived. The burned poles pointed squarely to the sky amid the crumbling adobe walls. The moon burnished the four charred stumps with a hue of milky whiteness. But this was not the most important thing. On a window ledge at the rear of the hut, for example, a tiny flowerpot still persisted: a rusty little tin can from which there emerged the stem of a carnation singed by the flames. There it persisted in spite of everything, like a forgotten memory, oblivious to change, surrounded by the eternal shining of the moon, like the eye of a blind child that has witnessed a crime without seeing it.

The hut lay at a strategic point. It commanded the only exit from the marshy zone, where the searching was taking place and where it was assumed that the last rebel guerrilla group of that region was hiding. The hut was something like the center of operations for the government patrol.

The weapons and the crates of ammunition were piled up in what had been the hut's only room. Amid the weapons and the crates of ammunition was an old splintered bench. A soldier, with his cap over his eyes, was sleeping on it. By the feeble flickering of the fire which, despite the officer's strict orders, the soldiers had kindled to protect themselves from the cold, one could see the worn edges of the bench, made smooth by years and years of rural weariness and sweat. Elsewhere, a piece of the wall shadowed a nearly intact small stone step with a black bottle dripping with tallow and a half-burned candle stuck in its neck. Behind the hut, leaning against the trunk of a sour orange tree, a small iron plough, with its ploughshare shining opaquely, seemed to await the early morning pull of the yoke on its splinter bar, and on its plough handles, the wrinkled and soft fists which now would probably be rotting in who knows what forsaken fold of the earth. These traces brought back the memory of life. The soldiers meant nothing, nor did the automatic weapons, the bullets, the violence. The only things that mattered were these scraps of a vanished tenderness.

Through them, one could see the invisible, feel in their hidden story the pulse of what is permanent. Between shots, which in turn seemed to echo other shots farther off, the hut propped itself up on its small relics. The rusty little tin can with the singed carnation was linked to someone's hands, someone's eyes. And those hands and those eyes had not completely faded away. They were there, they persisted as part of the undying aura that emanated from the hut, the aura of the life that had dwelt in it. The old shiny bench, the useless plough against the orange tree, the black bottle with its bit of candle and the tallow drippings stood out with a more intense and natural pathos than the total picture of the half-destroyed hut. One of the charred stumps with part of a beam still attached to it continued to smoke slightly. The thin column of smoke rose, disintegrating into bluish, cotton-like locks which the currents of wind fought over. It was like the breathing of the hard wood which would go on smouldering for many days yet. The heart of the *timbó* tree is as resistant to fire as it is to the ax and to time. But it was smoking too, and would end up as a somewhat pink ash.

On the earth floor of the hut, the other three soldiers of the squad warmed themselves by the feeble fire and fought off sleep with an incoherent chatter pierced by yawns and unrestrainable nodding. They had not slept for three nights now. The officer in charge of the detachment had kept his men in constant action since the moment of arrival.

A distant whistle coming from the thicket startled them. It was the password agreed upon. They grasped their rifles. Two of them quickly put out the fire with the butts of their weapons, and the other awoke the one who was sleeping on the bench, shaking him energetically:

"Get up . . . Saldívar! Epac-pue . . . Óuma, jhina,[1] Lieutenant . . . gonna settle things with you, kangüeaky[2] recruit. . . ."

The soldier stood up rubbing his eyes, as the rest rushed to man their supposed stations in the chilly night air.

One of the sentries answered the special whistle which was repeated, this time nearer. They heard approaching footsteps. A moment later, the patrol appeared. They could make out the officer walking ahead among the coconut palms because of his boots, his cap and his leather windbreaker. His short thick silhouette advanced under the moonlight which a film of cirrus clouds was beginning to dim. Three of the five soldiers who came behind were dragging the body of a man. Probably another hostage, Saldívar thought, like the old peasant the night before whom the officer had tortured in order to tear from him certain information about the rebels' hideout. The old man died unable to say anything. It was terrible. Suddenly, while they were beating him, the old man, his teeth firmly shut, began to sing quietly, with his teeth clenched, something like an unrecognizable polka, lively and mournful at the same time. It seemed that he had gone mad. Remembering this, Saldívar shuddered.

The manhunt gave no sign yet of coming to an end. Peralta was irritated, obsessed by this phantom redoubt which lay encysted somewhere in the marshes and which continued to elude his grasp.

Lieutenant Peralta was a hard man, and one obsessed—an appropriate trait for the clean-up operation that was being carried out. Formerly an officer in the military police during the Chaco War, he was in retirement from the service when the revolt broke out. Being neither timid nor lazy, Peralta reenlisted. His name was in no way mentioned during the fighting, but it began to make the rounds when the need arose for an expert and relentless man to track down the rebels. That is why he found himself in this spot of rebel resistance. He wanted to put an end to it as soon as possible, in order to return to the capital and enjoy his share of the victory celebration.

Evidently, Peralta had found a track during his scouting forays, and was preparing to unleash the final blow. Amid the almost total numbness

---

[1] "Hey, you, wake up! Come on!" common phrases in the Guaraní language, which is spoken by the indigenous people of Paraguay.
[2] In Guaraní, "tenderfoot."

of his senses, Saldívar vaguely heard Peralta's voice giving out orders. He also vaguely saw his comrades load two heavy machine guns and leave in the direction indicated by Peralta. He heard something about the guerrillas being trapped on a small wooded island in a marsh. He vaguely heard Peralta saying to him: "Saldívar, you'll remain here alone. We're gonna corner those outlaws in the marsh. I'm leaving you in charge of the prisoner and the supplies."

Saldívar made a painful effort to understand. He finally managed to understand only after the others had already left. The night had grown very dark. The wind wailed harshly through the coconut palms that completely surrounded the hut. On the earth floor lay the motionless body of the man. Maybe he was asleep, or dead. It was all the same to Saldívar. His mind moved among a variety of widely differing scenes, each one increasingly incoherent. Sleep was gradually anesthetizing his will. It was like a sticky rubber sheath around his limbs. He wanted only to sleep. But in a very confused way, he knew he should not sleep. On his neck, he felt a bubble of air. His tongue had become pasty; he felt that it was slowly swelling in his mouth and that at a given moment, it would cut off his breathing. He tried to walk around the prisoner, but his feet refused to obey him. He tottered like a drunk. He tried to think about something definite and concrete, but his jumbled memories slowly circled around weblike in confusion gliding through his head, formless and weightless. In one or two flashes of lucidity, Saldívar thought about his mother and his brother. They were like painful grooves in his soft and spongy dullness. Sleep no longer seemed to reside within him, it was something outside him, an element of nature which nuzzled against him from the night, from time, from violence, from the weariness of things, and forced him to bow lower, and lower. . . .

The boy's body trembled less from the cold than from that sleep which was doubling him over in painful exhaustion. But he still remained standing. The earth was calling him. The motionless body of the man on the earth floor called to him with its silent and comfortable example, but the boy resisted, his pulse trembling like a young bird on a thin branch.

At eighteen, Hugo Saldívar was one of the many draftees from Asunción who had been snatched into military service at the outbreak of the civil war. The bitter chain of chance events which had forced him to undergo countless absurd experiences had brought him here, absurdly, to serve in the detachment of headhunters led by Peralta in the marshes of the south, near the Paraná.

He was the only boy in the group, truly a misfit among those men from varied rural backgrounds who were yoked to the execution of a sinister task which fed on itself like a cancer. Hugo Saldívar thought several times about deserting, about running away. But in the end he decided that it was useless. Violence overwhelmed him, it was everywhere. He was but a squalid bud, a drooping leaf nourished on books and school, on the rotting tree which was collapsing.

His brother Víctor had in fact fought resolutely. But he was strong and vigorous, and had his deep ideas about brotherhood among men and the effort that was necessary to attain it. He felt his brother's words on his skin, but he would have wished them engraved in his heart: "We must all unite, Hugo, to overthrow all this which no longer has anything to offer, and erect in its place a social structure in which we may all live without feeling like enemies, where the desire to live as friends will be the natural goal of everyone. . . ."

Víctor had fought in the Chaco War and had brought back with him that turbulent and also methodical urgency to do something for his fellow-men. His older brother's transformation was a marvelous phenomenon for the ten-year-old child, who now, eight years later, was already an old man. Víctor had returned from the immense bonfire ignited by the petroleum in the Chaco with a deep scar on his forehead. But beneath the bullet's reddish furrow, he harbored an intelligent and generous conviction. And he had built himself a world in which, more than clouded memories and resentment, there was ample faith and precise hopes for the things which could be attained.

It would truly be beautiful to live for such a world as Víctor's, the boy often thought, moved but feeling distant from himself. Later, he saw and understood many things. Víctor's words were slowly penetrating from his skin to his heart. When they met again, everything would be different. But that was still very far off.

He did not even know where Víctor might be now. Nevertheless, he had the vague impression that his brother had gone south to the tea plantations, to organize a revolt among the farm laborers. What if Víctor were with those last guerrillas whom Peralta was pursuing through the marshes? This wild thought had occurred to him many times, but he tried to cast it off in horror. No, his brother had to live, he had to live. . . . He needed him.

The compelling pressure of sleep continued to nuzzle against his skin, against his bones. It wrapped itself around him like a viscous, relentless boa, slowly choking him. He was going to sleep, but there was the prisoner. He might escape, and then Peralta would be implacable with the negligent sentry. He had already shown this on other occasions.

Moving clumsily in his heavy rubber sheath, Saldívar poked around in the darkness searching for a piece of wire or rope to tie the prisoner. He might be a corpse, but perhaps he was pretending to be dead in order to escape in a moment of carelessness. His hands groped at every corner of the burned hovel in vain. Finally, he found a piece of vine—too dry and too short. It was no good. Then in a last, desperate flash of lucidity, Hugo Saldívar remembered that in front of the hut there was a deep hole, perhaps dug for a new post to support a roof which would never be raised. A man standing upright would fit in the hole up to his chest. Surrounding the hole was a pile of dirt which had been dug out. Hugo Saldívar leaned the Mauser against the remains of a wall, and began to drag the prisoner toward the hole. With an almost superhuman effort, he managed to put him into the black hole, which turned out to be like a pipe made to order. The prisoner stood upright in the hole. Only his head and his shoulders stuck out. Saldívar pushed the dirt from the mound with his hands and his boots, until he had somehow filled in all the open spaces around the man. The prisoner did not resist at any moment. Apparently, he accepted the sentry's act with absolute indifference. Hugo Saldívar barely noticed this. The effort expended revived him artificially for a little while. He even had enough energy to get his rifle and pack down the earth with the butt. Then, he dropped like a rock on the bench, as the hammering of the machine guns increased on the marshy plain.

Lieutenant Peralta returned with his men about noon. The mission was completed. A brutal smile illuminated his face, which was dark like that of a bird of prey. The soldiers prodded two or three bloody prisoners. They shoved them forward with curses, obscene insults, and rifle butts. They were more farm laborers from the upper Paraná. Only their bodies had been conquered. A glimmer of absurd happiness floated in their eyes. But that glimmer was already floating beyond death. They were only physically lingering a while longer on the impassive and thirsty earth.

Peralta called loudly:

"Saldívar!"

The prisoners blinked with a remnant of painful surprise.

Peralta called again furiously:

"Saldívar!"

No one answered. Then he glanced at the prisoner's head sticking out of the hole. It looked like a bust carved of moss-covered wood, a bust left behind long long ago. A line of ants was climbing the abandoned face to the forehead, like a dark ribbon from which the sun drew no glare. On the bust's forehead, there was a deep scar like a pale half moon.

The prisoners' eyes were fixed on the strange sculpture. Behind the greenish mask, crawling with ants, they recognized the comrade who had been captured the night before. They thought that Peralta's cry, calling the dead man by his real last name, was a supreme shout of triumph by the soldier tightly stuffed in the leather windbreaker.

Hugo Saldívar's rifle lay on the floor of the hut—the only clue of his desperate flight. Inside his narrow head Peralta was turning over fierce punishments for the deserter. He could not guess that Hugo Saldívar had fled at dawn like a madman, haunted by the bloody copper face of his brother, whom he himself had buried like a tree trunk in the hole.

The ants crawled up and down the face of Víctor Saldívar, the dead guerrilla.

The next day, Peralta's men found the corpse of Hugo Saldívar floating on the muddy waters of the marsh. His hair had gone completely gray, and all semblance of human expression had fled from his face.

1953

Juan Rulfo

1918–1986

CONSIDERED ONE OF the precursors of the Latin American "Boom" in literature, Juan Rulfo was born on May 16, 1918, in the state of Jalisco. He grew up in the small town of San Gabriel, its rich folklore becoming a major source of his fiction. The religious war of the *Cristeros* and his father's assassination, both during the 1920s, made profound and lasting impressions on him. Rulfo moved to Mexico City, studied law for some time, and worked in the Office of Immigration there and in Guadalajara. Even though he devoted most of his time to writing fiction, it wasn't until 1945 that Rulfo published his first story. His well-deserved fame rests on the short-story collection *El llano en llamas* (1953; *The Burning Plain and Other Stories,* 1967) and on his novel *Pedro Páramo* (1955), which appeared under the same title in English in 1959. Although Rulfo has specifically recognized William Faulkner as one of his masters, his themes are rooted in Mexico's history and culture. His experimental and highly innovative style has influenced the work of younger writers, especially that of Gabriel García Márquez.

Tell Them Not to Kill Me!

Translated by George Schade

"TELL THEM NOT to kill me, Justino! Go on and tell them that. For God's sake! Tell them. Tell them please for God's sake."

"I can't. There's a sergeant there who doesn't want to hear anything about you."

"Make him listen to you. Use your wits and tell him that scaring me has been enough. Tell him please for God's sake."

"But it's not just to scare you. It seems they really mean to kill you. And I don't want to go back there."

"Go on once more. Just once, to see what you can do."

"No. I don't feel like going. Because if I do they'll know I'm your son. If I keep bothering them they'll end up knowing who I am and will decide to shoot me too. Better leave things the way they are now."

"Go on, Justino. Tell them to take a little pity on me. Just tell them that."

Justino clenched his teeth and shook his head saying no.

And he kept on shaking his head for some time.

"Tell the sergeant to let you see the colonel. And tell him how old I am—how little I'm worth. What will he get out of killing me? Nothing. After all he must have a soul. Tell him to do it for the blessed salvation of his soul."

Justino got up from the pile of stones which he was sitting on and walked to the gate of the corral. Then he turned around to say, "All right. I'll go. But if they decide to shoot me too, who'll take care of my wife and kids?"

"Providence will take care of them, Justino. You go there now and see what you can do for me. That's what matters."

They'd brought him in at dawn. The morning was well along now and he was still there, tied to a post, waiting. He couldn't keep still. He'd tried to sleep for a while to calm down, but he couldn't. He wasn't hungry either. All he wanted was to live. Now that he knew they were really going to kill him, all he could feel was his great desire to stay alive, like a recently resuscitated man.

Who would've thought that old business that happened so long ago and that was buried the way he thought it was would turn up? That business when he had to kill Don Lupe. Not for nothing either, as the Alimas tried to make out, but because he had his reason. He remembered: Don Lupe Terreros, the owner of the Puerta de Piedra—and besides that, his compadre—was the one he, Juvencio Nava, had to kill, because he'd refused to let him pasture his animals, when he was the owner of the Puerta de Piedra and his compadre too.

At first he didn't do anything because he felt compromised. But later, when the drought came, when he saw how his animals were dying off one by one, plagued by hunger, and how his compadre Lupe continued to refuse to let him use his pastures, that was when he began breaking through the fence and driving his herd of skinny animals to the pasture where they could get their fill of grass. And Don Lupe didn't like it and ordered the fence mended, so that he, Juvencio Nava, had to cut open the hole again. So, during the day the hole was stopped up and at night it was opened again, while the stock stayed there right next to the fence, always waiting—his stock that before had lived just smelling the grass without being able to taste it.

And he and Don Lupe argued again and again without coming to any agreement.

Until one day Don Lupe said to him, "Look here, Juvencio, if you let another animal in my pasture, I'll kill it."

And he answered him, "Look here, Don Lupe, it's not my fault that the animals look out for themselves. They're innocent. You'll have to pay for it, if you kill them."

And he killed one of my yearlings.

This happened thirty-five years ago in March because in April I was already up in the mountains, running away from the summons. The ten cows I gave the judge didn't do me any good, or the lien on my house either, to pay for getting me out of jail. Still later they used up what was left to pay so they wouldn't keep after me, but they kept after me just the same. That's why I came to live with my son on this other piece of land of mine which is called Palo de Venado. And my son grew up and got married to my daughter-in-law Ignacia and has had eight children now. So it happened a long time ago and ought to be forgotten by now. But I guess it's not.

I figured then that with about a hundred pesos everything could be fixed up. The dead Don Lupe left just his wife and two little kids still crawling. And his widow died soon afterward too—they say from grief. They took the kids far off to some relatives. So there was nothing to fear from them.

But the rest of the people took the position that I was still summoned to be tried just to scare me so they could keep on robbing me. Every time someone came to the village they told me, "There are some strangers in town, Juvencio."

And I would take off to the mountains, hiding among the madrone thickets and passing the days with nothing to eat but herbs. Sometimes I had to go out at midnight, as though the dogs were after me. It's been that way my whole life. Not just a year or two. My whole life.

And now they've come for him when he no longer expected anyone, confident that people had forgotten all about it, believing that he'd spent at least his last days peacefully. "At least," he thought, "I'll have some peace in my old age. They'll leave me alone."

He'd clung to his hope with all his heart. That's why it was hard for him to imagine that he'd die like this, suddenly, at this time of life, after having fought so much to ward off death, after having spent his best years running from one place to another because of the alarms, now when his body had become all dried up and leathery from the bad days when he had to be in hiding from everybody.

Hadn't he even let his wife go off and leave him? The day when he learned his wife had left him, the idea of going out in search of her didn't even cross his mind. He let her go without trying to find out at all who she went with or where, so he wouldn't have to go down to the village. He let her go as he'd let everything else go, without putting up a fight. All he had left to take care of was his life, and he'd do that, if nothing else. He couldn't let them kill him. He couldn't. Much less now.

But that's why they brought him from there, from Palo de Venado. They didn't need to tie him so he'd follow them. He walked alone, tied by his fear. They realized he couldn't run with his old body, with those skinny legs of his like dry bark, cramped up with the fear of dying. Because that's where he was headed. For death. They told him so.

That's when he knew. He began to feel that stinging in his stomach that always came on suddenly when he saw death nearby, making his eyes big with fear and his mouth swell up with those mouthfuls of sour water he had to swallow unwillingly. And that thing that made his feet heavy while his head felt soft and his heart pounded with all its force against his ribs. No, he couldn't get used to the idea that they were going to kill him.

There must be some hope. Somewhere there must still be some hope left. Maybe they'd made a mistake. Perhaps they were looking for another Juvencio Nava and not him.

He walked along in silence between those men, with his arms fallen at his sides. The early morning hour was dark, starless. The wind blew slowly, whipping the dry earth back and forth, which was filled with that odor like urine that dusty roads have.

His eyes, that had become squinty with the years, were looking down at the ground, here under his feet, in spite of the darkness. There in the earth was his whole life. Sixty years of living on it, of holding it tight in his hands, of tasting it like one tastes the flavor of meat. For a long time he'd been crumbling it with his eyes, savoring each piece as if it were the last one, almost knowing it would be the last.

Then, as if wanting to say something, he looked at the men who were marching along next to him. He was going to tell them to let him loose, to let him go: "I haven't hurt anybody, boys," he was going to say to them, but he kept silent. "A little further on I'll tell them," he thought. And he just looked at them. He could even imagine they were his friends, but he didn't want to. They weren't. He didn't know who they were. He watched them moving at his side and bending down from time to time to see where the road continued.

He'd seen them for the first time at nightfall, that dusky hour when everything seems scorched. They'd crossed the furrows trodding on the tender corn. And he'd gone down there to tell them that the corn was beginning to grow. But that didn't stop them.

He'd seen them in time. He'd always had the luck to see everything in time. He could've hidden, gone up in the mountains for a few hours until they left, and then come down again. Already it was time for the rains to have come, but the rains didn't come and the corn was beginning to wither. Soon it'd be all dried up.

So it hadn't even been worthwhile, his going down and placing himself among those men like in a hole, never to get out again.

And now he continued beside them, holding back how he wanted to tell them to let him go. He didn't see their faces, he only saw their bodies, which swung toward him and then away from him. So when he started talking he didn't know if they'd heard him. He said, "I've never hurt anybody." That's what he said. But nothing changed. Not one of the bodies seemed to pay attention. The faces didn't turn to look at him. They kept right on, as if they were walking in their sleep.

Then he thought that there was nothing else he could say, that he would have to look for hope somewhere else. He let his arms fall again to his sides and went by the first houses of the village, among those four men, darkened by the black color of the night.

"Colonel, here is the man."

They'd stopped in front of the narrow doorway. He stood with his hat in his hand, respectfully, waiting to see someone come out. But only the voice came out, "Which man?"

"From Palo de Venado, Colonel. The one you ordered us to bring in."

"Ask him if he ever lived in Alima," came the voice from inside again.

"Hey, you. Ever lived in Alima?" the sergeant facing him repeated the question.

"Yes. Tell the colonel that's where I'm from. And that I lived there till not long ago."

"Ask him if he knew Guadalupe Terreros."

"He says did you know Guadalupe Terreros?"

"Don Lupe? Yes. Tell him that I knew him. He's dead."

Then the voice inside changed tone: "I know he died," it said. And the voice continued talking, as if it was conversing with someone there on the other side of the reed wall.

"Guadalupe Terreros was my father. When I grew up and looked for him they told me he was dead. It's hard to grow up knowing that the thing we have to hang on to, to take roots from, is dead. That's what happened to us.

"Later on I learned that he was killed by being hacked first with a machete and then an oxgoad stuck in his belly. They told me he lasted more than two days and that when they found him, lying in an arroyo, he was still in agony and begging that his family be taken care of.

"As time goes by you seem to forget this. You try to forget it. What you can't forget is finding out that the one who did it is still alive, feeding his rotten soul with the illusion of eternal life. I couldn't forgive that man, even though I don't know him; but the fact that I know where he is makes me want to finish him off. I can't forgive his still living. He should never have been born."

From here, from outside, all he said was clearly heard. Then he ordered, "Take him and tie him up awhile, so he'll suffer and then shoot him!"

"Look at me, Colonel!" he begged. "I'm not worth anything now. It won't be long before I die all by myself, crippled by old age. Don't kill me!"

"Take him away!" repeated the voice from inside.

"I've already paid, Colonel. I've paid many times over. They took everything away from me. They punished me in many ways. I've spent about forty years hiding like a leper, always with the fear they'd kill me at any moment. I don't deserve to die like this, Colonel. Let the Lord pardon me, at least. Don't kill me! Tell them not to kill me!"

There he was, as if they'd beaten him, waving his hat against the ground. Shouting.

Immediately the voice from inside said, "Tie him up and give him something to drink until he gets drunk so the shots won't hurt him."

Finally, now, he'd been quieted. There he was, slumped down at the foot of the post. His son Justino had come and his son Justino had gone and had returned and now was coming again.

He slung him on top of the burro. He cinched him up tight against the saddle so he wouldn't fall off on the road. He put his head in a sack so it wouldn't give such a bad impression. And then he made the burro giddap, and away they went in a hurry to reach Palo de Venado in time to arrange the wake for the dead man.

"Your daughter-in-law and grandchildren will miss you," he was saying to him. "They'll look at your face and won't believe it's you. They'll think the coyote has been eating on you when they see your face full of holes from all those bullets they shot at you."

1953

Elena Garro

b. 1920

ELENA GARRO WAS born in Puebla, Mexico, on December 15, 1920.
In 1937, she was studying philosophy at the UNAM (National University of Mexico) and was a choreographer at the University Theater. During that year she married writer Octavio Paz and started a
writing career of her own, at first in the field of journalism. After her
divorce from Paz, she lived in Spain, the United States, Mexico, and
France, working for various newspapers and also pursuing her own
work. Garro's major themes revolve around the concepts of time
and memory, which she explored fully in the prize-winning memoir
Recuerdos del porvenir (1963; *Recollections of Things to Come,* 1986).
In her short stories and plays, Garro also relates the plight of the
poor and the oppressed through haunting, often violent images.
Among her more recent works are the short-story collection *An-
damos huyendo Lola* (1980; We are fleeing Lola) and the novel *Testi-
monios sobre Mariana* (1981; Testimonies about Mariana).

The Day We Were Dogs

Translated by Tona Wilson

THE DAY WE were dogs was not just any day, even though it began the way
every day begins. We awoke at six in the morning and knew that it was a
day with two days inside it. Lying on her back, Eva opened her eyes and,
without changing her position, looked at one day and looked at the other.
I had opened mine just a few moments before and, so as not to see the
vastness of the empty house, I was looking at her. Why had we not gone
to Mexico City? I still do not know that. We asked to stay and no one

opposed our wish. The day before, the hall was filled with suitcases: everyone was fleeing the heat of August. Very early the suitcases left in a horse-drawn cart; on the table remained the half-finished cups of coffee and the oatmeal sticking to the bowls. Advice and suggestions rained down upon the tiles in the hall. Eva and I watched them disdainfully. We were the mistresses of the patios, the gardens, the rooms. When we took possession of the house, a great weight fell upon us. What could we do with the archways, the windows, the doors, and the furniture? The day turned solid, the violet sky clouded over with dark papers, and fear settled into the pillars and the plants. In silence we wandered about the house and watched our hair become rags. We had nothing to do, no one to ask what to do. In the kitchen, the servants clustered around the hearth, to eat and doze. The beds were not made; no one watered the ferns or took the dirty cups off the dining room table. At dusk, the songs of the servants filled with crimes and sorrows, and the house sank into that day, like a rock in a deep gorge.

We awoke determined not to repeat the preceding day. The new day shone double and intact. Eva looked at the two parallel days that glowed like two lines drawn in the water. Then she studied the wall, where Christ was in his white tunic. Then she turned her eyes to the other picture, which showed the image of Buddha wrapped in his orange tunic, pensive, in the middle of a yellowish landscape. Between the two pictures that guarded her bed, Eva had hung a clipping from a newspaper, with a photograph in which a lady in a beret was sailing on a yacht. "Madame Kroupuskaia on the Neva" said the caption.

"I like Russians," said Eva, and she clapped her hands to call the servants. No one responded to her call. We looked at each other without surprise. Eva clapped her hands in one of the days and her claps did not reach the day of the kitchen.

"Let's sniff around," she said to me.

And she jumped up on my bed to look at me up close. Her blonde hair covered her forehead. From my bed she jumped to the floor, put a finger to her lips and penetrated cautiously into the day that advanced parallel to the other. I followed her. No one. The day was alone, and it was as frightening as the other. The quiet trees, the rounded sky, green like a gentle meadow, without anyone either, without a horse, without a rider, abandoned. From the well rose the heat of August, which had caused the flight to Mexico City. Stretched out next to a tree was Toni. They had already chained him up. He looked at us attentively and we saw that he was in our day.

"Toni's good," said Eva and patted his open mouth.

Then she lay down next to him and I lay down on his other side.

"Did you already have breakfast, Toni?"

Toni didn't answer, only looked at us sadly. Eva got up and disappeared among the plants. She returned running and threw herself down next to Toni.

"I just told them to cook for three dogs and no people."

I didn't ask anything. Next to Toni the house had lost its weight. Two ants were walking on the ground of the day; an earthworm peeked out of a little hole, I touched it with my fingertip and it became a red ring. There were bits of leaves, little pieces of branches, tiny pebbles, and the black earth smelled of magnolia water. The other day was off to one side. Toni, Eva, and I watched without fear its gigantic towers and stationary winds, purple and mulberry colored.

"You, what's your name going to be? Look for your dog name, I'm looking for mine."

"I'm a dog?"

"Yes, we're dogs."

I accepted that and moved closer to Toni, who moved his head, disgusted. I remembered that he was not going to go to heaven; I would have the same fate. "Animals don't go to heaven." Our Lord Jesus Christ had not put a place for dogs in heaven. Nor had Lord Buddha put a place in Nirvana for dogs. In the house it was very important to be good so we could go to heaven. We couldn't hoard things, nor kill animals; we were vegetarians and on Sundays we threw Sunday from the balcony so someone could pick it up and we would learn not to keep anything. We lived up to date. The people of the town spied around the balconies of the house. "They're Spaniards," they said and looked at us askance. We didn't know that we weren't from there because we were going to heaven, either to one or the other: the white and blue or the orange and yellow one. Now there wouldn't be a place for the three of us in either of them. The alchemists, the Greeks, the anarchists, the romantics, the occultists, the Franciscans, and the Romans occupied the library shelves and dinnertable conversations. The Evangelists, the Vedas and the poets had a place apart. For the dogs there was nowhere but the foot of a tree. And afterwards? Afterwards we would be left lying on the ground.

"I just found my name."

"Already?" Eva sat up, curious.

"Yes: Christ."

Eva looked at me enviously.

"Christ? That's a good dog name."

Eva rested her head on her forepaws and closed her eyes.

"I found mine too," she said, sitting up suddenly.

"What?"

"Buddha!"

"That's a very good dog name."

And Buddha lay down next to Toni and began to growl with pleasure.

No one came to visit the day of Toni, Christ, and Buddha. The house was far away, within its other day. The chimes of the church clock told nothing. The ground began to get very hot: the worms crawled into their holes, the black beetles looked for the moist places underneath the stones, the ants cut acacia leaves, which they used as green sunshades. Where the dogs were, there was thirst. Buddha barked impatiently, asking for water, Toni imitated him and a moment later Christ joined in the barking. On a distant path appeared the feet of Rutilio, in huaraches. He brought three bowls of water. Indifferently he put a bowl in front of Toni, looked at Christ and Buddha, and placed a bowl of water near each of their snouts. Rutilio patted the heads of the dogs, and they gratefully wagged their tails. It was difficult to drink water with your tongue. Later the old servant brought food in a pot and served it in a big crock. The dogs' rice had bones and meat. Christ and Buddha looked at each other, astonished: weren't dogs vegetarians? Toni lifted his upper lip, growled fiercely through his white fangs, and quickly grabbed the chunks of meat. Christ and Buddha put their snouts in the crock and ate the rice moistened like gruel. Toni finished and drowsily watched his companions, who lapped up the rice. Later, they too rested on their forefeet. The sun beat down, the earth burned, and the dogs' food was heavy as a bag of rocks. They stayed sleeping in their day, separated from the day of the house. They were awakened by a blast that came from the other day. A long silence followed. Alert, they listened to the other afternoon. Another explosion, and the three dogs began running in the direction of the sound. Toni could not join in the race, because his chain stopped him close to the tree. Christ and Buddha jumped over the bushes in the direction of the gate.

"Where are you going, you wretched little brats?" Rutilio yelled at them, from the other day.

The dogs got to the gate; it was hard for them to open the door; the bolts were very high up. Finally they went out into the street, illuminated by the four o'clock sun. The street shone splendidly, like a fixed image. The stones glittered in the dust. There was nobody. Nobody but the two men bathed in blood, embraced in their struggle. Buddha sat down on the edge of the sidewalk and looked at them with eyes wide open. Christ settled down right next to Buddha and also looked at them with amazement. The men growled in the other day, "You'll see" . . . "Ayay! Son of a bitch!" Their smothered voices came from very far away. One restrained the hand of the one that held the pistol and with his free hand tattooed the other's chest with his knife. He was clasped to the body of the other, and, as though he hadn't enough strength, he slipped to the ground in the embrace. The man with the pistol stood firm in the splendid afternoon. His shirt and his white pants were soaked in blood. With a movement he freed his imprisoned hand and rested the pistol against the center of the forehead of his kneeling enemy. A dry sound divided the other afternoon in two, and opened a little hole in the forehead of the kneeling man. The man fell on his back and looked fixedly at the sky.

"Bastard!" yelled the man standing on the stones, while his legs continued to rain blood. Then he too raised his eyes to look at the same sky, and at the end of a few moments turned them on the dogs, who a couple of yards away, sitting on the edge of the sidewalk, stared at him openmouthed.

Everything was still. The other afternoon got so high that down below the street was outside of it. In the distance appeared several men with rifles. They were, like all the men, dressed in white, with palm sombreros on their heads. They walked slowly. The tread of their huaraches sounded from very far away. In the street there were no trees to deaden the sound of the footsteps; only white walls, against which echoed, closer and closer, the steps, like the roll of the drums on a day of fiesta. The roar stopped suddenly when they got to the wounded man.

"You killed him?"

"I sure did, ask the girls."

The men looked at the dogs.

"Did you see it?"

"Woof! Woof!" replied Buddha.

"Woof! Woof!" responded Christ.

"O.K. Take him away."

They took away the man and there remained no trace of him but the blood on the paving stones. He was writing his fate; the dogs read his bloody destiny and turned to look again at the dead man.

A time passed, the door of the house remained open, and the dogs, absorbed, sitting on the edge of the sidewalk, continued to look at the dead man. A fly appeared at the wound on his forehead, then cleaned its feet and moved to his hair. After an instant it returned to the forehead, looked at the wound, and again cleaned its feet. When the fly returned to the wound, a woman arrived and threw herself upon the dead man. But to him neither the fly nor the woman mattered. Unmoved, he continued to look at the sky. Other people came and bent down to see his eyes. It began to get dark and Buddha and Christ remained there, neither moving nor barking. They looked like two stray dogs and nobody paid any attention to them.

"Eva! Leli!" someone was calling from very high up. The dogs jumped, startled.

"Just wait till your parents get home! Just you wait and see!" Rutilio led them into the house. He placed a chair in the hallway, very close to the wall, and sat down to look at the dogs, who, lying at his feet, were watching him attentively. Candelaria brought a lighted paraffin lamp, and, strutting, returned to the kitchen. In a little while the songs flooded the house with mourning.

"It's your fault I can't go sing! . . . Wicked brats!" griped Rutilio.

Christ and Buddha listened to him from the other day. Rutilio, his chair, the lamp and the dead man, they were all in the parallel day, separated from the other day by an invisible line.

"Just wait and see, the witches will come and suck your blood. They say they love the blood of blondes. I'm going to tell Candelaria to leave the coals burning, so they can warm their calves. From the hearth they'll go straight up to your bed to enjoy themselves. It's what you deserve, for being wretches."

The hearth with the burning coals, Candelaria, Rutilio, the songs, and the witches, passed before the dogs' eyes like figures projected in another time. Rutilio's words circled through the hall without end and didn't touch them. On the floor of the day of the dogs, there were fat little bugs that were going to sleep. The sleepiness of the bugs was contagious and Christ and Buddha, curled up over their front paws, nodded.

"Supper time!"

They sat them down on the kitchen floor, in the circle of servants who were drinking alcohol and gave them a plate of beans with sausage. The dogs were falling asleep. Until yesterday they had still had oatmeal with milk for supper and the sausage made them feel queasy.

"Put them to bed, they're acting drunk!"

They put them both in the same bed, put out the lamp and left. The dogs slept in the other day, at the foot of the tree, with the chain around their necks, near the ants with their green sunshades and the red earthworms. After a short time they woke up, startled. The parallel day was there, sitting in the middle of the room. The walls were breathing burning coals; through the cracks the witches lurked, watching the blue veins of their temples. Everything was very dark. In one of the beds lay the dead man with his forehead open; at his side the man with the tattooed chest gushed blood. Very far away, at the back of the garden, slept the servants; Mexico City, with their parents and their brothers, who knew where that was? On the other hand, the other day was there, very close to them, without a bark, with its immobile dead men, in the immobile afternoon, with the enormous fly peering into the enormous wound and cleaning its feet. In sleep, without realizing it, we passed from one day to the other, and lost the day we were dogs.

"Don't be afraid, we're dogs . . ."

But Eva knew that it was no longer true. We had discovered that the heaven of men was not the same as the heaven of dogs.

The dogs did not share the crime with us.

1964

José Donoso

b. 1924

JOSÉ DONOSO WAS born into a middle-class family in the capital city of Santiago, Chile, in 1924. Rebellious by nature, Donoso dropped out of high school and became something of a drifter during the 1940s before resuming his education at the University of Chile, Santiago, and at Princeton University. He has worked as a journalist, editor, and translator, and has also taught at various universities, among them the University of Chile, the University of Iowa, and Colorado State University. Donoso has also lived in Argentina, Mexico, and Spain. His first novel, *Coronación* (1957; *Coronation,* 1965), a scathing portrayal of his country's upper classes, won the William Faulkner Foundation Prize and brought him international recognition. Other works followed in the 1960s, but it was in *El obsceno pájaro de la noche* (1970; *The Obscene Bird of Night,* 1973) that Donoso displayed his full powers as a highly experimental and challenging author. Considered by critics to be one of the best works of the Latin American literary "Boom," the novel continued to explore Donoso's central preoccupation with conflicts of class in a convoluted narrative style and highly subjective voice. (He has called it "the autobiography of my fears.") Later novels are *Casa de campo* (1978; *A House in the Country,* 1984), and *La desesperanza* (1986; *Curfew,* 1988). One of Donoso's best known works is his memoir *Historia personal del "boom"* (1972; *The Boom in Spanish American Literature: A Personal History,* 1977), which introduced the general reader to this most productive and innovative literary period in Latin America. His short stories have appeared in English in the collection entitled *Charleston and Other Stories* (1977), from which "The Walk" has been selected.

The Walk

For Mabel Cardahi

Translated by Andrée Conrad

1

IT HAPPENED WHEN I was very small, when my Aunt Matilde and Uncle Gustavo and Uncle Armando, my father's unmarried sister and brothers, and my father himself, were still alive. Now they are all dead. That is, I'd rather think they are all dead, because it's easier, and it's too late now to be tortured with questions that were certainly not asked at the opportune moment. They weren't asked because the events seemed to paralyze the three brothers, leaving them shaken and horrified. Afterwards, they erected a wall of forgetfulness or indifference in front of it all so they could keep their silence and avoid tormenting themselves with futile conjectures. Maybe it wasn't that way; it could be that my imagination and my memory play me false. After all, I was only a boy at the time, and they weren't required to include me in their anguished speculations, if there ever were any, or keep me informed of the outcome of their conversations.

What was I to think? Sometimes I heard the brothers talking in the library in low voices, lingeringly, as was their custom; but the thick door screened the meaning of the words, allowing me to hear only the deep, deliberate counterpoint of their voices. What were they saying? I wanted them to be talking in there about what was really important; to abandon the respectful coldness with which they addressed one another, to open up their doubts and anxieties and let them bleed. But I had so little faith that would happen; while I loitered in the high-walled vestibule near the library door, the certainty was engraved on my mind that they had chosen to forget, and had come together only to discuss, as always, the cases that fell within their bailiwick, maritime law. Now I think perhaps they were right to want to erase it all, for why should they live with the useless terror of having to accept that the streets of a city can swallow a human being, annul it, leave it without life or death, suspended in a dimension more threatening than any dimension with a name?

And yet . . .

One day, months after the incident, I surprised my father looking down at the street from the second-floor sitting room. The sky was narrow, dense, and the humid air weighed on the big limp leaves of the ailanthus trees. I went over to my father, anxious for some minimal explanation.

"What are you doing here, father?" I whispered.

214

When he answered, something closed suddenly over the desperation on his face, like a shutter slamming on an unmentionable scene.

"Can't you see? I'm smoking," he answered.

And he lit a cigarette.

It wasn't true. I knew why he was looking up and down the street, with his eyes saddened, once in a while bringing his hand up to his soft brown goatee: it was in hopes of seeing her reappear, come back just like that, under the trees along the sidewalk, with the white dog trotting at her heels. Was he waiting there to gain some certainty?

Little by little, I realized that not only my father but both his brothers, as if hiding from one another and without admitting even to themselves what they were doing, hovered around the windows of the house, and if a passerby chanced to look up from the sidewalk across the street, he might spot the shadow of one of them posted beside a curtain, or a face aged by suffering in wait behind the window panes.

2

Yesterday I passed the house we lived in then. It's been years since I was last there. In those days the street under the leafy ailanthus trees was paved with quebracho wood, and from time to time a noisy streetcar would go by. Now there aren't any wooden pavements, or streetcars, or trees along the sidewalk. But our house is still standing, narrow and vertical as a book slipped in between the thick shapes of the new buildings; it has stores on the ground floor and a loud sign advertising knit undershirts stretched across the two second-floor balconies.

When we lived there, most of the houses were tall and slender like ours. The block was always cheerful, with children playing games in the splashes of sunlight on the sidewalks, and servants from the prosperous homes gossiping as they came back from shopping. But our house wasn't happy. I say "wasn't happy" as opposed to "was sad," because that's exactly what I mean. The word "sad" wouldn't be correct because it has connotations that are too clearly defined; it has a weight and dimensions of its own. And what went on in our house was exactly the opposite: an absence, a lack, which, because it was unknown, was irremediable, something that had no weight, yet weighed because it didn't exist.

When my mother died, before I turned four, they thought I needed to have a woman around to care for me. Because Aunt Matilde was the only woman in the family and lived with my uncles Gustavo and Armando, the three of them came to our house, which was big and empty.

Aunt Matilde carried out her duties toward me with the punctiliousness characteristic of everything she did. I didn't doubt that she cared for me, but I never experienced that affection as something palpable that united us. There was something rigid about her feelings, as there was about those of the men in the family, and love was retained within each separate being, never leaping over the boundaries to express itself and unite us. Their idea of expressing affection consisted of carrying out their duties toward one another perfectly, and above all, of never upsetting one another. Perhaps to express affection otherwise was no longer necessary to them, since they shared so many anecdotes and events in which, possibly, affection had already been expressed to the saturation point, and all this conjectural past of tenderness was now stylized in the form of precise actions, useful symbols that did not require further explanation. Respect alone remained, as a point of contact among four silent, isolated relatives who moved through the halls of that deep house which, like a book, revealed only its narrow spine to the street.

I, of course, had no anecdotes in common with Aunt Matilde. How could I, since I was a boy and only half understood the austere motives of grown-ups? I desperately wanted this contained affection to overflow, to express itself differently, in enthusiasm, for example, or a joke. But she could not guess this desire of mine because her attention wasn't focused on me. I was only a peripheral person in her life, never central. And I wasn't central because the center of her whole being was filled with my father and my uncles Gustavo and Armando. Aunt Matilde was the only girl—an ugly girl at that—in a family of handsome men, and realizing she was unlikely to find a husband, she dedicated herself to the comfort of those men: keeping house for them, taking care of their clothes, preparing their favorite dishes. She carried out these functions without the slightest servility, proud of her role because she had never once doubted her brothers' excellence and dignity. In addition, like all women, she possessed in great measure that mysterious faith in physical well-being, thinking that if it is not the main thing, it is certainly the first, and that not to be hungry or cold or uncomfortable is the prerequisite of any good of another order. It wasn't that she suffered if defects of that nature arose, but rather that they made her impatient, and seeing poverty or weakness around her, she took immediate steps to remedy what she did not doubt were mere errors in a world that ought to be—no, *had* to be—perfect. On another plane, this was intolerance of shirts that weren't ironed exquisitely, of meat that wasn't a prime cut, of dampness leaking into the humidor through some-one's carelessness. Therein lay Aunt Matilde's undisputed strength, and through it she nourished the roots of her brothers' grandness and accepted their protection because they were men, stronger and wiser than she.

Every night after dinner, following what must have been an ancient family ritual, Aunt Matilde went upstairs to the bedrooms and turned down the covers on each one of her brothers' beds, folding up the bedspreads with her bony hands. For him who was sensitive to the cold, she would lay a blanket at the foot of the bed; for him who read before going to sleep, she would prop a feather pillow against the headboard. Then, leaving the lamps lit on the night tables beside their vast beds, she went downstairs to the billiard room to join the men, to have coffee with them and play a few caroms before they retired, as if by her command, to fill the empty effigies of the pajamas laid out on the neatly turned-down white sheets.

But Aunt Matilde never opened my bed. Whenever I went up to my room I held my breath, hoping to find my bed turned down with the recognizable expertise of her hands, but I always had to settle for the style, so much less pure, of the servant who did it. She never conceded me this sign of importance because I was not one of her brothers. And not to be "one of my brothers" was a shortcoming shared by so many people . . .

Sometimes Aunt Matilde would call me in to her room, and sewing near the high window she would talk to me without ever asking me to reply, taking it for granted that all my feelings, tastes, and thoughts were the result of what she was saying, certain that nothing stood in the way of my receiving her words intact. I listened to her carefully. She impressed on me what a privilege it was to have been born the son of one of her brothers, which made it possible to have contact with all of them. She spoke of their absolute integrity and genius as lawyers in the most intricate of maritime cases, informing me of her enthusiasm regarding their prosperity and distinction, which I would undoubtedly continue. She explained the case of an embargo on a copper shipment, another about damages resulting from a collision with an insignificant tugboat, and another having to do with the disastrous effects of the overlong stay of a foreign ship. But in speaking to me of ships, her words did not evoke the magic of those hoarse foghorns I heard on summer nights when, kept awake by the heat, I would climb up to the attic and watch from a roundel the distant lights floating, and those darkened blocks of the recumbent city to which I had no access because my life was, and always would be, perfectly organized. Aunt Matilde did not evoke that magic for me because she was ignorant of it; it had no place in her life, since it could not have a place in the life of people destined to die with dignity and then establish themselves in complete comfort in heaven, a heaven that would be identical to our house. Mute, I listened to her words, my eyes fixed on the length of light-colored thread which, rising against the black of her blouse, seemed to catch all the light from the window. I had a melancholy feeling of frustration, hearing those foghorns in the night and seeing that dark and starry city so much like the heaven in which Aunt Matilde saw no mystery at all. But I rejoiced at the world of security her words sketched out for me, that magnificent rectilinear road which ended in a death not feared, exactly like this life, lacking the fortuitous and unexpected. For death was not terrible. It was the final cutoff, clean and definite, nothing more. Hell existed, of course, though not for us, but rather to punish the rest of the city's inhabitants, or those nameless sailors who caused the damages that, after the struggle in the courts was over, always filled the family bank accounts.

Any notion of the unexpected, of any kind of fear, was so alien to Aunt Matilde that, because I believe fear and love to be closely related, I am overcome by the temptation to think that she didn't love anybody, not at that time. But perhaps I am wrong. In her own rigid, isolated way, it is possible that she was tied to her brothers by some kind of love. At night, after dinner, when they gathered in the billiard room for coffee and a few rounds, I went with them. There, faced with this circle of confined loves which did not include me, I suffered, perceiving that they were no longer tied together by their affection. It's strange that my imagination, remembering that house, doesn't allow more than grays, shadows, shades; but when I evoke that hour, the strident green of the felt, the red and white of the billiard balls, and the tiny cube of blue chalk begin to swell in my memory, illuminated by the hanging lamp that condemned the rest of the room to darkness. Following one of the many family rituals, Aunt Matilde's refined voice would rescue each of her brothers from the darkness as his turn came up: "Your shot, Gustavo . . ."

And cue in hand, Uncle Gustavo would lean over the green of the table, his face lit up, fragile as paper, the nobility of it strangely contradicted by his small, close-set eyes. When his turn was over, he retreated into the shadows, where he puffed on a cigar whose smoke floated lackadaisically off, dissolved by the darkness of the ceiling. Then their sister would say: "Your shot, Armando . . ."

And Uncle Armando's soft, timid face, his great blue eyes shielded by gold-framed glasses, would descend into the light. His game was generally bad, because he was the "baby," as Aunt Matilde sometimes called him. After the comments elicited by his game, he would take refuge behind the newspaper and Aunt Matilde would say: "Pedro, your shot . . ."

I held my breath watching my father lean over to shoot; I held it seeing him succumb to his sister's command, and, my heart in a knot, I prayed he would rebel against the established order. Of course, I couldn't know that that rigid order was in itself a kind of rebellion invented by them against the chaotic, so that the terrible hand of what cannot be explained or solved would never touch them. Then my father would lean over the green felt, his soft glance measuring the distances and positions of the balls. He would make his play and afterwards heave a sigh, his moustache and goatee fluttering a little around his half-open mouth. Then he would hand me his cue to chalk with the little blue cube. By assigning me this small role, he let me touch at least the periphery of the circle that tied him to his brothers and sister, without letting me become more than tangential to it.

Afterwards Aunt Matilde played. She was the best shot. Seeing her ugly face, built up it seemed out of the defects of her brothers' faces, descend into the light, I knew she would win; she had to win. And yet . . . didn't I see a spark of joy in those tiny eyes in the middle of that face, as irregular as a suddenly clenched fist, when by accident one of the men managed to defeat her? That drop of joy was because, although she might want to, she could never have *let* them win. That would have been to introduce the mysterious element of love into a game which should not include it, because affection had to remain in its place, without overflowing to warp the precise reality of a carom.

3

I never liked dogs. Perhaps I had been frightened by one as a baby, I don't remember, but they have always annoyed me. In any case, at that time my dislike of animals was irrelevant since we didn't have any dogs in the house; I didn't go out very often, so there were few opportunities for them to molest me. For my uncles and father, dogs, as well as the rest of the animal kingdom, did not exist. Cows, of course, supplied the cream that enriched our Sunday dessert brought in on a silver tray; and birds chirped pleasantly at dusk in the elm tree, the only inhabitant of the garden behind our house. The animal kingdom existed only to the extent that it contributed to the comfort of their persons. It is needless to say, then, that the existence of dogs, especially our ragged city strays, never even grazed their imaginations.

It's true that occasionally, coming home from Mass on Sunday, a dog might cross our path, but it was easy to ignore it. Aunt Matilde, who always walked ahead with me, simply chose not to see it, and some steps behind us, my father and uncles strolled discussing problems too important to allow their attention to be drawn by anything so banal as a stray dog.

Sometimes Aunt Matilde and I went early to Mass to take communion.

I was almost never able to concentrate on receiving the sacrament, because generally the idea that she was watching me without actually looking at me occupied the first plane of my mind. Although her eyes were directed toward the altar or her head bowed before the Almighty, any movement I made attracted her attention, so that coming out of church, she would tell me with hidden reproach that doubtless some flea trapped in the pews had prevented my concentrating on the thought that we shall all meet death in the end and on praying for it not to be too painful, for that was the purpose of Mass, prayer, and communion.

It was one of those mornings.

A fine mist was threatening to transform itself into a storm, and the quebracho paving extended its neat glistening fan shapes from sidewalk to sidewalk, bisected by the streetcar rails. I was cold and wanted to get home, so I hurried the pace under Aunt Matilde's black umbrella. Few people were out because it was early. A colored gentleman greeted us without tipping his hat. My aunt then proceeded to explain her dislike of persons of mixed race, but suddenly, near where we were walking, a streetcar I didn't hear coming braked loudly, bringing her monologue to an end. The conductor put his head out the window: "Stupid dog!" he shouted.

We stopped to look. A small white bitch escaped from under the wheels, and, limping painfully with its tail between its legs, took refuge in a doorway. The streetcar rolled off.

"These dogs, it's the limit the way they let them run loose . . ." protested Aunt Matilde.

Continuing on our way, we passed the dog cowering in the doorway. It was small and white, with legs too short for its body and an ugly pointed nose that revealed a whole genealogy of alleyway misalliances, the product of different races running around the city for generations looking for food in garbage cans and harbor refuse. It was soaking wet, weak, shivering with the cold or a fever. Passing in front of it, I witnessed a strange sight: my aunt's and the dog's eyes met. I couldn't see the expression on my aunt's face. I only saw the dog look at her, taking possession of her glance, whatever it contained, merely because she was looking at it.

We headed home. A few paces further on, when I had almost forgotten the dog, my aunt startled me by turning abruptly around and exclaiming: "Shoo, now! Get along with you!"

She had turned around completely certain of finding it following us and I trembled with the unspoken question prompted by my surprise: "How did she know?" She couldn't have heard it because the dog was following us at some distance. But she didn't doubt it. Did the glance that passed between them, of which I had only seen the mechanical part—the dog's head slightly raised toward Aunt Matilde, Aunt Matilde's head slightly turned toward it—did it contain some secret agreement, some promise of loyalty I hadn't perceived? I don't know. In any case, when she turned to shoo the dog, her voice seemed to contain an impotent desire to put off a destiny that had already been accomplished. Probably I say all this in hindsight, my imagination imbuing something trivial with special meaning. Nevertheless, I certainly felt surprise, almost fear, at the sight of my aunt suddenly losing her composure and condescending to turn around, thereby conceding rank to a sick, dirty dog following us for reasons that could not have any importance.

We arrived home. We climbed the steps and the animal stayed down below, watching us through the torrential rain that had just begun. We went inside, and the delectable smell of a post-communion breakfast erased the dog from my mind. I had never felt the protectiveness of our house so deeply as I did that morning; the security of those walls delimiting my world had never been so delightful to me.

What did I do the rest of the day? I don't remember, but I suppose I did the usual thing: read magazines, did homework, wandered up and down the stairs, went to the kitchen to ask what was for dinner.

On one of my tours through the empty rooms—my uncles got up late on rainy Sundays, excusing themselves from church—I pulled a curtain back to see if the rain was letting up. The storm went on. Standing at the foot of the steps, still shivering and watching the house, I saw the white dog again. I let go of the curtain to avoid seeing it there, soaking wet and apparently mesmerized. Suddenly, behind me, from the dark part of the sitting room, Aunt Matilde's quiet voice reached me, as she leaned over to touch a match to the wood piled in the fireplace: "Is she still there?"

"Who?"

I knew perfectly well who.

"The white dog."

I answered that it was. But my voice was uncertain in forming the syllables, as if somehow my aunt's question was pulling down the walls around us, letting the rain and the inclement wind enter and take over the house.

4

That must have been the last of the winter storms, because I remember quite vividly that in the following days the weather cleared and the nights got warmer.

The white dog remained posted at our door, ever trembling, watching the window as though looking for somebody. In the morning, as I left for school, I would try to scare it away, but as soon as I got on the bus, I saw it peep timidly around the corner or from behind a lamppost. The servants tried to drive it away too, but their attempts were just as futile as my own, because the dog always came back, as if to stay near our house was a temptation it had to obey, no matter how dangerous.

One night we were all saying good night to one another at the foot of the stairs. Uncle Gustavo, who always took charge of turning off the lights, had taken care of all of them except that of the staircase, leaving the great dark space of the vestibule populated with darker clots of furniture. Aunt Matilde, who was telling Uncle Armando to open his window to let some air in, suddenly fell silent, leaving her good nights unfinished. The rest of us, who had begun to climb the stairs, stopped cold.

"What's the matter?" asked my father, coming down a step.

"Go upstairs," murmured Aunt Matilde, turning to gaze into the shadows of the vestibule.

But we didn't go upstairs.

The silence of the sitting room, generally so spacious, filled up with the secret voice of each object—a grain of dirt slipping down between the old wallpaper and the wall, wood creaking, a loose window pane rattling—and those brief seconds were flooded with sounds. Someone else was in the room with us. A small white shape stood out in the shadows near the service door. It was the dog, who limped slowly across the vestibule in the direction of Aunt Matilde, and without even looking at her lay down at her feet.

It was as if the dog's stillness made movement possible for us as we watched the scene. My father came down two steps, Uncle Gustavo turned on the lights, Uncle Armando heavily climbed the stairs and shut himself into his room.

"What is this?" my father asked.

Aunt Matilde remained motionless.

"How could she have got in?" she asked herself suddenly.

Her question seemed to imply a feat: in this lamentable condition, the dog had leaped over walls, or climbed through a broken window in the basement, or evaded the servants' vigilance by slipping through a door left open by accident.

"Matilde, call for somebody to get it out of here," my father said, and went upstairs followed by Uncle Gustavo.

The two of us stood looking at the dog.

"She's filthy," she said in a low voice. "And she has a fever. Look, she's hurt . . ."

She called one of the servants to take her away, ordering her to give the dog food and call the veterinarian the next day.

"Is it going to stay in the house?" I asked.

"How can she go outside like that?" Aunt Matilde murmured. "She has to get better before we can put her out. And she'll have to get better quickly, because I don't want any animals in the house." Then she added: "Get upstairs to bed."

She followed the servant who was taking the dog away.

I recognized Aunt Matilde's usual need to make sure everything around her went well, the strength and deftness that made her the undoubted queen of things immediate, so secure inside her limitations that for her the only necessary thing was to correct flaws, mistakes not of intention or motive, but of state of being. The white dog, therefore, was going to get well. She herself would take charge of that, because the dog had come within her sphere of power. The veterinarian would bandage the dog's foot under her watchful eyes, and, protected by gloves and a towel, she herself would undertake to clean its sores with disinfectants that would make it whimper. Aunt Matilde remained deaf to those whimpers, certain, absolutely certain, that what she was doing was for the dog's good.

And so it was.

The dog stayed in the house. It wasn't that I could see it, but I knew the balance between the people who lived there, and the presence of any stranger, even if in the basement, would establish a difference in the order of things. Something, something informed me of its presence under the same roof as myself. Perhaps that something was not so very imponderable. Sometimes I saw Aunt Matilde with rubber gloves in her hand, carrying a vial full of red liquid. I found scraps of meat on a dish in a basement passageway when I went down to look at a bicycle I had recently been given. Sometimes, the suspicion of a bark would reach my ears faintly, absorbed by floors and walls.

One afternoon I went down to the kitchen and the white dog came in, painted like a clown with the red disinfectant. The servants threw it out unceremoniously. But I could see it wasn't limping anymore, and its once droopy tail now curled up like a plume, leaving its hindquarters shamelessly exposed.

That afternoon I said to Aunt Matilde: "When are you going to get rid of it?"

"What?" she asked.

She knew perfectly well what I meant.

"The white dog."

"She's not well yet," she answered.

Later on, I was about to bring up the subject again, to tell her that even if the dog wasn't completely well yet, there was nothing to prevent it from standing on its hind legs and rooting around in the garbage pails for food. But I never did, because I think that was the night Aunt Matilde, after losing the first round of billiards, decided she didn't feel like playing anymore. Her brothers went on playing and she, sunk in the big leather sofa, reminded them of their turns. After a while she made a mistake in the shooting order. Everybody was disconcerted for a moment, but the correct order was soon restored by the men, who rejected chance if it was not favorable. But I had seen.

It was as if Aunt Matilde was not there. She breathed at my side as always. The deep, muffling rug sank as usual under her feet. Her hands, crossed calmly on her lap—perhaps more calmly than on other evenings—weighed on her skirt. How is it that one feels a person's absence so clearly when that person's heart is in another place? Only her heart was absent, but the voice she used to call her brothers contained new meanings because it came from that other place.

The next nights were also marred by this almost invisible smudge of her absence. She stopped playing billiards and calling out turns altogether. The men seemed not to notice. But perhaps they did, because the matches became shorter, and I noted that the deference with which they treated her grew infinitesimally.

One night, as we came out of the dining room, the dog made its appearance in the vestibule and joined the family. The men, as usual, waited at the library door for their sister to lead the way into the billiard room, this time gracefully followed by the dog. They made no comment, as if they hadn't seen it, and began their match as on other nights.

The dog sat at Aunt Matilde's feet, very quiet, its lively eyes examining the room and watching the players' maneuvers, as if it was greatly amused. It was plump now, and its coat, its whole body glowed, from its quivering nose to its tail, always ready to wag. How long had the dog been in the house? A month? Longer, perhaps. But in that month Aunt Matilde had made it get well, caring for it without displays of emotion, but with the great wisdom of her bony hands dedicated to repairing what was damaged. Implacable in the face of its pain and whimpers, she had cured its wounds. Its foot was healed. She had disinfected it, fed it, bathed it, and now the white dog was whole again.

And yet none of this seemed to unite her to the dog. Perhaps she accepted it in the same way that my uncles that night had accepted its presence: to reject it would have given it more importance than it could have for them. I saw Aunt Matilde tranquil, collected, full of a new feeling that did not quite overflow to touch its object, and now we were six beings separated by a distance vaster than stretches of rug and air.

It happened during one of Uncle Armando's shots, when he dropped the little cube of blue chalk. Instantly, obeying a reflex that linked it to its picaresque past in the streets, the dog scampered to the chalk, yanked it away from Uncle Armando who had leaned over to pick it up, and held it in its mouth. Then a surprising thing happened. Aunt Matilde, suddenly coming apart, burst out in uncontrollable guffaws that shook her whole body for a few seconds. We were paralyzed. Hearing her, the dog dropped the chalk and ran to her, its tail wagging and held high, and jumped on her skirt. Aunt Matilde's laughter subsided, but Uncle Armando, vexed, left the room to avoid witnessing this collapse of order through the intrusion of the absurd. Uncle Gustavo and my father kept on playing billiards; now more than ever it was essential not to see, not to see anything, not to make remarks, not even to allude to the episode, and perhaps in this way to keep something from moving forward.

I did not find Aunt Matilde's guffaws amusing. It was only too clear that something dark had happened. The dog lay still on her lap. The crack of the billiard balls as they collided, precise and discrete, seemed to lead Aunt Matilde's hand first from its place on the sofa to her skirt, and then to the back of the sleeping dog. Seeing that expressionless hand resting there, I also observed that the tension I had never before recognized on my aunt's face—I never suspected it was anything other than dignity—had dissolved, and a great peace was softening her features. I could not resist what I did. Obeying something stronger than my own will, I slid closer to her on the sofa. I waited for her to beckon to me with a look or include me with a smile, but she didn't, because their new relationship was too exclusive; there was no place for me. There were only those two united beings. I didn't like it, but I was left out. And the men remained isolated, because they had not paid attention to the dangerous invitation to which Aunt Matilde had dared to listen.

5

Coming home from school in the afternoon, I would go straight downstairs and, mounting my new bicycle, would circle round and round in the narrow garden behind the house, around the elm tree and the pair of iron benches. On the other side of the wall, the neighbors' walnut trees were beginning to show signs of spring, but I didn't keep track of the seasons and their gifts because I had more serious things to think about. And as I knew nobody came down to the garden until the suffocations of midsummer made it essential, it was the best place to think about what was happening in our house.

Superficially it might be said nothing was happening. But how could one remain calm in the face of the curious relationship that had arisen between my aunt and the white dog? It was as if Aunt Matilde, after punctiliously serving and conforming to her unequal life, had at last found her equal, someone who spoke her innermost language, and as among women, they carried on an intimacy full of pleasantries and agreeable refinements. They ate bonbons that came in boxes tied with frivolous bows. My aunt arranged oranges, pineapples, grapes on the tall fruit stands, and the dog watched as if to criticize her taste or deliver an opinion. She seemed to have discovered a more benign region of life in this sharing of pleasantries, so much so that now everything had lost its importance in the shadow of this new world of affection.

Frequently, when passing her bedroom door, I would hear a guffaw like the one that had dashed the old order of her life to the ground that night, or I would hear her conversing—not soliloquizing as when talking to me—with someone whose voice I could not hear. It was the new life. The culprit, the dog, slept in her room in a basket—elegant, feminine, and absurd to my way of thinking—and followed her everywhere, except into the dining room. It was forbidden to go in there, but waited for its friend to emerge, followed her to the library or the billiard room, wherever we were going, and sat beside her or on her lap, and from time to time, sly looks of understanding would pass between them.

How was this possible? I asked myself. Why had she waited until now to overflow and begin a dialogue for the first time in her life? At times she seemed insecure about the dog, as if afraid the day might come when it would go away, leaving her alone with all this new abundance on her hands. Or was she still concerned about the dog's health? It was too strange. These ideas floated like blurs in my imagination while I listened to the gravel crunching under the wheels of my bicycle. What was not blurry, on the other hand, was my vehement desire to fall seriously ill, to see if that way I too could gain a similar relationship. The dog's illness had been the cause of it all. Without that, my aunt would never have become linked to it. But I had an iron constitution, and furthermore it was clear that inside Aunt Matilde's heart there was room for only one love at a time, especially if it were so intense.

My father and uncles didn't seem to notice any change at all. The dog was quiet, and abandoning its street manners it seemed to acquire Aunt Matilde's somewhat dignified mien; but it preserved all the impudence of a female whom the vicissitudes of life have not been able to shock, as well as its good temper and its liking for adventure. It was easier for the men to accept than reject it since the latter would at least have meant speaking, and perhaps even an uncomfortable revision of their standards of security.

One night, when the pitcher of lemonade had already made its appearance on the library credenza, cooling that corner of the shadows, and the windows had been opened to the air, my father stopped abruptly at the entrance to the billiard room.

"What is this?" he exclaimed, pointing at the floor.

The three men gathered in consternation to look at a tiny round puddle on the waxed floor.

"Matilde!" Uncle Gustavo cried.

She came over to look and blushed with shame. The dog had taken refuge under the billiard table in the next room. Turning toward the table, my father saw it there, and suddenly changing course he left the room, followed by his brothers, heading toward the bedrooms, where each of them locked himself in, silent and alone.

Aunt Matilde said nothing. She went up to her room followed by the dog. I stayed in the library with a glass of lemonade in my hand, looking out at the summer sky and listening, anxiously listening to distant fog-horns and the noise of the unknown city, terrible and at the same time desirable, stretched out under the stars.

Then I heard Aunt Matilde descend. She appeared with her hat on and her keys jingling in her hand.

"Go to bed," she said. "I'm taking her for a walk on the street so she can take care of her business there."

Then she added something that made me nervous: "The night's so pretty . . ."

And she went out.

From that night on, instead of going upstairs after dinner to turn down her brothers' beds, she went to her room, put on her hat, and came down again, her keys jingling. She went out with the dog, not saying a word to anybody. My uncles and my father and I stayed in the billiard room, or, as the season wore on, sat on the benches in the garden, with the rustling elm and the clear sky pressing down on us. These nightly walks of Aunt

Matilde's were never mentioned, there was never any indication that anybody knew anything important had changed in the house; but an element had been introduced there that contradicted all order.

At first Aunt Matilde would stay out at most fifteen or twenty minutes, returning promptly to take coffee with us and exchange a few commonplaces. Later, her outings inexplicably took more time. She was no longer a woman who walked her dog for reasons of hygiene; out there in the streets, in the city, there was something powerful attracting her. Waiting for her, my father glanced furtively at his pocket watch, and if she was very late, Uncle Gustavo went up to the second floor, as if he had forgotten something there, to watch from the balcony. But they never said anything. Once when Aunt Matilde's walk had taken too long, my father paced back and forth along the path between the hydrangeas, their flowers like blue eyes watching the night. Uncle Gustavo threw away a cigar he couldn't light satisfactorily, and then another, stamping it out under his heel. Uncle Armando overturned a cup of coffee. I watched, waiting for an eventual explosion, for them to say something, for them to express their anxiety and fill those endless minutes stretching on and on without the presence of Aunt Matilde. It was half past twelve when she came home.

"Why did you wait up for me?" she said smiling.

She carried her hat in her hand and her hair, ordinarily so neat, was disheveled. I noted that daubs of mud stained her perfect shoes.

"What happened to you?"

"Nothing," was her answer, and with that she closed forever any possible right her brothers might have had to interfere with those unknown hours, happy or tragic or insignificant, which were now her life.

I say they were her life, because in those instants she remained with us before going to her room, with the dog, muddy too, next to her, I perceived an animation in her eyes, a cheerful restlessness like the animal's, as if her eyes had recently bathed in scenes never before witnessed, to which we had no access. These two were companions. The night protected them. They belonged to the noises, to the foghorns that wafted over docks, dark or lamplit streets, houses, factories, and parks, finally reaching my ears.

Her walks with the dog continued. Now she said good night to us right after dinner, and all of us went to our rooms, my father, Uncle Gustavo, Uncle Armando, and myself. But none of us fell asleep until we heard her come in, late, sometimes very late, when the light of dawn already brightened the top of our elm tree. Only after she was heard closing her bedroom door would the paces by which my father measured his room stop, and a window be closed by one of her brothers to shut out the night, which had ceased being dangerous for the time being.

Once after she had come in very late, I thought I heard her singing very softly and sweetly, so I cracked open my door and looked out. She passed in front of my door, the white dog cuddled in her arms. Her face looked surprisingly young and perfect, although it was a little dirty, and I saw there was a tear in her skirt. This woman was capable of anything; she had her whole life before her. I went to bed terrified that this would be the end.

And I wasn't wrong. Because one night shortly afterwards, Aunt Matilde went out for a walk with the dog and never came back.

We waited up all night long, each one of us in his room, and she didn't come home. The next day nobody said anything. But the silent waiting went on, and we all hovered silently, without seeming to, around the windows of the house, watching for her. From that first day fear made the harmonious dignity of the three brothers' faces collapse, and they aged rapidly in a very short time.

"Your aunt went on a trip," the cook told me once, when I finally dared to ask.

But I knew it wasn't true.

Life went on in our house as if Aunt Matilde were still living with us. It's true they had a habit of gathering in the library, and perhaps locked in there they talked, managing to overcome the wall of fear that isolated them, giving free rein to their fears and doubts. But I'm not sure. Several times a visitor came who didn't belong to our world, and they would lock themselves in with him. But I don't believe he had brought them news of a possible investigation; perhaps he was nothing more than the boss of a longshoremen's union who was coming to claim damages for some accident. The door of the library was too thick, too heavy, and I never knew if Aunt Matilde, dragged along by the white dog, had got lost in the city, or in death, or in a region more mysterious than either.

1971

Clarice Lispector

1925–1977

ONE OF BRAZIL'S most respected writers, Clarice Lispector was born in the Ukraine on December 10, 1925, but her family emigrated to Brazil when she was two months old. A lawyer by training, Lispector was also one of Brazil's first female journalists and an editor for a major news agency. Her reputation as an important writer has been established by acclaimed critical reception of her many novels and short stories and by several literary awards. The short-story collection *Laços de família* (1960; *Family Ties,* 1960) and the novel *A maça no escuro* (1960; *The Apple in the Dark,* 1961) represent some of her best work. She was influenced by the French existentialists, especially Sartre, and by Virginia Woolf. In many of her texts, Lispector analyzes the female experience through the use of interior monologue and stream of consciousness.

The Imitation of the Rose

Translated by Giovanni Pontiero

BEFORE ARMANDO CAME home from work the house would have to be tidied and Laura herself ready in her brown dress so that she could attend her husband while he dressed, and then they would leave at their leisure, arm in arm as in former times. How long was it since they had last done that?

But now that she was "well" again, they would take the bus, she looking like a wife, watching out of the bus window, her arm in his: and later they would dine with Carlota and João, sitting back intimately in their chairs. How long was it since she had seen Armando sit back with intimacy and converse with another man? A man at peace was one who, oblivious of his wife's presence, could converse with another man about the latest news in the headlines. Meantime, she would talk to Carlota about women's things, submissive to the authoritarian and practical goodness of Carlota, receiving once more her friend's attention and vague disdain, her natural abruptness, instead of that perplexed affection full of curiosity—watching Armando, finally oblivious of his own wife. And she herself, finally returning to play an insignificant role with gratitude. Like a cat which, having spent the night out of doors, as if nothing had happened, had unexpectedly found a saucer of milk waiting. People fortunately helped to make her feel that she was "well" again. Without watching her, they actively helped her to forget, they themselves feigning forgetfulness as if they had read the same directions on the same medicine bottle. Or, perhaps, they had really forgotten. How long was it since she last saw Armando sit back with abandon, oblivious of her presence? And she herself?

Interrupting her efforts to tidy up the dressing table, Laura gazed at herself in the mirror. And she herself? How long had it been? Her face had a domestic charm, her hair pinned behind her large pale ears. Her brown eyes and brown hair, her soft dark skin, all lent to that face, no longer so very young, the unassuming expression of a woman. Perhaps someone might have seen in that ever so tiny hint of surprise in the depths of her eyes, perhaps someone might have seen in that ever so tiny hint of sorrow the lack of children which she never had?

With her punctilious liking for organization—that same inclination which had made her as a school-girl copy out her class notes in perfect writing without ever understanding them—to tidy up the house before the maid had her afternoon off so that, once Maria went out, she would have nothing more to do except (1) calmly get dressed; (2) wait for Armando once she was ready; (3) what was the third thing? Ah yes. That was exactly what she would do. She would wear her brown dress with the cream lace collar. Having already had her bath. Even during her time at the Sacred Heart Convent she had always been tidy and clean, with an obsession for personal hygiene and a certain horror of disorder. A fact which never caused Carlota, who was already a little odd even as a school girl, to admire her. The reactions of the two women had always been different. Carlota, ambitious and laughing heartily; Laura, a little slow, and virtually always taking care to be slow. Carlota, seeing danger in nothing; and Laura ever cautious. When they had given her *The Imitation of Christ* to read, with the zeal of a donkey she had read the book without understanding it, but may God forgive her, she had felt that anyone who imitated Christ would be lost—lost in the light, but dangerously lost. Christ was the worst temptation. And Carlota, who had not even attempted to read it, had lied to the Sister, saying that she had finished it.

That was decided. She would wear her brown dress with the cream collar made of real lace.

But when she saw the time, she remembered with alarm, causing her to raise her hand to her breast, that she had forgotten to drink her glass of milk.

She made straight for the kitchen and, as if she had guiltily betrayed Armando and their devoted friends through her neglect, standing by the refrigerator she took the first sips with anxious pauses, concentrating upon each sip with faith as if she were compensating everyone and showing her repentance.

If the doctor had said, "Take milk between your meals, and avoid an empty stomach because that causes anxiety," then, even without the threat of anxiety, she took her milk without further discussion, sip by sip, day by day—she never failed, obeying blindly with a touch of zeal, so that she might not perceive in herself the slightest disbelief. The embarrassing thing was that the doctor appeared to contradict himself, for while giving precise instructions that she chose to follow with the zeal of a convert, he had also said, "Relax! Take things easy; don't force yourself to succeed—completely forget what has happened and everything will return to normal." And he had given her a pat on the back that had pleased her and made her blush with pleasure.

But in her humble opinion, the one command seemed to cancel out the other, as if they were asking her to eat flour and whistle at the same time. In order to fuse both commands into one, she had invented a solution: that glass of milk which had finished up by gaining a secret power, which almost embodied with every sip the taste of a word and renewed that firm pat on the back, that glass of milk she carried into the sitting room where she sat "with great naturalness," feigning a lack of interest, "not forcing herself"—and thereby cleverly complying with the second order. It doesn't matter if I get fat, she thought, beauty has never been the most important thing.

She sat down on the couch as if she were a guest in her own home, which, so recently regained, tidy and impersonal, recalled the peace of a stranger's house. A feeling that gave her great satisfaction: the opposite of Carlota who had made of her home something similar to herself. Laura experienced such pleasure in making something impersonal of her home; in a certain way perfect, because impersonal.

Oh, how good it was to be back, to be truly back, she smiled with satisfaction. Holding the almost empty glass, she closed her eyes with a pleasurable weariness. She had ironed Armando's shirts, she had prepared methodical lists for the following day, she had calculated in detail what she had spent at the market that morning; she had not paused, in fact, for a single minute. Oh, how good it was to be tired again!

If some perfect creature were to descend from the planet Mars and discover that people on the Earth were tired and growing old, he would feel pity and dismay. Without ever understanding what was good about being people, about feeling tired and failing daily; only the initiated would understand this nuance of depravity and refinement of life.

And she had returned at last from the perfection of the planet Mars. She, who had never had any ambitions except to be a wife to some man, gratefully returned to find her share of what is daily fallible. With her eyes closed she sighed gratefully. How long was it since she had felt tired? But now every day she felt almost exhausted. She had ironed, for example, Armando's shirts; she had always enjoyed ironing and, modesty aside, she pressed clothes to perfection. And afterward she felt exhausted as a sort of compensation. No longer to feel that alert lack of fatigue. No longer to feel that point—empty, aroused, and hideously exhilarating within oneself. No longer to feel that terrible independence. No longer that monstrous and simple facility of not sleeping—neither by day nor by night—which in her discretion had suddenly made her superhuman by comparison with her tired and perplexed husband. Armando, with that offensive breath which he developed when he was silently preoccupied, stirring in her a poignant compassion, yes, even within her alert perfection, her feeling and love . . . she, superhuman and tranquil in her bright isolation, and he—when he had come to visit her timidly bringing apples and grapes that the nurse, with a shrug of her shoulders, used to eat—he visiting her ceremoniously like a lover with heavy breath and fixed smile, forcing himself in his heroism to try to understand . . . he who had received her from a father and a clergyman, and who did not know what to do with this girl from Tijuca, who unexpectedly, like a tranquil boat spreading its sails over the waters, had become superhuman.

But now it was over. All over. Oh, it had been a mere weakness: temperament was the worst temptation. But later she had recovered so completely that she had even started once more to exercise care not to plague others with her former obsession for detail. She could well remember her companions at the convent saying to her, "That's the thousandth time you've counted that!" She remembered them with an uneasy smile.

She had recovered completely: now she was tired every day, every day her face sagged as the afternoon wore on, and the night then assumed its old finality and became more than just a perfect starry night. And everything completed itself harmoniously. And, as for the whole world, each day fatigued her; as for the whole world, human and perishable. No longer did she feel that perfection or youth. No longer that thing which one day had clearly spread like a cancer . . . her soul.

She opened her eyes heavy with sleep, feeling the consoling solidity of the glass in her hand, but closed them again with a comfortable smile of fatigue, bathing herself like a *nouveau riche* in all his wealth, in this familiar and slightly nauseating water. Yes, slightly nauseating: what did it matter? For if she, too, was a little nauseating, she was fully aware of it. But her husband didn't think so and then what did it matter, for happily she did not live in surroundings which demanded that she should be more clever and interesting, she was even free of school which so embarrassingly had demanded that she should be alert. What did it matter? In exhaustion—she had ironed Armando's shirts without mentioning that she had been to the market in the morning and had spent some time there with that delight she took in making things yield—in exhaustion she found a refuge, that discreet and obscure place from where, with so much constraint toward herself and others, she had once departed. But as she was saying, fortunately she had returned.

And if she searched with greater faith and love she would find within her exhaustion that even better place, which would be sleep. She sighed with pleasure, for one moment of mischievous malice tempted to go against that warm breath she exhaled, already inducing sleep . . . for one moment tempted to doze off. "Just for a moment, only one tiny moment!" she pleaded with herself, pleased at being so tired, she pleaded persuasively, as one pleads with a man, a facet of her behavior that had always delighted Armando. But she did not really have time to sleep now, not even to take a nap, she thought smugly and with false modesty. She was such a busy person! She had always envied those who could say "I couldn't find the time," and now once more she was such a busy person.

They were going to dinner at Carlota's house, and everything had to be organized and ready, it was her first dinner out since her return and she did not wish to arrive late, she had to be ready. "Well, I've already said this a thousand times," she thought with embarrassment. It would be sufficient to say it only once. "I did not wish to arrive late." For this was a sufficient reason: if she had never been able to bear without enormous vexation giving trouble to anyone, now more than ever, she should not. No, no, there was not the slightest doubt: she had no time to sleep. What she must do, stirring herself with familiarity in that intimate wealth of routine—and it hurt her that Carlota should despise her liking for routine—what she must do was (1) wait until the maid was ready; (2) give her the money so that she could bring the meat in the morning, top round of beef; how could she explain that the difficulty of finding good meat was, for her, really an interesting topic of conversation, but if Carlota were to find out, she would despise her; (3) to begin washing and dressing herself carefully, surrendering, without reservations to the pleasure of making the most of the time at her disposal. Her brown dress matched her eyes, and her collar in cream lace gave her an almost childlike appearance, like some child from the past. And, back in the nocturnal peace of Tijuca, no longer that dazzling light of ebullient nurses, their hair carefully set, going out to enjoy themselves after having tossed her like a helpless chicken into the void of insulin—back to the nocturnal peace of Tijuca, restored to her real life.

She would go out arm in arm with Armando, walking slowly to the bus stop with those low thick hips which her girdle parceled into one, transforming her into a striking woman. But when she awkwardly explained to Armando that this resulted from ovarian insufficiency, Armando, who liked his wife's hips, would saucily retort, "What good would it do me to be married to a ballerina?" That was how he responded. No one would have suspected it, but at times Armando could be extremely devious. From time to time they repeated the same phrases. She explained that it was on account of ovarian insufficiency. Then he would retort, "What good would it do me to be married to a ballerina?" At times he was shameless and no one would have suspected it.

Carlota would have been horrified if she were to know that they, too, had an intimate life and shared things she could not discuss, but nevertheless she regretted not being able to discuss them. Carlota certainly thought that she was only neat and ordinary and a little boring; but if she were obliged to take care in order not to annoy the others with details, with Armando she let herself go at times and became boring. Not that this mattered because, although he pretended to listen, he did not absorb everything she told him. Nor did she take offense, because she understood perfectly well that her conversation rather bored other people, but it was nice to be able to tell him that she had been able to find good meat, even if Armando shook his head and did not listen. She and the maid conversed a great deal, in fact more so she than the maid, and she was careful not to bother the maid, who at times suppressed her impatience and became somewhat rude—the fault was really hers because she did not always command respect.

But, as she was saying . . . her arm in his, she short and he tall and thin, though he was healthy, thank God, and she was chestnut-haired. Chestnut-haired as she obscurely felt a wife ought to be. To have black or blonde hair was an exaggeration, which, in her desire to make the right choice, she had never wanted. Then, as for green eyes, it seemed to her that if she had green eyes it would be as if she had not told her husband everything. Not that Carlota had given cause for any scandal, although Laura, were she given the opportunity, would hotly defend her, but the opportunity had never arisen. She, Laura, was obliged reluctantly to agree that her friend had a strange and amusing manner of treating her husband, not because "they treated each other as equals," since this was now common enough, but you know what I mean to say. And Carlota was even a little different, even she had remarked on this once to Armando and Armando had agreed without attaching much importance to the fact. But, as she was saying, in brown with the lace collar . . . her reverie filled her with the same pleasure she experienced when tidying out drawers, and she even found herself disarranging them in order to tidy them up again.

She opened her eyes and, as if it were the room that had taken a nap and not she, the room seemed refurbished and refreshed with its chairs brushed and its curtains, which had shrunk in the last washing, looking like trousers that are too short and the wearer looking comically at his own legs. Oh! how good it was to see everything tidy again and free of dust, everything cleaned by her own capable hands, and so silent and with a vase of flowers as in a waiting room. She had always found waiting rooms pleasing, so respectful and impersonal. How satisfying life together was, for her who had at last returned from extravagance. Even a vase of flowers. She looked at it.

"Ah! how lovely they are," her heart exclaimed suddenly, a bit childish. They were small wild roses which she had bought that morning at the market, partly because the man had insisted so much, partly out of daring. She had arranged them in a vase that very morning, while drinking her sacred glass of milk at ten o'clock.

But in the light of this room the roses stood in all their complete and tranquil beauty. "I have never seen such lovely roses," she thought enquiringly. And, as if she had not just been thinking precisely this, vaguely aware that she had been thinking precisely this, and quickly dismissing her embarrassment upon recognizing herself as being a little tedious, she thought in a newer phase of surprise, "Really, I have never seen such pretty roses." She looked at them attentively. But her attention could not be sustained for very long as simple attention, and soon transformed itself into soothing pleasure, and she was no longer able to analyze the roses and felt obliged to interrupt herself with the same exclamation of submissive enquiry: "How lovely they are!"

They were a bouquet of perfect roses, several on the same stem. At some moment they had climbed with quick eagerness over each other but then, their game over, they had become tranquilly immobilized. They were quite perfect roses in their minuteness, not quite open, and their pink hue was almost white. "They seem almost artificial," she uttered in surprise. They might give the impression of being white if they were completely open, but with the center petals curled in a bud, their color was concentrated and, as in the lobe of an ear, one could sense the redness circulate inside them. "How lovely they are," thought Laura, surprised. But without knowing why, she felt somewhat restrained and a little perplexed. Oh, nothing serious, it was only that such extreme beauty disturbed her.

She heard the maid's footsteps on the brick floor of the kitchen, and from the hollow sound she realized that she was wearing high heels and that she must be ready to leave. Then Laura had an idea which was in some way highly original: why not ask Maria to call at Carlota's house and leave the roses as a present?

And also because that extreme beauty disturbed her. Disturbed her? It was a risk. Oh! no, why a risk? It merely disturbed her; they were a warning. Oh! no, why a warning? Maria would deliver the roses to Carlota.

"Dona Laura sent them," Maria would say. She smiled thoughtfully: Carlota would be puzzled that Laura, being able to bring the roses personally, since she wanted to present them to her, should send them before dinner with the maid. Not to mention that she would find it amusing to receive the roses . . . and would think it "refined."

"These things aren't necessary between us, Laura!" the other would say with that frankness of hers which was somewhat tactless, and Laura would exclaim in a subdued cry of rapture, "Oh, no! no! It is not because of the invitation to dinner! It is because the roses are so lovely that I felt the impulse to give them to you!"

Yes, if at the time the opportunity arose and she had the courage, that was exactly what she would say. What exactly would she say? It was important not to forget. She would say, "Oh, no! no! It is not because of the invitation to dinner! It is because the roses are so lovely that I felt the impulse to give them to you!"

And Carlota would be surprised at the delicacy of Laura's sentiments— no one would imagine that Laura, too, had her ideas. In this imaginary and pleasurable scene which made her smile devoutly, she addressed herself as "Laura," as if speaking to a third person. A third person full of that gentle, rustling, pleasant, and tranquil faith, Laura, the one with the real lace collar, dressed discreetly, the wife of Armando, an Armando, after all, who no longer needed to force himself to pay attention to all of her conversation about the maid and the meat . . . who no longer needed to think about his wife, like a man who is happy, like a man who is not married to a ballerina.

"I couldn't help sending you the roses," Laura would say, this third person so, but so. . . . And to give the roses was almost as nice as the roses themselves.

And she would even be rid of them.

And what exactly would happen next? Ah yes; as she was saying, Carlota, surprised at Laura who was neither intelligent nor good but who had her secret feelings. And Armando? Armando would look at her with a look of real surprise—for it was essential to remember that he must not know the maid had taken the roses in the afternoon! Armando would look with kindness upon the impulses of his little wife and that night they would sleep together.

And she would have forgotten the roses and their beauty. No, she suddenly thought, vaguely warned. It was necessary to take care with that alarmed look in others. It was necessary never to cause them alarm, especially with everything being so fresh in their minds. And, above all, to spare everyone the least anxiety or doubt. And that the attention of others should no longer be necessary—no longer this horrible feeling of their watching her in silence, and her in their presence. No more impulses.

But at the same time she saw the empty glass in her hand and she also thought, " 'He' said that I should not force myself to succeed, that I should not think of adopting attitudes merely to show that I am."

"Maria," she called, upon hearing the maid's footsteps once more. And when Maria appeared she asked with a note of rashness and defiance, "Would you call at Dona Carlota's house and leave these roses for her? Just say that Dona Laura sent them. Just say it like that. Dona Laura. . . ."

"Yes, I know," the maid interrupted her patiently.

Laura went to search for an old sheet of tissue paper. Then she carefully lifted the roses from the vase, so lovely and tranquil, with their delicate and mortal thorns. She wanted to make a really artistic bouquet: and at the same time she would be rid of them. And she would be able to dress and resume her day. When she had arranged the moist blooms in a bouquet, she held the flowers away from her and examined them at a distance, slanting her head and half-closing her eyes for an impartial and severe judgment.

And when she looked at them, she saw the roses. And then, irresistibly gentle, she insinuated to herself, "Don't give the roses away, they are so lovely."

A second later, still very gentle, her thought suddenly became slightly more intense, almost tempting, "Don't give them away, they are yours." Laura became a little frightened: because things were never hers.

But these roses were. Rosy, small, and perfect: they were hers. She looked at them, incredulous: they were beautiful and they were hers. If she could think further ahead, she would think: hers as nothing before now had ever been.

And she could even keep them because that initial uneasiness had passed which had caused her vaguely to avoid looking at the roses too much.

"Why give them away then? They are so lovely and you are giving them away? So when you find something nice, you just go and give it away? Well, if they were hers," she insinuated persuasively to herself, without finding any other argument beyond the previous one which, when repeated, seemed to her to be ever more convincing and straightforward.

"They would not last long—why give them away then, so long as they were alive?" The pleasure of possessing them did not represent any great risk, she pretended to herself, because, whether she liked it or not, shortly she would be forced to deprive herself of them and then she would no longer think about them, because by then they would have withered.

"They would not last long; why give them away then?" The fact that they would not last long seemed to free her from the guilt of keeping them, in the obscure logic of the woman who sins. Well, one could see that they would not last long (it would be sudden, without danger). And it was not even, she argued in a final and victorious rejection of guilt, she herself who had wanted to buy them; the flower seller had insisted so much and she always became so intimidated when they argued with her. . . . It was not she who had wanted to buy them . . . she was not to blame in the slightest. She looked at them in rapture, thoughtful and profound.

"And, honestly, I never saw such perfection in all my life."

All right, but she had already spoken to Maria and there would be no way of turning back. Was it too late then? She became frightened upon seeing the tiny roses that waited impassively in her own hand. If she wanted, it would not be too late. . . . She could say to Maria, "Oh Maria, I have decided to take the roses myself when I go to dinner this evening!"

And of course she would not take them. . . . And Maria need never know. And, before changing, she would sit on the couch for a moment, just for a moment, to contemplate them. To contemplate that tranquil impassivity of the roses. Yes, because having already done the deed, it would be better to profit from it . . . she would not be foolish enough to take the blame without the profit. That was exactly what she would do.

But with the roses unwrapped in her hand she waited. She did not arrange them in the vase, nor did she call Maria. She knew why. Because she must give them away. Oh, she knew why.

And also because something nice was either for giving or receiving, not only for possessing. And above all, never for one *to be*. Above all, one should never *be* a lovely thing. A lovely thing lacked the gesture of giving. One should never keep a lovely thing, as if it were guarded within the perfect silence of one's heart. (Although, if she were not to give the roses, would anyone ever find out? It was horribly easy and within one's reach to keep them, for who would find out? And they would be hers, and things would stay as they were and the matter would be forgotten. . .)

"Well then? Well then?" she mused, vaguely disturbed.

Well, no. What she must do was to wrap them up and send them, without any pleasure now; to parcel them up and, disappointed, send them; and, terrified, be rid of them. Also, because a person had to be coherent, one's thoughts had to be consistent: if, spontaneously, she had decided to relinquish them to Carlota, she should stand by that decision and give them away. For no one changed their mind from one minute to another.

But anyone can repent, she suddenly rebelled. For if it was only the minute I took hold of the roses that I noticed how lovely they were, for the first time, actually, as I held them, I noticed how lovely they were. Or a little before that? (And they were really hers.) And even the doctor himself had patted her on the back and said, "Don't force yourself into pretending that you are well, because you *are* well!" And then that hearty pat on the back. So she was not obliged, therefore, to be consistent, she didn't have to prove anything to anyone, and she would keep the roses. (And in all sincerity—in all sincerity they were hers.)

"Are they ready?" Maria asked.

"Yes," said Laura, surprised.

She looked at them, so mute in her hand. Impersonal in their extreme beauty. In their extreme and perfect tranquillity as roses. That final instance: the flower. That final perfection; its luminous tranquillity.

Like someone depraved, she watched with vague longing the tempting perfection of the roses . . . with her mouth a little dry, she watched them.

Until, slowly, austerely, she wrapped the stems and thorns in the tissue paper. She was so absorbed that only upon holding out the bouquet she had prepared did she notice that Maria was no longer in the room—and she remained alone with her heroic sacrifice.

Vacantly, sorrowfully, she watched them, distant as they were at the end of her outstretched arm—and her mouth became even dryer, parched by that envy and desire.

"But they are mine," she said with enormous timidity.

When Maria returned and took hold of the bouquet, for one tiny moment of greed Laura drew back her hand, keeping the roses to herself for one more second—they are so lovely and they are mine—the first lovely thing and mine! And it was the flower seller who had insisted. . . . I did not go looking for them! It was destiny that had decreed! Oh, only this once! Only this once and I swear never more! (She could at least take one rose for herself, no more than this! One rose for herself. And only she would know and then never more; oh, she promised herself that never more would she allow herself to be tempted by perfection, never more.)

And the next moment, without any transition, without any obstacle, the roses were in the maid's hand, they were no longer hers, like a letter already in the post! One can no longer recover or obliterate statements! There is no point in shouting, "That was not what I wanted to say!" Her hands were now empty but her heart, obstinate and resentful, was still saying, "You can catch Maria on the stairs, you know perfectly well that you can, and take the roses from her hand and steal them—because to take them now would be to steal them." To steal what was hers? For this was what a person without any feeling for others would do: he would steal what was his by right! Have pity, dear God. You can get them back, she insisted, enraged. And then the front door slammed.

Slowly, she sat down calmly on the couch. Without leaning back. Only to rest. No, she was no longer angry, not even a little. But that tiny wounded spot in the depths of her eyes was larger and thoughtful. She looked at the vase.

"Where are my roses?" she said then very quietly.

And she missed the roses. They had left an empty space inside her. Remove an object from a clean table and by the cleaner patch which remains one sees that there has been dust all around it. The roses had left a patch without dust and without sleep inside her. In her heart, that one rose, which at least she could have taken for herself without prejudicing anyone in the world, was gone. Like something missing. Indeed, like some great loss. An absence that flooded into her like a light. And also around the mark left by the roses the dust was disappearing. The center of fatigue opened itself into a circle that grew larger. As if she had not ironed a single shirt for Armando. And in the clearing they had left, one missed those roses.

"Where are my roses?" she moaned without pain, smoothing the pleats of her skirt.

Like lemon juice dripping into dark tea and the dark tea becoming completely clear, her exhaustion gradually became clearer. Without, however, any tiredness. Just as the firefly alights. Since she was no longer tired, she was on the point of getting up to dress. It was time to start getting ready.

With parched lips, she tried for an instant to imitate the roses deep down inside herself. It was not even difficult.

It was just as well that she did not feel tired. In this way she would go out to dinner feeling more refreshed. Why not wear her cameo brooch on her cream-colored collar? The one the Major had brought back from the war in Italy. It would add a final touch to her neckline. When she was ready she would hear the noise of Armando's key in the door. She must get dressed. But it was still early. With the rush-hour traffic, he would be late in arriving. It was still afternoon. An extremely beautiful afternoon. But, in fact, it was no longer afternoon. It was evening. From the street there arose the first sounds of darkness and the first lights.

Moreover, the key penetrated with familiarity the keyhole.

Armando would open the door. He would press the light switch. And suddenly in the frame of the doorway that face would appear, betraying an expectancy he tried to conceal but could not restrain. Then his breathless suspense would finally transform itself into a smile of utter relief. That embarrassed smile of relief which he would never suspect her of noticing. That relief which, probably with a pat on the back, they had advised her poor husband to conceal. But which had been, for this woman whose heart was filled with guilt, her daily recompense for having restored to her husband the possibility of happiness and peace, sanctified at the hands of an austere priest who only permitted submissive happiness to humans and not the imitation of Christ.

The key turned in the lock, that dark, expectant face entered, and a powerful light flooded the room.

And in the doorway, Armando himself stopped short with that breathless expression as if he had run for miles in order to arrive in time. She was about to smile. So that she might dispel the anxious expectancy on his face, which always came mixed with the childish victory of having arrived in time to find his boring, good-hearted, and diligent wife. She was about to smile so that once more he might know that there would no longer be any danger in his arriving too late. She was about to smile in order to teach him gently to confide in her. It had been useless to advise them never to touch on the subject: they did not speak about it but they had created a language of facial expressions whereby fear and confidence were communicated, and question and answer were silently telegraphed. She was about to smile. She was taking her time, but meant to smile.

Calmly and sweetly she said, "It came back, Armando. It came back."

As if he would never understand, he averted his smiling, distrusting face. His main task for the moment was to try and control his breathless gasps after running up the stairs, now that, triumphantly, he had arrived in time, now that she was there to smile at him. As if he would never understand.

"What came back?" he finally asked her in an expressionless tone.

But while he was seeking never to understand, the man's face, ever more full of suspense, had already understood without a single feature having altered. His main task was to gain time and to concentrate upon controlling his breath. Which suddenly was no longer difficult. For unexpectedly he noticed to his horror that the room and the woman were calm and showing no signs of haste. Still more suspicious, like someone about to end up howling with laughter upon observing something absurd, he meantime insisted upon keeping his face averted, from where he spied her cautiously, almost her enemy. And from where he already began to feel unable to restrain himself, from seeing her seated with her hands folded on her lap, with the serenity of the firefly that is alight.

In her innocent, chestnut gaze, the embarrassed vanity of not having been able to resist.

"What came back?" he asked suddenly with severity.

"I couldn't help myself," she said and her final compassion for this man was in her voice, one last appeal for pardon which already came mingled with the arrogance of an almost perfect solitude.

"I couldn't prevent it," she repeated, surrendering to him with relief the compassion which she with some effort had been able to contain until he arrived.

"It was on account of the roses," she said modestly.

As if a photograph were about to capture that moment, he still maintained the same disinterested expression, as if the photographer had asked him only for his face and not his soul. He opened his mouth and involuntarily his face took on for an instant an expression of comic detachment which he had used to conceal his annoyance when he had asked his boss for an increase in salary. The next moment, he averted his eyes, mortified by his wife's shamelessness as she sat there unburdened and serene.

But suddenly the tension fell. His shoulders dropped, the features of his face relaxed and a great heaviness settled over him. Aged and strange, he watched her.

She was seated wearing her little housedress. He knew that she had done everything possible not to become luminous and remote. With fear and respect he watched her. Aged, tired, and strange. But he did not even have a word to offer. From the open door he saw his wife sitting upright on the couch, once more alert and tranquil as if on a train. A train that had already departed.

1960

The Departure
of the Train

Translated by Alexis Levitin

THE DEPARTURE WAS from Central Station, with its enormous clock, the largest in the world. It showed the time as six in the morning. Angela Pralini paid for her taxi and picked up her small suitcase. Dona Maria Rita Alvarenga Chagas Souza Melo emerged from her daughter's Opala and set off toward the tracks. A well-dressed elderly lady with jewels. From the wrinkles that masked her came the pure form of a nose lost in age and of a mouth that once must have been full and sensitive. But what does it matter. You reach a certain point—and what once was, no longer matters. A new race begins. An old woman cannot make herself understood. She received a cold kiss from her daughter, who left before the train departed. She had first helped her up into the car. Since no middle seats were free, she had taken a place to one side. When the locomotive began to move, it surprised her a bit: she hadn't expected the train to go in that direction and had seated herself facing backward.

Angela Pralini noticed her startled movement and asked: "Would you like to change places with me?"

Dona Maria Rita, delicately surprised, said no, thank you, for her it was all the same. But she seemed troubled. She passed her hand over her cameo, with its gold filigree, pinned to her breast, fumbled at her broach, took her hand away, lifted it to her felt hat with its cloth rose, and again took it away. Stiff. Offended? Finally she asked Angela Pralini:

"Could it be for my sake you're offering to change seats?"

Surprised, Angela Pralini said no, and the old woman was surprised for the same reason: one doesn't accept favors from an old lady. She smiled a little too much, and her stretched lips covered with talcum powder split into dry furrows: she was enchanted. And a bit excited:

"How very nice of you," she said, "how very kind."

There was a moment of confusion as Angela Pralini also laughed, and the old woman continued to laugh, showing her spotless dentures. She gave a discreet little pull downward on her belt, which was too tight.

"How kind of you," she repeated.

She then composed herself again, rather suddenly, crossing her hands over her purse, which held everything you could imagine. Her wrinkles, when she laughed, had taken on meaning, thought Angela. Now they were once again incomprehensible, superimposed once again on a face unmalleable. But Angela had already broken her tranquillity. She had already seen many nervous young ladies telling themselves: if I laugh anymore I will ruin everything, it will be ridiculous, I have to stop—and it had been impossible. The situation was very sad. With great pity, Angela saw a cruel wart on her chin, a wart from which emerged a stiff black hair. But Angela had taken her peace away. You could see she was about to smile at any moment: Angela had the old woman on tenterhooks. Now she was one of those little old ladies who seem to think that they are always late, that the hour has passed. A moment later she couldn't contain herself and got up to look out the window, as if it were impossible to stay seated.

"Are you trying to close the window, ma'am," said a young fellow listening to Handel on a transistor radio.

"Ah," she exclaimed, terrified.

Oh, no, thought Angela, everything was getting spoiled, the young man shouldn't have said that, it was too much, no one should have touched her again. For the old woman, almost on the point of losing the attitude which had sustained her throughout life, almost about to lose a certain bitterness, quavered like harpsichord music between a smile and the deepest enchantment:

"No, no, no," she said with a false tone of authority, "not at all, thank you, I only wanted to look out."

She sat down immediately as if being observed by the politeness of the young man and the girl. The old woman, before getting into the train, had made the sign of the cross three times over her heart, discreetly kissing her fingertips. She was in a black dress with a genuine lace collar and a cameo of pure gold. On her dark left hand were a widow's two thick wedding rings, thick the way they don't make them anymore. From the next car you could hear a group of girl scouts singing their high-pitched praises of "Brazil." Luckily it was in the next car. The music on the young fellow's radio merged with the music of another fellow: he was listening to Edith Piaf singing "J'attendrai."

It was then that the train suddenly gave a jolt and the wheels began to move. The departure had begun. The old woman said softly: Ah, Jesus! She had soaked herself in sweet Jesus. Amen. A woman's transistor informed them that it was six-thirty in the morning, a chilly morning. The old woman thought: Brazil was improving its road signs. A certain Kissinger seemed to be running the world.

No one knows where I am, thought Angela Pralini, and this frightened her somewhat, she was a fugitive.

"My name is Maria Rita Alvarenga Chagas Souza Melo—Alvarenga Chagas was my father's surname," she added, as if begging pardon for having to say so many words just in telling her name. "Chagas," she added modestly, "were the Chagas, the 'stigmata,' of Christ. But you can call me Dona Maria Ritinha. And your name? What might one call you?"

"My name is Angela Pralini. I'm going to spend six months with my uncles on their farm. And you?"

"Ah, I'm going to my son's farm. I'm going to stay there for the rest of my life, my daughter took me to the train, and my son will pick me up with his cart at the station. I am like a package being passed from hand to hand."

Angela's uncles had no children and treated her like a daughter. Angela remembered the note she had left for Eduardo: "Don't look for me. I am vanishing from your life forever. I love you more than ever. Farewell. I would have been more yours had you wished it so."

They remained silent. Angela Pralini gave herself up to the rhythmic sound of the train. Dona Maria Rita looked again at that ring of diamonds and pearls on her finger and smoothed down her golden cameo: "I am old but I am rich, richer than anyone in this car. I am rich, I am rich." She glanced at her watch, but in order to see the thick gold plate rather than the time. "I am very rich, I am not just any old lady." But she knew, ah, how well she knew, that she was indeed any old lady, just a little old lady frightened of the littlest things. She remembered herself, the whole day all alone in the rocking chair, alone with the servants, while her "public relations" daughter spent the whole day out, only returning at eight in the evening, and not even giving her a kiss. She had gotten up this morning at five o'clock, everything still dark; and it had been cold.

After the kindness of the young man she had been extraordinarily excited, and all smiles. She looked drained. With her laugh she revealed herself as one of those little old ladies with a mouthful of teeth. The discordant cruelty of teeth. The young man had already moved off. She opened and shut her eyelids. Suddenly she tapped Angela on the thigh, quickly and gently:

"Today everyone is truly, but truly friendly. How really nice, how very nice!"

Angela smiled. The old woman continued to smile without taking her deep and empty eyes from those of the girl. "Come on, let's go, let's go," they snapped at her from all sides, and she looked here and there as if to choose. "Let's go, let's go." They jostled against her, laughing from all sides, and she fluttered, there, smiling, dainty, refined.

"How friendly everyone is on this train," she said.

Suddenly she tried to recompose herself, she cleared her throat unnecessarily, she drew herself in. It was going to be difficult. She feared that she had reached the point where she wouldn't be able to stop herself. She held herself severe and trembling, closing her lips over her innumerable teeth. But she couldn't fool anyone: her face had such hope in it that it disturbed the eyes of whoever looked at her. She no longer depended on anyone: now that they had touched her, she could go away—she, alone, tall, thin, radiant. She still would have liked to say something and in fact was preparing a sociable nod of the head, full of studied grace. Angela wondered if she would know how to express herself. She seemed to be thinking and thinking and then to find with tenderness a thought all ready-made in which somehow or other she could cradle her feelings. She said with the care and wisdom of the aged, as if it were necessary to put on such an air in order to speak like an elderly person:

"Youth! Gracious youth."

Her laughter was somewhat forced. "Was she going to have an attack of nerves?" thought Angela Pralini. For she was so marvelous. But now she cleared her throat again with austerity, tapping the seat with her fingertips as if urgently calling an orchestra to order for a new piece. She opened her purse, took out a small square of newspaper, unfolded it, unfolded it until it had become a large and normal newspaper from three days before—as Angela saw from the date. She began to read.

Angela had lost seven kilos. On the farm she would eat herself sick: bean stew and cabbage à la Mineira, to regain the precious lost kilos. She was this thin from having tried to keep up with Eduardo's brilliant, uninterrupted chain of thought: she had drunk coffee without sugar endlessly in order to stay awake. Angela Pralini had very pretty breasts, they were her strong point. She had pointed ears and a pretty, kissable, rounded mouth. Eyes with dark shadows. She took advantage of the scream of the train's whistle so that it might become her own scream. It was a sharp cry, hers, but turned inward. She was the woman who had drunk the most whiskey in Eduardo's group. She could take six or seven in a row, retaining a terrifying lucidity. At the farm she would drink thick cow's milk. One thing linked the old woman to Angela: both were going to be received with open arms, but neither knew this of the other. Angela suddenly shivered: who would give the dog its last day of deworming pills. Ah, Ulysses, she thought, to the dog, I didn't abandon you because I wanted to, it's that I had to flee Eduardo, before he destroyed me completely with his lucidity: a lucidity that illumined too much and singed everything. Angela knew that her uncles had a medicine for snakebite: she intended to enter the heart of the thick, verdant forest, with high boots smeared with insect repellent. As if leaving the Transamazonico highway behind, she, the explorer. What beasts would she encounter? It would be better to take along a rifle, food, and water. And a compass. Since having discovered—but having *really* discovered, with a shock—that she would die one day, she had no longer feared life and, thanks to death, now had all her rights: she would risk everything. After having had two relationships that had ended in nothing, this third that had ended in love—adoration, cut short by the fated desire to survive. Eduardo had transformed her: he had given her eyes within. But now she was looking out. Through the window, she saw the mountains, the breasts of the earth. Little birds exist, Eduardo! Clouds exist, Eduardo! There is a world of stallions and mares, and cows, Eduardo, and when I was a girl I raced bareback on a horse, without a saddle! I am fleeing my suicide, Eduardo. I'm sorry, Eduardo, but I don't want to die. I want to be fresh and rare as a pomegranate.

The old woman pretended to be reading the newspaper. But she was thinking: her world was a sigh. She didn't want the others to suppose that she was abandoned. God gave me good health so that I could travel alone. Also my mind is sound, I don't talk to myself, and I bathe on my own every day. She smelled of rose water, of withered macerated roses, her aged and musty perfume. That rhythmic respiration, thought Angela of the old woman, was the most beautiful thing remaining to Dona Maria Rita from her birth. It was life.

Dona Maria Rita was thinking: after getting old, she had begun to disappear for others, had become a passing glimpse. Old age: the supreme moment. She was a stranger to the general strategy of the world and her own was negligible. She had lost the longest-range objectives. She was, in fact, already the future.

Angela thought: I think that if I were to find the truth, I wouldn't be able to think it. It would be mentally unpronounceable.

The old woman had always been a bit empty, a little bit, anyway. Death? It was strange, it wasn't part of the passing days. And even "not to exist" didn't exist, it was impossible not-to-exist. Not to exist didn't fit into our daily life. Her daughter wasn't loving. On the other hand, her son was very loving, good-natured, a bit chubby. The daughter was as bone dry as her rapid little kisses, "public relations." The old woman had a certain laziness about living. It was monotony, however, that sustained her.

Eduardo listened to music with his thoughts. And he understood the dissonance of modern music, he only knew how to understand. His intelligence smothered her. You are temperamental, Angela, he said to her once. And so? What's wrong with that? I am what I am and not what you think I am. The proof that I am is in the departure of this train. My proof is also Dona Maria Rita, there across from me. Proof of what? Yes. She had already had plenitude. When she and Eduardo had been so passionately in love that being beside each other in bed, holding hands, they had felt their lives complete. Few people have known plenitude. And since plenitude is also an explosion, she and Eduardo had, like cowards, begun to live "normally." For you cannot prolong the ecstasy without dying. They had separated for a frivolous, almost artificial reason: they didn't want to die of passion. Plenitude is one of the truths you encounter. But the necessary break was surgery for her, just as there are women whose uteruses and ovaries have been removed. Empty within.

Dona Maria Rita was so ancient that in her daughter's house they were accustomed to her as if to an old piece of furniture. She was news to no one. But it never entered her head that she was a solitary. Just that she had nothing to do. It was an enforced leisure that at times pierced her to the bone: she had nothing to do in the world. Just live like a cat or a dog. She wished she could be an attentive companion to some lady, but such things didn't exist anymore, and anyway no one would believe in her strength at seventy-seven. They would all think she was weak. She didn't do anything, she only did this: to be old. Sometimes she would get depressed: she would feel that she was of no use, no use even to God. Dona Maria Ritinha didn't have an inferno within. Why is it that the old, even those who don't tremble, suggest something delicately tremulous? Dona Maria Rita had a brittle trembling like the music from a hurdy-gurdy.

But when it's a question of life itself—who can shore us up? for each one is a one. And each life has to be supported by its own life, only that one. Each one of us: that's all we can count on. Since Dona Maria Rita had always been an ordinary person, she thought that to die was not a normal thing. To die was surprising. It was as if she wasn't up to the act of death, since until now nothing extraordinary in life had happened to her that could justify all of a sudden another extraordinary event. She spoke and even thought about death, but deep down she was skeptical and suspicious. She believed that you died when there was an accident or when someone killed someone. The old woman had little experience. Sometimes she had palpitations: the heart's bacchanal. But that's all, and it had been with her since girlhood. At her first kiss, for example, her heart had gone out of control. And it had been a good thing alongside the bad. It was something that recalled her past, not as events, but as life: a sensation of vegetation in shadows, ferns, maidenhair, green coolness. When she felt this anew, she smiled. One of the most erudite words she used was "picturesque." It was good. It was like hearing the bubbling of a spring and not knowing where it had its source.

A conversation she carried on with herself:

"Are you doing something?"

"Yes, I am: I'm being sad."

"Doesn't it disturb you to be alone?"

"No, I'm thinking."

Sometimes she didn't think. Sometimes a person just is. She didn't need to be doing. To be was already a doing. One could *be* slowly or somewhat quickly.

On the seat behind, two women talked and talked without end. Their continuous sound mingled with the noise of the train wheels on the tracks.

Indeed, Dona Maria Rita had hoped that her daughter would remain on the platform to give her a little farewell, but it hadn't happened. The train immobile. Until the first lurch came.

"Angela," she said, "a woman never tells her age, so I can only tell you that I am very old. But no, for you—may I speak this way?—I'll tell you a secret: I am seventy-seven years old."

"I'm thirty-seven," said Angela Pralini.

It was seven in the morning.

"When I was young I was quite a little liar. I would lie for nothing just like that."

Later, as if she had become disenchanted with the magic of lies, she had stopped lying.

Angela, looking at old Dona Maria Rita, was afraid of growing old and dying. Hold my hand, Eduardo, so that I won't fear death. But he never held anything. The only thing he did was: think, think, and think. Oh, Eduardo, I need the gentleness of Schumann! Her life was dissolving, an evanescent life. She lacked hard bone, rough and strong, against which no one could do a thing. Who would be that essential bone? To keep at bay her feeling of enormous need, she thought: how did they manage to live in the Middle Ages without telephone and airplane? A mystery. Middle Ages, I adore you, you and your black-laden clouds that streamed into the luminous and fresh Renaissance.

As for the old woman, she had retreated. She was staring at nothingness.

Angela gazed at herself in her little pocket mirror. I look like a swoon. Beware the abyss, I say to the one who looks like a swoon. When I die I will have such a longing for you, Eduardo! The sentence could not stand up to logic, though there was an improbable sense to it. It was as if she had wished to express one thing and had expressed another.

The old woman was already the future. She seemed ashamed. Ashamed of being old? At some point in her life there surely must have been a mistake, and the result was this strange state she was in. Which, however, had not carried her to death. Death was always such a surprise for the one who died. She was, however, proud that she didn't dribble or make weewee in her bed, as if this form of brute health had been the meritorious result of an act of her will. Only she wasn't a lady, an elderly lady, for she had no arrogance: she was a dignified little old creature who suddenly would take on a frightened look. She—well, then, she praised her very self, considering herself an old woman full of precocity like a precocious child. But the true purpose of her life, that she did not know.

Angela dreamed of the farm: there you heard cries, barks, and howling at night. Eduardo, she thought to him, I was tired of trying to be what you assumed I was. I have a bad side—it is the stronger, and it prevailed, although I tried to hide it because of you—on this strong side I'm a cow. I'm a mare running free who paws the ground, I'm a woman of the streets, I'm a slut—and not a "woman of letters." I know that I am intelligent and that sometimes I hide it in order not to offend others with my intelligence, I who am of the subconscious. I fled from you, Eduardo, because you were killing me with your genius—intellect that practically forced me to cover my ears with my hands and scream out in horror and exhaustion. And now I will remain six months on the farm, you don't know where I'll be, and every day I'll bathe in the river, mixing with its clay my own blessed mud. I am vulgar, Eduardo! I want you to know that I like to read true romance magazines, my love, oh my love! how I love you and how I love your terrifying spells, ah, how I adore you, your slave, slave that I am. But I am physical, my love, I am physical, and I had to hide from you the glory of being physical. And you, who are the very splendor of rational thought, though you don't know it, you were nourished by me. You, superintellectual and brilliant, leaving everyone filled with wonder, mouths agape.

I believe, the old woman said to herself slowly, I believe that that pretty girl is not interested in talking to me. I don't know why, but no one speaks with me anymore. And even when I am right there with people, they seem not to remember me. And after all, it's not my fault I'm old. But it doesn't matter, I'll keep myself company. And I still have Nandinho, my dear son who adores me.

The long-suffering pleasure of scratching oneself! thought Angela. I, eh, I who don't go for this or for that, am free!!! I'm getting healthier, oh to swear out loud and startle everyone. Wouldn't the old lady understand? I don't know, she must have given birth a few times. Unhappiness is the only certainty—I'm not going to fall for that, Eduardo. I want to savor everything and then die and may I be damned! damned! damned! Though the old woman may in fact be unhappy without knowing it. Passivity. I'm not going to fall for that either, no passivity for me. I want to bathe naked in the muddy river that looks like me, naked and free! Viva! Three vivas! I'm leaving everything behind! everything! and therefore I am not abandoned, I don't want to depend on anyone but some three people and as for the rest: Hello, how are you? O.K. Edu, you know? I'm leaving you. You, in the depths of your intellectualism, aren't worth the life of a dog. I'm leaving you, then. And I'm leaving the pseudo-intellectual group that demanded of me an unending vain and nervous exercise of a false and hurried intelligence. I needed for God to abandon me before I could feel his presence. I need to kill someone within me. You ruined my intelligence with yours, which is that of a genius. And you forced me to know, to know, to know. Ah, Eduardo, don't worry, I'm taking along the books you gave me in order "to do a home study course," as you wished. I will study philosophy beside the river, for the love I bear you.

Angela Pralini had such deep thoughts that there were no words to express them. It was a lie to say that one could only have one thought at a time: she had numerous thoughts that crossed each other, and they were all different. Not to mention the "subconscious" that explodes in me, whether I want it or you don't. I'm a fountain, thought Angela, thinking at the same time where she had put her kerchief, wondering whether the dog had drunk the milk she had left for him, thinking of Eduardo's shirts, and of his extreme physical and mental exhaustion. And of old Dona Maria Rita. I will never forget your face, Eduardo. It was a somewhat surprised face, surprised at its own intelligence. He was ingenuous. And he loved without knowing that he loved. He would be stunned when he discovered that she had gone off, leaving the dog and him. I'm leaving for lack of nourishment, she thought. At the same time she was thinking of the old lady seated across from her. It wasn't true that you thought only one thought at a time. She was able, for example, to write a perfect check, without an error, while thinking of her life. Which wasn't a good one but at least was hers. Hers once again. Coherence, I don't want it anymore. Coherence is mutilation. I want disorder. I only sense through a vehement incoherence. In order to meditate I draw myself before myself and feel the emptiness. It is in emptiness that time passes. She who loved a good beach, with sun, sand and sun. The man is abandoned, he has lost contact with the earth, with the sky. He no longer lives, he exists. The atmosphere between her and Eduardo Gomes was that of an emergency. He had transformed her into an urgent woman. And, one who, to keep the urgency awake, took drugs, stimulants that made her thinner and thinner and killed her appetite. I want to eat, Eduardo, I'm hungry, Eduardo, I'm hungry for lots of food! I'm organic!

"Meet tomorrow's supertrain today." *Reader's Digests* that she used to read behind Eduardo's back. It was like the *Digests* that said: Meet tomorrow's supertrain today. She was positively not meeting it today. But Eduardo was the supertrain. Super everything. She knew today the super of tomorrow. And she couldn't stand it. She couldn't stand the perpetual motion. You are the desert, and I'm going to Oceania, to the South Seas, to Tahiti. Even if it's ruined by tourism. You are no more than a tourist, Eduardo. I am going toward my own life, Edu. And I say, like Fellini: in darkness and ignorance I create more. The life she had with Eduardo smelled like a newly painted pharmacy. She preferred the living smell of manure no matter how nauseating it might be. He was as proper as a tennis court. In fact, he played tennis to keep in shape. When all was said and done, he was a bore, whom she used to love and almost loved no longer. She was recovering here in the train itself her mental health. She remained in love with Eduardo. And he, unknowingly, with her as well. I who can't manage to do anything right, except make omelettes. With one hand alone I would break eggs with incredible speed, and empty them into the bowl without spilling a drop. Eduardo would die of envy before such elegance and efficiency. He sometimes gave lectures at universities, and they adored him. She, too, attended; she, too, adored him. How was it exactly that he began? "I feel ill at ease seeing people rise upon hearing that I am about to speak." Angela always was afraid that the others would withdraw, leaving them alone.

The old woman, as if she had received a thought transmission, thought: may they not leave me alone. How old am I really? Humph, I don't even remember.

Quickly, then, she emptied her mind. And she was peacefully nothing. Barely existing. It was good like that, really very good. Plunges into nothingness.

Angela Pralini, in order to calm herself, told herself a most calming, most tranquil story: once upon a time there was a man who loved the jaboticaba fruit. So he went to an orchard where there were trees covered with black protuberances, smooth and glistening, which fell with abandon into his hands and from his hands spilled down to his feet. The jaboticaba berries were so abundant that he gave himself the luxury of stepping on them. And they made a most delicious sound. They went: cloc-cloc-cloc etc. Angela calmed down like the jaboticaba man. On the farm they had jaboticaba, and she would make a moist and soft cloc-cloc-cloc with her bare feet. She never knew whether or not you ought to swallow the pits. Who would answer that question? No one. Only perhaps a man who, like Ulysses the dog, and unlike Eduardo, would answer: "Mangia, bella, que te fa bene." She knew a bit of Italian but was never sure of being right. And, after the man spoke those words, she would swallow the pits. Another delicious tree was one whose scientific name she had forgotten but which, in childhood, everyone had known quite directly, without science, one which in the Botanical Garden in Rio made a dry little cloc-cloc. See? See how you are being reborn? A cat's seven breaths. The number seven always accompanied her, was her secret, her strength. She felt beautiful. She wasn't. But that's how she felt. She also felt generous. With tenderness for old Maria Ritinha, who had put on her glasses and was reading the paper. Everything was slow about old Maria Rita. Near her end? ah, how it hurts to die. In life one suffers, but you have something in your hand: ineffable life. But what about the question of death? You had to have no fear: to go forward, always.

Always.

Like the train.

Somewhere there is something written on a wall. And it is for me, thought Angela. From the flames of hell a fresh telegram will come for me. And never again will my hopes be deceived. Never. Never again.

The old woman was as anonymous as a hen, as a certain Clarice had said speaking of a shameless old woman, madly in love with Roberto Carlos. That Clarice made you uncomfortable. She made the old woman cry out: there   must   be   a   way   o u t! And there was, too. For example, the way out for that old lady was her husband, who would return the next day, her acquaintances, her housemaid, intense and fruitful prayer in the face of despair. Angela repeated to herself as if madly biting herself: there must be a way out. For me just as well as for Dona Maria Rita.

I could not stop time, thought Maria Rita Alvarenga Chagas Sousa Melo. I failed. I am old. And she pretended to read the newspaper just to give herself composure.

I need shadows, moaned Angela. I need shadows and anonymity.

The old woman thought: her son was so kind, so warm-hearted, so gentle! He called her "Mom." Yes, perhaps I'll spend the rest of my life on the farm, far from "public relations," who doesn't need me. And my life ought to be very long, to judge by my parents and grandparents. I could easily, easily, reach a hundred, she thought comfortably. And die suddenly in order not to have time to feel fear. She crossed herself discreetly and begged God for a good death.

Ulysses, if his face were seen from a human point of view, would be monstrous and ugly. He was lovely from a dog's point of view. He was filled with vigor like a horse, white and free, only he was a soft brown, orangeish, whiskey-color. But his coat was beautiful like that of an energetic, prancing horse. The muscles of his neck were vigorous, and you could hold those muscles in your hands with knowing fingers. Ulysses was a man. Without a dog's world. He was gentle like a man. A woman must treat a man well.

The train coming to the fields: the crickets cricketing, high pitched and shrill.

Eduardo, once in a while, awkwardly, like someone forced to fulfill a function—would present her with the gift of an icy, uncut, diamond stone. She who preferred them cut. Well, she sighed, things are as they are. At times, looking down from her apartment, she had felt like killing herself. Ah, not because of Eduardo, but because of a kind of fatal curiosity. She wouldn't tell this to anyone, for fear of influencing a latent suicide. She wanted life, life flat and full, really nice, reading *Reader's Digest* for all to see. She wanted to die at ninety, not before, in the middle of an act of life, without feeling a thing. The ghost of madness stalks us. What are you doing? I am awaiting the future.

When the train had finally set in motion, Angela Pralini had lit her cigarette in hallelujah: she had feared before the train had left that she wouldn't have the courage to go and would end up getting off. But after a bit they had become aware of the action of shock-absorbers and, despite this, the sudden jolts of the wheels. The train was moving. And old Maria Rita sighed: she was closer to her beloved son. With him she could be a mother, she who was castrated by her daughter.

Once when Angela had had menstrual cramps, Eduardo had tried, quite awkwardly, to comfort her. And he had said something horrid to her: It was enough to make you blush with shame. You've got a tummy ache, don't you?

The train rushed on as fast as it could. The engineer delighted: this is the good life, and he blew the whistle at every curve. It was the long, heavy whistle of a train underway, clicking off the miles. The morning was cool and full of high green grasses. Yes, that's the way, onward, onward, said the engineer to the engine. The engine responded joyfully.

The old woman was nothing. And gazed into the air as one looks at God. She was made of God. That is, of all or nothing. The old woman was vulnerable, Angela thought. Vulnerable to love, love of her son. The mother was Franciscan, the daughter pollution.

God, thought Angela, if you exist, reveal yourself! For the hour has come. It is this hour, this minute, and this second.

And the result was that she had to hide the tears that came to her eyes. God in some way had answered her. She was happy and swallowed a muffled sob. How painful life was. Living was an open wound. To live is to be like my dog. Ulysses has nothing in common with Joyce's Ulysses. I tried to read Joyce, but I stopped because he was boring, sorry, Eduardo. Only he's a boring genius. Angela was feeling love for the old woman who was nothing, the mother she lacked. A mother, gentle, ingenuous, long-suffering. Her mother who had died when she was nine years old. Even sick, just being alive was enough. Even paralyzed.

Between her and Eduardo the air tasted like Saturday. And suddenly the two of them were rare, a rarity in the air. They felt rare, apart from the thousand people walking in the streets. At times the two were accomplices, they had a secret life because no one would have understood them. And also because rare ones are persecuted by the people who do not tolerate the insulting offence of those who are different. They hid their love in order not to wound the eyes of others with envy. In order not to wound them with a spark too luminous for eyes.

Bowwow wow, yapped my dog. My big puppy.

The old woman thought: I am an involuntary person. So much so that when she laughed—which was rare—you didn't know if she were laughing or crying. Yes. She was involuntary.

Meanwhile Angela Pralini, fizzling like the bubbles in Caxamba mineral water, was one too: all of a sudden. Just like that. All of a sudden what? Just all of a sudden. Zero. Nothing. She was thirty-seven years old and always intending to begin her life anew. Like the fizzling effervescent bubbles of Caxamba water. The seven letters of Pralini gave her strength. The six letters of Angela made her anonymous.

With a drawn-out wailing whistle, they arrived at the small station where Angela Pralini was going to jump out. She picked up her suitcase. In the space between the porter's cap and the nose of a young woman, there was the old lady sleeping, inflexible, her head priggishly erect beneath its felt hat, her fist closed over the newspaper.

Angela stepped down from the train.

Naturally this hadn't the slightest importance: there are people who always tend to regret, it's a trait of certain guilty natures. But the vision of the old woman waking up, the image of her face, surprised by Angela's empty seat, began to disturb her. In the end no one could know if she had fallen asleep thanks to her trust in Angela.

Trust in the world.

1974

Rosario Castellanos

1925–1974

ONE OF MEXICO'S most distinguished and versatile writers, Rosario Castellanos was born in Mexico City on May 25, 1925, into a family of provincial landowners. The family soon returned to their native Chiapas near the Guatemalan border, where the author grew up as a member of the Creole elite amidst a mostly indigenous population. Castellanos moved to Mexico City in 1944, started publishing poems and stories, and earned a graduate degree in philosophy from the National University of Mexico (UNAM) in 1950. Over the next ten years, she served as cultural director for the state of Chiapas. During the 1960s, Castellanos taught at the UNAM and at several universities in the United States. During the early seventies, she served as Mexican ambassador to Israel. A prolific writer of poems, essays, drama, and fiction, Castellanos examines in her work two major themes: the status of women and the social and racial oppression of the Chiapas indigenous peoples. Her first novel, *Balún-Canán* (1957; *The Nine Guardians,* 1958), portrays the mythical bicultural worlds of Chiapas, as narrated by a seven-year-old girl. Other well-known works are the novel *Los convidados de agosto* (1964; The guests of August), a feminist exploration of the Mexican middle-class, and *El uso de la palabra* (The right to speak), a collection of essays published posthumously in 1974.

Cooking Lesson

Translated by Maureen Ahern

THE KITCHEN IS shining white. It's a shame to have to get it dirty. One ought to sit down and contemplate it, describe it, close one's eyes, evoke it. Looking closely, this spotlessness, this pulchritude lacks the glaring excess that causes chills in hospitals. Or is it the halo of disinfectants, the rubber-cushioned steps of the aides, the hidden presence of sickness and death? What do I care? My place is here. I've been here from the beginning of time. In the German proverb woman is synonymous with *Küche, Kinder, Kirche.* I wandered astray through classrooms, streets, offices, cafés, wasting my time on skills that now I must forget in order to acquire others. For example, choosing the menu. How could one carry out such an arduous task without the cooperation of society—of all history? On a special shelf, just right for my height, my guardian spirits are lined up, those acclaimed jugglers that reconcile the most irreducible contradictions among the pages of their recipe books: slimness and gluttony, pleasing appearance and economy, speed and succulence. With their infinite combinations: slimness and economy, speed and pleasing appearance, succulence and . . . What can you suggest to me for today's meal, O experienced housewife, inspiration of mothers here and gone, voice of tradition, clamoring secret of the supermarkets? I open a book at random and read: "Don Quijote's Dinner." Very literary but not very satisfying, because Don Quijote was not famous as a gourmet but as a bumbler. Although a more profound analysis of the text reveals etc., etc., etc. Ugh! More ink has flowed about that character than water under bridges. "Fowl Center-Face." Esoteric. Whose face? Does the face of some one or something have a center? If it does, it must not be very appetizing. "Bigos Roumanian." Well, just who do you think you're talking to? If I knew what tarragon or *ananas* were I wouldn't be consulting this book, because I'd know a lot of other things, too. If you had the slightest sense of reality, you yourself or any of your colleagues would take the trouble to write a dictionary of technical terms, edit a few prolegomena, invent a propaedeutic to make the difficult culinary art accessible to the lay person. But you all start from the assumption that we're all in on the secret and you limit yourselves to stating it. I, at least, solemnly declare that I am not, and never have been, in on either this or any other secret you share. I never understood anything about anything. You observe the symptoms: I stand here like an imbecile, in an impeccable and neutral kitchen, wearing the apron that I usurp in order to give a pretense of efficiency and of which I will be shamefully but justly stripped.

I open the refrigerator drawer that proclaims "Meat" and extract a package that I cannot recognize under its icy coating. I thaw it in hot water, revealing the title without which I never would have identified the contents: Fancy Beef Broil. Wonderful. A plain and wholesome dish. But since it doesn't mean resolving an antimony or proposing an axiom, it doesn't appeal to me.

Moreover, it's not simply an excess of logic that inhibits my hunger. It's also the appearance of it, frozen stiff; it's the color that shows now that I've ripped open the package. Red, as if it were just about to start bleeding.

Our backs were that same color, my husband and I, after our orgiastic sunbathing on the beaches of Acapulco. He could afford the luxury of "behaving like the man he is" and stretch out face down to avoid rubbing his painful skin . . . But I, self-sacrificing little Mexican wife, born like a dove to the nest, smiled like Cuauhtémoc under torture on the rack when he said, "My bed is not made of roses," and fell silent. Face up, I bore not only my own weight but also his on top of me. The classic position for making love. And I moaned, from the tearing and the pleasure. The classic moan. Myths, myths.

The best part (for my sunburn at least) was when he fell asleep. Under my fingertips—not very sensitive due to prolonged contact with typewriter keys—the nylon of my bridal nightgown slipped away in a fraudulent attempt to look like lace. I played with the tips of the buttons and those other ornaments that make whoever wears them seem so feminine in the late night darkness. The whiteness of my clothes, deliberate, repetitive, immodestly symbolic, was temporarily abolished. Perhaps at some moment it managed to accomplish its purpose beneath the light and the glance of those eyes that are now overcome by fatigue.

Eyelids close and behold, once again, exile. An enormous sandy expanse with no juncture other than the sea, whose movement suggests paralysis, with no invitation except that of the cliff to suicide.

But that's a lie. I'm not the dream that dreams in a dream that dreams; I'm not the reflection of an image in a glass; I'm not annihilated by the closing off of a consciousness or of all possible consciousness. I go on living a dense, viscose, turbid life even though the man at my side and the one far away ignore me, forget me, postpone me, abandon me, fall out of love with me.

I, too, am a consciousness that can close itself off, abandon someone, and expose him to annihilation. I . . . The meat, under the sprinkling of salt, has toned down some of its offensive redness and now it seems more tolerable, more familiar to me. It's that piece I saw a thousand times without realizing it, when I used to pop in to tell the cook that . . .

We weren't born together. Our meeting was due to accident. A happy one? It's still too soon to say. We met by chance at an exhibition, a lecture, a film. We ran into each other in the elevator; he gave me his seat on the tram; a guard interrupted our perplexed and parallel contemplation of the giraffe because it was time to close the zoo. Someone, he or I, it's all the same, asked the stupid but indispensable question: Do you work or study? A harmony of interests and of good intentions, a show of "serious" intentions. A year ago I hadn't the slightest idea of his existence and now I'm lying close to him with our thighs entwined, damp with sweat and semen. I could get up without waking him, walk barefoot to the shower. To purify myself? I feel no revulsion. I prefer to believe that what links him to me is something as easy to wipe away as a secretion and not as terrible as a sacrament.

So I remain still, breathing rhythmically to imitate drowsiness, my insomnia the only spinster's jewel I've kept and I'm inclined to keep until death.

Beneath the brief deluge of pepper the meat seems to have gone gray. I banish this sign of aging by rubbing it as though I were trying to penetrate the surface and impregnate its thickness with flavors, because I lost my old name and I still can't get used to the new one, which is not mine either. When some employee pages me in the lobby of the hotel I remain deaf with that vague uneasiness that is the prelude to recognition. Who could that person be who doesn't answer? It could be something urgent, serious, a matter of life or death. The caller goes away without leaving a clue, a message, or even the possibility of another meeting. Is it anxiety that presses against my heart? No, it's his hand pressing on my shoulder and his lips smiling at me in benevolent mockery, more like a sorcerer than a master.

So then, I accept, as we head toward the bar (my peeling shoulder feels like it's on fire) that it's true that in my contact or collision with him I've undergone a profound metamorphosis. I didn't know and now I know; I didn't feel and now I do feel; I wasn't and now I am.

It should be left to sit for a while. Until it reaches room temperature, until it's steeped in the flavors that I've rubbed into it. I have the feeling I didn't know how to calculate very well and that I've bought a piece that's too big for the two of us—for me, because I'm lazy, not a carnivore; for him, for aesthetic reasons because he's watching his waistline. Almost all of it will be left over! Yes, I already know that I shouldn't worry: one of the good fairies that hovers over me is going to come to my rescue and explain how one uses leftovers. It's a mistake, anyhow. You don't start married life in such a sordid way. I'm afraid that you also don't start it with a dish as dull as broiled beef.

Thanks, I murmur, while I wipe my lips with a corner of the napkin. Thanks for the transparent cocktail glass, and for the submerged olive.

Thanks for letting me out of the cage of one sterile routine only to lock me into the cage of another, a routine which according to all purposes and possibilities must be fruitful. Thanks for giving me the chance to show off a long gown with a train, for helping me walk up the aisle of the church, carried away by the organ music. Thanks for . . .

How long will it take to be done? Well, that shouldn't worry me too much because it has to be put on the grill at the last minute. It takes very little time, according to the cookbook. How long is little? Fifteen minutes? Ten? Five? Naturally the text doesn't specify. It presupposes an intuition which, according to my sex, I'm supposed to possess but I don't, a sense I was born without that would allow me to gauge the precise minute the meat is done.

And what about you? Don't you have anything to thank me for? You've specified it with a slightly pedantic solemnity and a precision that perhaps were meant to flatter but instead offended: my virginity. When you discovered it I felt like the last dinosaur on a planet where the species was extinct. I longed to justify myself, to explain that if I was intact when I met you it was not out of virtue or pride or ugliness but simply out of adherence to a style. I'm not baroque. The tiny imperfection in the pearl is unbearable to me. The only alternative I have is the neoclassic one, and its rigidity is incompatible with the spontaneity needed for making love. I lack that ease of the person who rows or plays tennis or dances. I don't play any sports. I comply with the ritual but my move to surrender petrifies into a statue.

Are you monitoring my transit to fluidity? Do you expect it, do you need it? Or is this hieraticism that sanctifies you, and that you interpret as the passivity natural to my nature, enough for you? So if you are voluble it will ease your mind to think that I won't hinder your adventures. It won't be necessary—thanks to my temperament—for you to fatten me up, tie me down hand and foot with children, gag me on the thick honey of resignation. I'll stay the same as I am. Calm. When you throw your body on top of mine I feel as though a gravestone were covering me, full of inscriptions, strange names, memorable dates. You moan unintelligibly and I'd like to whisper my name in your ear to remind you who it is you are possessing.

I'm myself. But who am I? Your wife, of course. And that title suffices to distinguish me from past memories or future projects. I bear an owner's brand, a property tag, and yet you watch me suspiciously. I'm not weaving a web to trap you. I'm not a praying mantis. I appreciate your believing such a hypothesis, but it's false.

This meat has a toughness and consistency that is not like beef. It must be mammoth. One of those that have been preserved since prehistoric times in the Siberian ice, that the peasants thaw out and fix for food. In that terribly boring documentary they showed at the Embassy, so full of superfluous details, there wasn't the slightest mention of how long it took to make them edible. Years, months? And I only have so much time . . .

Is that a lark? Or is it a nightingale? No, our schedule won't be ruled by such winged creatures as those that announced the coming of dawn to Romeo and Juliet but by a noisy and unerring alarm clock. And you will not descend to day by the stairway of my tresses but rather on the steps of detailed complaints: you've lost a button off your jacket; the toast is burned; the coffee is cold.

I'll ruminate my resentment in silence. All the responsibilities and duties of a servant are assigned to me for everything. I'm supposed to keep the house impeccable, the clothes ready, mealtimes exact. But I'm not paid any salary; I don't get one day a week off; I can't change masters. On the other hand, I'm supposed to contribute to the support of the household and I'm expected to efficiently carry out a job where the boss is demanding, my colleagues conspire, and my subordinates hate me. In my free time I transform myself into a society matron who gives luncheons and dinners for her husband's friends, attends meetings, subscribes to the opera season, watches her weight, renews her wardrobe, cares for her skin, keeps herself attractive, keeps up on all the gossip, stays up late and gets up early, runs the monthly risk of maternity, believes the evening executive meetings, the business trips and the arrival of unexpected clients; who suffers from olfactory hallucinations when she catches a whiff of French perfume (different from the one she uses) on her husband's shirts and handkerchiefs and on lonely nights refuses to think why or what so much fuss is all about and fixes herself a stiff drink and reads a detective story with the fragile mood of a convalescent.

Shouldn't it be time to turn on the stove? Low flame so the broiler will start warming up gradually, "which should be greased first so the meat will not stick." That did occur to me; there was no need to waste pages on those recommendations.

I'm very awkward. Now it's called awkwardness, but it used to be called innocence and you loved it. But I've never loved it. When I was single I used to read things on the sly, perspiring from the arousal and shame. I never found out anything. My breasts ached, my eyes got misty, my muscles contracted in a spasm of nausea.

The oil is starting to get hot. I let it get too hot, heavy handed that I am, and now it's spitting and spattering and burning me. That's how I'm going to fry in those narrow hells, through my fault, through my fault, through my most grievous fault. But child, you're not the only one. All your classmates do the same thing or worse. They confess in the confessional, do their penance, are forgiven and fall into it again. All of them. If I had continued going around with them they'd be questioning me now, the married ones to find things out for themselves, the single ones to find out how far they can go. Impossible to let them down. I would invent acrobatics, sublime fainting spells, transports as they're called in the Thousand and One Nights—records! If you only heard me then, you'd never recognize me, Casanova!

I drop the meat onto the grill and instinctively step back against the wall. What a noise! Now it's stopped. The meat lies there silently, faithful to its deceased state. I still think it's too big.

It's not that you've let me down. It's true that I didn't expect anything special. Gradually we'll reveal ourselves to one another, discover our secrets, our little tricks, learn to please each other. And one day you and I will become a pair of perfect lovers and then, right in the middle of an embrace, we'll disappear and the words, "The End," will appear on the screen.

What's the matter? The meat is shrinking. No, I'm not seeing things; I'm not wrong. You can see the mark of its original size by the outline that it left on the grill. It was only a little bit bigger. Good! Maybe it will be just the right size for our appetites.

In my next movie I'd like them to give me a different part. The white sorceress in a savage village? No, today I don't feel much inclined to either heroism or danger. Better a famous woman (a fashion designer or something like that), rich and independent, who lives by herself in an apartment in New York, Paris, or London. Her occasional *affaires* entertain her but do not change her. She's not sentimental. After a breakup scene she lights a cigarette and surveys the urban scenery through the picture window of her studio.

Ah, the color of the meat looks much better now, only raw in a few obstinate places. But the rest is browned and gives off a delicious aroma. Will it be enough for the two of us? It looks very small to me.

If I got dressed up now I'd try on one of those dresses from my trousseau and go out. What would happen, hmmmm? Maybe an older man with a car would pick me up. Mature. Retired. The only kind who can afford to be on the make at this time of day.

What the devil's going on? This damned meat is starting to give off horrible black smoke! I should have turned it over! Burned on one side. Well, thank goodness it has another one.

Miss, if you will allow me . . . Mrs.! And I'm warning you, my husband is very jealous. . . . Then he shouldn't let you go out alone. You're a temptation to any passerby. Nobody in this world says passerby. Pedestrian? Only the newspapers when they report accidents. You're a temptation for anyone. Mean-ing-ful silence. The glances of a sphinx. The older man is following me at a safe distance. Better for him. Better for me, because on the corner—uh, oh—my husband, who's spying on me and who never leaves me alone morning, noon, or night, who suspects everything and everybody. Your Honor. It's impossible to live this way, I want a divorce.

Now what? This piece of meat's mother never told it that it was meat and ought to act like it. It's curling up like a corkscrew pastry. Anyhow, I don't know where all that smoke can be coming from if I turned the stove off ages ago. Of course, Dear Abby, what one must do now is open the window, plug in the ventilator so it won't be smelly when my husband gets here. And I'll so cutely run right out to greet him at the door with my best dress on, my best smile, and my warmest invitation to eat out.

It's a thought. We'll look at the restaurant menu while that miserable piece of charred meat lies hidden at the bottom of the garbage pail. I'll be careful not to mention the incident because I'd be considered a somewhat irresponsible wife, with frivolous tendencies but not mentally retarded. This is the initial public image that I project and I've got to maintain it even though it isn't accurate.

There's another possibility. Don't open the window, don't turn on the ventilator, don't throw the meat in the garbage. When my husband gets here let him smell it like the ogres in all the stories and tell him that no, it doesn't smell of human flesh here, but of useless woman. I'll exaggerate my compunction so he can be magnanimous. After all, what's happened is so normal! What newlywed doesn't do the same thing that I've done? When we visit my mother-in-law, who is still at the stage of not attacking me because she doesn't know my weak points yet, she'll tell me her own experiences. The time, for example, when her husband asked her to fix coddled eggs and she took him literally . . . ha, ha. Did that stop her from becoming a fabulous widow, I mean a fabulous cook? Because she was widowed much later and for other reasons. After that she gave free rein to her maternal instincts and spoiled everything with all her pampering . . .

No, he's not going to find it the least bit amusing. He's going to say that

I got distracted, that it's the height of carelessness and, yes, condescendingly, I'm going to accept his accusations.

But it isn't true, it isn't. I was watching the meat all the time, watching how a series of very odd things happened to it. Saint Theresa was right when she said that God is in the stewpots. Or matter is energy or whatever it's called now.

Let's backtrack. First there's the piece of meat, one color, one shape, one size. Then it changes, looks even nicer and you feel very happy. Then it starts changing again and now it doesn't look so nice. It keeps changing and changing and changing and you just can't tell when you should stop it. Because if I leave this piece of meat on the grill indefinitely, it will burn to a crisp till nothing is left of it. So that piece of meat that gave the impression of being so solid and real no longer exists.

So? My husband also gives the impression of being solid and real when we're together, when I touch him, when I see him. He certainly changes and I change too, although so slowly that neither of us realizes it. Then he goes off and suddenly becomes a memory and . . . Oh, no, I'm not going to fall into that trap; the one about the invented character and the invented narrator and the invented anecdote. Besides, it's not the consequence that licitly follows from the meat episode.

The meat hasn't stopped existing. It has undergone a series of metamorphoses. And the fact that it ceases to be perceptible for the senses does not mean that the cycle is concluded but that it has taken the quantum leap. It will go on operating on other levels. On the level of my consciousness, my memory, my will, changing me, defining me, establishing the course of my future.

From today on, I'll be whatever I choose to be at the moment. Seductively unbalanced, deeply withdrawn, hypocritical. From the very beginning I will impose, just a bit insolently, the rules of the game. My husband will resent the appearance of my dominance, which will widen like the ripples on the surface of the water when someone has skipped a pebble across it. I'll struggle to prevail and, if he gives in, I'll retaliate with my scorn, and, if he doesn't give in, I'll simply be unable to forgive him.

If I assume another attitude, if I'm the typical case, femininity that begs indulgence for her errors, the balance will tip in favor of my antagonist and I will be running the race with a handicap, which, apparently, seals my defeat, and which, essentially, guarantees my triumph by the winding path that my grandmothers took, the humble ones, the ones who didn't open their mouths except to say yes and achieved an obedience foreign to even their most irrational whims. The recipe of course is ancient and its efficiency is proven. If I still doubt, all I have to do is ask my neighbor. She'll confirm my certainty.

It's just that it revolts me to behave that way. This definition is not applicable to me, the former one either; neither corresponds to my inner truth, or safeguards my authenticity. Must I grasp some one of them and bind myself to its terms only because it is a cliché accepted by the majority and intelligible to everyone? And it's not because I'm a *rara avis*. You can say about me what Pfandl said about Sor Juana, that I belong to the class of hesitant neurotics. The diagnosis is very easy, but what consequences does the assumption hold?

If I insist on affirming my version of the facts my husband is going to look at me suspiciously; he's going to live in continual expectation that I'll be declared insane.

Our life together could not be more problematic! He doesn't want conflicts of any kind, much less such abstract, absurd, metaphysical conflicts as the one I would present him with. His home is a haven of peace where he takes refuge from all the storms of life. Agreed. I accepted that when I got married and I was even ready to accept sacrifice for the sake of marital harmony. But I counted on the fact that the sacrifice, the complete renunciation of what I am, would only be demanded of me on The Sublime Occasion, at The Time of Heroic Solutions, at The Moment of the Definitive Decision. Not in exchange for what I stumbled on today, which is something very insignificant and very ridiculous. And yet . . .

1971

Carlos Fuentes

b. 1928

CARLOS FUENTES WAS born in Mexico City on November 11, 1928, into an affluent professional family (his father was a career diplomat). He was educated at the National University of Mexico (UNAM), the Institute of International Studies in Geneva, Switzerland, and Princeton University. Between 1950 and 1959, he served extensively at various cultural institutions in Mexico and was his country's ambassador to France from 1975 to 1977. Fuentes has taught and lectured at numerous universities, among them UNAM, University of Concepción (Chile), the University of Paris, Columbia University, and the University of Pennsylvania. Although Fuentes is also one of the most "international" of Latin American writers, his work centers almost exclusively on the exploration of Mexican history, culture, and identity. His novel *La muerte de Artemio Cruz* (1962; *The Death of Artemio Cruz,* 1964), one of the best-known novels of the Latin American literary "Boom," is a technically complex text that captures the history of post-Revolutionary Mexico through the life of one of its patriarchs. Other novels that analyze similar themes are *Cambio de piel* (1967; *A Change of Skin,* 1968) and *Terra Nostra* (1975; *Terra Nostra,* 1976). Although he is best known as a novelist, Fuentes's short stories are masterful examples of the genre. *Burnt Water* (1980) is an anthology of stories from the collections *Cantar de ciegos* (1964; Blind men's songs) and *Chac Mool y otros cuentos* (1973; Chac Mool and other stories). More recent works by Fuentes are *Cristóbal Nonato* (1989; *Christopher Unborn,* 1990), a retelling of the life of Christopher Columbus and the cultural encounter between Europe and America, and *Constancia y otras novelas para vírgenes* (1989; *Constancia and Other Stories for Virgins,* 1990), a collection of novellas. The story reprinted here, "In a Flemish Garden," links Mexico's present to its past through the historical figure of the Empress Carlotta.

In a Flemish Garden

Translated by Margaret Sayers Peden

SEPT. 19. THAT attorney Brambila gets the most harebrained ideas! Now he's bought that old mansion on Puente de Alvarado, sumptuous, but totally impractical, built at the time of the French Intervention. Naturally, I thought it was just another of his many deals, and that he intended, as he had on other occasions, to demolish the house and sell the land at a profit, or at least to build an office and commercial property there. That is, that's what I thought at first. I was astounded when he told me his plan: he meant to use the house, with its marvelous parquet floors and glittering chandeliers, for entertaining and lodging his North American business associates—history, folklore, and elegance all in one package. And he wanted me to live for a while in his mansion, because this Brambila, who was so impressed with everything about the place, had noticed a certain lack of human warmth in these rooms, which had been empty since 1910, when the family fled to France. A caretaker couple who lived in the rooftop apartment had kept everything clean and polished—though for forty years there hadn't been a stick of furniture except a magnificent Pleyel in the salon. You felt a penetrating cold (my attorney friend had said) in the house, particularly noticeable in contrast to the temperature outside.

"Look, my handsome blond friend. You can invite anyone you want for drinks and conversation. You'll have all the basic necessities. Read, write, do whatever it is you do."

And Brambila took off for Washington, leaving me stunned by his great faith in my power to create warmth.

Sept. 19. That very afternoon, with one suitcase, I moved into the mansion on Puente de Alvarado. It is truly beautiful, however much the exterior with its Second Empire Ionic capitals and caryatids seems to refute it. The salon, overlooking the street, has gleaming, fragrant floors, and the walls, faintly stained by spectral rectangles where paintings once hung, are a pale blue somehow not merely old but antique. The murals on the vaulted ceiling (Zobenigo, the quay of Giovanni e Paolo, Santa Maria della Salute) were painted by disciples of Francesco Guardi. The bedroom walls are covered in blue velvet, and the hallways are tunnels of plain and carved wood, elm, ebony, and box, some in the Flemish style of Viet Stoss, others more reminiscent of Berruguete and the quiet grandeur of the masters of Pisa. I particularly like the library. It's at the rear of the house, and its French doors offer the only view of a small, square garden with a bed of everlasting flowers, its three walls cushioned with climbing vines. I haven't yet found the keys to these doors, the only access to the garden. But it will be in the garden, reading and smoking, that I begin my humanizing labors in this island of antiquity. Red and white, the everlastings glistened beneath the rain; an old-style bench of greenish wrought iron twisted in the form of leaves; and soft wet grass, partly the result of love, partly perseverance. Now that I'm writing about it, I realize that the garden suggests the cadences of Rodenbach . . . Dans l'horizon du soir où le soleil recule . . . la fumée éphémère et pacifique ondule . . . comme une gaze où des prunelles sont cachées; et l'on sent, rien qu'à voir ces brumes détachées, un douloureux regret de ciel et de voyage . . .

Sept. 20. In this house I feel very far removed from the "parasitical ills" of Mexico City. For less than twenty-four hours I've been inside these walls that emanate a sensitivity, a flow, suggestive of other shores. I've been invaded by a kind of lucid languor, a sense of imminence; with every moment I become increasingly aware of certain perfumes peculiar to my surroundings, certain silhouettes from a memory that formerly was revealed in brief flashes but today swells and flows with the measured vitality of a river. Amid the rivets and bolts of the city, when have I noticed the change of season? We don't notice the season in Mexico City: one fades into another with no change of pace, "the immortal springtime, and its tokens." Here the seasons lose their characteristic reiterated novelty of parameters with rhythms, rites, and pleasures of their own, of boundaries about which we entwine our nostalgia and our projects, of signs that nurture and solidify consciousness. Tomorrow is the equinox. Today, in this place, I have with a kind of Nordic indolence noted, not for the first time, the approach of autumn. A gray veil is descending over the garden, which I am observing as I write; overnight, a few leaves have fallen from the arbor, carpeting the lawn; a few leaves are beginning to turn golden, and an incessant rain is fading the greenness, washing it into the soil. The smoke of autumn hovers over the garden, as far as the walls, and one could almost believe one heard, heavy as deep breathing, the sound of slow footsteps among the fallen leaves.

Sept. 21. I finally succeeded in opening the French doors in the library. I went out into the garden. The fine rain continues, imperceptible and tenacious. If in the house I seemed to caress the skin of a different world, in the garden I touched its nerves. In the garden those silhouettes of memory, of imminence, that I noticed yesterday make my nerves tingle. The everlastings are not the flowers I know: these are permeated with a mournful perfume, as if they had been gathered from a crypt after years among dust and marble. The very rain stirs colorings in the grass I want to identify with other cities, other windows; standing in the center of the garden, I closed my eyes . . . Javanese tobacco and wet sidewalks . . . herring . . . beer fumes, the haze of forests, the trunks of great oaks . . . Turning in a circle, I tried to absorb the totality of this quadrangle of vague light that even in the rain seems to filter through yellow stained glass, to glimmer in braziers, made melancholy before it became light . . . and the verdant growth of the vines was not that of the burnt earth of the plateau; this was a different, soft, green shading into blue in the distant treetops, covering rocks with grotesque slime . . . Memling! Between the eyes of a Virgin and reflections of copper, I had seen this same landscape from one of your windows! I was looking at a fictitious, an invented landscape. This garden was not in Mexico! This misty rain . . . I ran into the house, raced down the hallway, burst into the salon, and pressed my nose to the window: on the Avenida Puente de Alvarado, a blast of jukeboxes, streetcars, and sun, the monotonous sun. A Sun God without shading or effigies in its rays, a stationary Sun Stone, a sun of shortened centuries. I returned to the library: the rain still fell on the old, hooded garden.

Sept. 21. I've been standing here, my breath misting the door panes, gazing out at the garden and the reflection of my blue eyes. Hours perhaps, staring at the small, enclosed space, fingering my beard absentmindedly. Staring at a lawn that minute by minute is buried beneath new leaves. Then I heard a muted sound, a buzzing that might have come from within me, and I looked up. In the garden, almost opposite mine, another head, slightly tilted, its eyes staring into mine. Instinctively, I leaped back. The face in the garden never varied its gaze, impenetrable in the deep shadows beneath its brows. The figure turned away; I saw only a small body, black and hunched, and I covered my eyes with my hands.

Sept. 22. There's no telephone in the house, but I could go out on the Avenida, call up some friends, go to the Roxy . . . After all, this is my city; these are my people! Why can't I leave this house; more accurately, my post at the doors looking onto the garden?

Sept. 22. I am not going to be frightened because someone leaped over the wall into the garden. I'm going to wait all evening—it continues to rain, day and night!—and capture the intruder . . . I was dozing in the armchair facing the window when I was awakened by the intense scent of the everlastings. Unhesitatingly, I stared into the garden—yes, there. Picking the flowers, the small yellow hands forming a nosegay. It was a little old woman, she must have been at least eighty. But how had she dared intrude? And how had she got in? I watched as she picked the flowers: wizened, slim, clad all in black. Her skirts brushed the ground, collecting dew and clover; the cloth sagged with the weight, an airy weight, a Caravaggio texture. Her black jacket was buttoned to the chin, her torso was bent over, hunched against the cold. Her face was shadowed by a black lace coif which covered tangled white hair.

I could see nothing but her bloodless lips, the paleness of her flesh repeated in the firm line of a mouth arched slightly in the faintest, saddest, eternal smile devoid of any motivation. She looked up; her eyes were not eyes . . . what seemed to emerge from beneath the wrinkled lids was a pathway, a nocturnal landscape, leading toward an infinite inward journey. This ancient woman bent down to pluck a red bud; in profile, her hawk-like features, her sunken cheeks, reflected like the vibrating planes of the reaper's scythe. Then she walked away toward . . . ? No, I won't say she walked through the vines and the wall, that she evaporated, that she sank into the ground or ascended into the sky; a path seemed to open in the garden, so natural that at first I didn't notice it, and along it as if—I knew it, I'd heard it before—as if treading a course long-forgotten, heavy as deep breathing, my visitor disappeared beneath the rain.

Sept. 23. I locked myself in the bedroom and barricaded the door with everything I could lay my hands on. I was sure it would do no good, but I thought I could at least give myself the illusion of being able to sleep with tranquillity. Those measured footsteps, always as if on dry leaves; I thought I heard them every moment. I knew they weren't real, that is, until I heard the faintest rustle outside the door, and then the whisper of something passed beneath the door. I turned on the light; the corner of an envelope was outlined against the velvety floor. For a moment I held its contents in my hand: old paper, elegant, rosewood.

Written in a spidery hand, large, erect letters, the message consisted of one word:

Tlactocatzine

Sept. 23. She will come, as she did yesterday and the day before, at sunset. I will speak to her today; she can't escape me, I will follow her through the hidden entry among the vines . . .

Sept. 23. As the clock was striking six, I heard music in the salon; it was the magnificent old Pleyel, playing waltzes. As I approached, the sound ceased. I turned back to the library. She was in the garden. Now she was skipping about, pantomiming . . . a little girl playing with her hoop. I opened the door, went out, I don't know exactly what happened; I felt as if the sky, as if the very air descended one level to press down on the garden; the air became motionless, fathomless, and all sound was suspended. The old woman stared at me, always with the same smile, her eyes lost in the depths of the world; her mouth opened, her lips moved; no sound emanated from that pale slit, the garden was squeezed like a sponge, the cold buried its fingers in my flesh . . .

Sept. 24. After the apparition at dusk, I came to my senses sitting in the armchair in the library; the French doors were locked, the garden solitary. The odor of the everlastings has permeated the house; it is particularly intense in my bedroom. There I awaited a new missive, a new sign from the aged woman. Her words, the flesh of silence, were struggling to tell me something . . . At eleven that evening I could sense beside me the dull light of the garden. Again the whisper of the long, starched skirts outside my door; and the letter:

My beloved
    The moon has risen and I hear it singing; everything is indescribably beautiful.

I dressed and went downstairs to the library; a veil-become-light enveloped the old woman, who was sitting on the garden bench. I walked toward her, again amid the buzzing of bumblebees. The same air, void of any sound, enveloped her. Her white light ruffled my hair, and the aged woman took my hands and kissed them; her skin pressed against mine. I *saw* this; my eyes told me what touch would not corroborate: her hands in mine were nothing but wind—heavy, cold wind; I intuited the opaque ice in the skeleton of this kneeling figure whose lips moved in a litany of forbidden rhythms. The everlastings trembled, solitary, independent of the wind. They smelled of the grave. Yes, they grew there, in the tomb: there they germinated, there they were carried every evening in the spectral hands of an ancient woman . . . and sound returned, amplified by the rain, and a coagulated voice, an echo of spilled blood copulating still with the earth, screamed:

"Kapuzinergruft! Kapuzinergruft!"

I jerked free from her hands and ran to the front door of the mansion— even there I heard the mad sound of her voice, the drowned dead echoing in the cavernous throat—and I sank to the floor trembling, clutching the doorknob, drained of the strength to turn it.

I couldn't; it was impossible to open.

It is sealed with a thick red lacquer. In the center, a coat of arms glimmers in the night, a crowned double eagle, the old woman's profile, signaling the icy intensity of permanent confinement.

And that night I heard behind me—I did not know I was to hear it for all time—the whisper of skirts brushing the floor; she walks with a new, ecstatic joy; her gestures are repetitious, betraying her satisfaction. The satisfaction of a jailer, of a companion, of eternal prison. The satisfaction of solitude shared. I heard her voice again, drawing near, her lips touching my ear, the breath fabricated of spume and buried earth:

". . . and they didn't let us play with our hoops, Max; they forbade us; we had to carry them in our hands during our walks through the gardens in Brussels . . . but I told you that in a letter, the letter I wrote from Bouchot, do you remember? Oh, but from now on, no more letters, we'll be together forever, the two of us in this castle . . . We will never leave; we will never allow anyone to enter . . . Oh, Max, answer me, the everlastings, the ones I bring in the evenings to the Capuchin crypt, to the Kapuziner- gruft, don't they smell fresh? They're the same flowers the Indians brought you when we arrived here: you, the Tlactocatzine . . . *Nis tiquimopielia inin maxochtzintl* . . . Remember? Lord, we offer you these flowers . . ."

And on the coat of arms I read the inscription:

Charlotte, Kaiserin von Mexiko

1954

Gabriel García Márquez

b. 1928

BORN IN THE small coastal town of Aracataca, Colombia on March 6, 1928, Gabriel García Márquez is perhaps the best-known Latin American author alive. The oldest of twelve children, he was raised by his grandparents, absorbing the rich folklore of Aracataca (the fictionalized Macondo of many of his works). He studied law at the University of Colombia in Bogotá during the late 1940s while at the same time pursuing a career in journalism and literature. He was deeply influenced by the Mexican writer Juan Rulfo and by William Faulkner. Over the past forty years, he has lived in Cuba, France, Mexico, Spain, and the United States, working as a journalist some of the time, and continuing to build a solid reputation as one of Latin America's most distinguished writers. In 1982, he received the Nobel Prize for Literature. Although he had written several novellas and a collection of short stories between 1955 and 1962, it was in 1967 that García Márquez achieved almost instantaneous fame with the publication of *Cien años de soledad* (1967; *One Hundred Years of Solitude,* 1970). A monumental fiction that captures the essence of the Latin American "Boom" in literature, this work has been viewed by some critics as the "culmination and synthesis" of Hispanic literature. Eight years later, García Márquez published his now classic novel of dictatorship, *El otoño del patriarca* (1975; *The Autumn of the Patriarch,* 1976). More recent works include *El amor en los tiempos del cólera* (1985; *Love in the Time of Cholera,* 1988), an engrossing family saga woven around the theme of obsessive love, and *El general en su laberinto* (1989; *The General in his Labyrinth,* 1990), a recreation of Simón Bolívar's last days. Even though García Márquez has been known as a committed socialist and as a supporter of Fidel Castro's Marxist government, he has avoided facile interpretations of history and politics in his works, having been more concerned with the realm of the imagination. In texts that range from "magical realism" to chronicles of actual events, García

Márquez succeeds in portraying intensely believable characters that transcend the forces of history, culture, and family in their indomitable humanity. The following two stories are from the collections *La hojarasca* (1955; *Leaf Storm and Other Stories,* 1972) and *Los funerales de la mamá grande* (1962; included in *No One Writes to the Colonel and Other Stories,* 1968).

Monologue of Isabel Watching It Rain in Macondo

Translated by Gregory Rabassa

WINTER FELL ONE Sunday when people were coming out of church. Saturday night had been suffocating. But even on Sunday morning nobody thought it would rain. After mass, before we women had time to find the catches on our parasols, a thick, dark wind blew, which with one broad, round swirl swept away the dust and hard tinder of May. Someone next to me said: "It's a water wind." And I knew it even before then. From the moment we came out onto the church steps I felt shaken by a slimy feeling in my stomach. The men ran to the nearby houses with one hand on their hats and a handkerchief in the other, protecting themselves against the wind and the dust storm. Then it rained. And the sky was a gray, jellyish substance that flapped its wings a hand away from our heads.

During the rest of the morning my stepmother and I were sitting by the railing, happy that the rain would revive the thirsty rosemary and nard in the flowerpots after seven months of intense summer and scorching dust. At noon the reverberation of the earth stopped and a smell of turned earth, of awakened and renovated vegetation mingled with the cool and healthful odor of the rain in the rosemary. My father said at lunchtime: "When it rains in May, it's a sign that there'll be good tides." Smiling, crossed by the luminous thread of the new season, my stepmother told me: "That's what I heard in the sermon." And my father smiled. And he ate with a good appetite and even let his food digest leisurely beside the railing, silent, his eyes closed, but not sleeping, as if to think that he was dreaming while awake.

It rained all afternoon in a single tone. In the uniform and peaceful intensity you could hear the water fall, the way it is when you travel all afternoon on a train. But without our noticing it, the rain was penetrating too deeply into our senses. Early Monday morning, when we closed the door to avoid the cutting, icy draft that blew in from the courtyard, our senses had been filled with rain. And on Monday morning they had overflowed. My stepmother and I went back to look at the garden. The harsh gray earth of May had been changed overnight into a dark, sticky substance like cheap soap. A trickle of water began to run off the flower-pots. "I think they had more than enough water during the night," my stepmother said. And I noticed that she had stopped smiling and that her joy of the previous day had changed during the night into a lax and tedious seriousness. "I think you're right," I said. "It would be better to have the Indians put them on the veranda until it stops raining." And that was what they did, while the rain grew like an immense tree over the other trees. My father occupied the same spot where he had been on Sunday afternoon, but he didn't talk about the rain. He said: "I must have slept poorly last night because I woke up with a stiff back." And he stayed there, sitting by the railing with his feet on a chair and his head turned toward the empty garden. Only at dusk, after he had turned down lunch, did he say: "It looks as if it will never clear." And I remembered the months of heat. I remembered August, those long and awesome siestas in which we dropped down to die under the weight of the hour, our clothes sticking to our bodies, hearing outside the insistent and dull buzzing of the hour that never passed. I saw the washed-down walls, the joints of the beams all puffed up by the water. I saw the small garden, empty for the first time, and the jasmine bush against the wall, faithful to the memory of my mother. I saw my father sitting in a rocker, his painful vertebrae resting on a pillow and his sad eyes lost in the labyrinth of the rain. I remembered the August nights in whose wondrous silence nothing could be heard except the millenary sound that the earth makes as it spins on its rusty, unoiled axis. Suddenly I felt overcome by an overwhelming sadness.

It rained all Monday, just like Sunday. But now it seemed to be raining in another way, because something different and bitter was going on in my heart. At dusk a voice beside my chair said: "This rain is a bore." Without turning to look, I recognized Martín's voice. I knew that he was speaking in the next chair, with the same cold and awesome expression that hadn't varied, not even after that gloomy December dawn when he started being my husband. Five months had passed since then. Now I was going to have a child. And Martín was there beside me saying that the rain bored him. "Not a bore," I said. "It seems terribly sad to me, with the empty garden and those poor trees that can't come in from the courtyard." Then I turned to look at him and Martín was no longer there. It was only a voice that was saying to me: "It doesn't look as if it will ever clear," and when I looked toward the voice I found only the empty chair.

On Tuesday morning we found a cow in the garden. It looked like a clay promontory in its hard and rebellious immobility, its hooves sunken in the mud and its head bent over. During the morning the Indians tried to drive it away with sticks and stones. But the cow stayed there, imperturbable in the garden, hard, inviolable, its hooves still sunken in the mud and its huge head humiliated by the rain. The Indians harassed it until my father's patient tolerance came to its defense. "Leave her alone," he said. "She'll leave the way she came."

At sundown on Tuesday the water tightened and hurt, like a shroud over the heart. The coolness of the first morning began to change into a hot and sticky humidity. The temperature was neither cold nor hot; it was the temperature of a fever chill. Feet sweated inside shoes. It was hard to say what was more disagreeable, bare skin or the contact of clothing on skin. All activity had ceased in the house. We sat on the veranda but we no longer watched the rain as we did on the first day. We no longer felt it falling. We no longer saw anything except the outline of the trees in the mist, with a sad and desolate sunset which left on your lips the same taste with which you awaken after having dreamed about a stranger. I knew that it was Tuesday and I remembered the twins of Saint Jerome, the blind girls who came to the house every week to sing us simple songs, saddened by the bitter and unprotected prodigy of their voices. Above the rain I heard the blind twins' little song and I imagined them at home, huddling, waiting for the rain to stop so they could go out and sing. The twins of Saint Jerome wouldn't come that day, I thought, nor would the beggar woman be on the veranda after siesta, asking, as on every Tuesday, for the eternal branch of lemon balm.

That day we lost track of meals. At siesta time my stepmother served a plate of tasteless soup and a piece of stale bread. But actually we hadn't eaten since sunset on Monday and I think that from then on we stopped thinking. We were paralyzed, drugged by the rain, given over to the collapse of nature with a peaceful and resigned attitude. Only the cow was moving in the afternoon. Suddenly a deep noise shook her insides and her hooves sank into the mud with greater force. Then she stood motionless for half an hour, as if she were already dead but could not fall down because the habit of being alive prevented her, the habit of remaining in one position in the rain, until the habit grew weaker than her body. Then she doubled her front legs (her dark and shiny haunches still raised in a last agonized effort) and sank her drooling snout into the mud, finally surrendering to the weight of her own matter in a silent, gradual, and dignified ceremony of total downfall. "She got that far," someone said behind me. And I turned to look and on the threshold I saw the Tuesday beggar woman who had come through the storm to ask for the branch of lemon balm.

Perhaps on Wednesday I might have grown accustomed to that overwhelming atmosphere if on going to the living room I hadn't found the table pushed against the wall, the furniture piled on top of it, and on the other side, on a parapet prepared during the night, trunks and boxes of household utensils. The spectacle produced a terrible feeling of emptiness in me. Something had happened during the night. The house was in disarray; the Guajiro Indians, shirtless and barefoot, with their pants rolled up to their knees, were carrying the furniture into the dining room. In the men's expression, in the very diligence with which they were working, one could see the cruelty of their frustrated rebellion, of their necessary and humiliating inferiority in the rain. I moved without direction, without will. I felt changed into a desolate meadow sown with algae and lichens, with soft, sticky toadstools, fertilized by the repugnant plants of dampness and shadows. I was in the living room contemplating the desert spectacle of the piled-up furniture when I heard my stepmother's voice warning me from her room that I might catch pneumonia. Only then did I realize that the water was up to my ankles, that the house was flooded, the floor covered by a thick surface of viscous, dead water.

On Wednesday noon it still hadn't finished dawning. And before three o'clock in the afternoon night had come on completely, ahead of time and sickly, with the same slow, monotonous, and pitiless rhythm of the rain in the courtyard. It was a premature dusk, soft and lugubrious, growing in the midst of the silence of the Guajiros, who were squatting on the chairs against the walls, defeated and impotent against the disturbance of nature. That was when news began to arrive from outside. No one brought it to the house. It simply arrived, precise, individualized, as if led by the liquid clay that ran through the streets and dragged household items along, things and more things, the leftovers of a remote catastrophe, rubbish and dead animals. Events that took place on Sunday, when the rain was still the announcement of a providential season, took two days to be known at our house. And on Wednesday the news arrived as if impelled by the very inner dynamism of the storm. It was learned then that the church was flooded and its collapse expected. Someone who had no reason to know said that night: "The train hasn't been able to cross the bridge since Monday. It seems that the river carried away the tracks." And it was learned that a sick woman had disappeared from her bed and had been found that afternoon floating in the courtyard.

Terrified, possessed by the fright and the deluge, I sat down in the rocker with my legs tucked up and my eyes fixed on the damp darkness full of hazy foreboding. My stepmother appeared in the doorway with the lamp held high and her head erect. She looked like a family ghost before whom I felt no fear whatever because I myself shared her supernatural condition. She came over to where I was. She still held her head high and the lamp in the air, and she splashed through the water on the veranda. "Now we have to pray," she said. And I noticed her dry and wrinkled face, as if she had just left her tomb or as if she had been made of some substance different from human matter. She was across from me with her rosary in her hand saying: "Now we have to pray. The water broke open the tombs and now the poor dead are floating in the cemetery."

I may have slept a little that night when I awoke with a start because of a sour and penetrating smell like that of decomposing bodies. I gave a strong shake to Martín, who was snoring beside me. "Don't you notice it?" I asked him. And he said: "What?" And I said: "The smell. It must be the dead people floating along the streets." I was terrified by that idea, but Martín turned to the wall and with a husky and sleepy voice said: "That's something you made up. Pregnant women are always imagining things."

At dawn on Thursday the smells stopped, the sense of distance was lost. The notion of time, upset since the day before, disappeared completely. Then there was no Thursday. What should have been Thursday was a physical, jellylike thing that could have been parted with the hands in order to look into Friday. There were no men or women there. My stepmother, my father, the Indians were adipose and improbable bodies that moved in the marsh of winter. My father said to me: "Don't move away from here until you're told what to do," and his voice was distant and indirect and didn't seem to be perceived by the ear but by touch, which was the only sense that remained active.

But my father didn't return: he got lost in the weather. So when night came I called my stepmother to tell her to accompany me to my bedroom. I had a peaceful and serene sleep, which lasted all through the night. On the following day the atmosphere was still the same, colorless, odorless, and without any temperature. As soon as I awoke I jumped into a chair and remained there without moving, because something told me that there was still a region of my consciousness that hadn't awakened completely. Then I heard the train whistle. The prolonged and sad whistle of the train fleeing the storm. *It must have cleared somewhere,* I thought, and a voice behind me seemed to answer my thought. "Where?" it said. "Who's there?" I asked looking. And I saw my stepmother with a long thin arm in the direction of the wall. "It's me," she said. And I asked her: "Can you hear it?" And she said yes, maybe it had cleared on the outskirts and they'd repaired the tracks. Then she gave me a tray with some steaming breakfast. It smelled of garlic sauce and boiled butter. It was a plate of soup. Disconcerted, I asked my stepmother what time it was. And she, calmly, with a voice that tasted of prostrated resignation, said: "It must be around two-thirty. The train isn't late after all this." I said: "Two-thirty! How could I have slept so long!" And she said: "You haven't slept very long. It can't be more than three o'clock." And I, trembling, feeling the plate slip through my fingers: "Two-thirty on Friday," I said. And she, monstrously tranquil: "Two-thirty on Thursday, child. *Still* two-thirty on Thursday."

I don't know how long I was sunken in that somnambulism where the senses lose their value. I only know that after many uncountable hours I heard a voice in the next room. A voice that said: "Now you can roll the bed to this side." It was a tired voice, but not the voice of a sick person, rather that of a convalescent. Then I heard the sound of the bricks in the water. I remained rigid before I realized that I was in a horizontal position. Then I felt the immense emptiness. I felt the wavering and violent silence of the house, the incredible immobility that affected everything. And suddenly I felt my heart turned into a frozen stone. *I'm dead,* I thought. *My God, I'm dead.* I gave a jump in the bed. I shouted: "Ada! Ada!" Martín's unpleasant voice answered me from the other side. "They can't hear you, they're already outside by now." Only then did I realize that it had cleared and that all around us a silence stretched out, a tranquillity, a mysterious and deep beatitude, a perfect state which must have been very much like death. Then footsteps could be heard on the veranda. A clear and completely living voice was heard. Then a cool breeze shook the panel of the door, made the doorknob squeak, and a solid and monumental body, like a ripe fruit, fell deeply into the cistern in the courtyard. Something in the air revealed the presence of an invisible person who was smiling in the darkness. *Good Lord,* I thought then, confused by the mixup in time. *It wouldn't surprise me now if they were coming to call me to go to last Sunday's Mass.*

(1955)

Artificial Roses

Translated by J. S. Bernstein

FEELING HER WAY in the gloom of dawn, Mina put on the sleeveless dress which the night before she had hung next to the bed, and rummaged in the trunk for the detachable sleeves. Then she looked for them on the nails on the walls, and behind the doors, trying not to make noise so as not to wake her blind grandmother, who was sleeping in the same room. But when she got used to the darkness, she noticed that the grandmother had got up, and she went into the kitchen to ask her for the sleeves.

"They're in the bathroom," the blind woman said. "I washed them yesterday afternoon."

There they were, hanging from a wire with two wooden clothespins. They were still wet. Mina went back into the kitchen and stretched the sleeves out on the stones of the fireplace. In front of her, the blind woman was stirring the coffee, her dead pupils fixed on the stone border of the veranda, where there was a row of flowerpots with medicinal herbs.

"Don't take my things again," said Mina. "These days, you can't count on the sun."

The blind woman moved her face toward the voice.

"I had forgotten that it was the first Friday," she said.

After testing with a deep breath to see if the coffee was ready, she took the pot off the fire.

"Put a piece of paper underneath, because these stones are dirty," she said.

Mina ran her index finger along the fireplace stones. They were dirty, but with a crust of hardened soot which would not dirty the sleeves if they were not rubbed against the stones.

"If they get dirty you're responsible," she said.

The blind woman had poured herself a cup of coffee. "You're angry," she said, pulling a chair toward the veranda. "It's a sacrilege to take Communion when one is angry." She sat down to drink her coffee in front of the roses in the patio. When the third call for Mass rang, Mina took the sleeves off the fireplace and they were still wet. But she put them on. Father Angel would not give her Communion with a bare-shouldered dress on. She didn't wash her face. She took off the traces of rouge with a towel, picked up the prayer book and shawl in her room, and went into the street. A quarter of an hour later she was back.

"You'll get there after the reading of the gospel," the blind woman said, seated opposite the roses in the patio.

Mina went directly to the toilet. "I can't go to Mass," she said. "The sleeves are wet, and my whole dress is wrinkled." She felt a knowing look follow her.

"First Friday and you're not going to Mass," exclaimed the blind woman.

Back from the toilet, Mina poured herself a cup of coffee and sat down against the whitewashed doorway, next to the blind woman. But she couldn't drink the coffee.

"You're to blame," she murmured, with a dull rancor, feeling that she was drowning in tears.

"You're crying," the blind woman exclaimed.

She put the watering can next to the pots of oregano and went out into the patio, repeating, "You're crying." Mina put her cup on the ground before sitting up.

"I'm crying from anger," she said. And added, as she passed next to her grandmother, "You must go to confession because you made me miss the first-Friday Communion."

The blind woman remained motionless, waiting for Mina to close the bedroom door. Then she walked to the end of the veranda. She bent over haltingly until she found the untouched cup in one piece on the ground. While she poured the coffee into the earthen pot, she went on:

"God knows I have a clear conscience."

Mina's mother came out of the bedroom.

"Who are you talking to?" she asked.

"To no one," said the blind woman. "I've told you already that I'm going crazy."

Ensconced in her room, Mina unbuttoned her bodice and took out three little keys which she carried on a safety pin. With one of the keys she opened the lower drawer of the armoire and took out a miniature wooden trunk. She opened it with another key. Inside there was a packet of letters written on colored paper, held together by a rubber band. She hid them in her bodice, put the little trunk in its place, and locked the drawer. Then she went to the toilet and threw the letters in.

"I thought you were at church," her mother said when Mina came into the kitchen.

"She couldn't go," the blind woman interrupted. "I forgot that it was first Friday, and I washed the sleeves yesterday afternoon."

"They're still wet," murmured Mina.

"I've had to work hard these days," the blind woman said.

"I have to deliver a hundred and fifty dozen roses for Easter," Mina said.

The sun warmed up early. Before seven Mina set up her artificial-rose shop in the living room: a basket full of petals and wires, a box of crêpe paper, two pairs of scissors, a spool of thread, and a pot of glue. A moment later Trinidad arrived, with a pasteboard box under her arm, and asked her why she hadn't gone to Mass.

"I didn't have any sleeves," said Mina.

"Anyone could have lent some to you," said Trinidad.

She pulled over a chair and sat down next to the basket of petals.

"I was too late," Mina said.

She finished a rose. Then she pulled the basket closer to shirr the petals with the scissors. Trinidad put the pasteboard box on the floor and joined in the work.

Mina looked at the box.

"Did you buy shoes?" she asked.

"They're dead mice," said Trinidad.

Since Trinidad was an expert at shirring petals, Mina spent her time making stems of wire wound with green paper. They worked silently without noticing the sun advance in the living room, which was decorated with idyllic prints and family photographs. When she finished the stems, Mina turned toward Trinidad with a face that seemed to end in something immaterial. Trinidad shirred with admirable neatness, hardly moving the petal tip between her fingers, her legs close together. Mina observed her masculine shoes. Trinidad avoided the look without raising her head, barely drawing her feet backward, and stopped working.

"What's the matter?" she said.

Mina leaned toward her.

"He went away," she said.

Trinidad dropped the scissors in her lap.

"No."

"He went away," Mina repeated.

Trinidad looked at her without blinking. A vertical wrinkle divided her knit brows.

"And now?" she asked.

Mina replied in a steady voice.

"Now nothing."

Trinidad said goodbye before ten.

Freed from the weight of her intimacy, Mina stopped her a moment to throw the dead mice into the toilet. The blind woman was pruning the rosebush.

"I'll bet you don't know what I have in this box," Mina said to her as she passed.

She shook the mice.

The blind woman began to pay attention. "Shake it again," she said. Mina repeated the movement, but the blind woman could not identify the objects after listening for a third time with her index finger pressed against the lobe of her ear.

"They are the mice which were caught in the church traps last night," said Mina.

When she came back, she passed next to the blind woman without speaking. But the blind woman followed her. When she got to the living room, Mina was alone next to the closed window, finishing the artificial roses.

"Mina," said the blind woman. "If you want to be happy, don't confess with strangers."

Mina looked at her without speaking. The blind woman sat down in the chair in front of her and tried to help with the work. But Mina stopped her.

"You're nervous," said the blind woman.

"Why didn't you go to Mass?" asked the blind woman.

"You know better than anyone."

"If it had been because of the sleeves, you wouldn't have bothered to leave the house," said the blind woman. "Someone was waiting for you on the way who caused you some disappointment."

Mina passed her hands before her grandmother's eyes, as if cleaning an invisible pane of glass.

"You're a witch," she said.

"You went to the toilet twice this morning," the blind woman said. "You never go more than once."

Mina kept making roses.

"Would you dare show me what you are hiding in the drawer of the armoire?" the blind woman asked.

Unhurriedly, Mina stuck the rose in the window frame, took the three little keys out of her bodice, and put them in the blind woman's hand. She herself closed her fingers.

"Go see with your own eyes," she said.

The blind woman examined the little keys with her fingertips.

"My eyes cannot see down the toilet."

Mina raised her head and then felt a different sensation: she felt that the blind woman knew that she was looking at her.

"Throw yourself down the toilet if what I do is so interesting to you," she said.

The blind woman ignored the interruption.

"You always stay up writing in bed until early morning," she said.

"You yourself turn out the light," Mina said.

"And immediately you turn on the flashlight," the blind woman said. "I can tell that you're writing by your breathing."

Mina made an effort to stay calm. "Fine," she said without raising her head. "And supposing that's the way it is. What's so special about it?"

"Nothing," replied the blind woman. "Only that it made you miss first-Friday Communion."

With both hands Mina picked up the spool of thread, the scissors, and a fistful of unfinished stems and roses. She put it all in the basket and faced the blind woman. "Would you like me to tell you what I went to do in the toilet, then?" she asked. They both were in suspense until Mina replied to her own question:

"I went to take a shit."

The blind woman threw the three little keys into the basket. "It would be a good excuse," she murmured, going into the kitchen. "You would have convinced me if it weren't the first time in your life I've ever heard you swear." Mina's mother was coming along the corridor in the opposite direction, her arms full of bouquets of thorned flowers.

"What's going on?" she asked.

"I'm crazy," said the blind woman. "But apparently you haven't thought of sending me to the madhouse so long as I don't start throwing stones."

1962

Alicia Yáñez Cossío

b. 1929

ALICIA YÁÑEZ COSSÍO, born in Quito in 1929, is one of Ecuador's foremost women writers. She studied in Madrid, and has worked as a journalist and teacher. Her first novel, *Bruna, soroche y los tíos* (1972; Bruna, altitude sickness, and the uncles), received the Ecuadorean National Prize. The following story, from the collection *El beso y otras fricciones* (1975; The kiss and other frictions), is a humorous satire of a military dictator.

Sabotage

Translated by Nina Scott

He who turns into a beast saves himself the trouble of living like a man.

—S. Johnson

THE PRESIDENT WAS a tall, strong, corpulent man. Politics was his life and the prime reason for his existence. He had numerous enemies because his actions were inhuman and even horrifying. He lacked the instinct and the intuition for command. He was a robust simpleton with power. Nevertheless, he had a female admirer who each day awaited his comings and goings. Because of her persistence she had gotten him to notice her, arousing a certain attraction which flattered his ego.

One morning, as he was about to leave for the new building he was supposed to inaugurate, he verified through the peephole in the door that the lovely young woman was waiting across the street for him to come out. He smiled with satisfaction, but immediately thereafter his face was contorted by a grimace of disgust—as sour as though he were sucking on a lemon—when he saw that his admirer was accompanied, as usual, by a little cocker spaniel bitch.

When he left, he ran his eyes caressingly over the young woman. She responded with her brightest smile, sustaining positive vibrations between them. The only obstacle barring his way was the little dog who growled more menacingly every moment, making him feel her barks on the most sensitive parts of his ankles. He hated dogs and could figure out neither a way to approach the young woman nor how to make her acquaintance. His twisted political career had caused him to lose all sense of human relationships.

All dogs produced in him a kind of allergic reaction. But that morning he hated the dog more than ever. He had conceived the embryo of an idea and was busily hatching a law against dogs. He knew his enemies would make fun of him. The law against dogs would make things worse, but he would tell his critics to go to hell. Meanwhile his admirer was out there waiting, and he, deprived of affection for so long, felt that he was losing precious time.

Spitting out a series of oaths, he got into his car. Dogs had always barked at him in a special way, perhaps because they sensed the current of aversion against small creatures that emanated from his very skin.

He arrived at the building he was to inaugurate. There was a large crowd and a tight cordon of security warded off his unpopularity. While he was reading his perfectly dreadful speech, the catastrophe happened: there was a deafening noise and the entire building collapsed, trapping the President and all of his supporters in the ruin.

With the noise, the confusion, and the clouds of dust, no one noticed the shot which was aimed at his head. Numerous casualties were taken immediately to clinics, and others were cleared away by sanitation trucks. Many government supporters died but by one of those twists of fate, he, who had been the central target of the sabotage, was saved.

For a long time he was eye-to-eye with Death. The two of them fought for room in the narrow hospital bed, but finally his corpulence won out and he pushed her out onto the floor. Death picked up her bones and walked away disconcertedly. During the assassination attempt one of the walls had fallen on him and he was pulled out of the rubble practically in pieces. The bullet had missed by millimeters the place where his new idea was located. His enemies were dumbfounded at what had happened, but continued their plots to get rid of him.

He was saved by the skill of the surgeons who sewed him up, who stitched and patched his entire body, consuming in the process whole meters of human epidermis, liters of plasma, plastic bones and organs manufactured exclusively for him. He emerged a new scientific creation, for though he was able to keep his own heart and part of his brain, all the rest of him was extraneous matter.

Every day the surgeons noted his steady improvement. The sharply-reduced number of his surviving supporters were very pleased. Among the gifts which he received were flowers sent by his admirer, which were carefully screened by the hospital laboratory before being allowed into the patient's room.

At last the day came when he was permitted to go home. He walked out a rejuvenated man with many political plans. He himself would get on the trail of the saboteurs. Aside from this he had a specific romantic plan in mind for the young woman who had sent the flowers and who owned the dog; however, he had simultaneously acquired a light prickle of fear after he had discovered the hidden powers of his enemies. A strong escort of police and detectives were constantly at his side while he attempted to resume his interrupted functions as though nothing had actually happened.

He had no sooner gotten home than he saw the beautiful young woman, and without stopping to reconsider, he crossed the street to thank her for the flowers. When he approached, the little dog barked at him with less hostility than before. He did not even feel her teeth on his ankles, perhaps because they weren't the same legs he had had before. His conversation with the young woman was hasty because he felt himself watched and criticized by the members of his guard.

The following day the same scene took place and was repeated on subsequent days. However, he did not feel attracted to the young woman. More and more compellingly he was drawn towards the little dog. Her skin was silkier and more lustrous than that of the young woman. Her damp, dark muzzle was more tempting than any smile. Her raised tail was more disturbing than the slender and elegant figure of her mistress. Besides, the little animal no longer barked as she had done before, but in a manner that sounded to him both musical and caressing.

At his office he was increasingly distracted and unaware of what was going on around him. Officials glanced at each other with surprise. The most urgent political problems had ceased to interest him. The idea he had been incubating in his head took shape in the form of a law which decreed that the largest item in the national budget was to be earmarked for the benefit of dogs, principally for female cocker spaniels. He was not his old self and no one knew the reason for the change. He spent his time thinking obsessively about the size, the color, and even the peculiar odor of the little dog.

Whenever he opened the door of his house he would cross the street at a bound, not bothering to greet the animal's mistress, who regarded him attentively, but instead flung himself on the ground to caress the little dog. The contact of his hands on the lustrous skin gave him inexplicable pleasure and when, pressed by his escort, he had to leave her, he moved away sorrowfully, turning his head with each step to look back at her, dilating his nostrils to catch the scent of her body.

His bodyguards never ceased being astonished: here was the President himself wasting minutes of his precious time on a miserable dog!

One day he was nearly run over. "Be careful!" his companions warned, but he was already on the ground petting the little dog, oblivious to the world around him and to the spectacle he was making of himself.

His doctors urged him to take a vacation. The government tottered as though caught in a grotesque dance. The President was so completely demented that the things he did and said were greeted with howls of laughter by his opponents and were commented upon unhappily by his astonished supporters.

The surgeons were very upset. The operations, the skin grafts, and the treatments had been perfect, except perhaps for. . . . But no, it was only a small patch on his left arm, hardly four square centimeters of skin. Nevertheless, the doctors began to glance with a certain measure of distrust at the surgeons.

One night the head of the medical staff was violently awakened. The President had disappeared from his bed. Caretakers and nurses went looking for him throughout the entire hospital. Alarms sounded. Policemen and detectives, believing him kidnapped, began to search the city streets. Highways and airports were sealed off until someone, quite by accident, discovered his whereabouts: the President was in back of his own house, padding along on all fours behind the little cocker spaniel.

It took several men to restrain him. He shouted at them ferociously and even appeared to bark. When the nurse uncovered his left arm to inject him with a tranquilizer designed to put him out, she broke into a horrified scream. She knew that the President had a skin graft on this arm, not of human skin but of a type she could not diagnose. But the graft had disappeared. His entire arm was covered with shaggy fur—like that of a

Saint Bernard—with the fur rapidly spreading over his chest and thorax.

"We can't deal with this case any longer," the dumbfounded doctors stated. "Have some veterinarians come in."

"That's one president who'll never growl again," said his enemies when the dog's mistress reported the extraordinary case.

1972

Nélida Piñón

b. 1937

NÉLIDA PIÑÓN WAS born in Rio de Janeiro, Brazil, in 1937. She has worked as a journalist and has taught at various universities in Brazil and in the United States. Piñón has pursued a writing career since the 1950s. Among her better-known works are the prize-winning novel *A Casa de Paixao* (1972; The House of Passion), and a short-story collection, *Sala de Armas* (1973; Fencing room). Although the themes that Piñón explores are common enough, dealing as they do with human relationships and motivations, her style, influenced by surrealism and existentialism, is experimental and hermetic.

Adamastor

Translated by Giovanni Pontiero

ADAMASTOR WAS LESS than five foot tall. Women were his great weakness even to the extent of taking them home when they didn't really appeal to him. "They all look a little like the Madonna," he once explained in order to justify his devotion. He would buy them frocks and gaudy prints covered with red roses and enhance their smile with gold fillings. He would play them an old-fashioned samba on the record player and arrange regular visits to a doctor for a check-up. Not a single woman had ever come to him in a decent state of health. It was his destiny in life to rescue the afflicted, he thought to himself as he shaved each morning.

And when they were back on their feet, with some money in their purse saved from the tips which Adamastor deposited daily in the little plastic piggy-bank by the bedside table, they would plan their escape. Sometimes, he could almost tell to the hour, the moment they had chosen. Their furtive movements reminded him of tiny birds at play. But he never tried to stop them and invariably took pity on them. After all, he himself had spent years taking refuge in some city or other on the coast.

"Apart from men, who else needs to escape?", he frequently asked himself, as he imagined his tiny frame weaving through gardens among the fruit trees, attentive to the sounds of elfin intrigues. "Adamastor," he would reply to himself in a loud voice.

No one had ever seen him weep or lament his lack of inches. For if anyone suggested that he was a weakling, he would react at once, assuring them with a broad grin: "What I possess is enough to convince anyone of my manhood."

He opened a bar near the docks. This was a quarter of the city in which he could prosper, for here the women whom he craved surged forth like spray from the sea. And such was his dedication to the job that everyone commented upon the atmosphere of contentment which reigned in that establishment. "Forever and ever, amen," rejoined Adamastor, who became boastful when questioned about life in the dock area and the growing popularity of his bar.

Women and pederasts shouted after him in the street, "Take pity on me, Adamastor." He would only smile, "sorting out the wheat from the chaff," for his other great weakness was to quote from the Bible at every possible opportunity. He had such a way with people that no one could recall a single instance of him ever having quarrelled with anyone. "Only women enter into the esteem and space of my body," he would claim.

Yet whenever anyone brought up the subject of the past, Adamastor would coil up like a periwinkle and his skin became covered in goose-pimples which he tried to conceal by rolling down his shirt-sleeves. His reminiscences never went back further than a few weeks. He confined his conversation to the day's happenings, to the meal which he had just eaten, to a certain woman he had brought home that very week. And this behavior became difficult to understand for it was common knowledge that Adamastor had led an adventurous life.

Adamastor looked after his friend João Manco as if he were an adopted son. He made sure that he was well provided with women and rum, the two main obsessions in João's existence. And Adamastor arranged these benefits so discreetly that João not only became deeply attached to his benefactor but carried all the gossip and information which Adamastor needed in order to prosper.

The sailors from the ships always headed straight for Adamastor's bar, dying of thirst and clamoring for women. The fame of Adamastor's bar was such that his women were thought to be the most desirable of all. He tolerated caressing and petting but barred anyone whom he found trying to take liberties—not on moral grounds or because of any fear of the police, as he was always at pains to remind his clients, for he had lost any hope of respectability the day he decided to take on this business. He was simply convinced that certain things should be restricted to the privacy of one's bedroom.

Refusing to discuss the matter further, he would put on a grave expression and assume the posture of a sea-captain. João Manco always backed him up when he voiced this conviction. Desperate for female company, the offending sailors found themselves obliged to leave the bar in the middle of the night protesting as they went: "We came here to spend the night, Adamastor, so why turn us away?" They tried to make him see that food and drink were not enough and that what they needed most of all was a woman, a comfortable bed and a welcoming home where they might enjoy sex at their ease. They finished up by persuading Adamastor that he had been too severe in forbidding them to relax like friends who had returned after a long absence.

To satisfy their needs he bought the house next door with direct access from the bar, and he brightened the place up with vases of flowers, some furniture and cheerful curtains. A picture of Saint George slaying the dragon was hung prominently on the wall and the house even boasted vicuna mattresses, a gift from an Argentinian seaman who had enjoyed his stay so much that he had given Adamastor the mattresses saying: "Please accept these and use them so that I shall recognize my home away from home when I return."

João supervised the bar's activities because Adamastor insisted upon decent behavior and only allowed one couple to use a room at a time. The room service itself was so meticulous that the guests often found towels embroidered with their initials, a refinement which moved some to tears.

Adamastor cautioned João that the facilities of the house were open to everyone with the exception of themselves, making it absolutely clear that they must not be seen frequenting the bedrooms—it was a question of formality. "We can enjoy our women elsewhere," he assured João. "If necessary, you can even use my house."

After this conversation, João began to take full advantage of Adamastor's house, his bed and any woman whom he happened to find there. Adamastor, when he discovered what was going on, did not lose his temper with João, for he much preferred that his women should take up with someone whom he trusted.

The two men lived together in perfect harmony. Whoever dared to offend Adamastor knew that João Manco—whose surname (denoting lameness) did not imply any physical defect, for not only was his skin as smooth as that of any youth, but women fell in love with him at first sight—would roll up his sleeves, bare his teeth ferociously, and flex his muscular torso which could match the swiftness of a fighting cock. Adamastor felt proud of João at such moments, admiring as he did, "valor unto death."

Every day they shared breakfast at the same table and each morning Adamastor would greet him by enquiring: "And how is my friend today ... happy?" João would scratch his hairy chest and button up his trousers concealing his underpants. He knew that Adamastor enjoyed these little rituals. "I asked God to send me a friend," he would reply, "and God sent you." Adamastor was struck by such delicate sentiments and the way in which this uninhibited young stud sought favors from God and then expressed his gratitude so spontaneously.

João's instinctive wisdom made Adamastor determined to look after the lad's future by willing him a piece of land, a little house and medical insurance in case he should need it. For João could not stay here on land watching the stars forever with winter approaching and nothing to occupy him.

Adamastor would mount the platform behind the bar where, looking over the cash desk, he could command a good view of the salon whenever he had something important to say. He had grown a moustache and his hair was so long that it crept under his shirt collar, his oriental features giving the impression that his hair was braided.

"And what about your future, my son?" João looked at him as if to say: "What are you talking about, old chap—some plant perhaps, some tree or sunflower?" Adamastor explained to João that it was the common fate of all men to grow old . . . "one's energy was suddenly sapped up and disappeared, heaven knows where—perhaps even to hell itself where we shall all be reunited sooner or later. It all starts when one's teeth begin to fall out, the first unmistakable sign of encroaching frailty, so that we cannot say that we haven't been warned and should start taking some precautions before it is too late. Our future means spending everything we have managed to save throughout our lifetime."

João became alarmed at all this wisdom. He trusted Adamastor completely in these matters and listened attentively before asking: "So the future comes with old age?" appealing to Adamastor's good nature. Both men laughed heartily. Adamastor found João's nonsensical quips irresistible, like the smell of rum on his breath and his habit of picking up women as if they were his private property. "If a man cannot tame a woman, Adamastor, what other animal can he hope to tame?"

Adamastor liked to think of himself as the captain of a great ship, gauging the direction of the wind under the threat of an impending storm. In the midst of these daydreams he invariably saved the ship at the eleventh hour because of some last minute change of course. And should he ever lose his life in these adventures it was never a question of cowardice or failure. In fact, he preferred the latter denouement which came closer to his idea of a truly dramatic situation.

"Well now, young man. Do I buy you a house or don't I?" João replied boldly: "Why should I want a house? Your home is my home, too, and your women are my women, because women don't really belong to anyone in particular and so long as you are alive I shall never go thirsty for want of rum."

Irritated by this flippant reply, Adamastor consulted his lawyer explaining the situation.

"It's not that I need an heir because I don't have any fortune to dispose of, but what do you suggest I should do?"

"Is he a relative?" the lawyer enquired.

"He is as dear to me as a son, but he is only a friend." In the end he bequeathed him the bar, which was to pass into João's name after his death. He returned home exhausted after his interview and felt considerably older, like a tree without roots which suddenly rebels, following a different course from that originally ordained by nature. He did not intend to remain there forever caring for João, holding the same conversation morning after morning.

"Whoever tried to escape while holding the reins of power?" he asked himself with some feeling. Understanding was beginning to penetrate his life.

One day a sailor asked him outright:

"Is Adamastor the name of some hero, or don't you know?" And others posed the same question until he began to feel haunted.

He said to João: "Look after things while I take a trip into town."

At the public library he tried to explain his query to the assistant so that there wouldn't be any misunderstanding: "I am not interested in education. All I want is a straightforward answer to a simple question: 'Who was Adamastor'?"

After some hesitation, she brought him a copy of Camoens' *Lusiads* indicating those passages which refer to the epic's hero. "Would you like to read it?" she asked.

Adamastor was puzzled by the book, by the woman's tinted spectacles, and by the terrifying discovery that the hero Adamastor had been a giant, a fact which the librarian carefully emphasized as she looked him over from head to toe. Adamastor suddenly felt unpleasantly feverish, his body shaking with anger. For the first time in his life he could not understand why a man less than five feet tall should have been called Adamastor. A cruel joke had been played on him. And this was something which had not dawned on him before, for he had been living in all innocence for some considerable time. A joke, no doubt, on the part of his father who had abandoned his mother when she became pregnant and run off leaving her not even enough money to buy food. He had been shown his father's farewell note many years later and had destroyed it immediately, certain of memorizing *every* single word of the message it contained: "Should the child be a boy, for reasons which I cannot explain, call him Adamastor."

And they baptized him Adamastor, respecting his father's wishes. And when he, too, ran away from home he only looked back once for it struck him that this was a moment for shedding tears as other men had done before him.

"Every time they christen someone Adamastor, are they paying homage to the hero of *Lusiads?*" he enquired, consulting the text in order to ascertain the truth.

"Is your name Adamastor?" the librarian asked him bluntly. To hide his embarrassment, he shook his head in denial.

"Adamastor is the name of my god-child who is soon to be baptized. As you know, the Church can sometimes be awkward in these matters if one doesn't choose a saint's name."

He entered the bar crestfallen. He was now a dwarf on public exhibition. He took out his identity card and there he saw recorded: Four foot, eleven inches, and not an inch more. And him with the name of a giant. He didn't know on whom to vent his exasperation, for João was incapable of understanding his dilemma. João could never find any fault with Adamastor. Even were he to break a limb, upon coming to his assistance João in all probability would reassure him: "Adamastor you look better now than you ever did."

"Women are no good when it comes to confiding in someone". . . . thought Adamastor aloud. . . . "Women are foolish," he would say to compensate for his lack of height. And in the bar he would adopt an attitude of indignation and outrage, refusing to acknowledge even the most gracious compliment or politeness. Out of caution, he had taken to wearing a brown tie with a white suit.

João put up with his friend's silence which had abruptly put an end to their customary banter each morning. He would slip quietly into the room in order not to disturb him.

"If it's a question of bumping off someone, I'll do the job for you. Just give me his name."

Even though wallowing in self-pity, Adamastor savored the idea of a man killing a complete stranger on a friend's behalf. And he mused to himself: "Only men are capable of such generosity. Women on the other hand, are only good for sex." But he made no reply to João's offer.

He did not intend to bother João with his problems, but simply to tell him: "I have been deeply wronged by my father's perverse behavior. Don't forget that I am a man of the world and I can judge things quite impartially" . . . or to cry out that nature had bungled somewhere in his case. Since there was no mistaking the fact, someone must take the blame, he reflected sadly.

"Do you like my name?" he finished up by asking. João nodded in the affirmative and said in a detached voice: "It's the name of a cowboy." Adamastor knew, however, he was no cowboy. There had been an Adamastor before him who had outclassed him so skillfully that his name had become immortalized in one of the world's great epics, such was the fame achieved by the other's devilish exploits. He would no longer be able to compete among men and now even women made him feel uncomfortable. He began to avoid them, fearing that they might start becoming intimate and bring about his ruin. And all those newspaper reporters who had once given him so much satisfaction making him feel important, he now carefully avoided, cowering behind the counter the moment he saw them approach.

"These clever types are a damn nuisance," he would mutter, surprising those who knew him to be vain and affected in his manner of speaking. He treated everyone with distrust and feared that they might unexpectedly embrace him or call out to him amidst laughter and taunts: "Well now, if it isn't the giant Adamastor!"

He had murdered the image of his father on innumerable occasions but that simply wasn't enough, just as changing one's city wasn't enough or assuming another name. The certainty of being Adamastor tortured him. He had to plead martyrdom in order to maintain his self-respect.

"Is it possible that I've been fated to play the cuckold?" he thought, recalling the perceptions which had caused him to forgive João Manco and others.

"What's troubling you, my friend?" João questioned him gently.

"One of these days, I shall go off in search of some new land. There is nothing here for me anymore." He was putting his friend to the test and tracing out the scar which he was about to inflict on the other's face—the symbol of love's revenge.

João dragged himself around the chair, rubbed his belly, and practiced all the other little tricks which had once delighted Adamastor. "And what about my future?" he asked, anxious to please him.

Adamastor, ever susceptible to affection, reassured him: "What is mine is also yours. I was only joking. This time I intend to die right here."

He sat crouched behind the cash register in the hope that people would soon forget him. He no longer attended to the clients personally and kept out of their sight as much as possible. If any woman pestered him, he would severely rebuke her: "Is this all you women ever want?" The customers, as well as João, soon realized that Adamastor was a changed man. But they felt sorry for him. Nor did they stop frequenting his bar. For who other than Adamastor offered them a house adjacent to the bar, gaily decorated with vases of flowers and dedicated to the protection of St. George.

1973

Luisa Valenzuela

b. 1938

LUISA VALENZUELA WAS born in Buenos Aires in 1938 into a literary
family. At eighteen, she wrote her first published short story, "Ciu-
dad ajena," ("City of the Unknown"), which would later go into her
collection *Los heréticos* (1967; *The Heretics,* 1976). Since then she
has published four novels and five collections of short stories while
sustaining a career as a respected journalist, both in Argentina and
the United States. In addition, she has devoted her political energies
to the cause of free expression, working with Amnesty International,
Americas Watch, and the Freedom to Write Committee of PEN
International. Valenzuela's work has often focused on the connections among politics, language, and gender. Her novels include *Hay
que sonreír* (1966; *Clara,* 1976), *El gato eficaz* (1972; The efficacious
cat), and *Cola de lagartija* (1983; *The Lizard's Tail,* 1983).

Strange Things Happen Here

Translated by Helen Lane

IN THE CAFÉ on the corner—every self-respecting café is on a corner, every
meeting place is a crossing of two paths (two lives)—Mario and Pedro
each order a cup of black coffee and put lots of sugar in it because sugar
is free and provides nourishment. Mario and Pedro have been flat broke
for some time—not that they're complaining, but it's time they got lucky
for a change—and suddenly they see the abandoned briefcase, and just by
looking at each other they tell themselves that maybe the moment has

come. Right here, boys, in the café on the corner, no different from a hundred others.

The briefcase is there all by itself on a chair leaning against the table, and nobody has come back to look for it. The neighborhood boys come and go, they exchange remarks that Mario and Pedro don't listen to. There are more of them every day and they have a funny accent, they're from the interior. I wonder what they're doing here, why they've come. Mario and Pedro wonder if someone is going to sit down at the table in the back, move the chair, and find the briefcase that they almost love, almost caress and smell and lick and kiss. A man finally comes and sits down at the table alone (and to think that the briefcase is probably full of money, and that guy's going to latch onto it for the modest price of a vermouth with lemon, which is what he finally asks for after taking a little while to make up his mind). They bring him the vermouth, along with a whole bunch of appetizers. Which olive, which little piece of cheese will he be raising to his mouth when he spots the briefcase on the chair next to his? Pedro and Mario don't even want to think about it and yet it's all they *can* think about. When all is said and done the guy has as much or as little right to the briefcase as they do. When all is said and done it's only a question of chance, a table more carefully chosen, and that's it. The guy sips his drink indifferently, swallowing one appetizer or another; the two of them can't even order another coffee because they're out of dough as might happen to you or to me, more perhaps to me than to you, but that's beside the point now that Pedro and Mario are being tyrannized by a guy who's picking bits of salami out of his teeth with his fingernail as he finishes his drink, not seeing a thing and not listening to what the boys are saying. You see them on street corners. Even Elba said something about it the other day, can you imagine, she's so nearsighted. Just like science fiction, they've landed from another planet even though they look like guys from the interior but with their hair so well combed, they're nice and neat I tell you, and I asked one of them what time it was but didn't get anywhere—they don't have watches, of course. Why would they want a watch anyway, you might ask, if they live in a different time from us? I saw them, too. They come out from under the pavement in the streets and that's where they still are and who knows what they're looking for, though we do know that they leave holes in the streets, those enormous potholes they come out of that can't ever be filled in.

The guy with the vermouth isn't listening to them, and neither are Mario and Pedro, who are worrying about a briefcase forgotten on a chair that's bound to contain something of value because otherwise it wouldn't have been forgotten just so they could get it, just the two of them, not the guy with the vermouth. He's finished his drink, picked his teeth, left some of the appetizers almost untouched. He gets up from the table, pays, the waiter takes everything off the table, puts tip in pocket, wipes table with damp cloth, goes off and, man, the time has come because there's lots going on at the other end of the café and there's nobody at this end and Mario and Pedro know it's now or never.

Mario comes out first with the briefcase under his arm and that's why he's the first to see a man's jacket lying on top of a car next to the sidewalk. That is to say, the car is next to the sidewalk, so the jacket lying on the roof is too. A splendid jacket, of stupendous quality. Pedro sees it too, his legs shake because it's too much of a coincidence, he could sure use a new jacket, especially one with the pockets stuffed with dough. Mario can't work himself up to grabbing it. Pedro can, though with a certain remorse, which gets worse and practically explodes when he sees two cops coming toward them to . . .

"We found this car on a jacket. This jacket on a car. We don't know what to do with it. The jacket, I mean."

"Well, leave it where you found it then. Don't bother us with things like that, we have more important business to attend to."

More crucial business. Like the persecution of man by man if you'll allow me to use that euphemism. And so the famous jacket is now in Pedro's trembling hands, which have picked it up with much affection. He sure needed a jacket like this one, a sports jacket, well lined, lined with cash not silk who cares about silk? With the booty in hand they head back home. They don't have the nerve to take out one of the crisp bills that Mario thought he had glimpsed when he opened the briefcase just a hair—spare change to take a taxi or a stinking bus.

They keep an eye peeled to see whether the strange things that are going on here, the things they happened to overhear in the café, have something to do with their two finds. The strange characters either haven't appeared in this part of town or have been replaced: two policemen per corner are too many because there are lots of corners. This is not a gray afternoon like any other, and come to think of it maybe it isn't even a lucky afternoon the way it appears to be. These are the blank faces of a weekday, so different from the blank faces on Sunday. Pedro and Mario have a color now, they have a mask and can feel themselves exist because a briefcase (ugly word) and a sports jacket blossomed in their path. (A jacket that's not as new as it appeared to be—threadbare but respectable. That's it: a respectable jacket.) As afternoons go, this isn't an easy one. Something is moving in the air with the howl of the sirens and they're beginning to feel fingered. They see police everywhere, police in the dark hallways, in pairs on all the corners in the city, police bouncing up and down on their motorcycles against traffic as though the proper functioning of the country depended on them, as maybe it does, yes, that's why things are as they are and Mario doesn't dare say that aloud because the briefcase has him tongue-tied, not that there's a microphone concealed in it, but what paranoia, when nobody's forcing him to carry it! He could get rid of it in some dark alley—but how can you let go of a fortune that's practically fallen in your lap, even if the fortune's got a load of dynamite inside? He takes a more natural grip on the briefcase, holds it affectionately, not as though it were about to explode. At this same moment Pedro decides to put the jacket on and it's a little too big for him but not ridiculous, no not at all. Loose-fitting, yes, but not ridiculous; comfortable, warm, affectionate, just a little bit frayed at the edges, worn. Pedro puts his hands in the pockets of the jacket (*his* pockets) and discovers a few old bus tickets, a dirty handkerchief, several bills, and some coins. He can't bring himself to say anything to Mario and suddenly he turns around to see if they're being followed. Maybe they've fallen into some sort of trap, and Mario must be feeling the same way because he isn't saying a word either. He's whistling between his teeth with the expression of a guy who's been carrying around a ridiculous black briefcase like this all his life. The situation doesn't seem quite as bright as it did in the beginning. It looks as though nobody has followed them, but who knows: there are people coming along behind them and maybe somebody left the briefcase and the jacket behind for some obscure reason. Mario finally makes up his mind and murmurs to Pedro: Let's not go home, let's go on as if nothing had happened, I want to see if we're being followed. That's okay with Pedro. Mario nostalgically remembers the time (an hour ago) when they could talk out loud and even laugh. The briefcase is getting too heavy and he's tempted once again to abandon it to its fate. Abandon it without having had a look at what's inside? Sheer cowardice.

They walk about aimlessly so as to put any possible though improbable tail off the track. It's no longer Pedro and Mario walking, it's a jacket and a briefcase that have turned into people. They go on walking and finally the jacket says: "Let's have a drink in a bar. I'm dying of thirst."

"With all this? Without even knowing where it came from?"

"Yeah, sure. There's some money in one pocket." He takes a trembling hand with two bills in it out of the pocket. A thousand nice solid pesos. He's not up to rummaging around in the pockets anymore, but he thinks—he smells—that there's more. They could use a couple of sand-wiches, they can get them in this café that looks like a nice quiet place.

A guy says and the other girl's name is Saturdays there's no bread; anything, I wonder what kind of brainwashing . . . In turbulent times there's nothing like turning your ears on, though the bad thing about cafés is the din of voices that drowns out individual voices.

Listen, you're intelligent enough to understand.

They allow themselves to be distracted for a little, they too wonder what kind of brainwashing, and if the guy who was called intelligent believes he is. If it's a question of believing, they're ready to believe the bit about the Saturdays without bread, as though they didn't know that you need bread on Saturday to make the wafers for mass on Sunday, and on Sunday you need some wine to get through the terrible wilderness of workdays.

When a person gets around in the world—the cafés—with the antennae up he can tune in on all sorts of confessions and pick up the most abstruse (most absurd) reasoning processes, absolutely necessary because of the need to be on the alert and through the fault of these two objects that are alien to them and yet possess them, envelop them, especially now when those boys come into the café panting and sit down at a table with a nothing's-been-happening-around-here expression on their faces and take out writing pads, open books, but it's too late: they bring the police in on their heels and of course books don't fool the keen-witted guardians of the law, but instead get them all worked up. They've arrived in the wake of the students to impose law and order and they do, with much pushing and shoving: your identification papers, come on, come on, straight out to the paddy wagon waiting outside with its mouth wide open. Pedro and Mario can't figure out how to get out of there, how to clear a path for themselves through the mass of humanity that's leaving the café to its initial tran-quility. As one of the kids goes out he drops a little package at Mario's feet, and in a reflex motion Mario draws the package over with his foot and hides it behind the famous briefcase leaning against the chair. Sud-denly he's scared: he thinks he's gotten crazy enough to appropriate anything within reach. Then he's even more scared: he knows he's done it to protect the kid, but what if the cops take it into their heads to search *him?* They'd find a briefcase with who-knows-what inside, an inexplicable package (suddenly it strikes him funny, and he hallucinates that the pack-age is a bomb and sees his leg flying through the air accompanied out of sympathy by the briefcase, which has burst and is spilling out big counter-feit bills). All this in the split second that it took to hide the little package, and after that nothing. It's better to leave your mind a blank and watch out for telepathic cops and things like that. And what was he saying to himself a thousand years ago when calm reigned?—a brainwashing; a self-service brainwash so as not to give away what's inside this crazy head of mine. The kids move off, carted off with a kick or two from the bluecoats; the package remains there at the feet of those two respectable-looking gentlemen, gentlemen with a jacket and a briefcase (each of them with one of the two). Respectable gentlemen or two guys very much alone in the peaceful café, gentlemen whom even a club sandwich couldn't console now.

They stand up. Mario knows that if he leaves the little package, the waiter is going to call him back and the jig'll be up. He picks it up, thus adding it to the day's booty but only for a short while; with trembling hands he deposits it in a garbage can on a deserted street. Pedro, who's walking next to him, doesn't understand at all what's going on, but can't work up the strength to ask.

At times, when everything is clear, all sorts of questions can be asked, but in moments like this the mere fact of still being alive condenses everything that is askable and diminishes its value. All they can do is to keep walking, that's all they can do, halting now and then to see for example why that man over there is crying. And the man cries so gently that it's almost sacrilege not to stop and see what the trouble is. It's shop-closing time and the salesgirls heading home are trying to find out what's wrong: their maternal instinct is always ready and waiting, and the man is weeping inconsolably. Finally he manages to stammer: I can't stand it anymore. A little knot of people has formed around him with understanding looks on their faces, but they don't understand at all. When he shakes the newspaper and says I can't stand it anymore, some people think that he's read the news and the weight of the world is too much for him. They are about to go and leave him to his spinelessness. Finally he manages to explain between hiccups that he's been looking for work for months and doesn't have one peso left for the bus home, nor an ounce of strength to keep on looking.

"Work," Pedro says to Mario. "Come on, this scene's not for us."

"Well, we don't have anything to give him anyway. I wish we did."

Work, work, the others chorus and their hearts are touched, because this word is intelligible whereas tears are not. The man's tears keep boring into the asphalt and who knows what they find, but nobody wonders except maybe him, maybe he's saying to himself, my tears are penetrating the ground and may discover oil. If I die right here and now, maybe I can slip through the holes made by my tears in the asphalt, and in a thousand years I'll have turned into oil so that somebody else like me, in the same circumstances . . . A fine idea, but the chorus doesn't allow him to become lost in his own thoughts, which—it surmises—are thoughts of death (the chorus is afraid: what an assault it is on the peace of mind of the average citizen, for whom death is something you read about in the newspapers). Lack of work, yes, all of them understand being out of a job and are ready to help him. That's much better than death. And the good-hearted sales-girls from the hardware stores open their purses and take out some crum-pled bills, a collection is immediately taken up, the most assertive ones take the others' money and urge them to cough up more. Mario is trying to open the briefcase—what treasures can there be inside to share with this guy? Pedro thinks he should have fished out the package that Mario tossed in the garbage can. Maybe it was work tools, spray paint, or the perfect equipment for making a bomb, something to give this guy so that inac-tivity doesn't wipe him out.

The girls are now pressing the guy to accept the money that's been collected. The guy keeps shrieking that he doesn't want charity. One of the girls explains to him that it's a spontaneous contribution to help his family out while he looks for work with better spirits and a full stomach. The crocodile is now weeping with emotion. The salesgirls feel good, re-deemed, and Pedro and Mario decide that this is a lucky sign.

Maybe if they keep the guy company Mario will make up his mind to open the briefcase, and Pedro can search the jacket pockets to find their secret contents.

So when the guy is alone again they take him by the arm and invite him to eat with them. The guy hangs back at first, he's afraid of the two of them: they might be trying to get the dough he's just received. He no longer knows if it's true or not that he can't find work or if this is his work—pretending to be desperate so that people in the neighborhood feel sorry for him. The thought suddenly crosses his mind: if it's true that I'm a desperate man and everybody was so good to me, there's no reason why these two won't be. If I pretended to be desperate it means that I'm not a bad actor, and I'm going to get something out of these two as well. He decides they have an odd look about them but seem honest, so the three of them go off to a cheap restaurant together to offer themselves the luxury of some good sausages and plenty of wine.

Three, one of them thinks, is a lucky number. We'll see if something good comes of it. Why have they spent all this time telling one another their life stories, which maybe are true? The three of them discover an identical need to relate their life stories in full detail, from the time when they were little to these fateful days when so many strange things are happening. The restaurant is near the station and at certain moments they dream of leaving or of derailing a train or something, so as to rid themselves of the tensions building up inside. It's the hour for dreaming and none of the three wants to ask for the check. Neither Pedro nor Mario has said a word about their surprising finds. And the guy wouldn't dream of paying for these two bums' dinners, and besides they invited him.

The tension becomes unbearable and all they have to do is make up their minds. Hours have gone by. Around them the waiters are piling the chairs on the tables, like a scaffolding that is closing in little by little, threatening to swallow them up, because the waiters have felt a sudden urge to build and they keep piling chairs on top of chairs, tables on top of tables, and chairs and then more chairs. They are going to be imprisoned in a net of wooden legs, a tomb of chairs and who knows how many tables. A good end for these three cowards who can't make up their minds to ask for the check. Here they lie: they've paid for seven sausage sandwiches and two pitchers of table wine with their lives. A fair price.

Finally Pedro—Pedro the bold—asks for the check and prays that the money in the outside pockets is enough to cover it. The inside pockets are an inscrutable world even here, shielded by the chairs; the inner pockets form too intricate a labyrinth for him. He would have to live other people's lives if he got into the inside pockets of the jacket, get involved with something that doesn't belong to him, lose himself by stepping into madness.

There is enough money. Friends by now, relieved, the three go out of the restaurant. Pretending to be absentminded, Mario has left the briefcase—too heavy, that's it—amid the intricate construction of chairs and tables piled on top of each other, and he is certain it won't be discovered until the next day. A few blocks farther on, they say good-by to the guy and the two of them walk back to the apartment that they share. They are almost there when Pedro realizes that Mario no longer has the briefcase. He then takes off the jacket, folds it affectionately, and leaves it on top of a parked car, its original location. Finally they open the door of the apartment without fear, and go to bed without fear, without money, and without illusions. They sleep soundly, until Mario jumps up with a start, unable to tell whether the bang that has awakened him was real or a dream.

1975

Cristina Peri Rossi

b. 1941

CRISTINA PERI ROSSI was born in 1941 in Montevideo to a second-generation Italian-Uruguayan family. She started writing at an early age, earned a degree in literature at the University of Montevideo, and worked as a journalist and teacher in Uruguay. In the late 1960s, two of her books, the short-story collection *Los museos abandonados* (1968; The abandoned museums) and the novel *El libro de mis primos* (1969; My cousins' books) won distinguished literary prizes. Peri Rossi's support of leftist resistance to her country's military government made her an object of persecution, and in 1972 she left for exile in Spain, where she presently lives. Peri Rossi's work is difficult to classify. One of her most important texts, *La nave de los locos* (1984; Ship of fools) uses the well-known medieval motif to interweave a series of fragments about social injustice and political repression in contemporary life. The following story, from the collection *La tarde del dinosaurio* (1976; The afternoon of the dinosaur) uses the theme of exile in a biting satire of militarism and political persecution.

The Influence of Edgar Allan Poe on the Poetry of Raimundo Arias

Translated by Tona Wilson

"I'VE BEHAVED MYSELF well, I promise," said her father, looking her straight in the eye. He had the clear blue eyes of a young child. Later on in life, eyes grow darker. Alicia had noticed this characteristic of the pupils. Something in life made them turn cloudy; they lost that color of a quiet lake, where the geese see themselves. The still waters stirred, interior currents coming from the distance, from beyond the sea, altered the rhythm and the shade of eyes. Then children ceased to be children and became grown-ups with darkened eyes, grown-ups without eyes, they reflected nothing and could no longer look within, as his eyes still could. She liked to peer into those waters. She saw tombs, marine animals, stones, shimmering spaces, the serene and restless lunar geography. When he was no longer a child, surely one would no longer be able to see the seahorse suspended—slow navigator—nor the plant with white flowers and a golden stem. She blew on it and the stem moved. Her father closed his eyes.

"You're late," she said in her clear soprano voice, "thirty-five minutes two seconds late. You'll go without dessert, as punishment." She didn't look at him, to avoid those trembling waters.

"But Alicia," he defended himself, "the traffic was heavy. There were a lot of people walking in the other direction, so many that it was difficult to take one step after another. Most of the time I had to place one foot cautiously, taking advantage of a small space left free, and keep the other in the air. This probably sounds simple to you, you didn't have to pace the avenue this afternoon trying to sell Marvel soaps, three for the price of one, refresh your life, but I can assure you it was a difficult operation. At times the foot that was left suspended in the air got tired of that position. Don't forget, either, that the bag full of soap weighs a lot. I tried to distract myself and think of other things while I had one foot in the air and waited for a narrow little space of pavement to be free so I could move it forward. One time I had such an opportunity, but a man who was alongside me made an effort, advanced his enormous square foot, and reached the space before me.

"You should have pushed him off," she said severely. He lowered his eyes. The handbag full of bars of soap was at one side; it was black, made of shiny leather, and had a sign that said "Marvel Ltd. Makes life more pleasant."

"It wouldn't have been easy," he defended himself. "He was a bulky man, a huge lump of granite; he walked firmly and quickly forward, impelled by his own ferocity. He would have trampled me underfoot as one crushes an ant when walking, inadvertently, indifferently. That man and all the rest were going somewhere, hurrying, inexorably."

It was six months since they had arrived in that country but they still hadn't discovered the direction in which to run. He was not convinced, either, that running was the best thing.

"Where were they running to?" asked Alicia curiously.

"I don't know that," he confessed. He tried to light a cigarette surreptitiously, but she noticed the process.

"Four," she pronounced brutally. "You only have one left."

"I think three," he tried to fool her. "If you remember correctly the one this morning I shared with you and anyway I couldn't enjoy it in my hurry."

"Four," she repeated from her seat. With that blue dress and her long hair falling down her back, she looked extraordinarily like her mother. Her mother had never had a blue dress and always wore her hair short; to his mind, this difference accentuated enormously the similarity. Perhaps the one she resembled, actually, was her mother's sister, but he couldn't be sure, in fact he had seen her only once, when his wife abandoned the two of them. He met her by chance at a supermarket; they could not talk for long because both were in a hurry, he had to feed the child and prepare a paper on the influence of Edgar A. Poe on the poetry of a very famous writer that no one knew about because he had never left his non-European country, and she had to return to the secret hideout of the guerrillas for whom she served as a screen. She seemed to him a very nice young woman—he would never forget her red hair, surely a wig to better conceal her identity—and he thought that he would have liked very much to have shown her the paper he was writing on the influence of Edgar A. Poe on the poetry of Raimundo Arias, even though she had no time for such things; she looked at him with intelligence, an intelligence devoured by passion, according to a phrase of Raimundo Arias, who never knew her but must have intuited her, of that he was certain. She thought it a pity that he was an intellectual petit bourgeois, as her sister had said before abandoning him, for he had a gentle and intelligent look. Be that as it may, he would never forget the red or blue or green or yellow hair of that girl—I should have known my wife's sister a little better, he reproached himself, but the whole world moved in a hurry; one had to make the revolution, cook the food, stand in line to buy milk, bread, rice, garbanzos, oil, kerosene, one had to run from the army when they attacked, he had to take care of the little girl (fruit of a condom of very poor quality), besides, he was going to write a novel about the revolution, at times the novel moved ahead of the revolution, at times the revolution moved so fast that it managed to pull ahead of the novel, and in the midst of all this, his wife abandoned him, she had pulled ahead of both, the novel and the revolution; the child stayed with him, they agreed, it isn't sensible to involve oneself in guerrilla warfare with such a young child, to fool everyone they said that she had run off to Czechoslovakia with another man. I should have gotten to know my sister's husband better, she thought, but there wasn't much time, one had to work, to stand on line to buy milk, bread, flour, rice, garbanzos, oil, kerosene, one had to make the revolution, and sometimes one was sleepy.

"How many bars of soap did you sell today?" Alicia asked, without moving from her chair. In front of her there was a small wooden table covered with colored stones and a crystal giraffe. It was all that they had managed to rescue in the flight, when they had to leave the country because he had been accused of professing the Marxist-Leninist faith, and of writing articles that were true panegyrics to the guerrilla mobs who were trying to undermine the fatherland and the prestige of national institutions. Very dignified, he took his daughter's hand—I am not an object, that you can carry in your arms, she said—gathered together a few papers, a few clothes, and they boarded the ship, under control of the police.

"Why don't we kill him now?" asked the corporal. "We can always say as usual that they met their death trying to flee the forces of order."

"No one is waiting for us," said the girl, from the deck of the ship, when they arrived.

"My child," he answered, "you know very well that I'm not a soccer player."

Alicia looked at her father's legs, so very thin in the only pair of trousers that he had left, and reflected that as a daughter she had not had much luck. Her father was not a soccer player, nor a ship owner, nor a well known singer (the only thing she had ever heard him sing was *A Desalambrar*,[1] and that was out of tune; she sang much better "Tremble, tyrants," the phrase from the national anthem that had been prohibited by the government for its clearly subversive character), nor the president of some trust, nor a movie actor. She had to resign herself. Children don't choose their parents, though parents can choose their children, this one, yes, Alicia, this one, no, abortion, unnamed.

"I sold twenty-six, plus one I gave away to an old woman, twenty-seven. Or actually, I didn't give it away, she gave me in return three oranges. She was selling oranges, red, healthy La Rioja oranges."

"Twenty-six," reflected the girl. "Not much for a whole day."

"Have a little consideration, my child, it seems to me that in this

[1] A popular protest song.

country people only bathe on Sunday mornings: besides, one has to take into account the competition from the soap gels, the bath salts, soap powder, cleansing lotion, soap petals, liquid foam, solid foam, and foam solid."

Not only had no one been waiting for them in that country—or in any other—but moreover they were badly received. Immediately on arriving they were asked for an extraordinary number of papers: official identification card of the father, official identification card of the daughter, the father's passport, the daughter's passport, father's consular visa, certificate of good conduct for the father, certificate of good conduct for the daughter, baptism certificate of both, certificate of single status (how do you expect me to have a certificate of single status if I'm married? Well, then, the daughter's, and your marriage license), elementary school diploma for the father, high school diploma, university diploma, certificate of vaccination against smallpox for both, against tetanus, against hepatitis, against tuberculosis, against rabies, against polio, against meningitis, against asthma, against german measles. The girl handed them over to the authorities, one by one, with great care, yellow and black; the girl pocketed them afterwards, meticulously; her father was very disorganized. They also required the presence of his wife, for the girl to be allowed to enter the country.

"That's impossible," said the man. "My wife did not travel with us."

"Well then the girl can't enter," said the functionary.

"Why not?" he asked. "I'm her father. I'll be responsible for her."

"Who says you're the father of this little girl? Only the mother can know that."

"And the papers, eh?" he answered, "I suppose the papers don't say so?"

"The papers aren't sufficient proof of fatherhood," stated the functionary. "Only the mother can say for sure whether you are the father of this child."

"I am not a child," responded Alicia indignantly. "I am a woman-to-be." (She had learned this in her reading book.)

"The mother will have to confirm that the child is the fruit of matrimony with you," concluded the functionary menacingly. "You may be a delinquent, a rapist, a child abductor, and this little girl your hostage."

"Ask her," he protested.

"This man is my father," she affirmed, a few seconds later. Actually, she had the idea of denying it. It was the first time that being their daughter or not had depended on her and not on them; she could have said, for example, "By no means, this is not my father, he's an imposter," or something of the sort, as happened in the serial novels or on the TV soap operas. And afterwards she would choose some other father, or better, suddenly be left an orphan, but she was not convinced that this solution was really adequate for her happiness. It was hard to find a suitable father within one's own country; outside, it could be even more so. Becoming an orphan began to be interesting at about eighteen, when one could get into the X-rated movies, buy and sell in one's own name, and pay taxes. One could have children long before that, from about twelve or thirteen; it must be a much less important thing since one could do it before one could open a savings account.

They decided to do a blood test to prove his paternity. It wasn't so bad after all (even though he fainted, as he did every time he saw blood. You can't make revolutions that way, his wife had said), because they took them to a very nice clinic, where they fed them free, after having extracted a quarter-litre of blood more than necessary, as they always did with foreigners, simply because they were foreigners. She ate with a good appetite.

"That's my blood you're eating," he said. He was so queasy after the extraction that he could take advantage of nothing more than coffee with milk. So she ate two rations of bread with butter and peach jam. This fruit was not a peach in the country they came from. It was called something entirely different. The newspapers never carried news of the country they came from, which seemed to them a lack of manners.

"I'd like to know what happened to the four hours they stole from me on the ship," she said, as soon as the results of the blood test confirmed that the father of the child was he, or any other man with type-A blood.

At the beginning of the fourth day at sea, the captain's order, carried over the P.A. system, reminded the passengers that they should set their watches ahead thirty minutes. The first time, the girl resisted this order. She kept her watch set at twelve o'clock, when everyone else on the ship ran the minute hand half way around the face, an extremely frivolous way to treat time, in Alicia's opinion. He didn't make her do it; he was an anarchist, he believed in freedom.

"Eat your strawberry ice cream, who knows when we'll be able to eat again." Strawberries were something else; there was another name for strawberries, in the country they had decided to go to, to be among people who spoke the same language as they did.

"And bear in mind, my dear child, that any individual rebellion is destined to failure," he said, looking, undaunted, at the girl's wrist watch, which continued to function at its deliberate rhythm of minutes and seconds. It was a pretty watch, with a blue face and silver numbers, that her mother had given her before she left. Because there where she was going surely time was measured in other dimensions, and life was more intense. Alicia, her eyes brimming with tears, looked at the blue face of her little watch (as though it were a lake and the hands the necks of swans drifting across its surface) and said:

"I won't set it ahead for anything in the world."

When they disembarked, Alicia's watch was four hours behind.

"It's not that I'm slow, it's that they're fast," she said, looking at the two huge clocks in the plaza.

When she finally succumbed—as though betraying a trust—and adjusted her watch to those of that part of the world, she began to miss the four hours they had stolen from her on the ship.

"What have they done with my five-thousand-seven-hundred-and-sixty minutes?" she asked her father. He was not prepared to answer this. Actually, he was not prepared to answer anything. He had been someone's child, too, for many years. He had lived as best he could, which in itself says a lot, and he was accustomed to having things stolen from him. They had stolen much more than four hours, and he had been able to do almost nothing to change the order of things. The order of things was the order of the owners of things, and any individual rebellion was doomed to failure. As for his wife, wherever she might be—if indeed she was still somewhere—she too had been someone's child for many years, had lived as best she could, which in itself says a lot, and she had dedicated herself to changing the order of things, but the order of things was very resistant.

"My dear, when we return they'll give them back to you, if in fact we do return someday. If we return by ship."

The answer did not console her. She wasn't interested in long-term reimbursals. She felt herself affronted, swindled.

"What will they do with so many accumulated hours?" She thought of ships filled with stolen hours, silent ships that crossed the ocean with their secret cargo of time. She thought of phantom ships full of men who guarded the chambers where the stolen time was kept, she imagined traffickers in hours who awaited the ships in dark, grimy ports, bought and sold hours. She thought of desperate men, who bought tiny little boxes with a miniscule amount of time, because the dealers speculated in the hours they bought. In some port or other a man, anxious, sees the ship arrive, from the ship is lowered a blue box, and he buys half an hour, maybe less, he buys ten minutes stolen from the trusting passengers of a ship, from involuntary emigrants, like her and her father, from exiles. A desperate man who waits in the port, watching the great oil spills drift, anxiously scanning the ship, the little blue box, a minuscule time, a piece of time he needs for something, and the voice of the captain repeating unequivocally, "Ladies and gentlemen, please have the kindness to set your watches ahead thirty minutes." And it was no longer twelve, no longer was it twelve midnight, aboard the ship that moved with the rhythm of the waves, it wasn't the black night of the sea at midnight; the passengers, powerless, defeated in other battles, obeyed the order docilely, reset their watches, and suddenly, at that very instant, it was no longer twelve o'clock, thirty minutes had disappeared from their lives, gone to swell the supply of hours in the ship's hold, making the time dealers rich.

"Mother fucking ships!" she cried, desperate.

Twenty-six bars of soap were not much, even though they nourished themselves with milk and nuts. "They have lots of calories," said her father, who understood these things, thanks to a course in "parental capacitation" he had taken before she was born. In the course, they had taught him the calories in foods, the ten appropriate answers one could give children when they began to show sexual curiosity, how to sterilize bottles, and what to do until the doctor arrives; but they had never said a word about how to survive with children in exile.

So he said nothing, but contemplated the ceiling. It was an ordinary ceiling, white, without important geographical features. Alicia sighed, conscious of her responsibilities. It was not a pleasant task, having to be responsible for a father, or for a mother, in these difficult times. Although her father was not very rebellious, he did at times try to make decisions on his own, and the projects that he undertook as a result of those decisions were nearly always doomed to failure. So she didn't criticize him too much, because her father was very sensitive and she was afraid of discouraging him; one had to encourage the growth of his personality even if it were through such unfortunate initiatives. She had read a couple of instruction manuals on adults, and although she was not in complete agreement with Freud (she preferred his rebellious disciple Lacan), she tried to prevent her father's depressive neurosis from advancing. She was particularly concerned about his sex life, which she considered plenty irregular and unstable. But he refused to approach the subject directly, fending it off with any pretext.

At times he said he was tired, at others that he wasn't interested, and although whenever they walked together she made frequent allusions to the women they met along the way, he showed a stubborn indifference.

First he said that he had to adjust his aesthetic patterns, given that the women of this country were very different from his compatriots; then he insinuated something about the scant use of soap, and he ended by praising black women, when everyone knew that in this country they had put an end to all blacks many years ago.

Alicia went to the box of Chinese tea made in France, which was on the table, and examined its contents. There remained a few coins, each from a different country, with portraits of various oppressors. Almost none were legally in circulation, and as for the bills, they were from the country they had abandoned in the exodus and no bank would take them, because they weren't backed up by gold. She had thought of papering a part of the room with those blue bills, but then decided against it as too folkloric. And she was a citizen of the world. Unlike her father.

"We don't have any money," she commented without emphasis. Almost every day she said the same thing. Then her father would look in the pockets of his only suit for the notebook with the addresses of friends and acquaintances, review it thoroughly without the least result, given that the majority of those people had since died, didn't live at those addresses, or were many thousands of miles away. But it was a ritual he enjoyed. When it comes to friends, we're nearly always left with useless addresses.

"I think today we've no one to ask for money," said her father, also without emphasis.

Alicia sighed and went to the big hat box into which she had put a few clothes before setting out on the trip.

"I'll be home in three or four hours, wait for me," she said to her father when she left. Melancholically, he watched her go. Not bad, with that Indian costume he had given her once, for a party at school. The feathers were drooping a bit, and during the voyage many had been lost. Alicia had repainted them with watercolors, trying to give them an exotic and picturesque air. The feathers were blue, red, yellow, black, and white.

"Do you have any idea what kind of feathers the Charrua Indians used?" she had asked her father. None whatsoever; the Spanish had put to death every last Indian in that country, and as for a descendant said to be 104 years old, he looked about as much like an Indian as an Afghan. Nor was she certain that they had worn feathers, as Metro Goldwyn Mayer suggested.

"Today I'm going to put on three more yellow ones; no one will know the difference," said Alicia.

She picked up the brushes and began to paint her face, trying to make the grimaces very horrifying. The tomato sauce was very effective, but once she had had problems with a cat who jumped up on her, excited by the smell. He admired her silently. Her complexion was too fair for her to look really like an Indian, but Europeans didn't notice such details; at least, not the sort of Europeans who were apt to stop in the street and give a few coins to an Indian girl.

"Be careful of old men, my child, they tend to be very libidinous," recommended her father every time she went out. "Don't let them get near you; they're very given to raping little girls."

"And even more so if they're Indian virgins," concluded Alicia, reciting the part of the speech that she knew by heart.

She looked at herself in the mirror. This time she had managed to make her mouth into a blood-chilling grimace, very satisfactory. With a few shadows around her eyes and fake wrinkles, her eyebrows blue and a painted scar, she had an air of age she seldom achieved.

Looking at herself in the mirror, she said:

"I don't know whether to put out the sign that says 'Latin American Indian girl' or whether to make another, saying 'Aged Latin American dwarf.' "

"I'm not sure there were any dwarves among the Indians," said her father.

"Me neither," she reflected. It was incredible how ignorant one could be about one's own ancestors. This didn't often happen in Europe. People in Europe were better educated; they could always name their ancestors as far back as five or six generations, they never had revolutions, and almost all of the countries had parliaments. Some bicameral, others not.

Only once had there been a small incident during her display with the Latin American Indian girl costume; it was when a dreadful little boy, a little younger than she, came up to her, very Machiavellian, and began to tug with all his strength at her single Indian braid; then, forgetting that she should mutter unintelligible sounds, she insulted him in perfect Spanish, denouncing without delay the Spanish colonization of the autochthonous civilizations of the Rio de la Plata. The incident culminated in her thrusting him a perfect punch in the jaw, and sending the imperialist to the ground.

Her father looked at her with some anguish and a great deal of admiration. He thought that something had changed in the genes, from one generation to the next; some obscure modification in hereditary characteristics had made the children of today perfect and admirable parents of their progenitors.

This was another race, endowed with a singular resistance, and in the very womb they had assimilated the lessons of intimate, obscure defeats; in the maternal womb they had learned sadness, failure, desolation, and when they saw the light of the world, they knew how to live in spite of it all. Conceived in bitter nights, in nights of sorrow, persecution, uncertainty, misery and terror, conceived in houses that were like dungeons or in dungeons that were tombs, in beds that were coffins, the survivors of those nights of torture and of pain were born with the mark of resistance and strength.

Alicia looked at him before going out. She had her head covered with feathers and a grass skirt, below which peeked her white legs. Her chest was bare, with two incipient breasts, round and discreet, and their delicate pink tips. She had no bow nor arrows, for her father had never been able to buy them for her, he was always short of money. Their gazes crossed, different but transparent. They both knew how to decipher the codes of the eyes. They had learned this on the high seas, during the long nights of insomnia, when not even the moon illuminated the ship's crossing. There, while they smoked rationed cigarettes and thought of how to get their hands on a ham sandwich in the kitchen, they had learned to read the waters of the eyes; tame waters those of the father, restless waters those of the lake of the daughter. Alicia looked at him and read, read the mystifications, the daydreams and the sorrow.

So that when she opened the door and assumed a voice to go with the garb of Latin-American Indian girl, fugitive in Europe, she said, clearly:

"I am certain that what you are thinking about our generation is completely false."

1976

Rosario Ferré

b. 1942

ROSARIO FERRÉ WAS born in Ponce, Puerto Rico, to a distinguished upper-middle-class family, her father, Luis Ferré, having served as governor of the island. She studied at the University of Puerto Rico, and holds a Ph.D. in Comparative Literature from the University of Maryland. She was founder and director of the influential literary magazine *Zona de carga* in the early 1970s. In her short stories, novellas, and essays, Ferré has explored the theme of woman's marginality within a rigidly patriarchal culture. Among her better-known works are *Papeles de Pandora* (1976; Pandora's papers); *La caja de cristal* (1978; *The Glass Box,* 1986), and *Maldito amor* (1986; Damned love).

Sleeping Beauty
Translated by Diana Vélez and Rosario Ferré

December 1, 1973

Dear Don Felisberto:

I know you'll be surprised to get this letter. I feel the only decent thing for me to do, in view of what's going on, is to warn you. It seems your wife doesn't appreciate what you're worth, a handsome man and rich besides. It's enough to satisfy the most demanding woman.

For a few weeks now, I've watched her go by the window of the beauty parlor where I work, always at the same time. She takes the service elevator and goes up to the hotel. I can see you turning the envelope around to see if you can find out my identity, if there's a return address. But you'll never guess who I am; this city is full of fleabag hotels with beauty parlors on the lower level. She always wears dark glasses and covers her hair with a kerchief, but even so I recognized her easily from the pictures I've seen of her in the papers. It's just that I've always admired her. Being a ballerina and at the same time the wife of a business tycoon is no mean achievement. I say "admired" because I'm not sure I still do. That business of going into hotel service elevators disguised as a maid seems rather suspicious to me.

If you still care for her, I suggest you find out what she's up to. She's probably risking her reputation needlessly. You know that a lady's reputation is like a pane of glass, it smudges at the lightest touch. A lady mustn't simply be respectable, she must above all appear to be.

Sincerely Yours,
A Friend and Admirer

She folds the letter and puts it in an envelope. Painstakingly, using her left hand, she scrawls an address on it with the same pencil she used for the letter. Then she stretches before the mirror and stands on her toes. She walks to the barre and starts on her daily routine.

December 18, 1973

Dear Don Felisberto:

I have no way of knowing whether or not my last letter reached you. If it did, you didn't take it seriously, because your wife keeps up her daily visits to the hotel. Don't you love her? If you don't love her, why did you marry her? She's running around like a bitch in heat and it doesn't seem to bother you. The last time she was here I followed her. Now I'll do my duty and give you the room number (7B) and the hotel: Hotel Elysium. She's there every day from three to five-thirty. By the time you get this letter, you won't be able to find me. Don't bother checking; I quit my job at the beauty parlor and I'm not going back.

Sincerely Yours,
A Friend and Admirer

She folds the letter, puts it in an envelope, writes the address and leaves it on the piano. She picks up the chalk and painstakingly dusts the tips of her slippers. Then she gets up, faces the mirror, grasps the barre with her left hand and begins her exercises.

I. Coppelia

Social Column
Mundo Nuevo
April 6, 1971

Coppelia, the ballet by the famous French composer Leo Délibes, was marvelously performed here last Sunday by our very own Pavlova dance troupe. For all the Beautiful People in attendance (and there really were too many of the *crème de la crème* to mention all by name), people who appreciate quality in art, the *soirée* was proof positive that the BP's cultural life is reaching unsuspected heights. (Even at $100 a ticket there wasn't an empty seat in the house!)

Our beloved María de los Angeles Fernández, daughter of our honorable mayor Don Fabiano Fernández, performed the main role admirably. The ballet was a benefit performance for the many charitable causes supported by CARE. Elizabeth, Don Fabiano's wife, wore one of Fernando Peña's exquisite creations, done in sun-yellow with tiny feathers, which contrasted strikingly with her dark hair. There, too, were Robert Martínez and his Mary (fresh from a skiing trip to Switzerland) as well as George Ramírez and his Martha (Martha was also done up in a Peña original—I love his new look—pearl-gray egret feathers!). We also loved the theater's decorations and the pretty corsages donated by Jorge Rubinstein and his Chiqui. (Would you believe me if I told you their son sleeps in a bed made out of a genuine racing car? That's just one of the many fascinating things to be found in the Rubinsteins' lovely mansion.) Elegant Johnny Paris was there, and his Florence, dressed in jade-colored quetzal feathers in a Mojena original inspired by the Aztec *huipil*. (It almost seemed as if the

BP's had prearranged it, for the night was all feathers, feathers, and more feathers!)

And, as guest star for the evening, the grand surprise, none other than Liza Minelli, who once fell in love with a question mark-shaped diamond brooch she saw on Elizabeth Taylor and, since she couldn't resist it, has had an identical one made for herself which she wears every night on her show, as a pendant hanging from one ear.

But back to our Coppelia.

Swanhilda is a young village maiden, daughter of the burghermeister, and she is in love with Frantz. Frantz, however, seems uninterested. Each day he goes around the town square to walk by the house of Doctor Coppelius, where a girl sits reading on the balcony. Swanhilda, overcome with jealousy, goes into Doctor Coppelius' house while he is out. She discovers that Coppelia (the girl on the balcony) is just a porcelain doll. She places Coppelia's body on a table and, with a tiny dollmaker's hammer, smashes each and every one of her limbs, leaving only a mound of gleaming dust. She dresses up as Coppelia and hides in the doll's box, stiffening her arms and staring straight ahead.

The brilliant waltz danced by Swanhilda posing as the doll was the high point of the evening. María de los Angeles would bend her arms, moving them in circles as if they were screwed on at the elbows. Her legs went up and down stiffly, pausing slightly before each motion and accelerating until the hinges rotated in a frenzy. Then she began to dance round and round, spinning madly across the room. Both the dancer who played Doctor Coppelius and the one who played Frantz stood looking at her, aghast. It seems María de los Angeles was improvising, and her act did not fall in with her role at all. Finally, she sprang into a monumental *jeté,* leaving the audience breathless. Leaping over the orchestra pit, she pirouetted down the carpeted aisle and, flinging open the theater doors, disappeared down the street like a twirling asterisk.

We loved this new interpretation of Coppelia despite the confusion it evidently caused among the rest of the troupe.

The BP's thunderous applause was well-deserved.

like a flash, her toes barely touch, barely skim the felt, flight, light, first a
yellow then a gray, leaping from tile to tile her name was Carmen Merengue
Papa really loved her skipping over cracks, from crack to crack break your
mother's back light lightning feet dance dancing is what I love just dancing
when she was Papa's lover she was about my age I remember her well
Carmen Merengue the trapeze artist hurtling from one trapeze into the flying
knife, the human boomerang, the female firecracker, meteorite-red hair
going off around her jettisoned through the air hanging by her teeth, going
round and round on a silver string, whirling, faster faster till she disappeared,
dancing as if nothing mattered, whether she lived or died, pinned to the tent
top by reflectors, a multicolored wasp gyrating in the distance, the bulging
eyes staring at her from below, the open mouths, the shortness of breath, the
sweating brows, ants in the pants of the spectators who moved around in their
seats below, when the fair was over she'd visit all the bars in town, she'd
stretch her rope from bar to bar, the men would place one finger on her head
and Carmen Merengue would spin around, was on my way to Ponce cut
through to Humacao, wide-hipped gentlemen cheering, clapping, she was
nuts, taking advantage of her, hey lonnie lonnie, right foot horizontal, one
foot in front of the other, her body stretched out in an arc, her right arm over
her head trying to slow the seconds that slipped by just beyond her tiptoes,
concentrating all her strength on the silk cord that

April 9, 1971
Academy of the Sacred Heart

Dear Don Fabiano:

I am writing on behalf of our community of sisters of the Sacred Heart of
Jesus. Our great love for your daughter, a model student since kindergarten, requires that we write to you today. We cannot ignore the generous
help you have provided our institution, and we have always been deeply
grateful for your concern. The recent installation of a water heater, which
serves both the live-in students and the nuns' cells, is proof of your
generosity.

Your daughter's disgraceful spectacle, dancing in a public theater and
dressed in a most shameless manner, was all over the social pages of this
week's papers. We know that such spectacles are quite common in the
world of ballet, but, Señor Fernández, are you prepared to see your
daughter become part of a world so full of danger to both body and soul?
What good would it do her to gain the world if she lost her soul? Besides,

all that tossing of legs in the air, those cleavages down to the waist, all that leaping and legspreading, Sacred Heart of Jesus, where will it lead? I cannot keep from you that we had placed our highest hopes in your daughter. It was understood that, at graduation time, she would be the recipient of our school's highest honor—our Sacred Medallion. Perhaps you are not aware of the great prestige of this prize. It is a holy reliquary, surrounded by tiny sunbeams. Inside the locket is an image of our Divine Husband, covered by a monstrance. On the other side of the locket are inscribed all the names of those students who have received our Sacred Medallion. Many of them have heard the calling; in fact most have entered our convent. Imagine our distress at seeing those photographs of María de los Angeles on the front page.

The damage has already been done and your daughter's reputation will never be the same. But you could at least keep her from persisting down this shameful path. Only if she abandons the Pavlova Company will we see fit to excuse her recent behavior and allow her to continue at our school. We beg you to forgive this saddest of letters; we would have preferred never to have written it.

> Most cordially yours, in the
> name of Jesus Christ our Lord,
> Reverend Mother Martínez

like a flash, toes barely touching the suncracked pavement, leaping crack over crack, break your mother's back, Felisberto's my boyfriend, says we'll get married, Carmen Merengue would never marry, no, she'd shake her head, her white face framed by false curls, the circus left without her, she stayed in the tiny room my father rented, didn't want her to be a trapeze artist any more, wanted her to be a lady, forbade her to go to bars, tried to teach her to be a lady but she would lock herself in, practice practice all the time, blind to her surroundings, worn-out cot, chipped porcelain washbasin, one slippered foot in front of the other, lifting her leg slightly to draw circles in the air, touching the surface of a pool of water with her tiptoe, but one day the circus came, she heard the music from afar, her red curls shook, she sat on the cot and covered her ears so as not to hear, but she couldn't not hear, something tugged, tugged at her knees, at her ankles, at the tips of her dance shoes, an irresistible current pulled and pulled, the music pierced the palms of her hands, her eardrums aflame with the clatter of hooves, she rose to look at herself in the shard of mirror she'd hung on the wall, that's what I am, a

dancer, face framed by false curls, eyelashes loosened by the heat, thick
pancaked cheeks, falsies under my dress, and that very day she went back

April 14, 1971

Dear Reverend Mother:

Your letter made Elizabeth and I think long and hard. We both agreed
that the best thing would be to withdraw María de los Angeles from the
Pavlova Company. The matter of her dancing had gotten a little out of
hand lately, and we had already discussed the possibility. As you know,
our daughter is a child of artistic sensibilities, and she is also very religious.
We've often found her kneeling in her room with that same distant,
ecstatic expression that takes hold of her when she is dancing. Our greatest
hope for María de los Angeles, however, is to see her someday neither as
a ballerina nor as a nun, but rather, surrounded by loving children. That
is why we beg you to refrain from stimulating an inordinate piety in her,
Mother, at this critical time when she will be most vulnerable.

María de los Angeles will inherit a large fortune as our only child. It
truly concerns us that when we have passed away, our daughter might fall
into the hands of some heartless scoundrel who's just out for her money.
One has to protect one's fortune even after death, as you well know,
Mother, for you yourself have to watch over the considerable assets of the
Holy Church. You and I both know that money is like water, it flows away
to sea, and I'm not about to let some hustler take away what I had to work
so hard to get.

Elizabeth and I have always loved María de los Angeles deeply, and
no one can say we weren't the happiest couple on the island when she
was born. Though boys are, of course, more helpful later on, girls are
always such a comfort, and we certainly enjoyed our daughter when she
was a little girl. Mother, she was the light of our house, the apple of our
eye. Later we tried to teach her how to be both kind and smart, because
a loving young lady with a good education is a jewel coveted by any
man, but I don't know how well we succeeded! Only when I see María
de los Angeles safely married, Mother, as safe in her new home as she
was in ours, with a husband to protect and look out for her, will I feel at
ease.

Let me point out to you, Mother, that your suggestion that María de
los Angeles might someday enter your order was totally out of place. I
assure you that if this were the case, we would not be able to avoid feelings

of resentment and suspicion, in spite of our sincere devotion to your cause and the affection we feel toward you. The fortune accruing to the convent, in that event, would be no *pecata minuta.*

I beg your forgiveness, Mother, for being brutally honest, but truthfulness usually preserves friendship. Rest assured that, as long as I'm alive, the convent will lack nothing. My concern for God's work is genuine, and you are his sacred workers. Had Elizabeth and I had a son as well as a daughter, you would have met no resistance from us. On the contrary, we would have welcomed the possibility of her joining you in your sacred task of ridding this world of so much sin.

Please accept a most cordial greeting from an old and trusted friend,

Fabiano Fernández

April 17, 1971
Academy of the Sacred Heart

Dear Señor Fernández:

Thank you for your recent letter. Your decision to remove María de los Angeles from the harmful environment of ballet was wise. It will be just a matter of time before she forgets the whole thing, which will then seem only a fading dream. As to your suggestion that we divert her from a pious path, with all due respect, Señor Fernández, despite your being the major benefactor of our School, you know we cannot consent to that. The calling is a gift of God; we would never dare interfere with its fulfillment. As our good Lord said in the parable of the vineyard and the works, many will be called but few chosen. If María de los Angeles herself is chosen by our Divine Husband, she must be left free to heed the calling. I understand that your worldly concerns are foremost in your mind. Seeing your daughter join our community would perhaps be heart-rending for you. But that wound, Sr. Fernández, would heal in time. We must remember that the Good Lord has us here only on loan; we're in this vale of tears only for a spell. And if you ever come to believe that your daughter was lost to this world, you will have the comfort of knowing that she was found by angels. It seems to me that her given name is surely a sign that Divine Providence has been on our side since the child was born.

Respectfully yours in the
name of Jesus Christ our Lord,
Reverend Mother Martínez

April 27, 1971

Dear Reverend Mother:

You cannot imagine the suffering we are going through. The very day we told María de los Angeles about our decision to forbid her dancing, she fell gravely ill. We brought in the best specialists to examine her, but to no avail. I don't want to burden you with our sorrow; I write you these short lines because I know you are her friend and truly care for her. I beg you to pray for her, so the Lord will bring her back to us safe and sound. She's been unconscious for ten days and nights now, on intravenous feeding, without once coming out of her coma.

Your friend,
Fabiano Fernández

II. Sleeping Beauty

It was her birthday, she was all alone, her parents had gone for a ride in the woods on their dappled mares, she thought she'd make a tour of the castle, it was so large, she'd never done that before because something was forbidden and she couldn't remember what, she went through the hallway taking tiny steps tippytoes together in tiny slippers, going up the circular stairs tippytoes together tiny steps through the dark, couldn't see a thing but she could feel something tugging at her shoes, each time more insistently, like Moira Shearer on tippytoes tapping the floor with the tips of her toes, trying to hit the note on the nose that would remind her just what it was she was forbidden to do, but no she couldn't, she bourréed without stopping to rest, she opened door after door as she went up the spiraled steps, it seemed days she was going up and up and she never reached the top, she was tired but she couldn't stop, her shoes wouldn't let her, she finally reached the cobwebbed door at the end of the tunnel, the doorknob went round and round in the palm of her hand, her fingertip pinched, a drop of blood oozed, fell, she felt herself falling, PLAFF! everything slowly dissolving, melting around her, the horses in their stalls, their saddles on their backs, the guards against the door, the lances in their hands, the cooks, the bakers, the pheasants, the quails, the fire in the fireplace, the clock under the cobwebs, everything lay down and went to sleep around her, the palace was a huge ship rigged to set out into the great unknown, a deep wave of sleep swept over her and she slept so long her bones were thin needles floating around inside her, piercing her skin, one day she

*heard him from afar TATI! TATI! TATI! she recognized his voice, it was
Felisberto coming, she tried to get up but the heavy gold of her dress wouldn't
let her rise, dance DANCE! that's what was forbidden! Felisberto draws his
face closer to mine, he kisses my cheek, is it you my prince, my love, the one
I've dreamt of? You've made me wait so long! Her cheeks are warm, take
those blankets off, you're stifling her, wake up my love, you'll be able to
dance all you want, the hundred years are up, your parents are dead, the
social commentators are dead, society ladies and nuns are dead, you'll dance
forever now because you'll marry me and I'll take you far away, talk to me,
I can see you tiny, as though at the bottom of a well, you're getting bigger,
closer, coming up from the depths, my gold dress falls away, I feel it tugging
at my toes, I'm free of it now, light, naked, moving towards you, my legs
breaking through the surface, kiss me again, Felisberto, she woke up*

April 29, 1971

Dear Reverend Mother:

Our daughter is safe and sound! Thanks no doubt to Divine Providence,
she woke up from that sleep we thought would be fatal. While she was still
unconscious, Felisberto Ortiz, a young man we'd never met, paid us a
visit. He told us they had been going together for some time and that he
loved her deeply. What a wily daughter we have, to be able to keep a secret
from us for so long! He was with her for a while, talking to her as though
she could hear everything he said. Finally he asked us to remove the heavy
woolen shawls we had wrapped her in to keep the little warmth still left
in her body. He went on rocking her in his arms until we saw her eyelids
flutter. Then he put his face close to hers, kissed her, and Bless the Lord,
María de los Angeles woke up! I couldn't believe my eyes.

To sum it all up, Mother, the day's events made us agree to the young
couple's plans to be married and set up house as soon as possible. Felisberto
comes from a humble background, but he's a sensible young man, with feet
firmly planted on the ground. We agreed to their engagement and they'll be
married within a month. Of course, it saddens us that now our daughter will
never be the recipient of the Sacred Medallion, as you had so wished. But I
am sure that, in spite of it all, you will share our happiness, and be genuinely
pleased to see María de los Angeles dressed in white.

I am, as always,
your affectionate friend,
Fabiano Fernández

Social Column
Mundo Nuevo
January 20, 1972

Dear Beautiful People: without a doubt, the most important social event of the week was the engagement between the lovely María de los Angeles Fernández, daughter of our own Don Fabiano, and Felisberto Ortiz, that handsome young man who holds so much promise as a young executive.

María de los Angeles' parents announced that the wedding would be within a month. They are already sending out invitations, printed—where else?—at Tiffany's. So go right to it, friends, start getting yourselves together, because this promises to be the wedding of the year. It should be very interesting to see the Ten Best Dressed Men competing there with the Ten Most Elegant Ladies. The occasion will bring to the fore the contest that has been going on all year long on our irresistibly exciting little island.

The cultural life of our Beautiful People will reach unheard-of-levels on that day, as our beloved Don Fabiano has announced he will lend his dazzling Italian Baroque collection to the Mater Chapel, where the wedding will be held. He has also announced that he is so happy with his daughter's choice (the groom has a Ph.D. in marketing from Boston University) that he will donate a powerful Frigid King ($200,000) to the chapel, so as to free the BP's who will attend the ceremony from those inevitable little drops, as well as suspicious little odors, of perspiration brought about by the terrible heat of our island, a heat that not only ruins good clothing, but also makes elaborate hairdos turn droopy and stringy. That is why so many wedding guests skip the church ceremony these days, despite being devout and even daily churchgoers, opting instead to greet the happy couple at the hotel receiving line, where the air conditioning is usually turned on full blast. This results in a somewhat lackluster religious ceremony. But this wedding will be unique because, for the first time in the island's history, the BP's will be able to enjoy the glitter of our Holy Mother Church wrapped in a delightful Connecticut chill.

Now, the BP's have a new group which calls itself the SAP's (Super Adorable People). They get together every Sunday for brunch to comment on the weekend's parties. Then they go to the beach and tan themselves and sip piña coladas. If you consider yourself "in" and miss these beach parties, careful, because you might just be on your way "out." Oh, I almost forgot to tell you about the most recent "in" thing among BP's who are expecting a call from the stork: you must visit the very popular Lamaze Institute, which promises a painless delivery.

For my darling daughter, so as to herald her entry into the enchanted world of brides.

(Newspaper clippings pasted by María de los Angeles' mother in her daughter's Wedding Album.)

An idea for a shower

If you've recently been invited to a shower for an intimate friend or family member and it has been stipulated that presents should be for personal use, here's an idea that will tickle the guests pink: first, buy a small wicker basket, a length of plastic rope for a clothesline and a package of clothespins. Then look for four bra and panty sets in pastel colors, two or three sets of panty-hose, a baby doll set, a pretty and bouffant haircurler coverup and two or more chiffon hairnets. Stretch out the clothesline and pin the various items of clothing to it, alternating color according to taste, until you've filled the entire clothesline. Now, fold it up, clothes and all, and place it in the basket. Wrap the basket in several yards of nylon tulle and tie it with a bow surrounded by artificial flowers. You won't believe what a big hit this novel gift will be at the party.

A bride's graceful table

Despite recent changes in lifestyle and decor, brides still generally prefer traditional gifts such as silverware, stemware and china.

China is now being made of very practical and sturdy materials which make it quite resistant to wear. It also comes in all kinds of modern designs. However, these sets are just not as fine as the classic porcelain sets. Elegant china such as Limoges, Bernadot or Bavarian Franconia can be found in homes where they have been handed down from generation to generation.

Silverware comes in different designs and levels of quality, among them sterling silver, silver plate, and stainless steel. Of course, stainless is practical, but for a graceful table there is nothing like sterling.

What is known as silver plate is a special process of dipping in liquid silver. Many brides ask for Reed and Barton, as it is guaranteed for a hundred years. The stemware should match the china, and there are several fine names to choose from in stemware. Brides, depending on their budgets, tend to ask for Fostoria, St. Louis or Baccarat.

A bride who makes out her list requesting these brands will have gifts that last a lifetime. It depends on the means of her guests: they might get together and, piece by piece, get her the china set, for example. If they are of more abundant means, they will probably want to give her sterling trays, vases, pitchers, gravy servers, oil and vinegar sets, etc. These articles are the *sine qua non* of a well-set table.

What makes for happiness?

A beautiful house surrounded by a lovely garden, fine furniture, rugs and draperies? Trips abroad? Clothes? Plenty of money? Jewels? Latest model cars? Perhaps you have all these and are still not happy, for happiness is not to be found in worldly goods. If you believe in God and in His word, if you are a good wife and mother, one who knows how to manage the family budget and makes her home a shelter of peace and love, if you are a good neighbor, always willing to help those in need, you will be happy indeed.

From your loving mother,
Elizabeth

(Footnotes to María de los Angeles and Felisberto's Wedding Album, written in by Elizabeth, now mother to both.)

1. Exchanging rings and vowing to love each other in Sickness and in Health.

2. Drinking Holy Wine from the Golden Wedding Chalice during the Nuptial Mass.

3. María de los Angeles in profile, with the veil spilling over her face.

4. Marching down the church aisle! What a sacred little girl she was!

5. Married at last! A dream come true!

6. María de los Angeles, front shot. Veil pulled back, she smiles. A married woman!

III. Giselle

dressed in white like Giselle, happy because I'm marrying him I come to you and kneel at your feet, Oh Mater! pure as an Easter lily, to beg you to stand by me this most sacred day, I place my bouquet on the red velvet stool where your foot rests, looking once again at your modest pink dress, at your light blue shawl, the twelve stars fixed in a diamond arc around your head, Mater, the perfect homemaker, here I am all dressed in white, not dressed like you but like Giselle after she buried the dagger in her chest, because she suspected Loys her lover would not go on being a simple peasant as she had thought but was going to turn into a prince with vested interests, she knew Loys would stop loving her because Giselle was very clever, she knew whenever there are vested interests love plays second fiddle, that is why Giselle killed herself or perhaps she didn't perhaps she just wanted to meet the willis, to reach them she had to go through the clumsy charade of the dagger, bury it in her chest, her back to the audience, hands legs feet thrashing around unhinged, poor Giselle lost her mind, that's what the peasants said, crazy! they cried surrounding her fallen body, but she wasn't there, she hid behind the cross in the graveyard where she put on her white willis dress, she stretched it over her frozen flesh, then she donned her dance shoes never to remove them again because her fate was to dance dance dance through the woods and Mater smiled from heaven because she knew that for her dancing and praying were one and the same, her body light as a water clock, the Queen of Death startled to see her dance, she slid her hand through her body, pulled it back covered with tiny drops, Giselle had no body she was made of water, suddenly the willis fled in panic, they heard footsteps it was Loys intent on following Giselle, a tiny voice deep inside her warned be careful Giselle a terrible danger stalks you, Loys always succeeds in his attempts and he's not about to let Giselle get away from him, he's bent on finding her so as to shove a baby into her narrow clepsydra womb, so as to take away her dewdrop lightness, widen her hips and spread out her body so she can never be a willis again, but no, Giselle is mistaken, Loys truly loves her, he won't get her pregnant, he'll put on a condom light and pink he promised next to her deathbed, he takes her by the arm and twirls her around the altar till she faces the guests who fill the church, then he takes her hand in his so as to give her courage, take it easy darling it's almost over, and now as rosy-fingered dawn colors the horizon distant churchbells can be heard and the willis must make their retreat. They're not angels as they had so deceitfully seemed, they're demons, their dresses are filthy crinolines, their gossamer wings are tied to their backs with barbed wire. And what about Giselle, what will she do? Giselle sees the willis slipping through the trees, disappearing like sighs, she hears them calling to her but she knows it's too late, she cannot escape, she feels Felisberto's hand pressing her elbow, marching her down the center of the church aisle

Social Column
Mundo Nuevo
February 25, 1972

Well, my friends, it seems the social event of the year has come and gone and María de los Angeles' fabulous wedding is now just a luminous memory lingering in the minds of the elegant people of Puerto Rico.

All the BP's showed up at the Mater Chapel to see and be seen in their gala best. The pretty bride marched down an aisle lined with a waterfall of calla lilies. The main aisle of the church, off-limits to all but the bride and groom, was covered with a carpet of pure silk, imported from Thailand for the occasion. The columns of the chapel were draped from ceiling to floor with orange blossoms ingeniously woven with wires so as to give the guests the illusion that they were entering a rustling green forest. The walls were lined with authentic Caravaggios, Riberas and Carlo Dolcis, a visual feast for the BP's eyes, avid as always for the beauty that also educates. Our very own Don Fabiano kept his promise, and María de los Angeles' wedding was no less glorious than those of the Meninas in the Palace of the Prado. Now, after the installation of the air conditioning unit, the nuns will surely never forget to pray for the souls of Don Fabiano and his family. A clever way to gain entry into the kingdom of heaven, if ever there was one!

The reception, held in the private hall of the Caribe Supper Club, was something out of *A Thousand and One Nights*. The décor was entirely Elizabeth's idea, and she is used to making her dreams come true. The theme of the evening was diamonds, and all the decorations in the ballroom were done in silver tones. Three thousand orchids flown in from Venezuela were placed on a rock crystal base imported from Tiffany's. The bridal table was all done in Waterford crystal imported from Ireland; the menus were pear-shaped silver diamonds; and even the ice cubes were diamond shaped, just to give everything the perfect touch. The wedding cake was built in the shape of the Temple of Love. The porcelain bride and groom, strikingly like María de los Angeles and her Felisberto, were placed on a path of mirrors lined with lilies and swans of delicate pastel colors. The top layer was crowned by the temple's pavilion, which had crystal columns and a quartz ceiling. A tiny classic Cupid with wings of sugar revolved around it on tiptoe, aiming his tiny arrow at whoever approached.

The main attraction of the evening was Ivonne Coll, singing hits like "Diamonds are Forever" and "Love is a Many-Splendored Thing."

The bride's gown was out of this world. It was remarkable for the simplicity of its lines. Our BP's should learn a lesson from María de los Angeles, for simplicity is always the better part of elegance.

HELLO! I ARRIVED TODAY
NAME: Fabianito Ortiz Fernández
DATE: November 5, 1972
PLACE: Mercy Hospital; Santurce, Puerto Rico

WEIGHT: 8 lbs.
PROUD FATHER: Felisberto Ortiz
HAPPY MOTHER: María de los Angeles de Ortiz

December 7, 1972
Academy of the Sacred Heart

Dear Don Fabiano:

The birth announcement for your grandson Fabianito just arrived. My heartfelt congratulations to the new grandfather on this happy event. They certainly didn't waste any time. Right on target, nine months after the wedding! A child's birth is always to be celebrated, so I can well imagine the party you threw for your friends, champagne and cigars all around, right there in the hospital's waiting room. You've been anxious for a grandson for so many years, my friend, I know this must be one of the happiest moments of your life. But don't forget, Don Fabiano, that a birth is also cause for holy rejoicing. I hope to receive an invitation to the christening soon, though my advice is to avoid having one of those pagan Roman fiestas with no holds barred which have lately become fashionable in your milieu. The important thing is that the little cherub not continue a heathen, but that the doors of heaven be opened for him.

As always,
Your devoted friend in
Jesus Christ our Lord,
Reverend Mother Martínez

December 13, 1972

Dear Reverend Mother:

Thank you for your caring letter of a week ago. Elizabeth and I are going through a difficult trial; we are both grieved and depressed. It is always a comfort to know that our close friends are standing by us at a time like this.

As one would expect, our grandson's birth was a joyous occasion. Since we thought the christening would be soon, Elizabeth had gone ahead with the arrangements. The party was to take place in the Patio de los Cupidos, in the Condado Hotel's new wing, and of course, all our friends were to have been invited. These social events are very important, Mother, not only because they serve to tighten bonds of personal loyalties, but because they are good for business. Imagine how we felt, Mother, when we got a curt note from María de los Angeles telling us to cancel the party, because she had decided not to baptize her son.

This has been a hard test for us, Mother. María de los Angeles has changed a lot since she got married, she's grown distant and hardly ever calls to say hello. But we'll always have the pleasure of her child. He's a beautiful little urchin with sea-blue eyes. Let's hope they stay that way. We'll take him to the convent one of these days so you can meet him.

> Please accept our
> affectionate regards,
> Fabiano Fernández

> December 14, 1972
> Academy of the Sacred Heart

Dear María de los Angeles:

Your father wrote me of your decision not to baptize your son, and I am deeply shaken. What's wrong with you, my child? I fear you may be unhappy in your marriage and that has greatly saddened me. If you are unhappy, I can understand your trying to get through to your husband, to make him see that something is wrong. But you are being unfair if you are using your own son towards that end. Who are you to play with his salvation? Just think what would become of him if he were to die a pagan! I shudder to think of it. Remember this world is a vale of tears and you have already lived your life. Now your duty is to devote yourself heart and soul to that little cherub the good Lord has sent you. We have to think in practical terms, dear, since the world is full of unavoidable suffering. Why not accept our penance here, so as to better enjoy the life beyond? Leave aside your fancies, María de los Angeles, your ballet world filled with princes and princesses. Come off your cloud and think of your child. This is your only path now. Resign yourself, my child. The Lord will look out for you.

> I embrace you, as always,
> with deepest affection,
> Reverend Mother Martínez

December 20, 1973

Dear Don Fabiano:

Please excuse my long lapse in writing. My affection for you has always remained the same, despite my long silences, as I trust you know. Your grandson is handsome as can be and I take pleasure in him daily. With all the problems María and myself have been having, the child has been a real comfort.

Don Fabiano, I beg you to keep what I'm about to tell you in the strictest confidence, out of consideration for me and sympathy for her. Now I realize what a mistake it was for us to have moved to our new house in the suburbs, a year after Fabianito was born. When we were living near you, you were always my ally and my guide as to how to handle María de los Angeles, how to lovingly lead her down the right path, so she wouldn't guess it had all been planned.

You'll recall that, before we were married, I gave your daughter my word she could continue her career as a dancer. This was her only condition for marriage, and I have kept my word to the letter. But you don't know the rest of the story. A few days after our wedding, María de los Angeles insisted that my promise to let her dance included the understanding that we would have no children. She explained that once dancers get pregnant, their hips broaden and the physiological change makes it very difficult for them to become successful ballerinas.

You can't imagine the turmoil this threw me into. Loving María de los Angeles as I do, I had always wanted her to have my child. I felt it was the only way to keep her by me, Don Fabiano; perhaps because I come from such a humble background, I've always had a terrible fear of losing her.

I thought that perhaps the reason she didn't want my child was because I come from a humble family, and this suspicion hurt me deeply. But I won't always be poor, Don Fabiano, I won't always be poor. Compared to you I guess I am poor, with my measly one hundred thousand in the bank. But I've made that hundred thousand the hard way, Don Fabiano, because far from your daughter's having been an asset to me, she's been a weight, a drawback, an albatross. Despite her unbecoming reputation as a dancer, thanks to my financial success, no one in this town can afford to snub us, and we get invited to all of San Juan's major social events.

When María de los Angeles told me she didn't want to have a

child, I remembered a conversation you and I had had a few days before the wedding. You said you were glad your daughter was getting married, because you were sure she'd finally settle down and make her peace. And then you added with a laugh that you hoped we wouldn't take long in giving you a grandson, because you needed an heir to fight for your money when you were no longer around. But I didn't find your joke the least bit funny. I remember thinking, "Who does this man think he's talking to? A healthy stud he can marry his daughter off to?" Later I got over it, and I realized it was all a joke and that you really meant well. After all, it wasn't such a bad idea, that business of an heir; not a bad idea at all. But it would be *my* heir. A few days later I tried to convince María de los Angeles that we should have a child. I told her I loved her and didn't want to lose her. I was convinced that a child was the only way to make our marriage last. But when she refused doggedly, I lost my patience, Don Fabiano—dammit, I got her pregnant against her will.

Rather than bringing peace to our home, Fabianito was a curse to María de los Angeles from the start, and she soon abandoned him to the care of his nanny. Despite her fears of not being able to dance again, her recovery has been remarkable since she gave birth. We went on like this, keeping a precarious peace, until two weeks ago when, as the devil would have it, I took her to see a flying trapeze show at the astrodome. It had just come to town and I thought since she had been so depressed, it might cheer her up. The usual jugglers and strongmen came on, and then a redheaded woman wearing an afro walked into the arena. She danced on a tightrope up high near the tent top, and I don't know why, but María de los Angeles was very impressed. She's been surprisingly absent, totally wound up in herself since then. When I speak to her she doesn't answer, and I hardly see her except at dinner time.

To top it all off, yesterday—it's hard to tell you about it, Don Fabiano—I got an anonymous letter, the second one in several days; a disgusting note scrawled in pencil. Whoever wrote it must be sick. It implies that María de los Angeles meets regularly with a lover in a hotel, when she's supposed to be at the studio.

I suppose I should be angry, Don Fabiano, but instead I feel torn to pieces. The truth is, no matter what she does, I'll always love her, I can't live without her.

Tomorrow I'll go and find out what's going on in that hotel room. I'm sure it's all just vile slander. Unhappy people can't stand to see

other people's happiness. Still, I can't avoid feeling a sense of foreboding. You know a man can take anything, absolutely anything but
this kind of innuendo, Don Fabiano. I'm afraid of what may happen, and yet I feel I must go. . . .

Suddenly he stops writing and stares blankly at the wall. He crumples
the note he's been writing into a tight wad and tosses it violently into the
wastepaper basket.

The afternoon sun filters in through the window of room 7B, Hotel
Elysium. It lights up the dirty venetian blinds, torn on one side, and falls
in strips over the naked bodies on the sofa. The man, lying on the woman,
has his head turned away. The woman slowly caresses him, burying the
fingers of her left hand in his hair. In her right hand, she holds a
prayerbook from which she reads aloud. "María was a virgin in all she
said, did and loved." The man stirs and mutters a few indistinct words as
if he were about to wake up. The woman goes on reading in a low voice,
after adjusting her breast under his ear. "Mater Admirabilis, lily of the
valley and flower of the mountains, pray for us. Mater Admirabilis
purer than. . . ." She shuts the prayerbook and looks fixedly at the
termite-ridden woodwork of the ceiling, at the water stains on the
wallpaper. She'd finally worked up enough courage to do it, and
everything had turned out according to plan. She had picked the man up
that very afternoon, on the corner of De Diego and Ponce de León. The
Oldsmobile had pulled up and she had seen the stranger stare at her
through the windshield, eyebrows arched in silent query. The man had
offered her twenty-five dollars and she had accepted. She had specified the
hotel and they had driven in silence. She refused to look at his face even
once.
    Now that it was over she felt like dancing. The man slept soundly, one
arm dangling to the floor, face turned towards the sofa. She slowly slid out
from under the warm body, pulled a nylon rope out of her purse and
stretched it taut from the hooks she had previously put into the walls. She
slipped on her dancing shoes, tied the ribbons around her ankles and
leaped onto the rope. A cloud of chalk from the tips of her slippers hung
for a moment in the still air. She was naked except for her exaggerated
makeup: thick rouge, meteorite-red hair and huge black eyelashes. She felt
now she could be herself for the first time, she could be a dancer; a second
or third class dancer, but a dancer nonetheless. She began, placing one

foot before the other, feeling the sun cut vainly across her ankles. She didn't even turn around when she heard the door burst open violently, but went on carefully placing one foot before the. . . .

December 27, 1974

Dear Reverend Mother Martínez:

Thank you so much for the sympathy card you sent us almost a year ago. Your words, full of comfort and wisdom, were a salve for our pain. I apologize for not finding the courage to answer you until today. To speak of painful things is always to live them over again, with gestures and words which we would like to erase but can't. There are so many things we wish had been different, Mother. Our daughter's marriage, for one. We should have gotten to know her husband better before the wedding; a neurotic and ambitious young man as it turns out, now that it's too late. Perhaps if we had been more careful, María de los Angeles would still be with us.

I apologize, Mother, I know I shouldn't speak that way about Felisberto. He's also dead, and we shouldn't bear grudges against the dead. But try as I may, I just can't bring myself to forgive him. He made María de los Angeles so unhappy, tormenting her about her dancing, throwing at her the fact that she'd never been anything but a mediocre star. And what wakes me up in the middle of the night in a cold sweat, Mother, what makes me shake with anger now that it's too late, is that he was making money on her; that he had bought the Pavlova Company, and that it was paying him good dividends. My daughter, who never needed to work a day in her life, exploited by that heartless monster.

On the day of the accident, she was in her choreographer's hotel room, working on some new dance steps for her next recital, when Felisberto barged in. According to the choreographer, he stood at the door and began to hurl insults at her, threatening to thrash her right there unless she promised she'd stop dancing for good. It had always struck me that Felisberto didn't seem to mind María de los Angeles' dancing, and when he did speak against it, it was only halfheartedly. Of course, it never occurred to me he was making money on her. At the time of the accident, however, he had just received an anonymous letter, which had made him begin to be concerned about public opinion. So that afternoon, he set out to teach María de los Angeles a lesson.

The choreographer, who didn't know a thing about what was going on, stood up for María de los Angeles. He tried to force Felisberto out of the room, and Felisberto pulled out a gun. He then tried to grab María de los Angeles but stumbled, accidentally shooting her. The choreographer then struck Felisberto on the head, tragically fracturing his skull.

You can't imagine what we went through, Mother. I keep seeing my daughter on the floor of that hotel dump bleeding to death, away from her mother, away from me, who would gladly have given my life to save her. I think of the uselessness of it all, and a wave of anger chokes me. When the ambulance arrived, she was already dead. Felisberto was lying next to her on the floor. They took him to Presbyterian Hospital and he was in intensive care for two weeks, but never regained consciousness.

It's been almost a year now, Mother. There seems to be a glass wall between the memory of that image and myself; a wall that tends to fog up if I draw too near. I no longer look for answers to my questions; I've finally stopped asking them. It was God's will. It was a comfort to spare no expense at her funeral. All of high society attended the funeral mass. Elizabeth and I were both touched by such proof of our friends' loyalty. All those Beautiful People and Super Adorable People whom you always refer to a little disdainfully in your letters, Mother, aren't really so bad. Deep down inside, they're decent.

We buried María de los Angeles surrounded by her bridal veil as though by a cloud bank. She looked so beautiful, her newly-washed hair gleaming over the faded satin of her wedding dress. Those who had seen her dance remarked that she seemed to be sleeping, performing for the last time her role of Sleeping Beauty. Fabianito, of course, is with us.

If it hadn't been for our daughter's sufferings, Mother, I would almost say it was all divine justice. You remember how Elizabeth and I prayed vainly for a son, so that we could grow old in peace? The ways of God are tortuous and dark, but perhaps this tragedy wasn't all in vain. María de los Angeles was a stubborn, selfish child. She never thought of the suffering she was inflicting upon us, insisting on her career as a dancer. But God, in his infinite mercy, will always be just. He left us our little cherub, to fill the void of our daughter's ingratitude. While we're on the subject, you'll soon get an invitation to his christening. We hope you'll get permission to leave the convent to attend, because we would very much like you to be his godmother.

From now on you can rest assured the convent will want for nothing, Mother. When I die, Fabianito will still be there to look after you.

> I remain, as always,
> Your true friend,
> Fabiano Fernández

that ceiling is a mess looks like smashed balls up there I told you dancing was forbidden keep insisting on it and I'll break every bone in your forbidden it's forbidden so just keep on sleep sleep sleep sleep sleep sleep sleep sleep sleep sleep wake up my love I want you to marry me I'll let you dance all you want bar to bar no please not today, you'll make me pregnant I beg you Felisberto I beg you for the sake of a mess that ceiling's a mess dancing Coppelia dancing Sleeping Beauty dancing Mater knitting white cotton booties while she waits for the savior's child to grow in her oh Lord I don't mind dying but I hate to leave my children crying just forget about being a dancer forget about it you will praise him protect him so that later on he'll protect and defend you now and forever more amen now kneel down and repeat this world is a vale of tears it's the next one that counts we must earn it by suffering not with silver trays not with silver goblets not with silver pitchers not with silver slander not with words put in your mouth with a silver spoon say yes my love say you're happy dancing Giselle but this time in smelly torn crinolines with wings tied to your back with barbed wire no I'm not happy Felisberto you betrayed me that's why I've brought you here so you can see for yourself so you can picture it all in detail my whiteface my black eyelashes loosened by sweat my thick pancaked cheeks eastsidewestside onetwothree the stained ceiling the rotting wood the venetian blinds eastsidewestside onetwothree what is money made of one day the circus came to town again and she covered her ears so as not to hear but she couldn't help it something was tugging at her ankles at her knees at the tips of her shoes eastsidewestside onetwothree something was pulling dragging her far away neither safe nor sweet nor sound Maria de los Angeles be still with balls sheer balls money's made with sheer balls neither recant nor resign nor content nor

1976

Rodrigo Rey Rosa

b. 1958

THE YOUNGEST AUTHOR represented in this anthology, Rodrigo Rey Rosa was born to a middle-class family in Guatemala City on November 4, 1958. He left Guatemala, a country plagued by violence and political strife, in 1980. Rey Rosa has studied at the School of Visual Arts in New York City and has lived in Bonn, Germany. His two short-story collections, published in English as *The Beggar's Knife* (1985) and *Dust on Her Tongue* (1989), represent his collaboration with his translator, the distinguished British writer Paul Bowles. Although the stories in these collections are not overtly political and in fact do not identify Guatemala's repressive and bloody regime, they are permeated by violence, unease, and corruption. Rey Rosa's latest book, *The Pelcari Project* (1991) is a horrifying tale of enslavement through science and technology in contemporary Central America. Rey Rosa's sense of irony and terse, limpid style distinguish him as one of the most original and promising writers of his generation.

The Truth

Translated by Paul Bowles

THE RAIN HAD stopped and the sunlight, tempered by the translucent curtains, shone into the spacious dining-room. A man, seated at the head of the table, a woman, and three small girls were eating their dessert in silence. It was a heavy silence. To the father's right, there was an empty chair, a half-eaten pastry.

"You're a liar," the father had said. The son had glanced up at him without saying anything. Black hairs stuck out of the man's nostrils. He looked at the child almost scornfully. Not allowing himself to cry, the boy had left the table and gone to his room. He lay down on the bed and opened a book, hoping to lose himself in its pages.

Somewhat later he stood up and looked into the mirror. For some time now his face had begun to please him. His lips, which had always struck him as being too thick, now seemed to suggest an expression of strength and humour. He had brown eyes that, half shut under the dark brows, were like those of a man. He combed his hair and stepped out into the corridor. Softly he went down the stairs and into the garden, using the back door.

The stable was only a short distance from the house, a building of concrete blocks with a tin roof. The light entered obliquely through a skylight, skeins of garlic were hung here and there to keep out the bats, and the air smelled of bran and urine. One of the horses snorted when he became aware of the boy. He went into the stall of a black mare and saddled her.

Once in the saddle he ceased being his father's son, to become a warrior. He trotted out along the dirt lane, and rode towards the mountains that surrounded the city. Barefoot children, washerwomen, beggars and drunks watched him go by—envy, hatred, desire, admiration. Soon the huts had been left behind, and he began to climb a path among the trees. The far-off noise of traffic on the highway was a hostile sound. It was the road of the white man. The red sun went behind the clouds. When he got to the top he pulled on the reins and stood up in the stirrups to look around him. Then he went at a gallop toward the gap crossed by the ancient aqueduct, for from there he could, without being seen, watch the winding highway below.

He hitched the mare where he always left her when he came up here, hidden behind some evergreen oaks, and went down the hill to the foot-walk. In the middle of the bridge he stopped and leaned over. There were stones missing from the wall here, and through a crack he could see the army of cars which the city spewed out each afternoon. The old stones were dangerously loose. A few days ago the idea had occurred to him, the idea of letting a stone fall, and, like a god from on high, changing the life of a mortal.

"Why did you do it?" the owner of the long black car chosen by the rock, would ask him. "Why?" He would try to break free of the chauffeur's grip. At last, giving up, he would say: "If you'll allow me, sir, perhaps I can explain.

"I've been coming to this part of the bridge for some time, to watch the cars go by. It's something worth seeing, if you manage to forget everything else, forget yourself and the bridge and the road, so that there is nothing but the stream of lights, the two streams, one red and one white. The other evening I was thinking: God knows who might not be going by underneath me at this minute—a murderer, or a saint. Someone with the key to the puzzle of my life, or of my ruin. But, sir, who are you? Why did my stone land on your car?"

The rock he was leaning on was covered with moss. It moved slightly. He scratched off the moss with a fingernail: the stone was porous. It was beginning to get dark, and the drivers of the cars had turned on their lights. What would happen if the car that was hit by the stone were driven by a woman? The car would be red; he did not manage to picture the woman. His fingernail was black, and the rock had no moss on it. Perhaps an evil angel was lurking nearby, because he thought: Push it. Now. But the voice he heard was his own.

He pushed the rock.

There was a squeal of brakes, and then the noise of cars colliding—two, three, four. For a moment there was silence. He jumped up and began to run, bent over, hidden by the parapet. When he got to the end of the aqueduct he looked down. From the chaos in the middle of the road, a man raised his hand and pointed to where he stood.

"Hey there!" he shouted.

He jumped down to the path and went on running. The men were yelling; two of them began to climb the cliff behind him. He was running and slipping; the shouts were missiles being shot at his back. If he succeeded in reaching the oak grove before the men got to the level of the bridge, he would be safe. It struck him as strange that while he was bending all his efforts to avoid the roots and holes in the path, he was thinking that he would rather not have been alone, that it would have been good to have someone with whom he could discuss it afterward. He stumbled and rolled on the ground. He could not see the men, but their voices sounded near. He got to the grove and stopped to catch his breath. It was dark here among the trees. He came to the mare, and was starting to unhitch her, when a voice, that of a boy, made him turn.

"I saw you," it told him.

He looked at the other as if he did not understand.

"I saw you throw the stone." It was the voice of blackmail.

The mare's mane was twisted; a fly lit on her ear; she flicked it away. The reflection in her black eye gave him the answer. He and the other boy both wore white shirts.

"You saw me," he said, letting go of the reins. They were the same size; he was wearing boots and his enemy was barefoot. He lowered his head. His father's words were being borne out. The mare champed at the bit, and he jumped upon the other, who fell on his back on the ground. He sat astride him and said between his teeth:

"You didn't see me. I saw you."

He punched the other in the mouth, and squeezed his knees together more tightly. The boy squirmed.

When the two men arrived, out of breath, he stood up.

"I saw him," he said, pointing. "I saw him push the stone."

The boy spat blood and raised his hands to his mouth. One of the men, whose forehead was bleeding, seized the boy by his shirt and kicked him.

"Get up," he told him. "We'll see if you've killed my wife, you whelp."

The boy was crying. He tried to defend himself, but it was hard for him to speak with his mouth full of blood. He had not said three words before the man hit him. The mare lifted a leg and set it down. Her master put his foot in the stirrup.

"What's your name?" the other man asked, when he was astride her.

He told him. His voice had an uncomfortable ring to it. He hastened to add:

"I'm sorry about your wife."

The two men, with the barefoot boy, went out of the grove.

He turned the mare around and started ahead slowly because the path was narrow and there was no light.

Even though he told himself that there was nothing to fear, and that his word was worth more than that of the other, his legs trembled and he was worried. "There was no other way," he thought, and on the other hand: "You're a liar," his father insisted.

It was a good thing that it was night, and that the mare was black, and that in the world of men nothing was certain. From a curve in the path he caught a glimpse of the city with its lights; it was as though he had returned from somewhere far away. The jaunt had almost come to an end. Smoke rose from the huts, and the mare hastened her step.

When he dismounted he felt vulnerable. He took a handful of salt from a pail and gave it to the mare: he liked to feel her rough tongue on his palm. He patted her neck and chest, and ran toward the house.

Dinner was on the table. Everyone seemed to be in a good humour.

"How far did you go?" his mother asked him.

"Not very far," he said. He looked at his sisters and began to cut his meat. He did not want to be asked any more questions.

No one would believe him if he told what had happened. He would have liked to discuss it with someone, but it was good too to have a secret. It made him feel like laughing to think that his secret was impenetrable, that not even he would be able to betray it.

His father was staring at him.

"Look at your hands," he said.

The black fingernail stood out against the white tablecloth.

"What were you doing?"

He raised his hand as if he wanted to see it in a stronger light. Turning toward his father, he thought: "I'm not a liar," and he realized that he was going to tell him the truth.

"I'm not sure," he said. "I think I killed a woman."

His sisters laughed.

"It's not a joke," he said. "I let a stone fall off the bridge, and she was underneath."

"Swear it's the truth," said his youngest sister.

"I swear."

"Why do you enjoy telling lies?" asked his father.

He wiped his lips and looked at the napkin. He did not intend to answer. Folding his arms, he sat back in his chair.

His mother passed him the bowl of fruit.

"What are you thinking about?" she asked him.

He imagined the other, who was paying for him: a damp cell, the dark.

"Nothing," he answered.

There was a short silence. Then they finished eating their supper.

1989

Xquic*

Translated by Paul Bowles

IF THE BEST of all worlds is one in which at a given moment each thing can become the symbol of any other thing, then in this best of worlds the bottomless black hole which is to be found in a pasture on a ranch called El Retiro (in the lower corner of the Petén on the Mexican border) will become, in due course, the symbol of life for certain members of the faculty of New York University. But in our world life allows no substitutes for emptiness; thus it is not the best of all possible worlds.

One morning in June when the cattle grazed in the high green grass outside the fence that surrounded the aforementioned hole, two horsemen came slowly into view. The cattle dispersed and the men dismounted, hitching their horses to the fence. The sun rose higher into the sky; they talked, sweated, and did not smile. The fat one, dark-skinned and with grey hair, spoke quickly in a low voice. The other, young, with Indian features, made a sign of agreement with his head once, and then again. They shook hands before getting on to their horses. One went off at a trot toward Esperanza, and the other ambled back to the ruined ranch-house.

They did not meet again until several months later, far from that place, one evening during the series of lectures to celebrate the passage of a century and a half since the founding of New York University. The public that night had been amazed by the address delivered by a foreign professor, a plump man with dark skin and grey hair. He spoke of an animal of which there was only one in existence, genus and species at the same time. His arguments met with a cool reception; there were, however, those who were inclined to favour them.

A small group remained in the hall when the lecture was over. Clara Graf of the Science Department expressed an enthusiasm for the idea of the "unique being" which did not seem entirely sincere. She claimed that she herself had once imagined a similar being, although the foreigner's rigid strictures bore no resemblance to her own concepts, in which dreams were connected to the copulation of insects or the nightly emanations of a certain flower.

"Animals are like numbers," she explained to Antonio, a pale man who did not seem to understand. "Like numbers composed of other numbers."

"This being is a key cipher, something like zero or the incommensurable π," said Joaquín, the young man with Indian features.

*Xquic, pronounced *shkeek*, is a figure in Mayan mythology.

Antonio turned and recognized Joaquín, whom he had not seen for several years; seeing his face reminded him of his childhood. He shook hands with him and interrupted Clara to introduce him. Meanwhile someone remarked that to categorize the various forms of life according to genus and species was a useless task because each class and each individual is nothing in itself.

"To classify an animal according to the number of its legs would be like using numbers according to the size of the angles and arcs that form them."

"Life is like an enormous tapestry," said an older woman. "If a thread is moved in one place, others are moved in another."

"And Xquic the unique being is the central thread of the warp," said the foreign professor, who had approached silently. *It seems to me that things happened all at once,* writes Antonio in his travel notebook, sent to the University from El Retiro, *that each stage along the way bringing me to the place where I am is separated from the next by an impassable obstacle.* It was December. Urged by Clara on the one hand, and by Joaquín on the other, he had undertaken the trip to the place where, according to an article by the stout professor published in the faculty press, "the unique being" had been discovered. *A short while ago I was walking on the campus with Clara, discussing an impossible creature, a "unique being". Now I am writing by the light of an alcohol lamp, surrounded by darkness and the forest.* He speaks of the possibility of believing in the incredible; cites Francisco Sánchez, who four centuries ago wrote that the leaves of certain trees, upon falling into a river in Ireland, became fishes, and that the bear licks her cub to give it a shape.

Antonio had travelled up the Chixoy in a canoe made of the trunk of a ceiba tree, along with twelve people whose faces he could not see, except for a child sitting on his right, whom he looked at over his shoulder, and who from time to time put its hand into the water as if it wanted to change it into a fish.

The river there is narrow. On both banks, outside the forest, there is wire strung along live yucca stalks; farmhouses have roofs of thatched palm. Here a long paddock in the mud, with seven dirty horses standing motionless; there one grey heron surrounded by white ones. The weeds in the undergrowth have long sword-shaped leaves, or round star-like ones. They pass over the framework of a sunken bridge. A tributary pours brown water into the green river. A newly fallen tree causes the water to jump and splash.

He spent the first night in a village: eight or ten dingy houses beside the river, where the boat stopped when the quick dusk fell. The forest air, he says, made him feel heavy, as if from a drug.

His dreams, quickly forgotten, left an unpleasant taste with him. He breakfasted at sunrise in a hut by the river. A deaf-mute child with no tongue came to sit opposite him at his table.

He managed to get me to give him some food, and afterwards some coins. It made me feel better to have given him something. In his tortured sign language the boy recounted violent occurrences which it seemed he had witnessed: a man stabbed to death, a poisoning, a shipwrecked man devoured by a fish.

Antonio asked the woman who brought the food if she knew where the boy was from. She did not know him; he had appeared the night before on the path running parallel to the river, going in the direction in which Antonio was headed. Antonio found it strange that the child inspired respect in her—perhaps even fear.

He continued the trip in the same dugout, with a different boatman. The river was narrower, and the trees met overhead, forming a tunnel. Now Antonio sat in the stern of the boat, beside a shirtless man whose body was weather-beaten by the sun. Ahead were two young women, both with long tresses of oily black hair.

They stop at midday to lunch. Antonio complains of the heat, does not eat. He writes: *Clara, the reason for this journey, lives in the midst of books, in a cold climate, like a transplanted flower under glass. She believes in an orderly world in which disorder exists only to give us hope, so as to allow us to doubt. I, sweating and full of loathing for the mosquitos, can't believe that the world is anything but chaos. I'd like to have undertaken this voyage without any reason, with no object.*

He found the camp in the expected place, at a bend in the river. First he saw the limp flags: the rectangular one of the republic, and the university's triangular one. The camp consisted of a whitewashed hut a few feet from the shore, with four military tents arranged in a semicircle around it. When the boatman shut off the motor Antonio heard the sound of another motor on land which quickly stopped running. A short blonde woman came out of one of the tents. Another appeared in the doorway of the hut, which gave onto the dock over the river. She also was short, but her hair was black and her skin was the colour of the people of the region. Antonio got out of the canoe. From the beginning, he writes, there was a misunderstanding.

"Señor Inspector?" she asked him.

The dugout was leaving.

"Tomorrow at ten!" shouted the boatman, removing his hat to say goodbye.

The woman, whose name was Iris, was dressed like those of the village where Antonio had slept the preceding night. *I let her continue under the mistaken impression,* he explains, *because for some reason I felt like an intruder.* Nevertheless he admits to finding it unflattering that he should have been taken for a government inspector.

Soon he realized that he should not have accepted the error. The woman was not a simple servant as he had assumed when he had first seen her. She spoke Spanish as well as Mam (her native tongue) and on going into the hut Antonio noticed that she had been reading a German magazine.

"If you don't mind," he said, in order to avoid having to make conversation, "I'd like to have a walk around outside."

The pretext was a valid one: after a journey in a dugout one needs to stretch one's legs.

"Of course," she said. Turning toward the door she called: "Ann!"

Ann was the blonde woman he had seen coming out of one of the tents. Iris indicated that Ann should accompany him.

She came running, her cheeks flushed from the exertion.

The two women and Antonio walked toward the centre of the camp, where the generator was housed. From there one could see, to the north, a straight path which lost itself among the trees. And to the east was another, winding along beside the river.

"You can go out this way and come back that way," Iris said. "Or vice versa."

Antonio chose the straight path without knowing quite why. Ann was speaking of the research, something about balance and harmony and the interrelation of the species, statements which he had heard from Clara, and which wearied him. He wondered if Ann were not bored living here, but he did not dare ask her, because it seemed to him that it would not have been a proper subject for an inspector to discuss. The path, completely straight, made Antonio think of an aisle in a cathedral.

"How far does it go?" he asked.

"Don't you know?" Ann was surprised. "It's the path to the well of Xquic."

They walked in silence for several minutes.

"What are you thinking about?" Ann murmured when they stopped.

The water in the well was crystalline, he had written on the last page of the notebook, *and the stick Ann handed me to thrust into it did not modify its direction as it penetrated the surface. At the bottom, which was of grey sand, there were three concentric circles. An almost imperceptible motion, slow and regular, made me lean over the water. On the surface I saw my face, my mouth partially open; I moved back. There was a metallic odour in the air.*

In the centre of the well, near the bottom, appeared a point which drew the light to it. It did not touch the bottom; it cast a shadow over it in the form of a comma. It seemed to grow from within, to issue from itself, from the transparent water, from nothingness. It turned very slowly upon itself, and as it turned it changed, or took on, shape. I experienced a slight dizziness, a coldness on the nape of my neck, a feeling of unreality, as from a blow on the head.

What had taken shape was the fossil of a snail, carefully imperfect, with a crack here, a hole there. It grew until it reached the edge of the well, and disappeared.

The light was fading. Ann had begun to walk towards the camp along the river path. I followed her.

"There's no doubt, Professor," Clara said. "It's his handwriting."

The notebook, small and black, was the worse for wear. Clara stood up and let it fall onto the table. Feeling suddenly dizzy, she rested her hand on the back of the chair. "It's farcical," she thought. Antonio, she suspected, had no intention of returning. There was something—she did not know precisely what, about the professor, with his glassy eyes and grey hair—which inspired distrust. It was Antonio's handwriting, slightly smaller and more crowded than usual, which could have been due to his desire to save paper. But perhaps there was some other explanation. She turned toward the wide windows: it was night and snow was starting to fall, white, soft.

"The testimony of your friend is of the utmost value to us," the professor told her.

This was true. Antonio was a sceptic. Clara realized the irony: Antonio was credulous and she was beginning to doubt.

"He didn't believe," the professor continued. "But he went where few people have gone and saw for himself. Others believe without having to stir from where they are."

"Like me," said Clara. The image of Antonio following Ann flashed across her mind.

"Like you," agreed the professor, rising to escort her to the door.

The idea of its being a snail has produced results, said the note which the professor sent Joaquín, waiting for news at El Retiro. *The publication of*

*the Science Department has announced the granting of the necessary funds
for the continuation of studies regarding the well of Xquic. Best to Antonio.
Remember me to Iris and Ann.*

After reading the note Joaquín put on his boots and went out onto the
veranda, where the boards were rotten. He gave orders to a youth lying in
a hammock to go to Esperanza for ice and beer. He went around the
outside of the house and found Antonio lying on his back in the green
water of the narrow swimming pool. There was no Iris, no Ann.

1989

Acknowledgments

(continued from p. iv)

"The Dark Night of Ramón Yendía" by Lino Novás Calvo. From *Spanish Stories and Tales* by Harriet De Onis. Copyright © 1954 by Alfred A. Knopf, Inc. Reprinted by permission of Alfred A. Knopf, Inc.

"The Image of Misfortune" from *Goodbyes and Other Stories* by Juan Carlos Onetti, translated by Daniel Balderston. Copyright © 1990. By permission of the University of Texas Press.

"New Islands" from *New Islands* by María Luisa Bombal. Translation copyright © 1982 by Farrar, Straus & Giroux, Inc. Reprinted by permission of Farrar, Straus & Giroux, Inc.

"The Philanthropist" and "The One Who Came to Save Me" first published in English in *Cold Tales* by Virgilio Piñera, translated by Mark Schafer, Eridanos Press, Boston. Copyright © 1985 Juan Piñera Lleras, Luisa Piñera Lleras, Yadira Piñera Concepcíon and José Manuel Piñera Lleras. Translation copyright © 1988 Mark Schafer. Published by permission of Eridanos Press, Inc.

"Bestiary" and "Secret Weapons" from *End of the Game and Other Stories* by Julio Cortázar. Copyright © 1967 by Random House, Inc. Reprinted by permission of Pantheon Books, a division of Random House, Inc.

"The Southern Thruway" from *All Fires the Fire and Other Stories* by Julio Cortázar, translated by Suzanne Jill Levine. Copyright © 1973 by Random House, Inc. Reprinted by permission of Pantheon Books, a division of Random House, Inc.

"The Prisoner" by Augusto Roa Bastos. From Seymour Menton, *Spanish American Short Story: A Critical Anthology.* Copyright © 1980 The Regents of the University of California. Reprinted by permission.

"Tell Them Not to Kill Me" from *The Burning Plain and Other Stories* by Juan Rulfo, translated by George D. Schade. Copyright © 1967. By permission of the University of Texas Press.

"The Day We Were Dogs" by Elena Garro. From *Contemporary Women Authors of Latin America: New Translations,* ed. by Doris Meyer and Margarite Fernandez Olmos. Copyright © 1983 by Brooklyn College Press. Reprinted with permission of the editors.

"The Walk" from *Charleston and Other Stories* by José Donoso. Copyright © 1977 by José Donoso. Reprinted by permission of David R. Godine, Publisher.

"The Imitation of the Rose" from *Family Ties* by Clarice Lispector, translated by Giovani Pontiero. Copyright © 1960. By permission of the University of Texas Press.

355